AF564575

Pandemonium

PRAISE FOR THE BOOK

'Tamal has a deep understanding and a broad perspective of the banking and financial sector. His curiosity, willingness to listen, attention to detail and ability to simplify complexity, while posing inconvenient questions, are unique strengths. These are reflected in this book.'

– UdayKotak, MD & CEO, Kotak Mahindra Bank Ltd & President, CII

'No other financial journalist-cum-author can read the pulse of the Indian banking system as Tamal can. A one-stop narrative of nuances and insights a reader is unlikely to get elsewhere. It's a compelling read.'

– Deepak Parekh, Chairman, HDFC Ltd

'Tamal writes with honesty, based on hard facts and with no holds barred. The volume will surely add to his reputation as an astute and insightful observer of, and honest commentator on, banking sector.

'He has given us a financial sector policy thriller, difficult to put down once one starts the first chapter "Who Killed Indian Banking?" Successive chapters prove the point that investigative and analytical journalism can provide sharper insights than a whole host of heavy-duty essays.

'Tamal's real strength is his determination to dig deep, put lesser-known facts on decision making in the sector out in the public domain without being unduly normative or judgmental about the persons involved.'

– Rajiv Kumar, Vice Chairman, NITI Aayog

'Our national economy has been under siege, aggravated by malfunctioning of the banking sector. This book offers valuable insights on its origin, spread and possible measures for a way out... They [the four distinguished former governors] spoke freely with Tamal because of his formidable reputation as a thoughtful, meticulous and fiercely independent columnist. In fact, these qualities shine throughout this book. I recommend this important book to professionals as well as the general public. It will benefit us all.'

– Vijay Kelkar, Chairman, India Development Foundation

'The breadth of knowledge and attention to details shown by this veteran economic historian and journalist make fascinating reading for anybody interested in the Indian financial sector. Tamal's superb storytelling makes the book so gripping that the reader is transported to the scene where the action is taking place. It's an unbiased and candid account of the role played by the regulator, the investigating agencies, the business community, the bankers and the government. By the time one reaches the end of the book, it becomes clear why banking in India has been a tragedy.

'My only complaint with the book is that it's like binge-watching an engrossing TV series – I could not put it down until the end.'

– U.K. Sinha, Former Chairman, SEBI

'Tamal has an exceptional record as an observer of Indian banking... The interviews with past governors of the Reserve Bank are revelatory because of their different perspectives. Recommended reading for anyone interested in the subject.'

– T.N. Ninan, Chairman, Business Standard Pvt Ltd

'Tamal Bandyopadhyay's magnum opus provides insights into the most important question in Indian policymaking today. With a fine understanding of banking, finance and economy and willingness to respect different perspectives, Tamal has woven a compelling tale of what has gone wrong with India's banking system, starting from the 1990s. In telling this tale, he critically examines the role of governance, management, regulation and especially supervision of banks. In reforming these four pillars lies the solution to India's most important policy problem and thereby the path to India becoming a $5 trillion economy.'

– Krishnamurthy Subramanian, Chief Economic Adviser, GoI

TAMAL BANDYOPADHYAY

FOREWORD BY BIBEK DEBROY

Lotus Collection

First published in 2021

The Lotus Collection
An imprint of
Roli Books Pvt. Ltd
M-75, Greater Kailash II Market, New Delhi 110 048
Phone: ++91 (011) 40682000
E-mail: info@rolibooks.com
Website: www.rolibooks.com
Also at Bengaluru, Chennai, & Mumbai

Cover Design: Bhavi Mehta
Layout Design: Bhagirath Kumar
Production: Lavinia Rao & Jagriti Jaiswal

ISBN: 978-81-946433-5-7

Typeset in ITC Galliard Std by Roli Books Pvt Ltd
Printed at Saurabh Printers Pvt. Ltd.

To Tapan Jyoti, my elder brother, an inspiration for many in the small town where I grew up, and my sister-in-law Chhabi, for her love and affection. You know what you mean to me.

Contents

Part IV
GOVERNORSPEAK

Part V
CRYSTAL GAZING

Part VI

Foreword

In the preface, Tamal Bandyopadhyay refers to Akira Kurosawa's *Rashomon*, a metaphor for different, and often conflicting, versions of the same event.

For Indian banking, the metaphor is rather apt. Reams have been written on banking in India, not just research papers, but books too. C.D. Deshmukh, the first Indian to be appointed Reserve Bank of India (RBI) governor and later Union finance minister, did write his autobiography. Subsequent RBI governors also wrote books. Since Y.V. Reddy, it has become almost mandatory for ex-RBI governors (and a few ex-deputy governors) to author books focused on their RBI stints. At best, to use the same metaphor, it is the woodcutter's story, not the commoner's perspective. But I doubt *Rashomon* would have become such a great film without Kazuo Miyagawa as its cinematographer.

To chronicle what Tamal calls the great Indian banking tragedy, we need an external, objective and dispassionate observer as cinematographer. If you are inside the system, you may know everything about it, but you may have no sense about its place and function in the bigger picture. For years and years, Tamal has been, and still is, a widely read business journalist, across newspapers, especially on banking and finance. That brings an investigative flair and felicity in his use of language, aided no doubt by his specialisation in English literature. He is more than a columnist, having authored several books, mostly on banking.

In *Lady Windermere's Fan*, Oscar Wilde had Dumby say, 'In this world there are only two tragedies. One is not getting what one wants, and the other is getting it.' (Later, this quote was redone by George Bernard Shaw in *Man and Superman*.) Why should there be a great tragedy in Indian banking? Across indicators – prevention of bank failures, number of banks (commercial, payments banks and small finance banks), bank branches and ATMs, deposits, bank credit, gross domestic product (GDP), banking standards, use of technology, digitisation, measures of financial inclusion – there have been improvements over time. Reforms, however defined, have much to do with competition and efficiency in factor markets (land, labour, capital).

Banking constitutes a critical strand of capital market reform. While privatisation of public sector banks (PSBs) is not yet on the agenda, there has been competition through private sector entry. Competition requires exit, as well as entry. The 2016 Insolvency and Bankruptcy Code (IBC) has ensured an exit for errant promoters. There is a regulator for banks, though less starkly so for non-banking financial companies (NBFCs). Within that broad reform template, there is quite a bit the country has got.

However, in this five-part book (six, if you include the data charts), Tamal unveils the tragedy that lurks beneath.

Part I, titled 'The Conundrum', portrays symptoms of the malaise, familiar to most people. Non-performing assets (NPAs) mounted. With development finance institutions (DFIs) having died an unnatural death, banks started to lend in areas where they did not possess expertise. Bond markets did not develop deeply enough and infrastructure projects were financed via debt rather than equity. Compared with real sector growth, financial sector growth was disproportionately high. Add to that the NBFC problem. Hence, there are issues with (a) regulatory oversight; (b) governance oversight within banks; and (c) perverse behaviour of rating agencies. Cutting across all three, there is an information flow problem despite penetration of private sector banks, which have not always covered themselves with glory.

India's banking landscape is still dominated by PSBs. Therefore, in unpeeling the malaise further, in Part II, Tamal zeroes in on PSBs. There have been committees galore, replete with recommendations. Implementation of recommendations, when attempted (read: consolidation and capitalisation), have concentrated on symptoms, not the disease. In the book's diagnosis, and no one can possibly disagree, the core disease part of the DNA of PSBs has elements of (1) control over appointments; (2) multiple channels of control; (3) lack of independence of boards; (4) political interference; (5) perverse incentives and lack of accountability; and (6) conflict between social and commercial objectives. Though not listed in Part II, I would also mention the Prevention of Corruption Act (PCA) and vigilance enquiries.

But this, including the PCA, takes us on to Part III – questions that should be asked, but are rarely asked. In one of the richest parts of the book, Tamal takes us through frauds, and how they were worked. 'The public sector bankers in India, including the retired, are an embarrassed and a much-harassed lot. The investigative agencies are hounding them for loans that have gone bad, and frauds. Are we replicating the Chinese banking system where many borrowers are dishonest, many bankers corrupt, risk assessment is poor and legal system weak, leading to large lumps of loans not being backed by genuine collateral? The investigative agencies are quick to file chargesheets and arrest bankers, but in how many cases have they been able to prove their charges? The focus seems to be more on the demonstrative effect. By subjecting them to public humiliation, unending investigation and tarring the entire banking community with the same brush, the Indian economy becomes the biggest loser. The tardy credit growth tells the story – the bankers are a harassed and a scared lot. They know if they do not lend, they will not be chargesheeted or arrested. And, no one loses his or her job for not lending. But if a loan turns bad, they may end up spending sleepless nights on a *durrie* at a barrack in Mumbai's Arthur Road Jail.'

This quote says it all. There is the broad reform template and there can be no quarrels with that. However, as a critical ingredient in that reform template, we have the immediate problem described in Part III, not just one of the richest sections of the book, but also one of the most disturbing. Although the focus is PSBs, this part makes clear in its concluding chapter that the malaise also extends to private sector banks, which are hardly paragons of virtue.

RBI governors have had impeccable credentials, academic and otherwise. It is natural that they should have thought about the problem, though they need not always have articulated their views in public. In Part IV, we have the views of four respected ex-RBI governors – C. Rangarajan, Y.V. Reddy, D. Subbarao and Raghuram Rajan. The trouble with this part is that no public servant, former or current, will ever be candid in publicly stated views. So far, we have had a litany of woes, warts and blemishes of the tragedy, skilfully portrayed by the author.

Any reader is bound to ask – what next? How do we fix the system? If one is going to borrow an expression from Greek tragedies, there must not only be mimesis, but catharsis too. In fairness, it is not up to Tamal to suggest solutions. That is for the broader government – legislature, executive and judiciary – to work out. However, with the skill set that the author possesses, there must be ideas and these are stated in Part V – refinement of the IBC, and reform of the RBI and Securities and Exchange Board of India (SEBI).

'There are too many questions. Is it a crisis? A game played by corporate India? It does not matter how we describe it – the fact is it spilled over to the real sector and created a crisis of confidence. What lies in the future? Should the DFIs come back? What should be the new landscape of banking: Co-existence of big banks and small banks? Should we have more banks or fewer banks? Will the bad banks and good banks continue to cohabit by the government's indulgence? If all state-owned banks cannot be capitalised, the government must choose who should live and who should die. Can a few of them be privatised?' These are meant to be regarded as rhetorical questions.

I have always been amused by the preamble to the Reserve Bank of India Act, 1934, which continues unamended: 'And whereas in the present disorganisation of the monetary systems of the world it is not possible to determine what will be suitable as a permanent basis for the Indian monetary system; but whereas it is expedient to make temporary provision on the basis of the existing monetary system, and to leave the question of the monetary standard best suited to India to be considered when the international monetary position has become sufficiently clear and stable to make it possible to frame permanent measures.' The RBI was thus constituted.

The preamble does not matter, though in some cases, courts have considered preambles before delivering judgments. In practice, an unamended preamble does not matter, not for the RBI. But for Tamal's book, I think it is some kind of a metaphor. We need to find permanent solutions, not just temporary ones, to identify the catharsis in the tragedy that this book has described. We have come a long way since the days of bank nationalisation and bank failures.

Nonetheless, there is a tragedy in the works and this is a wonderful book to understand that. Indeed, in some parts, it reads like a mystery. All mysteries deserve to be solved.

– Bibek Debroy
31 July 2020

Preface

I am neither a banker nor an economist. As a journalist covering India's financial ecosystem, I have tried to explain the great Indian banking conundrum: Why is the banking system serving the world's second-largest population and Asia's third-largest economy such a poster child for chaos and non-performance?

The subject is complex and the story is still unfolding, almost every day. So, how should one deal with such a broad canvas? The choices before me included a linear, time-bound narration with facts and figures, citing central bank notifications, key research reports, court judgments and reports of investigative agencies. Or, I could go the easier, columnist route and offer pearls of wisdom on how the Indian banking system ended up piling up so much of bad debt and what I thought were the ways of stemming the rot.

I did not follow either of those paths because I did not want to write a historical case study. Nor do I want to presume that you know all that has transpired, and are only interested in how this mess can be fixed. What I have attempted to do is chronicle an important story, much of which has not fully been told, through real people who are integral to India's banking ecosystem. These are characters who, with very few exceptions, are known, and in some cases heard, but never really understood – at least, until now.

To explain how I went about unravelling the tale of what

happened in India's banking system, let me start with Akira Kurosawa's 1950 classic, *Rashomon*, which opens with a woodcutter and a priest sheltering from a downpour under the Rashomon gate of the ancient Japanese city of Kyoto. When a commoner joins them, they both begin recounting a disturbing incident.

The woodcutter says he found the body of a murdered Samurai in the forest three days ago. The priest adds that he saw the Samurai and a woman travelling the same day that the murder took place. Both men are later summoned to testify in court, where they are joined by a captured bandit, who claims responsibility for the rape and murder.

The film goes on to narrate three separate yet intertwined stories – of the bandit, the murdered woman and the Samurai – told with the help of a medium. Each story lends a fresh prism to what transpired, adding rich new layers of truth and perspective to the plot.

In the similar way, this book attempts to capture the multi-layered banking landscape in India through the distinct yet interlaced eyes of central bankers, commercial bankers, economists, analysts, bond and foreign exchange dealers and, finally, bank customers.

They all have different stories to relate but these are all threads of the same narrative, which I have tried to weave together across 17 chapters grouped into five sections and a series of charts. Each chapter could be a book by itself.

The first chapter, 'Who Killed Indian Banks?', tries to dispassionately examine how and why many public sector lenders are facing a mountain of bad assets that threatens to bury many of them.

The second chapter is about how the Reserve Bank of India (RBI) decided to tackle bad loans through an aggressive policy launched by then governor Raghuram Rajan, and continued even more zealously by his short-lived successor, Urjit Patel.

The third chapter deals with the crisis that gripped India's non-banking financial companies (NBFCs) because of classic asset–liability mismatches, while the fourth chapter takes a close look at the role of rating agencies in the NBFC crisis.

These four chapters make up the first section of the book.

The second section focusses on public sector banks (PSBs), the mainstay of India's banking system, across three chapters dealing with what ails them, the issues caused by endless capital infusions from the government, and the ultimate solution that the government has found – consolidation.

The third section of the book has three chapters dealing with the world of fraud, the fear psychosis that has gripped bankers because of hyperactive investigative agencies, and a look at two fallen angels: Chanda Kochhar, CEO of ICICI Bank Ltd and Rana Kapoor, founder and promoter of Yes Bank Ltd.

The fourth section is a critical insights-rich core of the book. It features candid interviews with not one but four past governors – C. Rangarajan, Y.V. Reddy, D. Subbarao and Raghuram Rajan – who, in theory and in practice, held immense power as independent custodians and regulators and with a few exceptions have rarely spoken publicly about this topic. They spoke with unusual candour on everything we wanted to know about what exactly transpired across Indian banking.

I got to know what went wrong, the how and why, and, critically, the possible way forward from four men – yes there has not yet been a woman governor of RBI in its 85 years – who know and care deeply about India and her future.

Two of the chapters in the fifth section deal with the changes to India's insolvency law, the need for the RBI to reinvest in its own capabilities to regulate and oversee the banking system and maintain financial stability.

The last chapter in this section is on the challenging road that lies ahead for India's banking system. Spread across 1.56 lakh branches, managed by 1.4 million employees, catering to over 1,000 million customers, a healthy banking sector is essential to drive India's domestic and global aspirations.

The last section offers up a series of charts that tell the story of Indian banking and how it has evolved through the past few decades.

Finally, why do I name this book *Pandemonium*?

The literal meaning of pandemonium is a wild and noisy disorder or confusion; uproar – a situation in which a crowd of people act in a wild, uncontrolled, or violent way because they are afraid, excited, or confused. This is typically short-lived but the chaos in Indian banking is decades old.

John Milton coined this word in his poem *Paradise Lost.* Pandæmonium, as the capital of Hell is known in the epic poem, combines the Greek prefix pan-, meaning 'all' or 'every', with the Late Latin daemonium, meaning 'little spirit', 'little angel', or, as Christians interpreted it, 'little daemon', and later, 'demon'. It roughly translates as 'All Demons' but can also be interpreted as 'all-demon-place'.

In Hindu mythology, when the *asuras* defeated the *devas* in a battle and took over the universe, what followed was churning the ocean or *samudra-manthan* to get the nectar of immortality. That released the lethal poison known as 'Halahala'. Shiva consumed the poison to protect the world. In the process, he got a blue hue in his throat – he became Nilkantha.

The Indian banking system has also been through the *manthan.* The RBI did the churning through its asset quality review (AQR), releasing the poison in the form of bad loans. The book chronicles the *manthan* and the search for a Shiva to consume the poison, protect the system and take it forward.

Dear reader, if you enjoyed this saga and have come away with a richer understanding of what happened and what might lie ahead, the credit goes to the countless people who spoke to me, narrating their personal and professional stories, explaining intricate nuances with patience and leading me through the journey that became this book. And, if you find the end result wanting, then the blame lies squarely with me.

Happy reading,
Tamal

Acknowledgements

This book, my sixth, is the outcome of painstaking research, analysis of reams of data and hundreds of hours of interviews on and off the record, in India and globally, with central bankers, commercial bankers, economists, treasury managers, research analysts, rating agency executives, lawyers and senior staff of investigative agencies, and many banking customers.

Let me start by thanking Bibek Debroy, chairman of the Prime Minister's Economic Advisory Council. I asked him to write the foreword to a book that I had not yet written even a single word. He agreed instantly, which in itself was a big vote of confidence ahead of a daunting task.

I also thank Deepak Parekh, chairman, HDFC Ltd; Krishnamurthy Subramanian, chief economic adviser, Government of India; Rajiv Kumar, vice chairman, NITI Aayog; T.N. Ninan, chairman, Business Standard Pvt Ltd; Uday Kotak, MD and CEO, Kotak Mahindra Bank Ltd; U.K. Sinha, former chairman, SEBI; and Vijay Kelkar, chairman, India Development Foundation, for their liberal endorsements of the book.

Four past governors of the RBI – C. Rangarajan, Y.V. Reddy, D. Subbarao and Raghuram Rajan – were equally forthcoming, making the book deeply insightful with their candid views on Indian banking. Each of them spent long hours with me, answering every question, however uncomfortable and pointed, and putting up with my initial lack of understanding on many of the nuances they lived with in their roles.

Six past RBI deputy governors – Anand Sinha, K.C. Chakrabarty, S.S. Mundra, R. Gandhi, H.R. Khan and N.S. Vishwanathan – and retired executive directors Sudarshan Sen, Meena Hemchandra and Uma Shankar helped me better understand the intricacies of many RBI policies.

Similarly, three former chairmen of SBI – Rajnish Kumar, Arundhati Bhattacharya and Pratip Chaudhuri – offered me rich insights into how a major lender functions, especially in times of difficulty.

I am also thankful to V.G. Kannan, former CEO of Indian Banks' Association; veteran bankers A.K. Khandelwal, Birendra Kumar, P.H. Ravikumar, R.K. Bansal and G. Padmanabhan, non-executive chairman of Bank of India.

Vishnu Vaidyanathan, a corporate banking professional with a multinational bank, was of immense help in my research on a wide range of subjects.

My former colleague Somnath Dasgupta, a veteran journalist and editor, was the first reader for many of the draft chapters. He corrected many mistakes and gave me ideas on how to improve the narration. Nabeel Mohideen, a friend and colleague for more than three decades, has always been a sounding board. And, Devangshu Datta, whose interests range from markets to chess, bridge, sex and religion, asked many questions and gave me ideas to make the text smarter.

My first boss in *Mint* and a friend for the past 14 years, Raju Narisetti, has always been one call away for any help I seek. Thank you.

I relied on research reports by Ashish Gupta of Credit Suisse, Vishal Goyal of UBS and Renny Thomas, senior partner, McKinsey & Company, as well as publications from Nomura, Macquarie, CRISIL, ICRA, Liases Foras, Jeffries, and have liberally quoted from the columns of Bloomberg columnist Andy Mukherjee.

I have also delved into many of my own 'Banker's Trust' columns that appeared in *Mint* from early 2007 until late 2018, and, since then, in *Business Standard.* I thank both newspapers, as well as the *Indian Express*, the *Economic Times*, *Money Control*, *Moneylife*, *Outlook Business*, the *Times of India*, BBC, Press Trust of India, Reuters and Bloomberg for some of the reporting that filled gaps in my writing for the book.

One chapter of this book is based on a series of articles I had written for *Mint*, along with Achintan Bhattacharya, former director of National Institute of Bank Management.

I have also quoted from a news story by Varun Sood that was posted on LinkedIn.

For helping source information and transcribe a few interviews, my thanks go to Pruvasha Sinha, an associate in equity sales with an investment bank; Sanchit Agarwal, an investment analyst with Windrose Capital; and my former colleague Ravindra Sonavane.

Kapil Kapoor of Roli Books came up with the idea of telling India's banking story and Pramod Kapoor, founder of the publishing house, was of great support along the way. I also thank Neelam Narula and the team at Roli Books for their sincere efforts.

If I have inadvertently missed out on mentioning any name, my sincere apology and there are many who spoke to me on background that I am grateful for but can't name here. You know who you are and how much you have helped me.

My son Sujan, studying in the US, religiously called every night (morning for him) to check on the progress of the book, while wife Rita took care of all household chores, especially during the Covid-19 lockdown in Mumbai, so I could spend as much time as I needed to complete the project. My love and gratitude to both of them.

Finally, Gogal, as always, was my constant companion until the wee hours, patiently lying at my feet, with an occasional disapproving yawn, when I stayed up beyond 3 am working away on the chapters.

Thank you

PART I
THE CONUNDRUM

In October 2019, India's Finance Minister Nirmala Sitharaman spoke about the Indian economy at Columbia University. After she listed the Narendra Modi government's achievements, she took questions. Somebody cited former Reserve Bank of India (RBI) governor Raghuram Rajan's comment that the first Modi government had not done well because it was 'extremely centralised'.

Sitharaman riposted that the government-owned banks had their worst phase when Rajan was the RBI governor and Manmohan Singh the prime minister.

'What ails our banks today? Where has it been inherited from?' she asked.

Attempting to answer that question leads us into the first part of this book. Multiple factors contributed to the piling up of the mountain of bad loans. These negative factors were interwoven into the fabric of Indian banking in such a way that it is hard to identify a single main culprit:

Was it the surge in bank credit during the golden growth era of 2006–08?

Was it the 1990s decision to bury development finance institutions?

Was it the shallow corporate bond market?

Was it the RBI's ultra-loose monetary policy after the 2008 financial crisis?

Were banks to blame for being innovative in concealing non-performing assets (NPAs) or bad loans?

Was it the so-called 'policy paralysis' in the latter stages of the United Progressive Alliance (UPA) regime that ended in 2014?

Rajan went to war against the piling up of NPAs and his successor Urjit Patel intensified the battle to recognise bad assets. But the contagion also spread as the non-banking financial companies (NBFCs) were engulfed by NPAs, after the 2016 demonetisation.

While the system was flush with money, the banks had turned cautious because they were already burdened with NPAs. The NBFCs rushed to fill the void but they committed the cardinal sin of borrowing short and lending long.

The collapse of Infrastructure Leasing & Financial Services Ltd (IL&FS) in July 2018 started a forest fire that spread quickly, singeing many in the financial sector. The government was eventually forced to take drastic action. We discuss alternative firefighting methods which could have been tried.

Finally, in this section, I dissect the role of rating agencies. Were some raters compromised, or was it just plain inefficiency or incompetence?

The section winds up with a brief outline on how the maladies could be treated.

1

Who Killed Indian Banking?

PART 1

Scene: The Jerome L. Greene Hall at Columbia University.
Date: Tuesday, 15 October 2019.
Dramatis Personae: India's Finance Minister Nirmala Sitharaman
Professor Arvind Panagariya, moderator.
A hundred-odd students of the School of International and Public Affairs (SIPA).
Many well-known economists, finance professionals and fund managers.

The Deepak and Neera Raj Center on Indian Economic Policies at Columbia University is a relatively young institution. But it has turned the hosting of Indian finance ministers into a tradition. At its inauguration in October 2015, the keynote address was delivered by the late Arun Jaitley, who was then the finance minister. Jaitley spoke at this venue again in October 2017.

This is Sitharaman's first visit. She read out a speech on 'Indian

Economy: Prospects and Challenges', after announcing that she looked forward to a free-wheeling audience interaction.

Professor Panagariya served as the first vice chairman of the Government of India think-tank, NITI Aayog, from January 2015 to August 2017 before he returned to his tenured position at Columbia. (The ex-officio chairman of NITI is the prime minister.)

The audience also included Panagariya's thesis adviser, Jagdish Bhagwati, the renowned professor of economics, law and international relations, at Columbia University. Sitharaman confessed Bhagwati's presence made her 'a bit nervous'.

In her 24-minute prepared speech, she claimed that India's vision of becoming a $5 trillion economy by 2024–25 was 'challenging but realisable'. She also touched upon other measures taken by the Indian government such as a commitment to fiscal consolidation, a new insolvency law, injection of capital into government-owned banks, consolidation of the banking sector, liquidity support to non-banking financial companies, corporate tax cuts, etc.

Panagariya moderated the interactive session that followed.

The first three questions were on a possible cut in personal income tax, the effects of the November 2016 demonetisation and the case for doing it again (amidst audience laughter) and the ease of doing business.

Sitharaman responded confidently.

Then a gentleman read out this question: 'Ma'am, so, there is no doubt that the Indian economy has done better since the NDA (Bharatiya Janata Party-led National Democratic Alliance) came to power in 2014. But you obviously had to face your fair share of criticism globally. I recently came across a lecture delivered by Dr. Raghuram Rajan at Brown University and one of the points he mentioned was why didn't Modi-1 do better on the Indian economy. [This is] Because the government is extremely centralised and the leadership does not appear to have a consistent, articulated vision on how to achieve economic growth. What would be your view on this?'

Sitharaman took her time: 'It has several layers of observations. Let me put it that way and I would want you to give me the benefit of reading it over again so that I can jot it down and I give you a pointed reply. Would you please do that again?'

The gentleman: 'Should I read it out again?'

Sitharaman's answer: 'Yeah. Read it out again.'

The gentleman: 'Sure. Because the government is extremely centralised and the leadership does not appear to have a consistent, articulated vision on how to achieve economic growth.'

Sitharaman paused, and looked disturbed. Then she smiled and said: 'I am taking a minute to respond because I do respect Raghuram Rajan as a great scholar, who chose to be in the central bank in India at a time when the Indian economy was all buoyant, yet I cannot but mention it now that the banks in India… and you are all aware only a few days ago the *Economist* has written about the state of Indian banks. Yet, to link with the statement, it was in his time that loans were given just based on phone calls from crony leaders and public sector banks (PSBs) in India till today are depending on government's equity infusion to get out of that mire.

'Dr. Manmohan Singh was the prime minister and I am sure Dr. Raghuram Rajan will agree that Dr. Manmohan Singh would have had a consistent, articulated vision for India. (Audience laughs.)

'With due respect, I am not making fun of anybody, but I certainly want to put this forward for a comment which has come like this.

'I have no reason to doubt that Dr. Raghuram Rajan feels every word of what he is saying and I am here today giving him his due respect, but also placing the fact before you that Indian public sector banks did not have a worst (sic) phase than when the combination of Dr. Manmohan Singh and Dr. Raghuram Rajan as prime minister and the governor of Reserve Bank had.

'At that time, none of us knew about it. There was an asset quality review which Dr. Raghuram Rajan did, which I am very happy about – very grateful that he did it. But I am sorry. Can all of us put together also think of what ails our banks today? Where has it been inherited from?

'So, it's very well… Dr. Bhagwati is here, Dr. Panagariya is here,

I am sure there are many more economists among us who can take a view of what prevails today; of what prevailed 50 years ago.

'But I would also want answers for the time when Dr. Raghuram Rajan was in the governor's post speaking about the Indian banks – for which today, to give a lifeline is the primary duty of the finance minister of India. And the lifeline, kind of an emergency, has not come overnight.

'So, if there is a feeling that there has been a centralised leadership now, I like to say that a very democratised leadership led to a whole lot of corruption... Very democratised leadership. The prime minister, after all, is the first among equals in any Cabinet. We have after all inherited the Westminster [model]. Haven't we?

'You need to have a country as diverse as India with an effective leadership. A rather too democratic leadership – which probably will have the approval of quite a lot of liberals – I am afraid, left behind such a nasty stink of corruption which we are cleaning up even today.

'So, very well, I respect his views but if I am given the opportunity – now that you have given me an opportunity – I like to give my view with due respects to Dr. Raghuram Rajan and his knowledge.'

The moment she stopped, many hands were raised (for asking questions) and the audience started clapping.

The moderator, Panagariya, said: 'Well, you know, the next time you go to hear Dr. Raghuram Rajan, you have got your question.'

That eased the tension. Everyone, including a visibly relaxing Sitharaman, laughed.

Who Killed Indian Banking?

A fortnight later, (31 October), the TV Channel CNBC did exactly what Panagariya suggested: It asked Rajan about Sitharaman's comment. He replied: 'I had eight months in the previous [UPA-II] government and I had 26 months under this [NDA] government. So much of my term [as RBI governor] was under this government.'

Rajan added, 'Let me not get into a political back and forth.

The reality is, there is a clean up which we started, which is underway, which needs to be completed fast. The recapitalisation has to be done, but it also has to be done in the non-bank financial sector which is seizing up. And, you need to clean up, and get the financial system going again if you want stronger growth.

'There are people who say "Why did we do the clean up, we could have gone on?" (But) we simply couldn't have gone on because banks were stopping lending because their balance sheets were getting clogged with non-performing loans. So, you had to force recognition and recapitalisation to set them back on track,' he added.

That job was, he said, 'half-finished right now' and 'it has to be finished.'

Two years after he stepped down as RBI governor in 2016, Rajan prepared a 17-page note on bad loans in September 2018. This was at the request of Dr. Murli Manohar Joshi, a member of India's Parliament and chairman of its Estimates Committee.

Through eight sections and seven charts, the note explains how bad loans were created, how the RBI tackled it, whether it could have been done differently and how to prevent a recurrence.

According to Rajan and others who track banking, the genesis of bad loans started in 2006–08. At that time, growth was strong and many infrastructure projects had been completed on time without cost overruns. So, the banks extrapolated past growth and performance and assumed this happy state of affairs would continue.

This led to a classic case of irrational exuberance, as the global financial crisis took hold and growth slowed down. Rajan, in this note, refers to a conversation with one promoter who said he was being wooed by bankers who were waving cheque books and asking him to quote the amount he wanted.

The Golden Era

India's golden era of growth was between financial years 2005–06 and 2007–08 (April 2005 to March 2008 – India follows an

April–March financial year), before the onset of the so-called Subprime crisis.

The gross domestic product (GDP) of the Indian economy grew at 9.5 per cent in 2005–06, 9.6 per cent in 2006–07 and 9.3 per cent in 2007–08, under the old national income accounts methodology. The average inflation (the yardstick for inflation calculation was the wholesale price index in those days) in 2006 was 4.42 per cent; in 2007, 6.59 per cent; and 2008, 4.74 per cent. The fiscal deficit, which was 3.96 per cent of GDP in 2006, dropped to 3.32 per cent in 2007 and further to 2.54 per cent in 2008.

The cocktail of high economic growth, even higher credit growth, low inflation and a reduced fiscal deficit led to risk-taking by corporations and banks. Bank credit grew at breakneck pace. Non-food credit – that is, commercial loans from banks – rose by 32.35 per cent year-on-year in 2006, 26.07 per cent in 2007 and 21.14 per cent in 2008. Economists say that bank credit should ideally grow at no more than three times the GDP growth rate. But in 2006, it clearly crossed that threshold.

In September 2008, the collapse of US investment bank, Lehman Brothers Holdings Inc., triggered a global financial crisis. Institutions all over the world with exposure to dodgy US mortgages suffered losses, or went bust.

The Reddy Regime

The RBI's 21st governor, Y.V. Reddy, is widely credited for protecting India's banking system from the impact of the global financial crisis. Reddy completed a five-year term in office on 5 September 2008, just over a week before Lehman went down.

In an interview with this author (Chapter 12), Reddy defends the high credit growth during his tenure, claiming it was not a bubble. An increase in household financial savings and a reduction in the government's revenue deficit created the ideal situation for genuine growth, he says.

But of course, there were elements of a bubble, particularly in sectors like housing and infrastructure. Reddy sensed the impending storm and he successfully ring-fenced Indian banks from global turmoil, through a policy of monetary and regulatory tightening.

As the crisis loomed, Reddy raised the risk weight on banks' exposure to commercial real estate, housing loans to individuals against mortgage of properties, consumer credit and capital market exposures.

Banks are required to keep capital in hand to be able to absorb the impact of potential bad loans. If a higher risk-weight is assigned to a given class of loans, the bank must set aside more capital for giving such loans. Hence, higher risk weights lead to higher cost of money for banks and higher interest rates for the borrowers. This discourages excessive lending and borrowing.

In central banking parlance, this is a 'counter-cyclical' measure. The RBI also hiked provisions for 'standard assets' (loans where interest and principal are repaid on time) progressively from 2005, and it clamped down on banks borrowing from other banks.

The banking sector's gross bad loans were 3.3 per cent of the overall loan portfolio in 2006. This declined to 2.5 per cent in 2007 and 2.25 per cent in 2008. After provisions, net bad loans dipped to 1.2 per cent in 2006, and further reduced to 1 per cent in 2007 and 2008. However, this did not last. By 2018, gross bad loans had risen to 11.2 per cent, and net bad loans had risen to 6 per cent in 2018.

Death of DFIs

Although the irrational exuberance of 2006–08 may have led to risk-taking, there were other factors contributing to the malaise in banking. One of these was a policy decision taken way back in the 1990s, which, in turn, reversed a policy decision taken just after Independence.

A special class of lenders called development finance institutions (DFIs) were created just after Independence. The DFIs were promoted, owned, and assisted by the government to offer long-term project financing, particularly for infrastructure. Banks were meant to focus on short-term loans such as the working capital needs of commercial borrowers.

The logic was that banks borrow their funds through short-term loans – savings accounts can be closed anytime and even fixed deposits mature in a few years. However, infrastructure projects need long-term capital since projects have longer gestation periods.

The DFIs were meant to service such long-term needs. This was possible so long as they had access to low-cost, long-tenure financing. For decades, they had access to the low-cost National Industrial Credit Long Term Operations Fund, which was created out of the profits of the RBI. (The RBI generates profits through the so-called seigniorage on every bank note it prints since the cost of printing is less than the face-value beside buying and selling bonds in the open market and deploying foreign exchange reserves, among others.) The DFIs also raised cheap money through bonds, backed by government guarantees.

The first DFI was the Industrial Finance Corporation of India Ltd (IFCI), set up in 1948, under an Act of Parliament, to meet medium- and long-term financial needs. The Industrial Credit and Investment Corporation of India Ltd (ICICI) followed in 1955 and the Industrial Development Bank of India (IDBI) was created in 1964 as a wholly-owned subsidiary of the RBI.

In the 1990s, policy changed and the DFIs started being phased out. It was assumed that long-term capital needs could also be serviced by scheduled commercial banks and the bond market.

The DFIs had to die because the windows for cheap money closed as reforms gathered pace after liberalisation in 1991. DFIs found themselves raising money through short-duration, high-cost financing and creating longer-maturity assets. This asset–liability mismatch was unsustainable.

Many believe that the death of the DFIs led to or contributed largely to a bad loan crisis in the 1990s. The peak of that wave of bad loans came in 1994 when 19.07 per cent of banking assets turned into gross bad loans, and 13.71 per cent turned into net bad loans after provisioning.

Nobody cares to look at IFCI today. It is now a listed penny stock which can be called a non-deposit-taking, non-banking financial company (NBFC) with a weak balance sheet.

Another DFI, IDBI struggled with increasing asset–liability mismatches before it became a 'full-service universal bank'. This required complicated legal manoeuvres:

First, the Industrial Development Bank (Transfer of Undertaking and Repeal) Act 2003 gave it the status of a company. Then the RBI turned it into a scheduled bank in September 2004. IDBI's own banking arm, which had been set up in 1994, was merged into the parent institution. This 'infanticide' was committed in 2005 to complete the transformation from DFI into bank.

A Government of India review in 2002 said, 'Financial sector reforms, involving interest rate deregulation, increased competition from banks, and lack of concessional funds have rendered the business models of DFIs unsustainable.'

Nobody sheds tears for the DFIs but banks, which used to focus on working capital loans, struggled to learn the art of project lending. Even two decades down the line, they continue to stumble in this area. A deep corporate bond market might have made a difference, but such a market does not exist.

Project Dreams

The third large DFI, ICICI became a universal bank in 2002 by merging with its child, ICICI Bank Ltd. That banking arm was born in 1994 when the RBI granted licences to ten new banks.

The ICICI merger was quite dramatic. On 5 October 2000, ICICI's managing director (MD) and chief executive officer (CEO), K.V. Kamath and his core team of Nachiket Mor, Chanda Kochhar and P.H. Ravikumar, along with ICICI Bank's MD and CEO, H.N. Sinor, unveiled a road map to universal banking. The presentation was made to three RBI deputy governors – Reddy, S.P. Talwar and Jagdish Kapoor – at the 18th floor of the RBI's headquarters on Mint Road, Mumbai.

Code-named 'Project Dreams', this was basically a reverse

merger, where the smaller banking arm would take over the larger DFI. In about 20 minutes, Kamath's team displayed 22 slides describing the path of migrating the DFI into a universal bank in most minute details.

Till 2013, ICICI Bank was among the biggest infrastructure lenders. But it then started to focus on retail and unsecured lending. In 2019, ICICI Bank would finally shut down its project financing division to reduce its exposure to long-term assets, especially in infrastructure.

Shallow Corporate Bond Market

'There is no liquidity!' A banker who started his career on the trading floor, and retired as the boss of a large PSB, once told me that in his 36-year career, he had never heard any other description of the corporate bond market.

This statement best sums up the problems. The lack of depth is one reason why long-term financing is high risk. Bonds are secured instruments, which allow funds to be raised for the long term, or even forever (in the case of perpetual bonds). If a bond-holder wishes to exit, she can sell the instrument in the secondary market. Hence, a bank which uses short-term financing, or a mutual fund facing redemption demands, can also pick up long-duration bonds without fears of asset–liability mismatch.

This of course, depends on a liquid secondary bond market where instruments are easily traded. This is the case in most developed markets, including the US. Trading volumes in debt markets are much higher than in stocks across most of the First World.

But India is a different story. There are few corporate bond investors – mostly insurance companies, pension retirement funds and mutual funds, apart from banks. The insurers and the Employees Provident Fund Organisation (EPFO) are not allowed to trade in the secondary market, leading to reduced volumes. Foreign investors are not too excited about investing in corporate bonds either.

There are many other problems. Most corporate bonds are privately placed with a select set of investors instead of being launched via the public issue route. This is done to save time and avoid disclosures but it leads to loss of transparency.

Holidays also lead to inconvenience. If the redemption falls on a holiday, the issuer is required to pay up on the last working day before the holiday. But different states have different sets of holidays.

Although there has been much talk about enhancing bond market liquidity, there has been little movement on the ground. The 2006 Union Budget appointed a high-level expert committee to look into the legal, regulatory, tax and market design issues in development of the corporate bond market.

R.H. Patil, founder and first MD of National Stock Exchange (NSE) India Ltd, headed the committee, which had 11 members of repute such as U.K. Sinha and C.B. Bhave (both of whom went on to chair India's capital market regulator), and Usha Thorat, an RBI deputy governor.

But nothing much happened in terms of real changes in liquidity even after the committee submitted its report. Succeeding budgets have seen many similar committees set up. In addition, the RBI and the Securities and Exchange Board of India (SEBI), have explored ways to develop this market.

In the 2019 Budget too, Finance Minister Sitharaman announced fresh measures to deepen the corporate bond market, including the formation of a Credit Guarantee Enhancement Corporation to help companies boost credit rating and raise cheaper funding.

Since 2016, the RBI has insisted on big corporations raising part of long-term borrowings from the corporate bond market. In fact, companies with large exposures must raise one-fourth of fresh borrowings from there. The regulations also ask every company that plans to raise at least ₹200 crore from the bond market to issue electronic instruments.

There is some hope of things getting better. The tri-party repo, for instance, could improve liquidity and make the secondary market livelier. This is a contract where a third entity (aside from the borrower and lender), called a Tri-Party Agent, acts as an intermediary between the two parties and facilitates the transaction.

The third party oversees selection of the bond that is offered as collateral to raise money, payment, settlement and custody – essentially doing due diligence and managing all the processes. Once the tripartite corporate bond repo market gathers volume, there will be more liquidity.

The financial market regulator SEBI has also mandated the consolidation of ISINs, or international securities identification numbers. ISIN, a 12-digit code, is the unique identification of a security. The consolidation of all securities of the same maturity under one ISIN will boost liquidity.

Take-out Financing Never Took Off

Yet another instrument in the financial tool kit is take-out financing. That has also not gained traction.

Take-out financing is a model for providing long-duration finance through medium-term loans. For instance, say a project needs to raise money for 15 years. There are three potential lenders but none of them can handle loans of more than five years tenure. Well, they can agree to finance the project by successively offering loans of five-year maturity each. Each lender takes out the previous lender's loan.

Alternatively, a single institution like the India Infrastructure Finance Company Ltd (IIFCL), can enter after commercial operation of the project (let us say, four years from sanction and disbursement of the first loan) and 'take out' the loan and carry it for the rest of its life.

This is an internationally accepted way of lending to infrastructure projects. The basic purpose is to address asset–liability mismatches and maintain banks' exposure to different sectors as prescribed by the RBI (banks cannot hold exposures of more than a certain percentage of their entire portfolio in any given sector). It solves asset–liability mismatch and also frees up commercial banks' funds for incremental credit to new projects.

The reason why this has not taken off in India is that under RBI norms, one entity needs to agree to take out the exposure of another entity to an infrastructure project on 'pre-determined basis'. That is, the terms of agreement of transferring the loan need to be agreed in advance. This ignores changes in the project's risk profile. Banks are also required to set aside higher capital for take-out exposures.

The take-out financing model has been in existence since 2006 when IIFCL, a special purpose vehicle for infrastructure financing, was set up. But the first such transaction only took place in October 2010.

The concept would have been more popular if there had been dynamic loan pricing, when a loan leaves one bank's books and migrates. Ideally, such arrangements should have a system of step-down pricing. The banks should charge higher interest rates at initial stages, when the risks are higher. At that stage, if a project stalls before commencement, there is no cash-flow. Once the project is up and running, risks reduce.

At first sight, external commercial borrowings could also have come in handy for long-term projects. But there is a cap on the interest rates for such borrowings and this makes them unpopular (apart from currency risks). In 2014, the RBI introduced a flexible structuring of long-term project loans for infrastructure but this was then withdrawn.

In 2016, the RBI allowed NBFCs to refinance any existing infrastructure loans and other project loans by way of take-out financing, without pre-determined agreements. But although the concept exists, it has not taken off.

The death of DFIs, an anaemic and illiquid corporate bond market and stillborn take-out financing are among the structural issues affecting banking. Some other unexpected developments have also added to the bankers' woes.

Flood of Money

In October 2008, just over a week before Lehman Brothers filed for bankruptcy, D. Subbarao took over as the RBI governor. Subbarao had been the finance secretary. He responded to the global crisis by flooding the system with money and cutting policy rates to historic lows.

The first rate-cut was announced on 20 October 2008 in response to an incipient liquidity crisis. The overnight inter-bank call money rates had soared and the commercial banks were running dry.

Banks had stopped lending to individuals as well as to corporations because they were worried about liquidity disappearing. They were also trying to raise money and retain it, by paying very high rates to depositors.

The RBI acted decisively to restore confidence and convince banks that liquidity would be maintained. It cut the policy rate from 9 per cent to 4.75 per cent between October 2008 and April 2009.

It also slashed the cash reserve ratio (CRR). This is the proportion of deposits that commercial banks must either keep with the central bank, or hold in cash. The CRR was cut from 9 per cent to 5 per cent and the minimum invested in government bonds was reduced from 25 per cent to 24 per cent. This freed more funds for commercial credit.

The Indian economy displayed a lot of resilience during the crisis. GDP growth dropped below 5 per cent for only one quarter – January–March 2009 – and it bounced back fast. After three successive years of 9 per cent-plus growth, growth sagged, albeit to a relatively healthy 6.72 per cent in 2009, even as the rest of the world struggled through what is now called the Great Recession.

In the next two years, growth rates recovered to 8.59 per cent and then 8.91 per cent. But this growth was due to an injection of steroids in the form of easy money and loan forgiveness.

Banks were allowed to repeatedly restructure bad loans. This helped borrowers – affected by global demand recession and the collapse of exports and thus, in no position to pay back loans.

India staged a sharp, V-shaped recovery. But the ultra-loose monetary policy and massive loan restructuring induced inflation and this led to the creation of bad assets. It was only after the inflation genie was bottled up that the RBI could wage war against NPAs.

Policy Paralysis

The second term of the UPA government (UPA-2) ran from May 2009 to April 2014. The latter half of UPA-2 is marked by policy paralysis and that added spice to the simmering bad-loan problem.

As Rajan's note details, a variety of governance problems such as the suspect allocation of coal mines coupled with the fear of investigation slowed down government decision-making.

Infrastructure Blues

Core industries such as metals production, and projects across the infrastructure sector generated the largest share of bad loans.

Metals, and the steel industry in particular, contributed the maximum chunk of bad loans. In March 2019, 28.5 per cent of all NPAs came from the metals sector, while it was as high as 46.3 per cent in March 2018.

In March 2019, infrastructure (power, roads and telecom, etc.) contributed about 18 per cent of all bad loans. This was lower than the 22.6 per cent infrastructure infra contributed to bad loans in March 2018.

The power sector accounted for about one-fifth of the banks' total exposure to industry at its peak. In March 2016, the share was 21.24 per cent. The share of basic metals, (including steel), was about 12 per cent in January 2020. At that time, the road sector contributed close to 7 per cent of all industrial loans, and telecommunications, close to 5 per cent.

Stalled projects saw costs shooting up. As debt became unserviceable, many became 'zombie' projects. There were bad loans generated across every infrastructure with stranded power plants, incomplete road projects and a huge mess in telecom.

Let us take a brief look at the causes of stalled projects.

Land acquisition and other issues

Any infrastructure project requires land and land acquisition is a roadblock, literally so, in the case of highway projects. A November 2019 Union government survey examined 190 delayed infrastructure projects and found that at least 70 per cent were stalled over land acquisition issues, with especial regard to the compensation payable. This survey was undertaken in consultation with state governments in order to identify projects that could be revived and to expedite completion of these.

Sixty projects implemented by the Indian Railways, 40 projects implemented by the National Highways Authority of India (NHAI) and 28 power projects across India faced difficulties in acquiring land. The delays varied. Some projects were delayed for a decade or even more.

In most cases, conflicts over land transfers arose due to differences of opinion between the Union and state governments on the amount of compensation to be paid to the landowners whose land was being acquired.

In several other projects, protests by displaced citizens either led to delays, or termination. As many as 20 more projects failed to receive environmental clearances from the respective state governments.

Bihar topped the list of states with issues pertaining to highway projects. In Uttar Pradesh, the NHAI was unable to acquire land for highway projects as the state government imposed a condition that the apex roads authority would have to guarantee the development of a 10-metre-wide strip of plantation along either side of the highways if the project involved the felling of existing trees.

According to a March 2009 report published in *Mint*, the Centre unsuccessfully tried for four years to get the state government to drop this clause.

Power Projects

Projects in the power sector suffered from generic land acquisition issues as well as issues specific to the sector. These included capacity additions without any Power Purchase Agreement (PPA) with distribution companies (discoms), coal supply issues, the inability of discoms to pay generators, regulatory challenges of various kinds, the inability of promoters to infuse equity and tardy project implementation.

A high-level empowered committee was set up by the Union government in 2018 to examine 34 'stressed' thermal power projects, (mostly private sector), with a total generation capacity of 40,130 MW.

The key findings were:

- After the Supreme Court cancelled the allocation of 204 coal mines in 2014, many projects were stranded without assured coal supply.
- Lower-than-anticipated growth in demand coupled to surplus supply resulted in under-utilisation of capacity. More stress arose because many projects had failed to tie up PPAs, and others suffered from termination or non-operationalisation of PPAs, and low off-take of expensive power.
- Delayed realisation of receivables from discoms was endemic. This impaired the ability to service debt and exhausted working capital. In some cases, discoms also pressed for renegotiating PPAs.
- Delay in land acquisition, inadequate transmission systems, slow statutory clearances, etc. delayed projects, affecting viability. Promoters were unable to infuse additional equity in many instances.

The Panel also blamed banks for delays in approval of working capital. This happened when banks hit the limit of permitted exposure to a sector (in this case, power). Even if the working capital was sanctioned, the banks avoided disbursal of even relatively insignificant amounts once it hit the limit.

The Telecom Story

The telecom story is also fascinating. Years of litigation came to a climax in October 2019 when the Supreme Court dismissed petitions seeking review of the definition of adjusted gross revenue (AGR). That judgment leaves telecom operators liable to pay tens of thousands of crores in pending dues.

The government is demanding pending licence fees and spectrum usage charges, including penalties, interest and interest on unpaid interest. The telcos say the government's interpretation of what it was owed under the 1999 revenue-sharing agreement is too broad and unfair, as it includes non-telecom revenue, such as interest and dividend income.

Banks are caught in this crossfire. The telecom industry already owes huge sums, some of which was borrowed by companies, which have gone bankrupt. Delivering its verdict in September 2020, the Supreme Court allowed the telecom companies a ten-year timeline for payment of AGR dues, beginning April 2021 after making an upfront payment of 10 per cent of the dues.

■ ■ ■

PART 2

Many macroeconomic factors beyond any banker's control may have contributed to the bad loan crisis. But this does not mean the banks were blameless. Seduced by the lure of credit growth, they failed to do due diligence and accept project appraisals done externally, at face value. And, when they ran into trouble, the banks also tried to cover up the extent of bad loans by using innovative instruments, evergreening through fresh loans and creative accounting measures.

Lazy Project Appraisals

Another factor which has contributed to the chaos is the fondness for outsourcing project appraisals.

Rajan's note says the bankers were over-confident and did too little due diligence for some loans. Many banks did no independent analysis, relying solely on external agencies. Such outsourcing is a weakness, and it multiplies possibilities for undue influence.

The RBI releases a biannual Financial Stability Report (FSR), which is a six-monthly health check of banking. The December

2019 edition mentions this outsourcing arrangement without naming any entity.

> The impairment crisis in the banks has also highlighted certain basic deficiencies with regard to the appraisal of long-term projects with a significant gestation time... A significant part of such projects undertaken was consortium lending with appraisals carried out by professional merchant bankers with built-in conflicts of interest (since they are paid by the borrowers).

SBI Caps

Many feel that India's largest lender's merchant banking arm – SBI Capital Markets Ltd, popularly known as SBI Caps – contributed to the messy situation that arose around project appraisals.

Corporations were always anxious to get SBI Caps to carry out project appraisal and loan syndication assignments. A stamp of approval more or less guaranteed being in the good books of the gigantic State Bank of India (SBI). Having SBI on board in turn meant other banks would queue up to offer money. This led to a classic conflict of interest.

Let us look at the origins of this toxic situation.

In the 1990s, project financing was done through a combination of rupee term loans and so-called 'deferred payment guarantees' against which external commercial borrowings facilities could be drawn by borrowers.

A deferred payment guarantee is issued by a bank, at the request of a customer for buying goods or machinery with a commitment to pay after a specified time in either lump sum, or instalments. The bank undertakes to pay the instalments due under the deferred payment schedule. In effect, it is a loan given by the seller of the goods (or services) to the buyer, with the guarantee of the bank bringing comfort to both parties.

In the late 1990s, commercial banks were allowed to participate in infrastructure financing only up to a limit of ₹1,000 crore with sublimits of ₹400 crore for rupee loans and ₹600 crore for guarantees.

In April 1999, the RBI cleared the decks for all commercial banks to participate in infrastructure lending. Loan syndication was also allowed. The banks could do their own project appraisals or follow the appraisal of a lead lender.

The SBI already had a merchant banking arm in SBI Caps, which had been set up in 1986 by hiving off SBI's merchant banking division. In 1995, the SBI set up a project finance business unit for assessing infrastructure and other projects. It created an infrastructure and project appraisal group within SBI Caps for this purpose.

SBI Caps has its fingers in all sorts of financial pies. It offers the gamut of investment banking and corporate advisory services such as project advisory, structured debt placements, manages public issues and private placements, mergers and acquisitions, private equity and stressed assets resolution.

But over time, loan syndication turned out to be its mainstay, generating over 90 per cent of SBI Caps' total revenues between 2010 and 2015. Typically, it earns 0.25–0.50 per cent commission on each syndication. The commission rate is reduced for very large projects.

As competition intensified, merchant bankers dropped their fees for handling initial public issues (IPOs). For example, fees for handling IPOs of public sector undertakings went down to a token ₹1. The SBI Caps headquarters in Cuffe Parade, Mumbai, used to display photographs of cheques of less than ₹2 as commission earned for jointly handling an IPO.

Once it saw dwindling market share in managing public issues, SBI Caps reinvented itself. It was already attracting talent from the Indian Institutes of Management (IIMs) and from other top management institutes, which meant it had a bunch of executives with degrees in engineering and management.

But around 2000, SBI Caps also started to recruit from DFIs, particularly IDBI, which was still a prominent term lending institution at the time. These recruits were typically engineers and chartered accountants who had exposure to infrastructure financing. This coincided with the focus on infrastructure lending by the banks.

SBI Caps also had a captive market due to its parent. Borrowers would approach it for project appraisal; at the next stage, SBI would often come in as a lender (not in all cases though); and, once SBI was on board, other banks would follow.

The formula was actually as simple as that. Banks were hungry for credit growth, but project appraisal and risk management were not their forte. SBI Caps cashed in on these lacunae.

The government also engaged SBI Caps for formulating policies and model concession agreements for different sectors to attract public–private participation in projects.

The overall focus was on generating financial analysis via excel spreadsheets, while consultants would do the technical analysis. SBI Caps relied on techno-economic viability studies undertaken by reputable technical consultants such as Development Consultants Pvt Ltd, Sargent & Lundy and Tata Consulting Engineers Ltd in power sector; Engineers India Ltd in oil and gas; and LEA Associates South Asia Pvt Ltd and STUP Consultants in road sector. It also relied on traffic studies undertaken by reputable consultants in roads and ports.

The Beginning

In 2009, SBI Caps handled a restructuring for Maytas Infra Ltd, a listed company promoted by the family of B. Ramalinga Raju. Raju was the CEO-founder of Satyam Computer Services Ltd, and was responsible for the first major fraud in the infotech sector.

SBI Caps engaged with the company's 17 lenders, led by SBI, ICICI Bank Ltd and IL&FS. IL&FS was at that time, the largest shareholder in Maytas Infra, with 37.1 per cent stake. IL&FS took over the troubled firm in August 2009. Maytas Infra was rechristened IL&FS Engineering & Construction Company Ltd in January 2011.

In 2010, SBI Caps handled debt restructuring at the now-defunct Kingfisher Airlines Ltd and at Air India.

By 2013, the floodgates of debt restructuring had opened up and SBI Caps was reeling in many clients. The game plan was as follows. SBI Caps would be appointed by the promoter. It would rely heavily on information made available by the promoter and by technical consultants to analyse the company. Once it had completed this exercise, it would hawk the restructuring product to banks.

SBI and its associate banks (which were merged into the parent in 2017) were the first port of call. Once SBI sanctioned a loan, it became a passport for other banks to participate.

By deploying a shrewd strategy of playing one bank against another, SBI Caps would create demand, and reduce the cost of loans. In their eagerness to get a slice of the pie, banks would often end up mispricing risks.

Many projects, particularly in road and power, went bust due to faulty government policies and court rulings. But one could argue that there have also been instances when SBI Caps turned a blind eye to the inevitable.

Take Nagarjuna Oil Refinery Ltd, for example. This became a classic case of evergreening of loans. In 2017, a cyclone damaged the tanks and port structure of this petroleum refinery project. The delay pushed up costs and made it unviable. But the banks poured good money after bad to keep the account 'standard' and not have it classified an NPA. Fresh loans were used to pay interest on the earlier loan (principal repayments were not required until project completion).

Simple Plot, Creative Storytelling

In its essentials, the evergreening plotline was simple. When a project got delayed, the banks approached an investment banker like SBI Caps to create some room for fresh loans.

This could be done through various creative means. In some cases, a sub-project was created, or the original project was expanded, or a product line was added. The company setting up the project could, for example, buy so-called 'line-balancing' equipment to make it more viable and efficient.

Let us say the new facility may need ₹300 crore. The cost can be padded up with frills like building improvement, retrofitting of equipment, repairs and other miscellaneous expenses (difficult to quantify), making it, say, ₹500 crore. Such practices were rampant in the power and steel sectors.

Lenders sanctioned additional loans, based on the investment banker's appraisal (with nominal or zero equity infusion from the promoter). The lending banks claimed the new loans helped the company service the interest and instalments, and so prevented the entire exposure from becoming an NPA.

There have been instances where SBI Caps did not go deep into the technological viability studies done by consultants. The banks ended up financing companies to ostensibly buy plants and machinery, based on quotes from entities that did not actually exist.

In one such case, the investment banker relied on the technical inputs given by the promoter firm, which was a media company, and did not verify the equipment supplier. The bankers later filed a case of fraud against the promoters. However, by the time the investigative agencies got into action, the promoters had fled the country.

Or, take the case of Electrosteel Steels Ltd. An integrated steel plant could not be completed on time. The promoters did not have enough money to push it through to completion. There was a taker for the project but the promoters did not wish to let it go. Instead of selling it off, the loan was restructured with the help of SBI Caps. Ultimately, it was sold to the old bidder but the bankers had to take a much bigger haircut due to the delay.

Creative Restructuring

As RBI examined and unfolded a series of restructuring schemes, more and more 'innovative products' started surfacing.

The Export Performance Bank Guarantee (EPBG) is one such innovation. Here, a company, with or without an export record, enters into a contract for exports with importers abroad, willing to advance cash against an export performance bank guarantee.

Now how does this work? First, a bank in India sanctions and releases an EPBG – a non-fund based facility. At the second stage, a bank overseas – normally a banker to the overseas importer – discounts this guarantee and provides funds to the company.

In effect, the overseas bank takes an exposure to a domestic bank. The money is actually used for regularising the domestic fund-based facilities. The company is 'saved' from becoming an NPA in the lending bank's books.

Thus, a non-fund-based facility is converted into fund-based facility. In due course, when the company fails to export enough (this is likely as it has not acquired adequate capacity), the EPBG is invoked, leading to payment of the funds by the Indian bank, rendering the account again an NPA.

Why was this done? Just to kick the problem down the road and postpone the inevitable in the fond hope that the situation would improve, and the company would come out of the woods.

Another such innovation is stand-by letters of credit or SBLC – a sort of financial guarantee. Raw materials for manufacturing goods are bought, using an SBLC. Once they are sold, the bills presented under the SBLC are honoured and borrowers make the payments.

For a genuine borrower, backed by exports, this is a good product which ensures access to cheap dollar funds during periods when the USD–INR rate is stable.

But it also comes in handy in preventing accounts being recognised as NPAs. This is done by issuing long-dated financial guarantees (generally in foreign currency by overseas branches of Indian banks and discounted in India) and crediting the proceeds to the domestic account.

The SBLC was rampantly misused by many companies, including Winsome Diamonds and Jewellery Ltd, Suzlon Power Ltd, Shree Ganesh Jewellery House (I) Ltd and Sterling Biotech Ltd. On many occasions, SBLCs were also rolled over (with a new

SBLC being issued as the old one was due for expiry) when the companies on whose behalf such a facility was issued did not have the funds to pay on the due date. So, eventually stress returned to these accounts.

Since SBLC is not a fund-based facility, both the bankers and the corporations were liberally using it to raise funds for buying raw materials. The problems were aggravated when the SBLC was not rolled over, or the overseas lending bank insisted on invoking it but no bank was willing to rescue borrowers who could not pay the dues.

Many bankers allege SBI held all sorts of troubled assets in its kitty and SBI Caps was making 'ridiculous' projections about the future of these companies.

One such case was a proposal for 'realignment' of bad loans given to the companies of a large domestic business group. These loans had been made by a consortium of lenders. The promoters had already been termed wilful defaulters and were also on the caution list of the ECGC Ltd (known as Export Credit Guarantee Corporation of India Ltd before 2014).

A wilful defaulter is one who has the capacity to service bank loans but does not do so. Fund diversion also makes one a wilful defaulter.

Banks are supposed to be cautious while dealing with exporters on the ECGC caution list. Many lending banks had already filed suits for recovery of loans and some had even secured winding-up notices.

The proposal envisaged the lenders converting their bad loans into 'standard' loans through a credit substitute, clearing all overdues. Essentially, it was an attempt to evergreen the account.

The plan was that the existing domestic lenders would issue SBLCs for the subsidiary of a group company, incorporated overseas. This company would then borrow from overseas banks against the SBLCs and lend these funds on to its subsidiary.

At the next stage, this subsidiary would use some of these funds to repay debt owed to some shell companies set up by the group in a tax haven. The shell companies, in the garb of investors unrelated to the group, would then invest these funds as foreign direct investment (FDI) in the domestic defaulting group companies to help them clear overdues.

This is how the stage was set for the domestic lenders to 'refinance' the debt of the domestic companies, which became 'standard' through this rerouting.

With effect from April 2015, the RBI directed that a 'standard' loan would immediately be downgraded to NPA upon restructuring. From that point onwards, public sector banking circles started talking about 'refinancing', 'realignment' and 'consolidation' of debt – all euphemisms for restructuring to circumvent the RBI regulation.

Yet another innovative product is securitisation of future profits from sale. Here, fresh money is given by calculating the net present value of future profits for servicing loans. This ignores the point that loans are supposedly sanctioned only after the bank has factored in future profits. In effect, this is like lending money twice against the same asset.

Confidence Tricks

If you walk down Mumbai's Fashion Street and you are offered Dolce & Gabbana T-Shirts and Louis Vuitton bags at fabulous discounts, it is common sense to suspect the labels are fake. You cannot buy a genuine Rolex watch on a footpath either (unless it is stolen).

Bankers failed to apply even this level of basic common sense while doing their due diligence. There has been blatant fakery in some cases.

In one such case, it was only after CBI officers entered the SBI Caps office in Cuffe Parade, that SBI Caps realised that it had been duped. Two senior employees of a public sector consulting firm had been involved in preparing a detailed project report (DPR) for a sick, large private sector steel company.

But this pair had actually left the consulting firm long ago. While doing the project appraisal, they were actually on the sick steel company's payroll! They had simply flaunted their old visiting cards to establish their credentials in SBI, and SBI Caps accepted the DPR printed on the letterhead of the PSU consulting firm at face value.

In some ways SBI Caps was the fall guy used by banks to dress up their loans and keep balance sheet looking apparently healthy. While SBI Caps and others can be blamed for sloppy project appraisals, why did not the bankers carry out basic checks? It is the duty of the bankers to go through the projections and question and look for inconsistencies.

Many projections were also simply based on copy-pasting government statistics on data, like road traffic and power consumption. There was no attempt to go deeper in appraisals.

In their greed for credit growth, many banks just lapped up any proposal vetted by SBI Caps. In a fiercely competitive market, they also cut interest rates, thus mispricing the risks.

The Defence

'It is unfair to blame SBI Caps for the mess. What can SBI Caps do? You must remember it never ever did the techno-economic viability of the projects... All the projects were approved for funding on so many assumptions which had gone wrong,' says Arundhati Bhattacharya, former SBI chairman, who had headed SBI Caps before taking up the bigger assignment.

Before moving to the corner room, Bhattacharya's successor Rajnish Kumar also served as the MD of SBI Caps. He had also been a chief general manager in SBI, overseeing project finance. He says, 'No one can question the capability of SBI Caps to appraise projects. But banks need to do their own due diligence before financing projects.

'When I was heading the project finance unit in the bank, I had rejected and amended many of the proposals done by SBI Caps. It is a fact that other banks draw a lot of comfort from SBI's association with a project as a lender but are they not supposed to do their own due diligence?'

The RBI draws up an annual risk mitigation plan for all banks. In 2016, it flagged its concerns about the role played by SBI Caps and the perceived conflicts of interest.

After that, to avoid potential conflict of interest, SBI started doing project financing and syndication in-house for private sector companies, leaving SBI Caps to focus only on government projects. This, of course, does not address the problem of PSBs' lack of expertise in the appraisal of project loans.

Hope Banking

This can be called 'hope banking'. The banks were living in hope. In many troubled projects, there was evergreening with the banks disbursing fresh loans to book artificial profits by recovering interest on previous loans.

A classic example of such 'hope banking' is the 400 MW Shree Maheshwar Hydel Power Corporation Ltd. This was the first privately-promoted hydro project in Madhya Pradesh. Conceived in 1992, the project on the Narmada ran smack into the agitation against the Narmada Dam project. It never took off. The promoters' equity was not enough to compensate for cost over-runs and it was apparent that the project was never going to start generating power.

However, it stayed alive! Banks kept up a continuous infusion of funds. By November 2010, 30 per cent of the project was completed. In 2011, the cost per unit of power produced was estimated at above ₹11. The PPA with the MP Electricity Board had originally pegged the cost at ₹2.64 a unit, and later revised this to ₹5.32.

The 2019 annual report of its promoter exudes confidence, saying 'even now several investors are interested' and they will be 'in a position to kick-start the project'. In April 2020, the Madhya Pradesh government finally terminated the PPA, dropping the curtain after 28 fruitless years. The banks would have probably been prepared to pump fresh money down this rabbit-hole without the PPA termination.

This is just one instance of hope banking. Such absurdities continued until Rajan decided to blow the whistle and cracked down on NPAs. Urjit Patel carried on the agenda of cleaning house.

The next chapter deals with that…

■ ■ ■

2

The War Against NPAs

PART 1

A retired deputy governor of the RBI once told me he had always wondered why PSBs postponed the recognition of bad loans.

It is true that once a bad loan is recognised, profits are reduced or even turn into losses. But compensation at PSBs is not linked to the bank's performance, so where is the harm in recognising bad loans?

Credit decisions or even bad loan recovery at PSBs can lead to the senior bankers being hounded by government investigative agencies. But there is no such fear when it comes to recognising a bad loan.

Paradoxically, private banks tend to recognise bad loans relatively quickly, despite the fact that compensation at private banks is linked to performance.

It is an interesting question. The answers are illuminating. A public sector banker says the RBI deputy governor's question can be answered with two words: Pride and hope.

The PSBs' share in bad loans is disproportionately higher than their market share of total loans. As of March 2020, among 34 listed Indian banks, the PSBs together held around 59.38 per cent of loans but they were responsible for 71.78 per cent of gross NPAs.

Any lender may see a given loan turn bad and become an NPA. Bad loans hurt in two different ways. The loan is not earning interest, and even the principal may be lost. In addition, the bank must set aside money to provide for NPAs. This double-whammy hits profits.

The problems get worse when the loss is larger than the bank's capacity to make provision comfortably – that is, profits earned elsewhere will not cover the loss. The bank then goes into denial mode.

The legendary P.C. Sorcar Jr used to perform a trick called 'Water of India', where an ordinary-looking jug would keep magically refilling itself no matter how often it was emptied. Similarly, the government, the majority owner of the PSBs, can continue to inject inexhaustible amounts of capital into them.

But PSBs are listed and the share price falls as the NPAs rise. It is traumatic for the CEO of a PSB to be reduced to watching that collapse playing out live across the TV screen.

This is why PSBs delay the recognition of bad loans. *Why* loans turn bad is a different story.

The Evolution of Restructuring

The definition of NPAs and loan restructuring are dynamic phenomena, and there is a chequered history.

The concept of loan restructuring can be traced to the Great Depression of 1929–39, when 'loan modification' was introduced in the USA. A series of mortgage modification schemes were put in place to prevent banks foreclosing and auctioning homes where buyers could not service debt. This was to check rising homelessness and its adverse economic impact.

The earliest Indian directives on restructuring of non-industrial accounts came about in 1978 when the Government of India and the RBI advised banks to reschedule the loans of people affected by floods and other natural calamities.

A structured framework was put in place in the early

1990s, after the introduction of Income Recognition and Asset Classification (IRAC) norms, following the Narasimham Committee recommendations. Initially, this framework was meant only for restructuring industrial accounts. In August 2008, its scope was widened to deal with stressed non-industrial accounts.

Until the mid-1980s, the management of NPAs was left to banks and their auditors. In 1985, the RBI introduced a 'Health Code' system, classifying loans into as many as eight categories – from 1 (satisfactory) to 8 (bad).

In April 1992, the RBI introduced prudential norms on capital adequacy. This was in response to the international banking regulations issued by the Basel Committee on Banking Supervision.

The first phase of the so-called Basel norms, an effort to coordinate banking regulations across the globe to strengthen banking systems, was introduced in 1988.

India adopted it in a gradual process. For instance, in 1993, a loan account used to become NPA if the borrower had not paid for four quarters. In 1994, the period was shortened to three quarters and, in 1995, to two quarters.

In 2001, the RBI replaced the concept of 'past dues' with 'overdues'. An amount is considered as past due when it remains outstanding for 30 days beyond due date. In sync with global standards, the RBI said any dues beyond 90 days would be tagged as an NPA, beginning from April 2003 (financial year 2003–04).

The First Impact

The 1992 prudential norms had a shocking impact as the extent of NPAs became apparent. By 1994, the gross NPAs for all scheduled banks was estimated to be 19.07 per cent of all assets; the PSBs did even worse with gross NPAs held at 24.8 per cent.

It took more than a decade to reduce those NPAs to more manageable levels. Falling interest rates in the early twenty-first century allowed banks to book huge treasury profits and they used these surpluses to provide for the bad loans. The rates started falling early this century and the 10-year bond yield dropped to its historic low of 4.953 per cent on 16 October 2003. The bond prices and yield move in opposite directions. When the prices rise, the yields fall. With interest rates falling, bond prices rose and banks made hefty treasury profits by selling bonds which they had bought earlier at a lower price.

Bad assets are classified as 'sub-standard', 'doubtful' and 'loss assets'. The RBI started tightening definitions.

On 31 March 2001, a sub-standard asset was one which had remained an NPA for up to 18 months; beyond 18 months, it became doubtful. Any loan a bank identified as unrecoverable would be called a loss asset. On 31 March 2005, the RBI decided a sub-standard loan would be treated as doubtful after 12 months, not 18.

The Fine Print

The 2001 review was in the light of international best practices following guidance from the Bank for International Settlements (BIS) and the US Financial Accounting Standards Board (FASB).

The BIS paper on 'Sound Practices for Loan Accounting and Disclosure' (July 1999), says:

> ...A loan should generally be identified as impaired when payments are in arrears for a minimum number of days. As an exception, loans need not be identified as impaired when the loan is fully secured and there is reasonable assurance of timely repayment of principal and interest (including full compensation for overdue payment)...

The FASB's statement number 114 on 'Accounting by Creditors for Impairment of Loan' provided that an 'allowance for credit losses' must be calculated on 'present value basis' when a loan is impaired.

Based on these, the new RBI regulations of March 2001 permitted restructuring on a 'standard' account before, or after the commencement of commercial production. The 'standard' classification could be retained if the instalments of principal alone were rescheduled, and the loan was fully secured.

Finally, for rescheduling of interest, the amount of sacrifice measured in present value terms must be provided for, or written off. That is, if the rescheduling meant the bank foregoing 'X' amount of interest, the net present value of X had to be calculated and provisioned, or subtracted, from the balance sheet.

The same rules would apply to a rescheduled 'sub-standard' account, allowing the 'sub-standard' classification to be retained. The rescheduled 'sub-standard' account could be upgraded to 'standard' category only after one year of satisfactory performance in terms of payment of interest or principal.

The date of commencement of commercial operation (DCCO) in a project plays a key role in deciding on classification of loans.

The Age of Forbearance

In early 2000, the prudential norms were held hostage to government policies. The PSBs held the bulk of the NPAs but since the government did not have the money to recapitalise PSBs, the thrust was on forbearance.

If the borrowers were not paying interest, PSBs would give them a longer rope by increasing the repayment period.

The biggest problem was the so-called evergreening by banks and the routing of additional loans through multiple banks. Multiple banking was, in fact, a tool to ensure that an asset does not turn bad. This was most prevalent in sectors like steel, infrastructure and real estate by around 2010.

At that time, infrastructure was the holy cow. There were a bunch of incentives, including a regulatory cushion, to lend to infrastructure. These loans were also continuously restructured, and enjoyed the standard tag.

This led to a peculiar situation. Banks were financing much more than the financials of companies justified. There was no discipline in lending, and there was also a huge gap in information with the regulators and supervisors.

Banks also need to make provision for standard assets. Typically, they need to provide 0.40 per cent or 40 basis points for standard assets and a lower amount (0.25 per cent) for agricultural loans. For many years, the provision for a restructured stressed asset was held at 2 per cent.

Restructuring is not a new phenomenon. As mentioned earlier, it started in 1978 when loans were restructured for borrowers affected by natural calamities. But the practice gained steam in 2009 after the collapse of Lehman Brothers.

D. Subbarao was then at the helm at the RBI. The system was flush with money and an ultra-loose monetary policy was adopted in the aftermath of the global financial crisis.

The RBI noticed the rise in restructured standard advances from ₹97,834 crore in March 2010 to ₹1,06,859 crore in March 2011, while the gross NPAs of the banking system were ₹81,816 crore and ₹94,088 crore, respectively. This trend prompted Subbarao to set up a working group on restructuring bad loans, chaired by Executive Director B. Mahapatra, in July 2012.

The group recommended raising the provision for restructured loans to 5 per cent. The working group also said that once a loan is restructured, it should be treated as a substandard/bad loan. Till then, restructured loans were treated as standard. The banking community vehemently opposed these recommendations and Subbarao did not implement them.

Tightening the Screw

Subbarao's successor Raghuram Rajan did raise provisioning when he took over in September 2013. Rajan felt that the RBI had given too long a rope to the banks for restructuring and he decided to tighten the screws. The RBI raised the provisioning requirement for restructured loans substantially for different categories, and different maturities.

Till then, asset classification norms called for provision only if an account was not serviced for 90 days, or the borrower had not paid interest and/or principal for three months. The borrowers, in 'consultation' with lenders, were taking advantage of this window. After not paying for 89 days, they would clear a month's due on the

90th day. In banking parlance, this was a 'critical amount'.

The banks were thus violating RBI norms – first by allowing a borrower not to pay for 89 days, and then taking only a month's dues. The new asset classification norm called this bluff.

The banking community was hugely upset about the regulator's new-found aggressiveness. To appease them, the RBI allowed 'rectification' – giving temporary liquidity in the form of loans to help borrowers tide over asset–liability mismatches.

Playing with Banks' Money

Raghuram Rajan identified a problem where risk was being misallocated. When he met an entrepreneur who was narrating a sob story, Rajan asked why he couldn't just sell the company? The entrepreneur explained he could not do this because he had hardly put any equity into the business.

In every normal business venture, the equity holders take the risk. But in India, Rajan found, lenders were taking the risks while the promoters were essentially playing with other people's money.

In September 2016, in his first speech as a deputy governor, N.S. Vishwanathan, also focused on the weak balance sheet of many promoters. He said, 'It appears that there was no adequate effort to assess corporate leverage. We therefore had situations of the promoters ending with much less skin in the game. What this does is to turn the problem of corporate insolvency into a problem of the banks rather than that of the promoters.'

If a business has no equity, the debt gets bloated. One possible solution is to divide such debt into two parts – sustainable and unsustainable. The unsustainable debt, which cannot be serviced, can be converted into equity, transferring the risk to the equity holder. Banks too can convert debt into equity, which gives them a stake in businesses.

If a debt is not serviced, the borrower becomes a defaulter. Equity is risk capital. While a dividend may be paid to equity-holders, there is no legal obligation to pay dividends.

This was the rationale behind the restructuring schemes of the

Rajan era. In June 2015, strategic debt restructuring (SDR) gave banks the power to convert a part of their debt in stressed companies into majority equity. It did not work because promoters delayed the restructuring, dangling promises of bringing in new investors.

Earlier, in February 2014, the RBI had allowed a change in management of stressed companies. The idea was to force shareholders (not lenders) to bear the so-called first loss and force promoters to have more skin in the game.

The London Approach

An earlier corporate debt restructuring (CDR) mechanism, put in place in August 2001, had failed to alleviate the pain of lenders. The objective of the CDR was to ensure a timely transparent mechanism for restructuring debts of ₹20 crore or more outside the purview of Board for Industrial and Financial Reconstruction (BIFR), Debt Recovery Tribunal (DRT) and other legal channels.

Until then, any account that was restructured was considered an NPA but banks were not barred from offering fresh advances to such borrowers. In March 2001, the RBI told banks that even if a sub-standard account is restructured, if it was backed by securities, it could continue to be classified as a sub-standard asset. What is more, it could bounce back to become a standard asset after a year.

The CDR may have arisen from this. Once a stressed asset was referred to the CDR platform, it was not downgraded, provided it was backed by securities.

The philosophy behind the CDR was the so-called London Approach, under which the Bank of England had played the role of an honest broker in the 1970s when the UK entered a recession.

Banks saw bad loans increasing after a sharp spike in petroleum prices led to a slowdown and high inflation. In the 1990s, many countries facing wide-scale corporate distress turned to the London Approach as a basis for developing guidelines to encourage out-of-court debt workouts. On a similar line, the Jakarta Initiative was launched in Indonesia, after the East Asian Crisis (the so-called 'Asian Flu') in 1997–98. By December 2003, at least 100 cases, involving close to $30 billion of corporate debt, were settled through this platform.

The CDR platform evolved through revisions in 2003 and 2005, following the recommendations of two working groups headed by deputy governors, and it was revised again in 2008. The regulations became progressively more stringent as the restructuring facility initially meant for infrastructure was extended to other segments, barring real estate, capital markets and consumer loans.

Typically, a standard restructured account needed some provisioning. The idea of the CDR was to allow bankers to restructure the account within a set timeframe. If they did not follow the norms, they could not get the benefit of the first time 'asset protection'.

Initially, there were very few proposals for restructuring on the CDR platform, mainly from the DFIs as bankers were still mostly into working capital loans. The scenario changed after the big government push for infrastructure financing between 2004 and 2009. There were truckloads of proposals then!

But progress on the CDR platform was slow and the results were manipulated as bankers and borrowers were scratching each other's backs. For every loan recast, a feasibility study was required. Who would do the study? Who would pay? The banks were paying upfront but charging it by debiting from the corporate accounts. So, the borrowers were paying, leading to clear conflict of interest.

The Turning Point

An RBI directive on 27 August 2008, a fortnight before the Lehman collapse, was the turning point. The RBI liberalised loan restructuring – the facility was extended to all loans, including working capital loans. The negative list featured only three types of loans – consumer and personal advances, capital market exposures and commercial real estate loans. What is more, the banks were allowed to do restructuring internally without moving to CDR.

After the Lehman collapse, banks were allowed a limited window for a second restructuring and, even real estate loans could be restructured. The banks abused this facility initially and the RBI apparently woke up late to the rot within the system.

It was flooded with requests from banks for extension of the second recast window when exports collapsed during the global crisis. The RBI had little choice by then but to accede to the banks' demands. Its primary concern was to protect bank balance sheets.

In June 2016, the Scheme for Sustainable Structuring of Stressed Assets or S4A scheme followed the SDR. This allowed banks to convert up to half the loans of stressed companies into equity, or equity-like securities. But, this scheme too, like the earlier ones, failed to resolve the bad loan problem.

However, the restructuring plans were forcing banks to recognise problems, take haircuts, make provisions for the true economic value of loans and restructure viable projects. Without the RBI's support and arm-twisting, the banks would not have done this for fear of harassment by investigative agencies.

'Pretend and Extend'

But the banks also chose to kick the can down the road. Instead of cleaning up their balance sheets, some of them indulged in what Rajan described as, 'pretend and extend'. They pretended that everything was fine and extended fresh loans to keep the books clean.

All instructions issued on restructuring required the banks to be satisfied with the viability of the given project. Banks used this opportunity to provide preposterous moratorium periods and absurd repayment schedules.

There was no insolvency law in India until 2016 but these restructuring schemes mimicked the features of insolvency code in developed markets.

There were problems on both sides of the fence.

Ideally, if a venture fails, the promoters should move ahead to start another without any emotional attachment. That is the spirit of the concept of limited liability. But unlike in developed markets, Indian promoters find it difficult to accept failure along with the attached social stigma.

Similarly, banks do not write down loans. Why? They do not have enough profits to write down a bad loan. Besides, the PSBs especially suffer from the fear of the three Cs – the Central Bureau of Investigation (CBI), the Central Vigilance Commission (CVC) and the Comptroller & Auditor General of India (CAG).

In most developed markets, writing down the value of loans is common when borrowers are under stress. Banks sometimes write down a loan when they sense trouble even when the account is still performing. In India, banks take haircuts typically at the very terminal stage. They also write off loans only to reduce their NPAs.

Data on a Platter

The RBI could sense that something was wrong but it was helpless as it did not possess the full picture. Until the establishment of the Central Repository of Information on Large Credits (CRILC) in June 2014, data on NPAs were disaggregated.

Before CRILC was set up, in 2007–08, the RBI tried to set up a credit information system where the banks could share data of bad loans but that did not work. The banking regulator often sought information from the lead bank in a consortium but the complete data was rarely available. So, the RBI did not have comprehensive credit information about any borrower.

The CRILC was Rajan's initiative. Once it was in place, the banks started supplying data in real time for all loans of ₹5 crore and above. For accounts turning bad, the data was weekly, while standard accounts were reported monthly.

Banks had to submit quarterly reports on all borrowers with an aggregate fund-based and non-fund-based exposure of ₹5 crore or more. They also had to classify borrowers as Special Mention Accounts (SMA) of various levels to gauge the probability of such accounts turning bad.

Going by the norms, if a borrower has not paid a loan instalment (principal or interest) for 90 days, the account turns NPA and the bank needs to make provision for it. Until the 90-day mark, when an account turns NPA for non-payment, it remains standard but stressed.

But in case a borrower is not able to pay one instalment (30 days), it signals incipient stress and the account is called SMA 0. For non-payment between 31 days and 60 days, it is SMA-1; and between 61 days and 90 days, SMA-2.

Apart from regular quarterly submissions, the banks were advised to keep the regulator informed on a real-time basis whenever a large borrower's account becomes overdue for 61 days (SMA-2) and/or banks were jointly planning to restructure such an account. The special mention accounts and the step-by-step classification of non-payment dealt a blow to the cosy relationships between banks and borrowers.

The RBI, as well as banks, could access this data. This gave a comprehensive view of the banking system's exposure to every large borrower, and how the exposure to the same borrower was classified differently by different banks. Most importantly, the central bank could see how funds were moved across banks to keep accounts 'standard'.

It was clear that the situation was far worse than what the RBI had envisaged. In its worst nightmare, the regulator could not have imagined the terrible asset quality.

One barometer was the movement of stressed assets – declared NPAs plus restructured loans. From 2009 onwards, the stressed assets started rising but the NPAs did not rise in tandem (as banks were hiding NPAs under the garb of restructured assets). In 2012, the number of restructured accounts increased sharply, outpacing both credit growth and growth rate of gross NPAs. After the AQR started (more on this later in this chapter), the scales tilted and the NPAs started rising.

These were bad loans but they were not recognised.

Anand Sinha, who handled regulation throughout his stint at the RBI, first as an executive director (with limited involvement with supervision) and later as deputy governor, told me about the empirical analysis undertaken by the central bank on bad loans since June 2000.

It indicated that the NPA growth typically follows the credit growth with a lag of two years. Robust credit growth in 2010–11 raised concerns about credit boom in the economy, which had an implication for asset quality. At the aggregate level, there was no credit boom during 2010–11 though the infrastructure sector showed some signs of a boom which moderated later.

'Soon serious concerns arose about asset quality when NPAs rose to 3.1 per cent on 31 March 2012, reflecting NPA generation with a lag of credit disbursed in the earlier years. The aggressive tightening of monetary policy during 2010–11 and 2011–12 due to near double-digit, persistent inflation and the sharply slowing economy would also have led to growth in NPAs,' he said.

Risk-Based Supervision

Just a year before CRILC came into existence, the RBI had changed its supervisory model – from CAMELS (capital adequacy, asset quality, management, earnings, liquidity and system and control) to RBS or risk-based supervision.

India's banks are heterogeneous in terms of size, nature of business models and risk-taking ability. Under CAMELS, based on their business model, the banks were grouped into five categories – SBI, other PSBs, old private banks, new private banks and foreign banks – for supervision purposes.

In the new supervisory regime, they were re-grouped on homogeneity. For instance, Citibank, Standard Chartered and HSBC had earlier been grouped as foreign banks; under the RBS, they migrated to 'medium-sized banks'.

Once this was done, RBI could see that even smaller banks had relatively large exposures to corporate accounts. Growth-hungry banks depended on the lead bank (in most cases, the SBI) for project appraisal and gave loans to large corporations even though their balance sheets could not justify such risk-taking. (More on this in the chapter 'What Ails Public Sector Banks'.) Technically, it is called multiple lending but, for all practical purposes, this was informal loan syndication.

No bank wanted to miss out the credit growth story. Between

2006 and 2009, bank credit grew at a scorching pace. It dipped after the Lehman crisis but started to pick up again in 2011.

Another factor that contributed to this trend was the memorandum of understanding PSBs were signing with the government every year for their performance. The CMDs and executive directors were given a bonus every year. This was a pittance but it was linked to balance sheet growth and not the quality of assets.

In many cases, the banks appeared to be drafting the proposals as well as appraising them. The large banks, the bullying big brothers, were calling the shots in making decisions on which borrower to finance and by how much. The smaller banks were forced to fall in line.

The RBS opened a new can of worms.

The RBI discovered the following:

- The default risk in almost all banks was extremely high. (Typically, the default risk is measured in standard asset portfolio of the banks over and above the declared NPAs.)
- The recovery risk was also equally high because enough security had not been taken when loans were sanctioned. In most PSBs and some private banks, it was usual for the higher officials to permit deviations in security norms.
- The stressed assets were relatively higher in industry and lower in agriculture.
- Certain banks, particularly a few private banks, had efficient managers and their quality of loans was better.
- The low-capitalised banks tended to take more risks for more returns as higher returns could help them build capital.
- Highly profitable banks, too, tended to take more risks for better returns.
- Banks with a diversified portfolio of retail and corporate loans had better balance sheets.
- There were issues with sectoral and geographical concentration – such as real estate, steel, tea gardens in Assam, among others.

- There were differences in the quality and quantity of collaterals held by different banks.
- There was rampant misuse of the general-purpose loans to companies for business. The banks were giving such loans to tide over liquidity crisis and thus, keep accounts performing.

Once the RBS was in place, most banks were downgraded at least by one notch and many even lower, subsequently.

The regulator's concerns were on multiple grounds:

- Poor credit assessment of banks.
- Lack of monitoring of loan accounts.
- The banks did not assess the high leverage of corporate borrowers.
- The borrowers were siphoning off money and the banks could not track that.
- The promoters' contribution and personal guarantee for loans were only on paper; in most cases, they were not charged to banks and hence unenforceable.
- The banks were restructuring the loans by giving fresh loans but the promoters were not bringing in any contribution in the form of equity.
- There was a concentration of risk as all banks were rushing to lend to certain sectors such as steel and infrastructure, without the skills required to appraise projects in those areas.
- The banks were putting in a lot of conditions before disbursing a loan but waiving many terms later. For instance, a large steelmaker threw in many pieces of prime real estate in Mumbai as collateral. But later it convinced the banks to release the real estate as the project itself (land, plant and machinery) was hypothecated to the banks. The problem was that the land of such projects could not fetch much money and the plant and machinery turned into scrap.

Were the banks compromised? The RBI did not explicitly say so. But it found that, after the sanction of loans, if the supervision was bad, monitoring was worse. Since the project appraisal was done by the lead bank, others were relaxed. Also, the bankers were taking borrowers' commitments at face value.

Another ingenious system of managing bad loans was discovered. When a string of accounts was on the verge of turning bad, the bank typically created a pool of debt covering all, got it rated by a not-so-reputable rating agency, and sold it to relatively smaller banks, including cooperative banks. This practice of down-selling or palming off of bad loans was invented by a private bank, which later came close to collapse.

Yet another clever way of managing bad assets was sanctioning two loans at the same time. While the first loan would be disbursed immediately, the disbursement of the second loan was typically kept on hold and, the second loan got disbursed to help the borrower if the first loan turned bad!

Three Lines of Defence

Theoretically, every bank has three lines of defence to protect the balance sheet: Internal control, risk management and audit. While both internal control and risk management were weak, the internal audit for most banks was tailored to make top managements feel comfortable.

A close look at the audit forms across PSBs (which the auditors need to fill after inspection) gives us a glimpse into their priorities. The focus was on deposits, advances, bad loans, interest income, non-interest income and other business parameters. The overarching theme of such audits was how the business was doing; there was no qualitative assessment.

Of course, such audits potentially could check frauds. But a focus on qualitative aspects would have been more efficient. For instance, in the $2 billion Nirav Modi scam that hit Punjab National Bank (PNB), the auditors completely missed out on the hefty commission the bank was earning from Modi's Group of companies.

CRILC Review

By November 2014, Rajan called for a review of CRILC, which had been in operation for six months by then. The focus was on how banks were reporting their bad loans. Every account worth ₹100 crore or more was scrutinised.

By that time, the banks had stopped 'restructuring' bad loans but 'rectification' was being done. To its horror, the RBI found that rectification had replaced restructuring and most large accounts were rectified. How could every large borrower have a cash crunch?

Around the same time, at a workshop on the new supervisory model, the RBI assessed the progress of the risk-based supervision. The Department of Banking Supervision (DBS) of the central bank decided that a thematic review should be undertaken on important aspects of credit, market and operational risks.

To start with, it was decided that the asset quality of the big banks be simultaneously reviewed. In March 2015, the process was complete and Rajan was informed.

The Cat out of the Bag

Around half-a-dozen large banks including SBI, PNB, ICICI Bank and Axis Bank were asked to make presentations to the RBI. The regulator got a clear sense of what was happening. The cat was out of the bag.

Deputy Governor S.S. Mundra and Governor Rajan decided to take a closer look. They put the largest 100 borrowing accounts in each bank under the scanner.

What started with a basket of 100 large accounts expanded manifold. What were small accounts for say a large bank such as SBI were large accounts for a smaller bank such as Dena Bank, or Bank of Maharashtra. Hence, even with the focus on 100 large accounts of each bank, the RBI ended up scrutinising thousands of accounts.

Rajan and Mundra discovered accounts which were registered as NPAs in one bank were supposedly performing assets in another. Many accounts were not restructured but these had been rectified repeatedly.

Rajan's patience was running out. Enough time had been given to the banks for restructuring stressed loans but they were misusing it, and trying to take the regulator for a ride.

First of its Kind

The exercise by Mundra–Rajan unearthed so many problems that the RBI decided that a system-wide audit was needed. This is how the asset quality review or AQR – a first-of-its-kind health check of Indian banking – was conceived.

Globally too, there was nothing comparable to the AQR anywhere. After the collapse of Lehman Brothers, the US Federal Reserve started conducting sensitivity tests and solvency tests to identify banks which could become basket cases, but the banking turf in the US is very different.

Most US banks have exposure to market instruments and this makes it easier to flag problems. If a bond is issued and not serviced, there is a problem. But Indian banks are primarily in the business of giving loans. Loans work via agreements between borrower and bank, and banks can accommodate borrowers in many ways.

Typically, the annual RBI inspection starts after July when the banks have released their audited results; this is the second quarter of the Indian financial year. The inspection continues through the financial year until the end in March of the next calendar year. Depending on the seriousness of the findings of inspection teams, interactions with the bankers can continue for months.

A simultaneous look at all banks through the AQR is a very different story.

Anxious Bankers

During financial year 2014–15, bankers were looking anxious. They were 'negotiating' for regulatory forbearance. The RBI could sense the unease in the same way that a doctor feels there is something wrong about a patient.

Everyone agreed that something had to be done. But when and how? Who will bell the cat? Did the banks have the capital to absorb the shock of new NPAs?

The AQR involved the focussed direction of supervisory resources. It would throw new light upon risks within the system. The DBS planned the scope, modalities and execution meticulously. An AQR team was constituted with the governor as its chairman, and all the proposals of the DBS were discussed by this team.

The Go-ahead

The AQR process started in June 2015, after Rajan gave the go-ahead. It was a three-month project, slated to be completed by August 2015 so that the recognition of bad assets could start from the September quarter. But it spilled over to October. The clean up process started from the December 2015 quarter.

This is how it worked.

India has over 100 banks. But very small ones, particularly foreign banks with small balance sheets and no corporate accounts, were left out of the exercise. The RBI used all the resources at its disposal to make a success of the AQR.

A team was formed for each bank, and all teams worked simultaneously. Typically, a senior supervisory manager (SSM) looks after the audit of a bank. The rank of the SSM depends on the bank being audited. An SSM supervising SBI could be a general manager at RBI, but the SSM of a relatively smaller bank could be a deputy general manager, or even an assistant general manager. For large banks, a team of four executives can work under the SSM.

The Control Room

The AQR team was like a financial bomb-disposal squad, trying to defuse explosives which could destroy the depositors' trust – the bedrock of banking.

A control room was set up on the third floor of RBI's Cuffe Parade office, away from its central office on Mint Road. Two general managers were collating the real time data; a third general manager was consolidating them under different heads; and a fourth one was looking at the big picture on the computer screen.

The chief general manager in charge of DBS was heading the

control room. For six months, the team hardly slept. All of them worked flat out, even over the weekends.

Every evening the Cuffe Parade team would come over to the central office to take stock of the situation. Over *poha* and coffee from the canteen, the meetings would carry on at least until 10 pm. But quite often, there would be calls at midnight, or later, from senior colleagues who stayed tuned in 24x7.

Slowly, the big picture emerged. Typically, the team discovered anomalies. Account 'A' was a performing asset on the book of Bank X but non-performing asset on Bank Y's book and a stressed asset on the book of Bank Z.

How could that happen?

Well, there are many ways:

- Routing the same credit through multiple banks.
- Raising temporary finance to service debt from other private and foreign banks under multiple bank finance.
- Switching to different finance models.
- Creative products such as capex loans – an all-purpose, no-appraisal sort of loan repayable at the borrowers' convenience with incredibly long tenures and full repayment only on maturity.
- Hiking the borrowers' cash credit limit, allowing them to draw more money to pay back loans.
- Misuse of export guarantee covers.
- When Letters of Credit (LCs) were devolving, banks were not recognising devolvement.
- Giving short-term overdrafts to borrowers to repay loans.
- Offering fresh loans at the next stage to adjust the overdraft.
- Artificially raising the sales volumes to lift the limit of bank borrowing.
- Blatantly misusing the CDR platform for restructuring.
- Seeking personal guarantees of the promoters but not invoking them.
- Arbitraging between fund-based and non-fund based exposure by manipulating respective limits.

- Most of the technical evaluation studies were rotten. While the borrowers were faltering on every business parameter, the studies were justifying higher credit limits.
- The date of commencement of commercial operation (DCCO), a critical milestone for any project loan, was manipulated. Often, there was a date on which a factory ceremonially opened. But there was no production. It was just a formality.

The DCCO is the date when the unit is supposed to begin operations. The sales and other financial projections, including the repayment schedules for the loans, are based on this date.

The more the date was postponed, the longer the tenure of the loan and the bigger the interest liability and hence the higher the probability of the loan going bad. The restructuring norms permitted postponements of DCCOs in certain circumstances, but this was rampantly misused.

The RBI found that the banks were delaying recognising large accounts as NPAs, even if projects were not starting up, and the 'project commencement' milestone was largely cosmetic.

In one such case, the RBI team found that a huge sum of money had been deployed overseas for oil and gas exploration. But just an Internet search revealed that the oil field the banks had funded in Africa had already been identified as dry by a major oil company.

This prompted the regulator to launch 'targeted scrutiny' of certain accounts and 'thematic scrutiny' of real estate, housing loans, bills and letter of credit discounting.

It also went for 'targeted audits' of certain accounts by external auditors to red-flag misdoings. The banks themselves were appointing such auditors, at the instance of the regulator.

House of Cards

Given the scale at which the system was being gamed, the RBI had to opt for carpet bombing.

Among other things, it found innovative usage of the so-called

SBLC (stand-by letter of credit). This is a guarantee by one bank, based on which another bank would lend. The RBI found these were used as chain letters – Bank A was giving money based on a guarantee by Bank B, then it was passed on Bank C, D, E, F and so on.

The same bank was becoming the guarantor as well as the lender. This was a house of cards but no bank involved in this chain would ever invoke a guarantee, since that would bring the house down. The borrowers had no skin in the game; the bankers were funding both debt and equity.

Instead of paying banks' money from their own pockets, the borrowers were also using accommodation bills to service the principal plus interest of previous bills. Backed by the new bill, they would get fresh and higher credit, which would enable them to clear the previous loans and the chain continued.

In banking parlance, such a practice is called kiting, or kite flying. When people use one or more credit cards to withdraw cash at an ATM and pay dues on another credit card, they do the same thing on a much smaller scale.

As if this was not enough, there was also round-tripping.

Round Tripping

One of the SSMs found a large account in a very large bank, let us call it Bank A, had not been serviced on the 90th day. Why was Bank A not classifying this loan as an NPA? The SSM was informed the required funds would flow into its account before the end of the 90th day. Indeed, the money arrived and the SSM was impressed – here was a banker who did not believe in hiding facts.

There was no need to classify that account as an NPA. So, it was maintained as a standard asset. But just out of curiosity, the SSM checked the CRILC data the very next day.

Lo and behold, to his horror, he found an equivalent amount of money had left Bank A and gone to another bank, Bank B. He couldn't believe his eyes. But one phone call to his counterpart in

Bank B confirmed his suspicions. But the story did not end there! The funds left Bank B a day later and entered the books of a third bank, Bank C.

What was going on?

These banks were keeping the account standard simply by transferring money from one bank to another, to yet another. In such chains, as many as ten banks might have sanctioned a loan to one borrower. But the dates of sanctions and disbursements were different, allowing for the round-tripping. It may be inferred that loans were applied for, and sanctioned, on different dates deliberately to enable this sidestep of the NPA recognition norms.

The Next Step

Broadly, the AQR findings can be divided into four categories:

- Banks were piling up NPAs but not recognising them.
- They were camouflaging NPAs through fresh loans and other innovative ways.
- The CDR platform for restructuring stressed assets had failed.
- The date of commencement was being gamed. Many projects had not got going on the formal commencement dates.

There were long discussions about the next step. Deputy Governor Mundra was conservative in his approach and wanted to give more time to banks. But his boss Rajan thought the rot was too deep. He could not accept the manipulation of the DCCO.

What next? It was decided to analyse all the findings once again, in stages.

At stage one, the focus was on what they call 'quality assurance'. Here, three CGMs and the CGM in-charge of DBS analysed the tabulated data. They followed up with a series of meetings with the group of SSMs to get a clearer picture before confirming each NPA account.

Once the consolidated picture emerged, at stage two, a

presentation was made to Mundra, Rajan and the executive director in charge of supervision, Meena Hemchandra.

At stage three, the RBI supervision team met the bankers one-on-one and discussed the findings. The venue was the Cuffe Parade office, which resembled a sort of Scotland Yard during these meetings. The bankers were not grilled but the RBI team had every detail on the table to confront them. There was documentary evidence to support each point they were making.

After the meeting with the bankers, at stage four, a second round of checks was undertaken, with the bankers' feedback and more facts.

At stage five, it was decided that 30 of the largest accounts must undergo a second level of quality assurance check. This was done by senior executives of the supervision team who had not been involved in the exercise. They were flown in from Delhi and Chennai for a third-party check.

At stage six, the control room did an assessment of the impact. If the banks were to recognise all bad loans at one go and set aside money, how would it affect their NPA pile, capital and profitability? The team looked at the last three years' profits, presumed a 5 per cent rise each year and worked out different scenarios on the assessed NPA figures to estimate the impact.

Once the exercise was over, the team went back to Rajan to make the final presentation, drawing up different scenarios about the capital requirement for PSBs.

Before biting the bullet, at the last stage, Rajan called a meeting of the bankers at the RBI central office on Mint Road. All big banks present there were vociferous in their protests. The boss of a large bank said the RBI was not following the rules, and the decision to force the banks to clean up the bad loans was principle-based.

A rules-based approach to regulation prescribes in detail a set of rules on how to behave as opposed to a principle-based approach to regulation, where outcomes and principles are set and the controls, measures and procedures on how to achieve that outcome is left for each organisation to determine.

Is this True?

In his typical style, Rajan asked the team one simple question: 'Is this true?'

The 15th-floor conference room at the central office has seldom seen a debate as animated as the one that followed. The team explained graphically to the governor how every rule was followed and nothing was left to principles.

It backed up this argument with multi-level evidence. The bankers had no choice but to accept what the RBI team was saying.

Immediately after the bankers' meeting, Rajan spoke to the junior minister of finance, Jayant Sinha, who had been his classmate at IIT Delhi, on a video conference.

Sensing the imminent collapse of all the creative scheming, borrowers and bankers started lobbying in Delhi to stop the inevitable. They sought the shoulders of influential ministers to cry on.

In November, Rajan, along with Mundra and the chief general manager in charge of DBS, flew to Delhi to meet Finance Minister Arun Jaitley. The mission was to convince Jaitley that the clean-up exercise could not be avoided.

The finance minister gave them a patient hearing, got a sense of the capital requirement for the banks and gave the go-ahead. His junior minister Sinha and Anjuly Chib Duggal, who had taken over as financial services secretary a couple of months back, were present at the meeting. The next day, Jaitley announced the government was ready to clean up the banking system.

The RBI's 555th Central Board meeting in Kolkata on 11 December spent much of its time discussing this.

■ ■ ■

PART 2

The banks were given the period from October–December 2015 to January–March 2017 – six quarters to clean up the mess. (The idea was to do half the job in the first two quarters – October–December

2015 and January–March 2016 and the rest over the next four quarters.) Before the exercise ended, there was a change of guard at the RBI. Urjit Patel, who was observing these developments as a deputy governor, moved into the corner room in August 2016.

Rajan forced the banks to start recognising the bad assets; Patel moved one step ahead to resolution. Viral Acharya, who moved into RBI as a deputy governor a few months after Patel became governor, was his chosen lieutenant. Acharya was in charge of monetary policy but, with inflation under control, he spent most of his time overseeing the clean-up exercise.

The Indian Banks' Association (IBA), a national body for the banking industry, lobbied hard for more time to make provisions but the RBI refused to extend the deadline.

Sharp Differences within RBI

Why were they given six quarters? Why not four or eight? There were sharp differences within the RBI on how much time should be given for the clean up. The views varied between giving them two quarters to as many as 16 quarters or four years to mute the disruption and let banks brace to absorb the shock.

Mundra felt, given the capital position of the banks and also that the RBI had allowed this to linger for years, ideally, information and the action agenda should be shared with each bank separately. He was in favour of giving them eight quarters and leaving it to each bank to manage the process internally. Depending on their health, they could do progressive provisioning.

His logic was that the banks did not have enough capital to absorb the shock and the RBI should own some responsibility. But Mundra was overruled. One of the board members, a former banker, who apparently had a close relationship with Rajan, pushed for tough action. Rajan too felt enough time had been given to bankers; they had to step up and start provisioning.

The idea was to use the first two quarters for making provisions for NPAs and the next four quarters to clean up accounts already restructured on the CDR platform, which had failed to meet the conditions of restructuring.

After the deadline ended, Patel examined the progress in 2017. It was not a normal inspection. The SSMs wanted to check what the banks had done – and what they had not – after they were told to clean up books.

They found the following:

- The promoters' contribution was not forthcoming. The banks lent to group companies to keep some accounts performing and, in the process, corporations were over-leveraged, leading to the much-discussed 'twin balance sheet problem'.
- The banks made attempts to create charges to protect their interests but these were either incomplete, or diluted. Essentially, they were not putting enough pressure on corporate borrowers.
- And, of course, they were not classifying all NPAs. They kept many accounts under the 'watch list' and called them 'critical' accounts but refused to classify them as NPAs. In these cases, banks argued that the concerned entity was facing a temporary problem, which it would soon tide over. One relatively large, new private bank was in most watchful mood – it was watching many, many accounts.

Lipstick on a Pig

Upset with the way bankers were handling bad loans, Rajan made his famous comment, 'You can put lipstick on a pig but that will not make the pig a princess.'

Once the progress report was on the table, the RBI held meetings with each bank to discuss what had been done and what needed to be done. The MD and chairman of the banks and the head of their audit committee had to meet up at the RBI central office.

When it came to meeting the larger banks, the RBI was represented by executive directors, and even by Deputy Governor Mundra. The CGMs headed the RBI teams holding meetings with smaller banks.

The bankers argued their case and all large bad accounts were discussed at length, with point-counterpoint presented by both sides. After this series of meetings, the RBI briefed its Board for Financial Supervision (BFS), a committee of the central board, on developments.

The BFS did not like the understatement of bad loans. It advised the RBI to be stricter. In September 2017, the regulator asked the banks to disclose under-provisioning of bad loans.

The idea originated from Y.H. Malegam, a respected chartered accountant who had headed the government's National Advisory Committee on Accounting Standards. He had also been the longest-serving director on the RBI board.

He made the point that given almost all banks were listed on the bourses, they owed it to shareholders to disclose their real health status, even if that meant a negative impact on balance sheets. After several rounds of discussion, it was decided that banks would have to disclose the situation if the under-provisioning gap was 15 per cent or more.

Da Vinci Code

The BFS suggested that the capital market watchdog, the SEBI, be kept informed. As the published financial statements of banks did not depict the true and fair view of their financial position, the RBI directed them to make adequate disclosures of such divergences in 'Notes to Accounts' in their annual financial statements. That is how it cracked the proverbial Da Vinci Code of balance sheet management by the banks.

As many as 23 banks under-reported bad loans in the first year after AQR – fiscal year 2015–16 and the figure rose to 30 banks in the next fiscal year. The amount of divergences in gross bad loans almost doubled from ₹43,463 crore to ₹83,206 crore, as pointed out in a report by the rating agency ICRA Ltd. For fiscal year 2018–19, at least 14 banks under-reported ₹29,431 crore in bad loans.

The first to admit the divergence was Yes Bank Ltd. For 2016, Yes Bank had disclosed gross NPAs of ₹748.9 crore, but the RBI's assessment of the correct level of gross NPAs was over six times higher at ₹4,925.6 crore. As far as net NPAs post-provisioning was concerned, there was a divergence of ₹3,319 crore between Yes Bank's reported figure and the RBI's assessment. The next year, the difference was even wider at ₹6,355 crore.

Yes Bank may have been among the worst offenders but it was certainly not alone. At ICICI Bank, the difference in gross NPAs was to the tune of ₹5,105 crore, leading to additional provisioning of ₹1,071 crore in 2015–16. At Axis Bank, the regulator found a gross NPA divergence of ₹9,478 crore, raising its bad loans to ₹15,566 crore.

Had Yes Bank assessed the quality of its loan assets as the RBI wanted, it would have reported 6 per cent gross NPAs instead of 0.8 per cent as it did. Similarly, Axis Bank's gross NPAs in 2016 would have made up 4.5 per cent of its loan book against the reported 1.78 per cent. At ICICI Bank, gross NPAs would have been 7 per cent against 5.85 per cent.

How could this sort of divergence and gross under-reporting occur? Beyond facts and figures, bankers do take a 'view' on whether a particular loan is good, or bad. There have also been instances when the auditors do not agree with the management's point of view on certain loan accounts and the auditors make their displeasure public in the notes to the accounts.

However, at times, the auditors also failed to identify hidden bad assets. To be fair, unlike the RBI inspectors who had access to all information about a bank and also a view of the entire banking system, auditors have limited access. The auditors must also have to complete their job within a specified timeframe, unlike the RBI supervisors who can take the time to dig for details.

The RBI has refrained from taking any action against banks for under-provisioning and left it to the market to punish them.

More Power to RBI

An ordinance was promulgated in 2017, amending the Banking Regulation Act, 1949. This amendment gave RBI the authority to push the banks hard to deal with bad assets. It authorised the RBI to direct banks to invoke the insolvency and bankruptcy code (IBC) against defaulters.

There is an interesting story behind the amendment. After the IBC was legislated in May 2016, there was a meeting at the finance ministry where RBI Governor Patel and the two deputy governors, Mundra and Acharya were present. Apart from Jaitley, the-then chief economic advisor to the Government of India, Arvind Subramanian, and the secretary of the DFS were also there.

The government's view was that as the IBC was already in place and the AQR done and dusted, the RBI should just go ahead and use the new law to complete the clean up. Patel insisted that the RBI must be specially equipped to deal with the cases to be referred to the IBC.

Jaitley, being a lawyer by profession, knew well that the Banking Regulation Act itself empowers the RBI with such powers and there was no need for anything else. But Patel kept pushing for this. He felt the AQR was over but the clean up was not being done with the desired zeal.

Two new sections – 35AA and 35AB – were added after Section 35A in the Banking Regulation Act, enabling the government to authorise the RBI to 'direct banking companies to resolve specific stressed assets by initiating insolvency resolution process, where required.'

Armed with the ordinance, the RBI forced banks to push 40 bad accounts into IBC in two phases during 2017. Together, these 40 bad accounts accounted for around 40 per cent of the bad assets then.

The RBI set up a committee with some of its board of directors to go through all the cases and make recommendations for IBC referrals. Deputy Governor N.S. Vishwanathan and Bharat Doshi, a director on the central board, were in the committee, along with a few others.

Finally, the RBI struck at the midnight on 12 February 2018, dismantling all existing frameworks for restructuring stressed assets as well as the joint lenders' forum, which was an institutional mechanism overseeing this process.

This forced the banks to classify all large loans worth at least ₹2,000 crore as NPAs immediately after restructuring. Such accounts must be inducted to the bankruptcy process if they are not resolved within 180 days of default. The clock started ticking from 1 March 2018.

This circular came back to haunt the RBI when the Supreme Court declared it was 'ultra vires' in April 2019. That means the RBI was deemed to lack the legal authority to issue this circular. (More on this in the chapter 'The Great Indian Asset Sale'.)

Flagging the Problem

Ashish Gupta, an analyst with Credit Suisse Securities (India) Pvt Ltd flagged the looming problems ahead of most others. The July 2011 report of Credit Suisse said it was expected that the next six months would see an end to the 'current benign asset quality cycle which has been buttressing bank profitability'. It pointed out explosive loan growth in the power sector and highly leveraged real estate developers.

Gupta's 'House of Debt' report in August 2012, once again exposed the ugly underbelly of Indian banking with 13 per cent of total bank loans and 98 per cent of the banking system's net worth concentrated in just ten corporate houses.

It also said the financials of seven of this pack of ten were too stretched. Calling 2014 'The year of reckoning', the 'House of Debt' report of 2013 dissected the balance sheets of the ten groups clinically and discovered that the rise in debt outpaced capital expenditure in most of these groups.

Bad Bank?

As banks started disclosing their bad assets following the AQR, the finance ministry explored the idea of floating a bad bank. On 16 February 2016, the ministry's Department of Economic Affairs held a 'North Block Policy Charcha: Workshop on Resolving Stressed Assets'.

The RBI was represented by Deputy Governor Vishwanathan. The others present included Birendra Kumar, MD & CEO of International Asset Reconstruction Company Pvt Ltd; Anil Bhatia, MD and CEO of JM Financial Asset Reconstruction Company; M.R. Umarji, an expert in banking laws; Gupta of Credit Suisse and Luis Cortavarria, a specialist on bad banks, from the International Monetary Fund (IMF).

The government was represented by Jayant Sinha, minister of state for finance; T.V. Somanathan, then joint secretary in the Prime Minister's Office, and Arvind Subramanian, the chief economic adviser.

They were trying to get the hang of the problem and build a consensus about a 'bad bank'. The discussion also veered around to sector-specific bad banks for distressed sectors like steel, power and telecom.

Subramanian was particularly fond of the idea and the Economic Survey 2016–17 proposed the setting up of a public sector asset rehabilitation agency, which is essentially a centralised bad bank. But there weren't too many takers.

By that time, the IBC was in place and an auction-based recovery platform was ready. Jaitley was not enamoured of the bad bank idea. In a post-budget interview, he said a bad bank was a potential solution but it could not be supported by the government alone.

Victory or Defeat?

Who won the war on NPAs? Was the price worth paying? Could this problem have been fought with a different strategy?

Opinions vary.

The gross NPAs of the banking sector were reported as 4.28 per cent of their loans in 2015. This rose sharply after the AQR. Gross NPAs rose to 11.21 per cent in 2018, before dropping to 9.1 per cent in 2019.

The PSBs held far more NPAs, and proportionately higher NPAs than their private sector counterparts; in some PSBs, bad assets exceeded one-fourth of loan books. The balance sheets of close to a dozen PSBs deteriorated to the extent where they were barred from making fresh loans.

Credit growth slumped, badly hitting Asia's third-largest economy. The government has kept on pumping in capital to shore up PSBs but that has not been enough. The solution, policymakers now believe, could be in consolidation in the public sector banking industry. We will have more to say on this subject in the chapters on bank recap and consolidation.

A Divided House

Even within the RBI, opinion is divided. While a senior central banker defends the AQR, quoting Samuel Johnson, 'When a man knows he is to be hanged... it concentrates his mind wonderfully,' another finds the measure too drastic. 'Can you shift from second gear to fifth while driving a car? There is a process.'

While RBI was correct in identifying the malaise, many thought the medicine too strong. Some banks ran the risk of 'slipping off the terrace of a skyscraper and dying' because the government could not ensure a soft landing. It could not provide a parachute in the form of immediate and adequate infusion of fresh capital.

'I agree that the recognition of bad loans is very important but it cannot be done in isolation. Recapitalisation of banks and resolution of bad assets also should have been planned simultaneously – it should have been a three-pronged strategy. The RBI should have chalked out a glide path,' says Arundhati Bhattacharya, who was heading SBI at that time.

She also makes a point that when the AQR was put in place, there was no sign of the insolvency code. 'We did not know what to do with the factories of the loan defaulters. The only agency around at that time which could keep a factory in a running condition if we take it away from the borrowers, was Alvarez & Marsal (a global agency that specialises in managing turnarounds). The ecosystem was not prepared for the shock...'

Her successor Rajnish Kumar, too, feels the same way. 'It (the AQR) was like putting the cart before the horse. The Bankruptcy

Code should have been made operational before the AQR. The bankers' mindset was rehabilitation (of projects) in the absence of a proper recovery mechanism.'

Historically, there have been higher bad loans at times within the Indian banking system and this could happen again in future, given the crisis caused by the Covid-19 pandemic.

The gross NPAs of the PSBs were 24.8 per cent in 1994. They remained in double-digits until 2002 (11.1 per cent) before dropping to 9.4 per cent in 2003. In that year, India accounted for little over 2 per cent of an estimated $1.3 trillion global NPAs, while Asia's share was 77 per cent.

If the banking industry could survive such a high level of bad loans for almost a decade, why can't it absorb the current shock? That question has more than theoretical significance for the financial sector.

India's government-owned banks are undergoing what the Roman Catholics call purgatory – this is a condition of suffering and purification that leads to union with God in heaven. Only banks that can endure this phase will come up trumps. After this, they will be wiser and avoid offering kid-glove treatment to powerful corporate borrowers. They will also temper their obsession for balance sheet growth by paying heed to risks.

■ ■ ■

3

India's Northern Rock Moment

On 4 September 2018, heavyweight infrastructure lender IL&FS was staring at two repayment obligations. There was a commercial paper (CP) of LIC Mutual Fund (MF) which had to be redeemed and a ₹1,000 crore short-term loan taken from Small Industries Development Bank of India (SIDBI).

LIC-MF, an associate company of the state-owned Life Insurance Corporation of India (LIC), initially agreed to roll over the CP but decided against it at the last minute. IL&FS chose to pay off LIC-MF and it was then left with no money to service the SIDBI debt. (I could not confirm the exact amount but sources in debt market say it could be ₹150 crore.)

IL&FS had been juggling with a liquidity problem for quite sometime and there were mutters in the corporate debt market about what was going on in the group.

One of its subsidiaries – technically an 'intermediate holding company', IL&FS Transportation Networks Ltd (ITNL), had delayed the repayment of ₹450 crore of inter-corporate deposits (ICDs) from SIDBI in June 2018.

In late August, about a week before the 4 September default,

IL&FS Financial Services Ltd (IFIN), the group's listed financial services arm, could not redeem one of its CPs on the day of maturity.

These were relatively small sums for a group, which had exposures to multiple infrastructure projects of close to a lakh crore. That was all the more cause for concern across the NBFC sector where people wondered how it was undergoing such a cash crunch.

The defaults led to a shake-up in management. In mid-September, the IL&FS board appointed the former LIC chairman, S.B. Mathur, as the group chairman. A fortnight later, on 1 October 2018, the government took drastic action.

The government used its powers under a special provision of The Companies Act, 2013 and dismantled the IL&FS board as 'the affairs of IL&FS were being conducted in a manner prejudicial to the public interest'. Kotak Mahindra Bank Ltd's MD and CEO Uday Kotak was asked to chair a new board, which was put in place to pilot a rescue.

This was the first instance of the government using the provision of Companies Act, 2013. It was a legal necessity since the NBFCs were not covered by the insolvency law at that time.

On 30 November, the Serious Fraud Investigation Office (SFIO), which is an agency controlled by the Ministry of Corporate Affairs, filed an interim report on IL&FS. That lit a fuse under India's dynamic NBFC industry, and sent it reeling.

The SFIO investigation revealed some damning facts:

> Nine directors and senior management persons, including Ravi Parthasarathy, chairman and managing director of IL&FS (non-executive chairman from October 2017); Hari Sankaran, vice chairman and managing director; Arun Kumar Saha, joint managing director and chief executive officer; and Vibhav Kapur, chief investment officer; exercised "control over the group". All of them had been at the helm of affairs for over 20 years.
>
> The SFIO found rampant evergreening of loans by the group; and it alleged "inflated profits, suppressed provisioning

and non-disclosure of possible NPAs" in the listed subsidiary, IFIN.

The group had hundreds of associate companies with complex intra-group transactions. The modus operandi of the group between 2015 and 2018 was to maintain an appearance of financial health in the holding company, IL&FS, and its immediate key subsidiaries.

This was done through an unsustainable form of pyramid funding by circulating funds around within the group through various step-down subsidiaries. The holding company or the subsidiary company would borrow short-term funds. The money was then moved around through other group companies to circumvent RBI norms of investment by NBFCs.

The holding companies which had borrowed, kept a spread by lending the funds to step-down subsidiaries at higher interest rates than their own cost of borrowing. They also charged the subsidiaries high fees for availing such loans. These step-down subsidiaries were thus, financially unviable. But these companies were not subject to scrutiny.

The key subsidiaries of IL&FS were projected as financially sound by showing those interest charges, as well as dividend and fee income, along with the evergreening of loans. This was to ensure the payment of regular dividends and also to maintain high credit ratings.

DNA Money *did an analysis which showed that on a consolidated basis, IL&FS paid ₹362.8 crore dividend in financial year 2015, ₹360.5 crore in 2016, ₹436.5 crore in 2017 and ₹258.3 crore in 2018, including dividend distribution tax. These pay-outs to shareholders happened even though cash flow from operations and investments was continually negative. The cash-flow was negative to the tune of as much as ₹11,311 crore in 2018. The listed subsidiary, IFIN, ignored its own net negative cash flow of over ₹2,000 crore in fiscal 2018, and approved ₹130 crore dividend for shareholders.*

Accounting magic aside, this was just a Ponzi scheme on a large scale. Some group companies had carefully manipulated good credit ratings. These companies took a series of loans and lent the money on to their subsidiaries at higher interest rates. Each loan was used to 'service' loans taken earlier, with subsidiaries making interest payments that gave apparent net interest income to the original borrower companies. The money was siphoned out of the group companies and distributed to shareholders through dividend pay outs.

This was a financial perpetual-motion machine. It would continue to run for as long as the group could raise funds by borrowing from the market.

The Gang of Nine

The gang of nine – the group of directors – at the helm had "amassed multiple immovable properties" and huge financial assets. Parthasarathy declared ₹98.98 crore in "movable properties besides four immovable properties".

The IL&FS Employees Welfare Trust (EWT), an unregistered trust set up in August 1990, was at the epicentre of the fraud. The gang of nine used EWT as a conduit for their activities as they enriched themselves at the cost of the IL&FS group companies.

The objective of the trust initially was to provide relief to employees in case of natural disasters. It also provided support for housing facilities and subsidised home loans and extended support for health, education and other welfare purposes.

Over time, EWT was used to carry out less laudable tasks. These included giving loans for buying shares of the group companies, and even for the distribution of shares and debentures, and the sale of such financial instruments, and the distribution of the sale proceeds.

"The trust was used as (a) fig leaf to perpetuate wrong doing(s) as the trust is an unregulated entity. The managerial personnel had adopted (the) 'trust route' to avoid reporting to the shareholders, thereby circumventing corporate governance requirements." The trustees – the gang of nine – were privy to privileged information and used them to time the sale of shares.

In financial year 2013–14, EWT had bought eight lakh shares of IL&FS from Housing Development Finance Corporation Ltd (HDFC) at ₹1,184.50 a share without doing any valuation (this was actually a regulatory requirement, as IL&FS is not listed). Those shares were bought by raising a loan of ₹94.76 crore from HDFC itself with an interest payment of ₹53.77 crore till 30 June 2018.

The Mystery

If the rise of IL&FS defied all logic and the creation of this 'business model' broke all sorts of laws and regulations, there was a lot of mystery shrouding its fall as well.

On 24 July 2018, Parthasarathy, who had run the group with the authority and flamboyance of a promoter, stepped down like a professional manager, citing ill health.

A last-ditch attempt was made to raise funds that could have alleviated the liquidity crisis. This was through a rights issue. It is an even bigger mystery how and why this rights issue was aborted.

The rights issue was approved at the company's annual general meeting on 29 September 2018. A resolution was passed to raise capital through a rights issue, to approach the National Company Law Tribunal (NCLT) for permission to sell assets, and generate liquidity to repay debtors.

Sankaran, the vice chairman and MD of IL&FS, unveiled this three-pronged strategy at its annual general meeting. The ₹4,500 crore rights issue was launched; a small amount from one shareholder did flow into an escrow account, kept with one of the lenders, which had given a short-term loan to IL&FS to tide over a temporary liquidity crisis. And yet, the rights issue was aborted.

The lender was IndusInd Bank Ltd. It had exposure to a few operating companies of the group, the largest account being a ₹750 crore loan to Chenani Nashri Tunnelway Ltd – this was classified as a standard asset.

Who pulled the plug on the issue? And, why?

Had it gone through, IL&FS could have continued to function as a 'going concern', giving it time to sell off assets at reasonable prices.

Apart from the rights issue, IL&FS also had plans to tap some lenders and equity holders for liquidity support of about ₹3,500 crore. Pending the rights issue and liquidity support, IL&FS approached IndusInd Bank for a short-term loan of ₹2,000 crore as it needed to meet running expenses and service debt. Several meetings were held at different levels.

The assets of the holding company were offered as security and the proceeds of the rights issue were earmarked as one of the repayment sources. IL&FS also offered to open the rights issue's escrow account with IndusInd Bank.

Before disbursing the money, IndusInd Bank brass met the senior management of LIC, the largest shareholder of IL&FS, to revalidate its claim about the rights issue and collected no-objection certificates from the security trustee for taking the assets as security.

There was a catch, though. Even though the security document was signed, it was not registered due to the sudden turn of events and the board was superseded. In the absence of registration, it may not be easy for IndusInd Bank to recover the money it gave. But that is a different story.

Valuation Collapse

IL&FS was set up in 1987 by Central Bank of India, HDFC and Unit Trust of India (UTI). As of 31 March 2019, LIC was the largest shareholder in IL&FS with a stake of 25.34 per cent, followed by Orix Corporation of Japan (23.54 per cent), Abu Dhabi Investment Authority (12.56 per cent) and IL&FS Employees Welfare Trust (12 per cent). Among others, HDFC held 9.02 per cent, Central Bank of India 7.67 per cent and SBI 6.42 per cent.

Three years before the default, the Piramal Group, a diversified group with a big presence in healthcare, life sciences, drug discovery, financial services and real estate, was looking to buy a big stake in IL&FS. But LIC put its foot down. Piramal wanted to acquire a 35 per cent stake in IL&FS in a deal that could have offered a lifeline to the cash-strapped infrastructure lender. But LIC was not happy about the valuation.

Piramal's offer was at ₹740–750 per share but LIC was not willing to accept anything below ₹1,200. Three years down the line, LIC chose not to subscribe to a rights issue priced at just ₹150 a share!

A 34-page affidavit, filed with NCLT by Sankaran, said LIC's decision in 2015 not to back the proposed merger with Piramal Group worsened the crisis at IL&FS. The group was already facing a cash crunch due to delayed projects and problems with refinancing. Piramal's entry would have generated ₹8,500 crore of investible funds in the entity.

The bulk of IL&FS's debts increased from ₹48,671 crore in 2014 to ₹94,216 crore by October 2018 when the edifice crumbled. LIC which apparently had reservations about welcoming the Piramal Group on board watched the unsustainable growth of the infrastructure funding juggernaut.

The state-owned insurer was busy 'privatising' IDBI Bank Ltd during that period. Up to March 2019, the state-owned insurer had invested ₹24,078 crore to raise its stake in the bank to 51 per cent by infusing fresh capital.

At the time of writing, in May 2020, the new board of IL&FS was able to complete the sale of only its wind energy assets. That sale helped lighten the outstanding debt of ₹94,000 crore by ₹4,300 crore.

A Family of 347!

India's NBFC sector is a 'shadow banking' industry. Similar 'shadow banks' exist in many Third World countries, notably China, Indonesia and Bangladesh, among others.

These are financial institutions that borrow and lend funds for all sorts of projects. But as they are not banks, they are subject to light-touch supervision and regulation. That has advantages since such firms can be nimble and take smart commercial decisions to create and exploit new markets. But less regulation may also open the door to more creative accounting and fraud.

IL&FS was registered as a 'core investment company' and grew into a group with businesses straddling infrastructure and financial services. It had 14 wholly-owned subsidiaries (called intermediate holding companies) – ten for infrastructure and four for finance.

The group had its finger in every pie. It had exposures in airports, education, information technology, maritime, power, ports, roads, technology, turnkey contracts, water and waste management… You name it. Even within the power sector for example, it was present in every segment – solar, wind and thermal.

Subsidiaries, joint ventures and associate companies in India and abroad ran these businesses. The group structure consisted of a maze of inter-connected companies.

Overall, IL&FS group consisted of 347 companies – 203 for transportation, the maximum number of companies for one sector, and one each for real estate and EPC (engineering, procurement and construction), the minimum. There were 44 joint-venture companies, 19 associate companies and 110 entities to manage the activities of the group along with so-called third parties and government agencies. Of these, 113 entities were housed around the world – in China, Dubai, Mexico, Portugal, Spain, the US, etc.

Some of these overseas entities have very intriguing profiles. For instance, Se7en Factor Corporation, based in Seychelles, had ₹21 crore of assets and no turnover in 2018; Grusamar Albania SHPK in Albania was under liquidation in the financial year 2018; and Nigeria-based ITNL Africa Projects has had no operational revenues in all years since its inception in 2012. The Spanish subsidiary, Elsamex S.A., itself had 11 subsidiaries and 56 joint-venture companies as per the 2017 annual report.

First Progress Report

The 'First Progress Report' prepared by its new board, dated 30 October 2018, estimated the fund-based facilities (as of 8 October 2018) at ₹94,215.6 crore. Of this, the parent held ₹18,052.5 crore, the intermediate holding companies ₹23,301.1 crore and the operating companies ₹52,862 crore.

IL&FS and IFIN together had lent ₹31,247.3 crore to the subsidiaries, joint ventures and associates.

The non-fund based facilities such as LCs and bank guarantees (as of 30 September 2018) were pegged at ₹5,138 crore.

Overall, IL&FS' exposure to group companies was ₹24,866 crore. It borrowed money to invest in equity in its group companies and gave intra-group loans to its subsidiaries and associates. This was a recipe for disaster as there was no return, in the absence of any cash flow in many subsidiaries.

Going by the RBI norms, a core investment company can borrow up to 2.5 times its networth but IL&FS stretched it to many times more. It tapped every available source in its borrowings. Its lenders included PSBs, private banks, foreign banks, financial institutions and NBFCs. It also raised money through market instruments such as non-convertible debentures (NCDs) and CPs. The PSBs held more than one-third of the IL&FS debt.

The Way Ahead

Kotak went on record saying that around ₹50,000–55,000 crore would be recovered. At the higher end of this estimated recovery, the lenders would get 58 per cent of their money back.

About half of this recovery will come in the form of cash, by selling assets; another large chunk will come from creating an Infrastructure Investment Trust (InvITs). This will keep IL&FS' mainstay, the infrastructure business, alive. (InvITs are another version of the REITs or real estate investment trust. These are designed to suit the specific needs of the infrastructure sector.) The lenders will also be able to carry on with a few large projects which are viable, and get their money back. This constitutes the third part of the recovery.

Why is it taking so long? The task before Kotak's team, which was assisted by business management consulting firm Alvarez & Marsal, financial and transaction advisors Arpwood Capital and JM Financial, and legal advisor, Cyril Amarchand Mangaldas and Shardul Amarchand Mangaldas – is herculean.

There is no precedent for untangling this sort of complex maze of inter-connected companies in the Indian financial system. The government-appointed board is looking at selling companies, monetising assets, closing down many, and reviving a few, and part-restructuring some through different schemes.

The SFIO looked into the activities of the group for the ten years until 2018. But there was muck even before 2008. Like Alexander the Great, Parthasarathy was trying to build a global financial empire. In the process, he strayed a long way from the original mandate. Instead of being a catalyst for infrastructure creation, the group ended up owning scores of outfits working in completely unrelated fields.

Why did IL&FS do this? The projects had problems at every level – the structure, funding pattern, leverage, and cost and delays. While the span of supervision got lost in the mesh of over 300 companies, board meetings hardly lasted beyond an hour, illustrating how casually this was 'managed'. The directors just danced to Parthasarathy's tune.

Who is to be blamed for the collapse of IL&FS? The responsibility must be shared between the CEO, management, the board, auditors, rating agencies as well as equity holders, who had representatives on the board but allowed it to be run the way the 'gang of nine' wanted.

Like other players in infra finance, IL&FS was also plagued by delayed payments or non-payment of dues by government agencies such as NHAI: payments adding up to at least ₹15,000 crore are still under arbitration.

Hence, Kotak's team cannot clean up things overnight. It also has to follow the process laid down by the insolvency law and overseen by former Supreme Court judge, Justice D.K. Jain. First, a committee of creditors has to prepare the resolution proposal, then the Ministry of Corporate Affairs vets it and, finally, this is sent to the NCLT. Kotak also needs to try to make sure assets are sold at a price higher than their liquidation value. This may lead to fresh auctions and bids for such sales which can further delay the resolution process.

Flawed DNA

The Bloomberg columnist Andy Mukherjee wrote about it in 2018 immediately after the IL&FS collapse. He explained how this started as an attempted Indian clone of the Macquarie Group and turned into an unwieldy, debt-fuelled empire.

There was something inherently wrong in the DNA of IL&FS, from the very beginning. But the authorities closed their eyes and allowed it to become a monster. By the time it fell, it was 'too big to fail' like Lehman Brothers and the government had to attempt a rescue in order to prevent the whole NBFC sector going down a rabbit hole.

What is in its DNA? Let us quote from Mukherjee's column verbatim:

> The $25 million that IL&FS arranged in 1997 via floating-rate notes – guaranteed by USAID and sold to Bear Sterns & Co. – illustrates the chutzpah that sank the firm. New Tirupur Area Development Corp., the borrower, was floated as a lifeline for a textile center in Tamil Nadu where industrial waste had polluted the groundwater. Tirupur's knitwear business and its households were suffering, but the state didn't have the $250 million required to draw river water, treat it and supply it to the town.
>
> IL&FS showed the way out. Let New Tirupur get a 30-year contract for private water supply and handling of sewage, and a reasonable 20 per cent annual return to lure investors who would share the equity risk with the government and IL&FS. The financial institution, which was also one of the

lenders to the project, paid its share in September 2002, just as work on the water-treatment facility was about to start. But instead of the committed 1.4 billion rupees in equity, senior and subordinate debt – $29 million at the time – Parthasarathy released less than 1 billion rupees.

The big hole was a 46 per cent shortfall in the 900 million-rupee ($25 million) senior debt, owing to an inexplicable 150 million-rupee deduction. IL&FS said it was "costs relating to the USAID loan." A third of it was a commitment fee, and the rest was precious Bear Sterns dollars that had lain in an escrow account and bled, with net losses compounding at 12 per cent a year.

Thus, before New Tirupur could put a single brick on the ground, its stakeholders lost money they never even got to touch. The economics of the project became shaky, and a tussle began between equity holders and creditors. The government of Tamil Nadu had to pump in more public money. As a Madras High Court judge would later note, "Water started flowing (or trickling down) to the common users, both industrial and domestic, in May 2005. What flowed thereafter appears to be only litigation."

This became a pattern of behaviour. For IL&FS to win, other stakeholders had to lose. Never mind if a 30-year concession on a toll road became a license to collect money from commuters in perpetuity. In New Tirupur, even LIC, the biggest shareholder in IL&FS, saw its equity interest diluted. As a result, it had to give up its board seat in the water company.

DHFL's Date with Destiny

Inevitably the default affected other NBFCs. Sixteen days after the IL&FS default, India's fourth-largest mortgage financier among the NBFCs (some of the banks have bigger home loan portfolios), Dewan Housing Finance Corporation Ltd (DHFL), another triple-A rated company, had its date with destiny.

On 21 September 2018, DSP Mutual Fund, a joint venture between India-based DSP Group and BlackRock Inc., an American investment management company, sold ₹300 crore worth of DHFL CP at a discount. This created panic in the debt market and sparked speculation that DHFL could be facing a liquidity crunch and headed for a default.

The news of the sale triggered a 60 per cent fall in the DHFL share price intraday, prompting a probe by SEBI. The stock closed 43 per cent lower, dragging down other NBFC stocks as well.

'The asset manager sold DHFL bonds at a net yield of 11 per cent compared with a coupon rate of 9.1 per cent at the time of issue. The bond was sold at a steep discount in third week of September of 2018 (₹100 bond was sold at ₹82),' according to a finance ministry note to the corporate affairs ministry.

The CP was maturing in June 2019. DSP MF sold the paper at a steep discount as it was facing redemption pressure. As on 31 August 2018, the DSP MF's asset under management was ₹1.12-lakh crore. By 19 September, it had shrunk to ₹1.06-lakh crore – which was largely in line with redemption pressures across the debt mutual fund industry.

Kalpen Parekh, president of DSP MF, was quoted in the media as saying that the sale of the paper at higher rates was an interest rate call rather than a credit call. 'With regards to the sale of NCD of DHFL, the last deal in the security happened at yield of 10.25–10.5 per cent. Since our volume was ₹300 crore, the yields went to 11 per cent. Even after this sale, we continue to hold Dewan Housing Finance paper worth around ₹800 crore in our debt portfolio.'

The Origin

That was the beginning of the end for DHFL but what was behind this panic?

DHFL's maiden bond issue of secured NCDs for ₹1,000 crore, with an option to retain over-subscription up to ₹4,000 crore, saw demand of ₹18,586 crore when it closed on 4 August 2016.

Kapil Wadhawan, its promoter and chairman of the board of directors, smelt an opportunity. Around the same time, another mortgage lender was looking for funds. Wadhawan wanted to queer the pitch for this rival.

DHFL immediately floated another public issue with a base size of ₹2,000 crore and an option to retain oversubscription up to ₹8,000 crore, to soak up all the available money. Opening on 29 August 2016, this issue mopped up ₹12,678 crore.

Two years later, in April 2018, an even bolder DHFL raised ₹1,000 crore by selling rupee-denominated bonds overseas – these were so-called masala bonds. Going by the Euro Medium Term Note (EMTN) programme filed by the company, it planned to raise up to ₹13,000 crore at the prevailing exchange rate through many tranches in that year.

By any yardstick, these were all record collections. Even before floating the masala bond, DHFL had started giving big loans to real estate developers and slum rehabilitation projects. It had sanctioned around ₹8,000 crore in loans towards slum rehabilitation and ₹20,000 crore to the developers.

In the three years, between March 2015 and March 2018, DHFL's assets almost doubled – from ₹54,638 crore to ₹1,07,572 crore.

Typically, the NCD issues earmarked 20 per cent each for qualified institutions and corporations and 30 per cent each for retail investors and high-net-worth individuals. Did these investors have a safety net? No.

These were fully secured issues in theory but the 'security' was flawed. There was general and not specific collateral, beside a floating charge on the company's assets. Unlike a fixed charge, which is created on a specific asset, a floating charge is created over receivables and stocks in general.

The money raised through these debentures was used to fund both retail and wholesale assets. An end-use clause could have prevented the diversion of funds, as was discovered later.

DHFL was one of the contenders vying to buy PNB Housing

Finance Ltd, another mortgage lender. An *Economic Times* report dated 12 September 2018 says seven bidders, including DHFL, submitted non-binding offers to acquire PNB Housing Finance in a deal estimated at around $2.3 billion.

Was the timing of the sale of DHFL debt paper at a discount and the company's bid for PNB Housing Finance purely a coincidence?

Wadhawan is cooling his heels in Taloja jail, Navi Mumbai, while I am writing this chapter. He was arrested by the Enforcement Directorate (ED) for his involvement in the alleged fraud case of Yes Bank. (More on this in the chapter 'Fallen Angels'.) The ED has also been probing his alleged links with global terrorist Dawood Ibrahim's aide, Iqbal Mirchi.

KPMG Special Review

KPMG conducted a 'special review' of the businesses of DHFL, covering its workings between April 2015 and March 2019. Union Bank of India, a PSB which is one of the lenders to DHFL, commissioned this review in February 2019. The finance ministry wanted this done.

A few weeks before, investigative news portal Cobrapost reported alleged fund diversion by the DHFL promoters and its link with Iqbal Mirchi. The exposé pegged the size of the scam at ₹31,000 crore.

The banking industry had an exposure of ₹28,195 crore to DHFL and the erstwhile mortgage regulator National Housing Bank (NHB), ₹2,484 crore. The company had overseas borrowings to the tune of ₹2,747 crore and domestic borrowings of ₹41,435 crore in the form of bonds and debentures, CPs and other debt instruments. Overall, it had debt of ₹84,868 crore in July 2019.

> The 86-page KPMG special review clinically describes how loans and advances worth ₹24,594 crore were disbursed with inadequate loan documentation to 65 entities with hardly any operations.
>
> It revealed that DHFL disbursed loans and advances to

inter-connected entities linked to its promoters, and ₹12,541 crore repayment by 28 such entities were untraceable, implying fund diversion.

It was found that 25 of the 40 entities related to DHFL reported minimal operations in terms of net worth, income, and profit before tax of less than ₹1 lakh. But these raised ₹14,361 crore loans and ICDs, with the outstanding held at ₹13,714 crore till the end of the audit period.

"These entities may not qualify as related parties under the Companies Act, 2013, and hence, such transactions may have not required clearance from the audit committee. However, these transactions should be examined further."

Tracking fund diversions, the KPMG report says:

- Twelve entities used the bank loans to buy preference shares and debentures worth ₹4,010 crore in companies "with commonalities to DHFL promoter entities".
- Seventeen entities had got ₹4,128 crore loans from DFHL and as "advances given for joint ventures under negotiations" and "other advances" without disclosing their names.
- Seven entities had invested ₹733 crore in debentures and preference shares using loans from DHFL. Here too, the names of the investee companies were missing.

KPMG could not access the financial data of any group companies beyond DHFL and thus could not ascertain the use of funds and the extent of involvement of the promoter. It had asked for details of 197 bank accounts but did not get all the data from the management. "Availability and access to critical system/data was a continuous challenge."

DHFL borrowed ₹27,215 crore from 27 banks during the period under review and a fund flow analysis by KPMG found that a sum amounting to 67 per cent of this – ₹15,040 crore

– was invested in mutual funds on the same day the company got the money from the banks.

The compliance culture in DHFL was terrible.

- Three potentially related party transactions of ₹424 crore were not approved by its audit committee.
- Thirty-five entities with ₹19,754 crore loans were directly or indirectly controlled by the promoters but this was never disclosed.
- Seventeen loans given to 17 entities worth ₹8,859 crore were rescheduled, despite defaults of more than 90 days.
- Loan documentation for ₹19,736 crore given to 45 entities was "insufficient".

The KPMG review found DHFL's finance committee, consisting of two promoters and one independent director was authorised to approve loans above ₹200 crore. This was in accordance with the norms laid down by the NHB.

The minutes of 12 such loan approvals, totalling ₹5,404 crore, were not available and half of the amount was given to "entities with commonalities to DHFL promoter".

A further nine loans worth ₹6,010 crore were sanctioned in violation of internal guidelines of corporate governance. They were approved after the money was disbursed.

Though 15 companies defaulted on loans to DHFL for more than 90 days, these entities were still classified as standard assets by the NBFC, as on December 2018. They could not be classified as on 31 March 2019 because there was no data. These 15 companies owed a total of ₹7,639 crore to DHFL.

Incidentally, in September 2018, NHB penalised DHFL the princely sum of ₹65,000 for classifying a bad loan good without following proper procedures.

The focus of the KPMG review was to look at the fund diversion.

But it could not do the job properly because it was denied access to data. In November 2019, once again KPMG was asked to do a forensic audit.

One cannot blame KPMG for not being able to access all relevant data as DHFL was running two parallel offices. While its headquarters in Bandra, a western suburb in Mumbai, was busy with business, at another place, a few trusted employees of the promoter were generating thousands of fake accounts, using special software to 'create' retail borrowers for the money flowing into various group companies.

The ED has told a dedicated court dealing with money laundering offences that ₹12,773 crore was allegedly siphoned off over the past decade from DHFL through about one lakh fictitious borrowers created to route the money into about 80 shell companies. During a raid in early 2020 at the DHFL premises, the directorate stumbled upon customised software used to create lakhs of fake accounts.

The modus operandi is very similar to that employed in the case of the Punjab and Maharashtra Cooperative Bank which had created 21,049 fictitious loan accounts to camouflage loan defaults by the HDIL Group which ran 44 loan accounts with the bank.

More dirt will emerge in due course but let us take a look at what DHFL did to stay alive.

Staying Alive

On 16 March 2019, the DHFL board approved the divestment of the company's entire 30 per cent shareholding in Avanse Financial Services Ltd to Olive Vine Investment, an affiliate of the Warburg Pincus Group. Avanse Financial Services, an education-focused NBFC, is an associate enterprise of DHFL in which International Finance Corporation held 20 per cent equity stake. The RBI approved the sale on 4 June 2019.

DHFL and its parent Wadhawan Global Capital also exited Aadhar Housing Finance Ltd, a specialised lender for low-income earners, on 10 June 2019 for about ₹2,200 crore. DHFL got ₹500 crore by selling its entire 9.15 per cent in Aadhar Housing. The stake was sold to BCP Topco VII Pte Ltd, which is controlled by private equity funds managed by Blackstone.

DHFL also exited the mutual fund industry by selling its 50 per cent stake in DHFL Pramerica Asset Managers to its joint-venture partner Premerica.

Apart from these deals, DHFL sold ₹2,000 crore worth of its loan portfolio to offshore investors in a transaction led by SC Lowy, a banking group based in Hong Kong. It also sold ₹1,375 crore of wholesale loans to foreign alternative investment management fund, Oaktree Capital, which buys distressed loan portfolios at a discount.

Between September 2018 and June 2019, DHFL shrunk its balance sheet from ₹1.15-lakh crore to ₹85,000 crore and it lived to tell the tale. In a regulatory filing on 25 June 2019, DHFL claimed that since September 2018, it had met liability obligations of over ₹41,000 crore.

But it could not come back from the hole it had dug for itself.

On 4 June 2019, DHFL missed interest payment on NCDs. It did pay up after a week but the rating agencies did not wait. On 5 June, DHFL was downgraded to default category. At least ₹750 crore worth of CPs was due for redemption that month and it was in talks with banks to arrange money for that.

The default sounded the death knell for DHFL. By the time, India's general elections were over and a new government (NDA-2) was in place.

Northern Rock Moment

Many more NBFCs were culled in what some analysts have defined as the Lehman moment for India. The right descriptor is actually the Northern Rock moment.

In September 2007, former building society-turned retail bank in UK, Northern Rock asked the Bank of England, as lender of the last resort, for liquidity support after it found its access to the short-term money market frozen. A depositor run followed. Northern

Rock used to build long-term assets on the back of short-term market borrowings.

A BBC report by Dominic O'Connell on the anniversary of its collapse says its chairman, Matt Ridley, summed up its rise in the 2007 annual report, lauding 'another excellent year' and saying 'our strategy of using growth, cost efficiency and credit quality to reward both shareholders and customers continues to run well'.

A few months later, Northern Rock's empire was in ruins. The fuel, it had used to grow so quickly, turned out to be toxic. Instead of using customer deposits as the source of funds to lend out to home owners, it borrowed in the international money markets. Post the Lehman crisis, when money markets were frozen, it collapsed.

This was the same game plan followed by many of India's NBFCs that have had a phenomenal run. They borrowed short term through money market instruments, primarily CPs, for cost efficiency. They just kept on rolling these over to fund long-term loan assets.

When interest rates started rising in 2018, many of them found themselves in a spot at the sudden rise in cost of money. The RBI also started hiking the policy rate from June 2018 on concerns over rising inflation, and the twin deficits of the Fiscal and Current Account.

Between June and August 2018, the policy rate was raised by half a percentage point from 6 per cent to 6.5 per cent. But the rates of corporate bonds rose by much more, tracking the yields of government bonds. At the shorter end, the rise in the cost of borrowing was even higher.

The surge in the volume of privately-placed debt around this time gives an idea of how the NBFCs were raising money. In financial year 2016–17, the private placement market recorded its highest-ever volume of ₹6.41-lakh crore. This dropped to ₹5.99-lakh crore in 2017–18 and, with rising rates, the volume declined further. The cost of borrowing for AAA-rated corporations rose by at least 2 percentage points in the bond market.

While there were other borrowers in the money market, the

NBFCs were borrowing the lion's share and doing this through private placement.

Two Factors

Two factors encouraged the NBFCs to go whole hog in raising cash. First, there was a liquidity sugar rush after the November 2016 demonetisation. Money flooded the system pulling down the yields of money market instruments. Second, many of the PSBs had withdrawn from the credit market.

The rise in bad loans hit the PSBs hard as they needed to provide for such loans. In the process, their capital got eroded and the RBI restrained many PSBs from giving fresh loans.

Now armed with bagful of cheap money, the NBFCs looked with greed at the new vistas opening up due to the banks' inability to lend. They also acted as intermediaries.

Not all PSBs were restrained by the RBI from lending. They had no problems loaning money to the NBFCs but were wary of lending directly to corporations for fear of piling up bad loans. Bank lending to NBFCs saw a jump of 43 per cent year-on-year in August 2018 and it constituted 20 per cent of the banking system's incremental loans.

In financial year 2015–16, the loan portfolio of NBFCs grew 11 per cent to ₹13.17-lakh crore; in 2017, the growth was 12.73 per cent to ₹14.85-lakh crore; and, in 2018, the growth was 18.8 per cent to ₹17.64-lakh crore. Bank credit grew at 10.3 per cent in 2016, 4.5 per cent in 2017 and 10.3 per cent in 2018. It was clear that the shadow banks were picking up market share.

Liquidity Sugar Rush

On 8 November 2016, when the government demonetised the high-denomination currency notes of ₹500 and ₹1,000, the liquidity shortage in Indian financial system was ₹35,000 crore.

By 25 November, there was ₹5.27-lakh crore surplus liquidity as people rushed to banks, depositing notes kept at home. The banking industry's deposit portfolio, which was ₹100-lakh crore on

11 November 2016, rose to ₹107.58-lakh crore by March 2017 and ₹114.26-lakh crore by March 2018. By March 2019, it was ₹125.73-lakh crore.

The NBFCs also got plenty of money from the mutual funds. The mutual funds were collecting even more money than the banks and channelling it into the NBFCs, through short-term CPs. Given the surpluses, there was no problem borrowing short-term money at low rates and then rolling over the loans. Hence, there were unprecedented incentives to accept asset–liability mismatches and create long-term assets using short-term funds.

Mutual fund assets under management or AUM, grew at impressive rates. In 2017, the AUM grew by 42.3 per cent to ₹17.55-lakh crore; the growth was 21.7 per cent in 2018 and 18 per cent in the first five months of fiscal 2019 (until August 2018 just before the September crisis started) to ₹25.2-lakh crore.

In absolute terms, mutual funds' AUM grew ₹6.16-lakh crore between April and August 2018 while only ₹1.64-lakh crore flowed into bank deposits in that time.

The balance sheets of the 'non-deposit taking systematically important NBFCs', which have 86 per cent market share, reveal that in the run-up to the crisis, in the financial year 2017, NBFCs borrowed more through debentures and CPs.

The share of secured borrowing fell to 48 per cent of total borrowings while unsecured borrowings rose to 52 per cent. The mutual funds' contribution to the NBFC borrowing through CPs was 64.2 per cent. NBFCs' borrowing from banks in 2017 dropped by 7 percentage points as mutual funds rushed in to fill in the gap.

The Core Problem

An October 2018 Credit Suisse report highlights the core problem: 'Over the last few years, NBFCs and housing finance companies (HFCs) have attracted a disproportionate amount of funds from mutual funds. As of August 2018, NBFC and HFCs accounted for 30 per cent of the total debt and liquid funds and 41 per cent of overall corporate debt investments.' More than half of the exposure of mutual funds to this segment was through CPs.

Another Credit Suisse report around that time pegged mutual funds' exposure to NBFC debt at 30 per cent of their overall debt assets under management and 55 per cent of this exposure was of short tenure.

India's capital market regulator's norms for mutual funds (which were amended in February 2017 before this rush) allowed up to 25 per cent of asset allocation for the debt schemes with a further 15 per cent limit for papers of HFCs. The regulator was behind the curve it appears.

Later, in October 2019, it introduced exit loads for liquid funds and made it mandatory for liquid funds to have 25 per cent exposure to sovereign papers, treasury bills, etc. But by that time, the damage was done.

The mutual funds' investment in the CPs of NBFCs jumped from close to ₹99,000 crore in August 2014 to over ₹2.65-lakh crore in July 2018. Then they started pulling out as they feared that not all NBFCs would be able to pay back.

A Nomura report in September 2018 on the liability profile of some of the large NBFCs, including HFCs, says short-term CPs accounted for as much as 30 per cent for one specific company and between 10 per cent and 20 per cent for many. If I include CPs and one-year NCDs, the share rises to 40 per cent of the debt of that company (which has 30 per cent funding from CPs) and between 10 per cent and close to 30 per cent for others.

A Global Phenomenon

Borrowing short and lending long is a worldwide phenomenon for this set of financial intermediaries. For instance, in the US, financial companies had 50 per cent share of the volume of the outstanding $1.11 trillion CPs as of December 2019.

But the problem in India was not only confined to asset–liability mismatches. There were other issues plaguing the NBFCs. For instance, in late 2018, one of them borrowed ₹800 crore from a film production house at a monthly interest rate of 2.25 per cent (which annualises to about 30 per cent).

Two HFCs subscribed to the Tier II capital of a private bank in the form of a long-term bond, and the bank, in turn, had given hefty loans to both. A quid pro quo of this sort may not be quite illegal but such incestuous relationships usually lead to systemic issues.

Given innovative products and superior delivery systems, the NBFCs made fast inroads in almost every segment of the credit business. They were in vehicle financing, housing mortgages and even wholesale financing. The total credit market of the NBFCs that had been giving home loans, auto and two-wheeler loans and consumer loans beside wholesale loans was around ₹28.43-lakh crore in 2018, a little less than a third of the ₹90-lakh crore bank credit.

The compounded annual growth rate (CAGR) of NBFCs in five years between 2013 and 2018, had been 17 per cent versus 9.4 per cent growth of the banking sector; among NBFCs, the HFCs grew even faster, at around 20 per cent.

The mushrooming of HFCs added fuel to this fire. There were 72 HFCs in 2015; by June 2019, when the NHB was the regulator for HFCs, the figure had risen to 99. A year down the line, in June 2020, there were 102 HFCs.

To be sure, the NBFCs do not compete with banks; they create a new credit market. Consumers need them. Most of them do not take public deposits (DHFL was one of the exceptions) but that does not mean they cannot create systemic risks.

The banking system had lent at least ₹57,000 crore to IL&FS. Overall, the banking system's exposure to this set of lenders was ₹5.13-lakh crore as of September 2019. Where do the banks get their money from? The depositors. So it comes back to household savings being funnelled into the NBFCs.

The Assets Side Problem

There were serious issues on the assets side as well with the NBFCs. Loans against property (LAP) was a popular product (and remains so).

Many argue that NBFCs keep enough margin for LAP and unless the property market crashes, such loans are literally as safe as houses.

However, as with so many other financial products, the problems lie in misuse.

A few NBFCs turned LAP into a game of passing-the-parcel.

For illustration, Company A has given a borrower ₹100 crore LAP and two years down the line, Company B picked up that loan at ₹120 crore (including interest, which the borrower defaulted on) and, in the third round, Company C picked that up at ₹150 crore (again, with interest). So, this loan has been ever-greened and this was common practice in the NBFC sector.

The high-margin 'super-priority' loan is another dicey product. Such loans are sought by desperate borrowers when no other avenue is open and the lender takes the first charge on the cash flow and assets – it has precedence above all others, in case the borrower defaults. However, at the insolvency court, the first charge for such loans does not hold water legally; this loan becomes *pari passu* or all lenders enjoy equal rights.

The Real Estate Sector

The fate of the NBFCs, particularly those that have large exposures to real estate developers, has been intertwined with India's real estate sector. A February 2019 report of Liases Foras, a real estate research firm, says the developers' sales in the past decade, between 2009 and 2018, have grown 1.28 times in units and 1.56 times in value but the inventory during the decade has grown 3.33 times in units and 4.72 times in value. The total debt of the industry has risen from ₹1.2-lakh crore to ₹4-lakh crore.

Analysing the business of the top 90 developers, including the listed ones, the study says they have a disposable income of ₹57,000 crore to meet the annual debt repayment obligation of ₹1.29-lakh crore.

The industry is at an inflexion point and the developers are stuck, like 'an elephant in a well' which cannot emerge unaided. A few of them drowned, and they pulled down the NBFCs in the process.

Jefferies analyst Bhaskar Basu and others said in 2019 that the NBFCs had raised their exposure to property firms by 46 per cent over three years, while bank loans to builders grew by just 4 per cent.

Yet another February 2019 report by Macquarie Research hits the nail on the head again. Between financial year 2014 and 2018, the incremental lending by NBFCs and HFCs to commercial real estate rose by 84 per cent. In contrast, commercial banks' exposure to this sector incrementally rose just 16 per cent. If I include the first half of 2019, when the crisis surfaced, the growth had been even higher.

Joint Statement

On 23 September 2018, just two days after DSP MF sold DHFL paper at a discount, India's banking and markets regulators issued a rare joint statement late on Sunday, saying 'The Reserve Bank of India and the Securities and Exchange Board of India are closely monitoring recent developments in financial markets and are ready to take appropriate actions, if necessary.'

The regulators' move to calm the frayed nerves of investors came after the BSE's benchmark Sensex lost nearly 1500 points on Friday over a rumoured default by DHFL which the home lender denied. Rajnish Kumar, then SBI chairman, had to step in to reassure investors on Sunday, saying there was no concern related to liquidity at mortgage lenders.

Kumar's bank, India's largest, stepped up the buying of loans from the stressed NBFCs, raising its portfolio purchase plan to ₹45,000 crore in 2019. A few other banks joined in, even as the mortgage regulator raised its refinance limit to HFCs for the July 2018–June 2019 period.

The RBI too committed to infusing ₹36,000 crore into the system in October 2018, buying government bonds off the market to ease pressure on liquidity. Many steps have been taken to fight the NBFC crisis – ranging from dismantling the boards of the rogue companies to conducting forensic audits, probe by investigative agencies, sending promoters to jail, taking companies to the insolvency court and arranging a lifeline of liquidity.

The weak mortgage regulator was stripped of its power of regulations. But NHB is still supposed to be committed to the task of supervision which is also not its forte. After taking over as the regulator of the mortgage market in August 2019, the RBI in June 2020 proposed to define home finance and change the rules for the HFCs. It also proposed to treat all deposit taking HFCs, and non-deposit taking HFCs with at least ₹500 crore loan books as systematically important. At least 46 of these HFCs will fall into this category.

The Way Forward

NBFCs which survived the crisis, or became stretcher cases, do not have too many choices. The banks cherry-picked their assets, leading to a shrinkage in the loan books and a rise in bad loans. They cannot compete with banks any more, which they were doing.

The NBFCs now need to reinvent themselves as niche players in high-margin businesses and focus on creating new markets in sectors where banks fear to tread. The other option is to convert themselves into banks. The merger of Capital First Ltd with IDFC Bank Ltd is the guiding beacon for this path. One large HFC tried to follow this path but did not get the RBI approval.

The licence for both universal banks as well as small finance banks can be applied for, on tap. However, unless the regulator changes its approach to what it defines as a 'fit and proper' candidate for a bank, it will be difficult for most NBFCs to convert. Many of them had applied for a licence in 2013 but none got it; quite a few are also owned by corporations that cannot get a banking licence until norms are changed.

The large NBFCs, at least some of them can also use their wide network to go big time into securitisation. They can originate loans and convert them into debt instruments and sell these instruments to banks.

Securitisation is the practice of pooling various types of debt – home loans, commercial mortgages, auto loans, etc – and selling their related cash flows to investors as securities in the form of bonds. The banks will be only too happy to buy such securities if they are convinced about their quality.

Around 9,600 NBFCs together possess a loan portfolio equal to 15 per cent of India's GDP but only 803 of them could boast of ₹100 crore or more of assets as of February 2020. While many fell to the wayside, a few have learnt their lessons and are in the process of changing their business models.

An investor presentation by Indiabulls Housing Finance Ltd in 2019 was titled 'The Phoenix Rises Again'. The third-largest mortgage lender, after an unsuccessful attempt to merge with a bank, has been shrinking its balance sheet.

An October 2019 notice to stock exchanges by Piramal Enterprises Ltd explained how its exposure to CPs was slashed by 90 per cent and the exposure to wholesale residential real estate loans pared substantially, while the retail loan portfolio grew three times.

Flashback 2001

Two decades ago, India's oldest mutual fund, the UTI, needed to be bailed out. How this was accomplished is the best illustration of how a systematically important financial institution can be rescued.

In 2000, the trust's flagship scheme US-64 boasted over 20 million investors and over ₹22,000 crore in assets. A year down the line, UTI was grappling with its worst crisis, with its reserves turning negative by at least ₹1,000 crore. The real value of the UTI unit dropped to below ₹6, against a face value of ₹10 and a quoted net asset value (NAV) of ₹13.

The stock market scam, perpetrated by Ketan Parekh, had led to massive erosion of the prices of shares the UTI scheme held. Investors rushed to redeem their units, which promised an assured return. UTI had no money in its kitty to meet those redemptions.

Its chairman P.S. Subramanyam announced the suspension of trading in US-64 on 2 July 2001. But the suspension was revoked within a week. Subramanyam was sacked the next month.

UTI was split into two – one entity was to hold the stressed assets and another, the healthy assets. The unitholders were offered an option of cash, or a tax-free six-year bond, offering better than market interest rates. The investors did not suffer any loss and the government eventually made money on its investment. The mess was cleared up at electrifying speed.

IL&FS not an NBFC

The IL&FS mess cannot be cleaned up that fast due to the incredibly complex group structure. But those who brood over the NBFC crisis will be foxed by a paradox. The IL&FS default became a flashpoint for the NBFC sector. But IL&FS itself is not an NBFC!

It is a core investment company in the business of acquisition of shares and securities. Under RBI norms, such a company needs to hold not less than 90 per cent of its net assets in the form of investment in equity shares, preference shares, bonds, debentures, debt or loans in group companies. (In November 2019, an RBI working group recommended a series of measures, including periodical inspection of the companies and the formation of board-level committees.)

The group had to pay the price of misgovernance but the fall of IL&FS should not have led to a systemic NBFC crisis had it been handled with care. Given that IL&FS is a systematically important financial institution, should it not have been ring-fenced?

The fire could have been doused and contagion stemmed if the regulator and the government had seen the crisis through a different prism. A one-line statement from the RBI and the government in the first week of September, immediately after the IL&FS default, would have helped solve the problem.

This could have been followed by a package of liquidity support to the infrastructure lender for the next two years or so, while freezing its activities and letting investors know the real profile of the IL&FS group. The rogue NBFCs could have been taken to task in due course.

The analyst community estimates that a ₹20,000 crore lifeline could have saved IL&FS, and by extension, the NBFCs from contagion. In the event, the losses are already much more and there is an ongoing fallout from the crisis.

Subsequently, Yes Bank was not allowed to fail because it has retail depositors. Did IL&FS have to go under because retail depositors had no exposure to it? After all, the money the banks had lent IL&FS came out of public deposits.

Could it have been handled differently? Rabindranath Tagore in one of his poems *The Invention of Shoes* provides an answer:

> One day King Hobuchandra told his minister Gobuchandra that he wished his feet should not get dirty when he stepped on the ground. Millions of brooms were then purchased to ensure a dust-free kingdom. But the whole kingdom, the king's palace, and even the sun, got covered by the dust raked up by these brooms. The king fell sick and started coughing and sneezing.
>
> The water from the lakes and ponds was then used liberally to settle the dust. The kingdom was flooded and, much to the king's annoyance, the dust turned into mud.
>
> When this experiment failed, it was decided to cover the earth with leather. Millions of sheep and goats were then slaughtered but their hides were not enough to do the trick.
>
> Finally, an old cobbler walked into the royal court seeking an audience with the king. Sitting at the king's feet, the cobbler stitched together a pair of simple leather sandals. Now the king could roam around in freedom; his feet would not get dirty again.

The simple approach of the cobbler could have solved the crisis. Neither the RBI nor the government saw any merit in this minimalist approach. Instead, they preferred to clean the kingdom with brooms and created a monstrous cloud of dust.

■ ■ ■

4

Who will Rate the Rater?

In January 2019, a chartered accountant who had worked at a premier rating agency walked into the cabin of the MD of a gems and jewellery company at the Bharat Diamond Bourse office in Mumbai's Bandra Kurla Complex.

The chartered accountant has been running a 'rating advisory company' for seven years. The MD ushered him in with a warm handshake. Those were the pre-Covid-19 days. The MD had been waiting anxiously for this meeting along with his chief financial officer (CFO).

The company was facing a liquidity crunch. It had a working capital loan facility from a bank and it could secure additional lines of credit if it had a rating. The adviser assured the MD that he would secure an investment-grade rating for the company from one of the top three rating agencies, provided his conditions were met.

There were just two conditions. The company would have to pay the adviser a fee of one per cent of the total loan amount before it accepted the rating. And, the company would not directly deal with the rater.

The CFO found the promises of the rating adviser an attractive quick-fix to his problems but the MD had his doubts. 'Can we manipulate the rating so easily?' he asked his colleague.

He was aware that in a credit rating agency (CRA) the call is taken through a vote of the rating committee members. All raters need to adhere to the analytic firewall policy – this is a Chinese wall between the sales executives and the analytical team. This ensures that the analysts do not know what the CRA is earning for a particular assignment and the sales executives do not have access to any information about the rating beyond what is in the public domain.

The system can therefore be rigged only if a rating agency is ready to break the code of governance at multiple levels.

The Process

The rating of a company is a well-documented process. A company seeking rating for its debt issue, or for a bank loan, has to pay the entire fee in advance and sign the agreement before the rating process kicks off. This way, a company unhappy with its rating cannot exit the process without paying.

The process starts only after the agreement is signed. Direct interactions with the entities being rated till such time are a strict no-no. As the rating symbol captures 'ability and willingness to pay interest and principal on time in full', the emphasis is on free cash flows and the rated entity's ability to service debt obligations including both interest and principal.

Typically, raters follow an unwritten rule that a minimum of two people meet their clients. This is to weed out any subjectivity in analysis. The focus is on the business model, competition and professional competence apart from parentage and succession planning, among other things.

Unlike an equity analyst, a rating analyst's task is to try and envisage what can go wrong and whether the company has the ability and resources to tide over potential risks. The team of analysts evaluates the strength of a company raising debt through a series of meetings with its management, suppliers, buyers and bankers.

For all rating exercises (new as well as surveillance), a CRA deploys a primary analyst, a principal analyst, a relationship head and a sector specialist.

The 'rating note' contains the rating recommendation and the rationale – why the company has been given a particular rating.

This note then travels to the rating committee, consisting of three to five experienced credit-risk professionals – typically former bankers or people with experience in credit analysis at a rating agency – for considering a fresh rating and/or continuation/ revision (upward or downward).

These members cast their votes either in favour of or against the recommendation of the analysts. The recommended rating is assigned only after a majority of the members vote in favour of it.

If the company believes that the rating is not fair, it can appeal to the rater with fresh information. This is heard by a different committee called 'Appeal Committee', consisting primarily of external members.

The rating committee members as well as the analysts use a rating methodology that is approved by the rating criteria committee. This committee, made of senior credit analysts, may include external members too. The job of the criteria committee is to set basic guidelines for certain credit scenarios. This helps analysts and rating committee members remain objective in their assessment.

The methodologies and criteria guidelines are also put up on the rating agency's website to ensure the investors can rely on the comparability of ratings and soundness of the methodology.

Neither the analysts nor any member of the committee should have any conflict of interest while assigning the rating and accepting the recommendation.

It is an apparently transparent process with built-in checks and balances; rigging the system is not easy. Still, the MD of the gems and jewellery company and his management team chose to use the services of the rating adviser. The stakes were too high.

They met again at the diamond bourse in October 2019. This

time, the adviser did not look so confident. The handshake was limp.

By then, the world of raters had changed. IL&FS had already defaulted on a short-term loan from SIDBI and the bank had begun disciplinary proceedings against the chief general manager of its risk management department.

The MD and the adviser exchanged wry smiles. Over a cup of ginger-tea, the MD told the adviser, 'Now I know how the rating agencies work!'

The IL&FS Fiasco

Just weeks before IL&FS went belly up in September 2018, three rating agencies – India Ratings & Research Pvt Ltd, ICRA Ltd and CARE Ratings Ltd – had given its debt papers AAA/AA+ ratings. IL&FS was enjoying the highest AAA rating even *after* its subsidiary, IL&FS Transport Networks Ltd, defaulted in June.

SEBI imposed penalties of ₹25 lakh each on ICRA, CARE and India Ratings for their 'lapses in their duty to investors by not taking timely action'. That was done in December 2019. In January 2020, the capital market regulator issued fresh show-cause notices to the rating agencies, seeking to raise the penalty after its board felt ₹25 lakh was too small for the magnitude of negligence. Defending the decision, the Securities Appellate Tribunal ruled that the SEBI has powers to enhance penalties, or levy higher penalty than originally imposed.

The three raters had rated close to ₹1-lakh crore worth of NCDs of IL&FS.

SEBI had also penalised another CRA, Brickwork Rating India Pvt. Ltd, for not adhering to the code of conduct. Brickwork had delayed recognition of default in debt repayment by two companies, Bhushan Steel Ltd and Gayatri Projects Ltd.

Many heads rolled across the rating ecosystem. SEBI told CARE to sack its chairman, S.B. Mainak, a former MD of LIC, after a forensic report said that he had asked analysts to hold back ratings and, in some cases, not change assessments.

The regulator's decision was based on the findings of a forensic report by EY, formerly Ernst & Young. CARE had commissioned EY after a whistle-blower complaint. Typically, such reports study telephone calls, WhatsApp messages and emails, and recorded statements of staff members.

CARE had appointed EY to find out whether the management had interfered in the assessment process.

Mainak was given marching orders in February 2020; he immediately resigned. In December 2019, CARE had also shown the door to its MD and CEO, Rajesh Mokashi.

ICRA had acted even earlier, on August 29, sacking Naresh Takkar, its MD and CEO. The EY audit had reportedly revealed the involvement of Mokashi as well.

As far as Takkar is concerned, another whistle-blower's complaint to SEBI had indicated that he used his position to influence the rating outcome, going against the facts presented by the analysts. On 12 September 2019, ICRA shared with the stock exchanges the representation of Takkar, a fortnight after it had sacked him.

'Regrettable Action'

Reacting to the board's 'regrettable action', Takkar harped on his contribution to the growth of the company. He did present facts and data as well to support his claim that he had acted with integrity.

> Our ratings team never expected and did not foresee such malfeasance by the (IL&FS) group, which was owned by such large and respectable institutional shareholders, overseen by highly experienced and reputed board members and the financial statements audited by auditors with such high repute and international standing. Given all these factors, management plans, policies and representations were relied upon with greater confidence. ICRA, and for that matter no rating agency is either expected or equipped to carry out investigations or forensic audits.
>
> ICRA followed all its regular process and practices, but could not be expected to anticipate and prevent what happened

> at IL&FS. ICRA since its inception, institutionalised checks and balances where all its rating decision are assigned by the rating committees, and each rating committee member has an equal vote, with a right to record dissent, and no individual has a veto right. There are strict guidelines for dealing with conflict of interest for all the analytical and rating committee members. ...It would be grossly incorrect and unfair, indeed illegal, if I am singled out and solely held responsible for any collective failure.

ICRA had sent Takkar on administrative leave on 1 July 2019, following concerns raised in the anonymous letter to SEBI. On 29 August, he got the sack.

In his representation, Takkar admitted that ICRA received an anonymous representation 'sometime in November 2018' and from day one, he had fully supported independent investigations.

> However, during the last few months, I had serious concerns about the lack of transparency, fairness and independence of the investigations, and also the board's reluctance to deal with the same.

He ended his note saying:

> After 27 years of dedicated service... I feel highly disappointed and aggrieved at the grossly unfair manner in which ICRA board has wrongly dealt with me, first by sending me on forced administrative leave... ignoring my offer to go on voluntary leave... and finally culminating into the most unfortunate decision to wrongfully terminate my services without assigning any reason... I reserve all my rights and remedies available to me, for such injustice rendered to me.

Project Icarus

The findings of the interim report of a forensic audit code-named Project Icarus, by Grant Thornton, an audit, tax and advisory firm, engaged by the government-appointed board of the disgraced IL&FS, exposed India's rating industry.

It graphically detailed goodies that senior CRA professionals allegedly enjoyed to maintain the rating of a company with shaky financials on a high pedestal.

Until the findings of the report were revealed in the media, CRAs used to be criticised for basking in the cool comfort of their offices, oblivious of ground realities, of failing miserably in due diligence and acting only when the writing on the wall was already visible to the entire world.

The report added a dirty dimension to that, alleging widespread corrupt practices across the raters. It detailed the favours extended by IL&FS to executives of some of the rating agencies. This goes well beyond white shirts and Fitbit watches.

Going by the report, between September 2012 and August 2016, Ramesh Bawa, the MD and CEO of IL&FS Financial Services Ltd, had facilitated the purchase of a villa in Gurgaon Espace Premiere Nirvana Country by Jyotsna Srivastava, wife of Ambreesh Srivastava, head of financial institutions, South and Southeast Asia, Fitch Ratings. This came with a discount of ₹43 lakhs. India Ratings is a 100 per cent subsidiary of Fitch Group. Bawa had even requested Ajay Chandra of Unitech Ltd, the builder, to resolve an issue Jyotsna was facing – namely, interest charged on delayed payments.

IL&FS also arranged tickets to the corporate box in Santiago Bernabeu Stadium in Spain's capital Madrid for D. Ravishankar, founder and director of Brickwork, so that he could watch Real Madrid play on home ground.

Ravishankar watched the match with his son, who was doing his PhD at the University of Barcelona, and profusely thanked Arun K. Saha, joint MD and CEO of IL&FS. Saha happened to be the point person for making such arrangements, including the distribution of generous gifts during Diwali.

The draft audit report also alleged the strategies deployed in the case of a ₹300 crore NCD raised by Gujarat Road and

Infrastructure Company Ltd, a joint venture between the Gujarat government and IL&FS. When CARE informed the company of its rating committee's decision to award an AA+ rating, it did not go down well with the officials as there was another rater willing to award the AAA rating.

It is not clear if this story is true, and if so, which agency was willing to give it a higher rating, but CARE ultimately gave it an AAA rating after Saha spoke to Mokashi.

Referring to another case, the Grant Thornton report says 'It appears that ICRA had earlier planned to assign "A- with outlook stable" ratings to IL&FS Rail Ltd (a group company), which was changed to "A with outlook stable" after meetings between the representatives of ICRA and IL&FS group.'

Cultural Roots

Let us take a look at the cultural roots of the CRAs. The big three – CRISIL Ltd (established 1987), ICRA (1991) and CARE (1993) were all promoted by now-defunct DFIs – ICICI Ltd, IFCI Ltd and IDBI, respectively.

When the legendary H.T. Parekh was chairman of ICICI in the 1970s (1972–78), his secretariat followed an informal process of handing out gifts. Every Diwali and New Year, gifts that landed in the company's office were numbered and kept in the conference room till they were distributed through a lottery draw among the peons, gardeners, canteen boys, sweepers and other service personnel.

Some gifts were also sent to an orphanage at Girgaum, Mumbai. And, of course, the chairman's secretariat would send a 'thank you' note to all senders, requesting them not to continue with the ritual in future. I am not aware of the processes followed by IFCI and IDBI during this period.

In the beginning, the bosses of all the rating agencies represented the sponsors and eminent professionals were on their boards. The rating committees were constituted mainly with members of the boards and ethics was an obsession.

The late R. Ravimohan, former MD & CEO of CRISIL, once

remarked: 'Credibility is the most valuable asset on our balance sheet; unfortunately accounting standards do not permit recording and valuing the same.'

Other rating agencies such as Acuité Ratings & Research Ltd (formerly SME Rating Agency of India Ltd, promoted by SIDBI and Dun & Bradstreet in 2005), Brickwork Rating (2008), and India Ratings (in early 2000 Fitch bought a stake from Duff & Phelps Corporation and raised it gradually) by and large adopted the culture of the big three.

The general perception is that international tie-ups and technical assistance – Standard & Poor's (S&P) for CRISIL, Moody's Investor Service for ICRA, Department for International Development, UK, for Acuité Ratings and Fitch Group for India Ratings – have given an added impetus to governance and transparency. This may not be entirely correct as the foreign partners do not actually have much operational influence on the rating committees and they do not set criteria.

In fact, the international agencies have actually benefited more from the outsourcing of research, expanding their footprint and nipping potential competition in the bud. The foreign partners are more into marketing and brand-building and do not seem to have made much contribution to changes in the rating culture.

The CRA boards have adopted governance policies defining conflict of interest, disclosure norms and rules for accepting gifts, favours and gratifications with predetermined monetary value. All these are documented, and established as a part of the employee engagement rules and ethics policy; compliance officers (usually company secretaries) are tasked with implementation.

Chocolates and Dry Fruits

Apart from chocolates and dry fruits, office utility articles such as calendars, pens and pen stands, potted plants and coffee table books feature in the permissible list. But employees are expected to return gold-plated idols of deities in the Hindu pantheon, Montblanc pens, smartphones and iPads.

Incidentally, the salary and emoluments (including stock options) of rating agency employees are on a par with, if not better than, compensations in the banking and finance industry.

Although the Grant Thornton report dealt with only IL&FS, people familiar with the industry say that internal norms are relaxed at least for a few CRAs. It was not uncommon for people from the rating fraternity to be seen on cruises to Greece, Spain and Alaska.

The not-so-senior managers enjoy free stays at cottages in beach resorts (Goa), tea plantations (Coorg), wildlife sanctuaries (Jim Corbett National Park) and hill stations (Shimla), courtesy the rated entities.

This is not exactly a recent trend. More than a decade back, a leading NBFC and a large industrial group used to hold their 'offsites' in Macau and Las Vegas. There the raters, along with bankers, addressed the senior management team on economic trends and opportunities in their sector, while enjoying all-expenses-paid holidays. Of course, some did not participate and some paid their own airfare.

At the beginning of the century, a few CRAs decided to try a new tactic to expand their market share. They introduced an unsolicited exercise in the garb of 'visibility ratings', or 'shadow ratings'.

They rated companies based on information available in the public domain. Such ratings were first informally shared with the companies and the rating exercise would start with an official mandate only after these were accepted. These products fizzled out after SEBI came down heavily even though this has been an accepted global practice.

Whatever the ethics of this shadow rating as a marketing ploy, the problem goes much deeper. The rating agencies can only blame themselves for cutting corners in their greed for growth and market share. The rating business enjoys fat margins of 50–70 per cent, and yet CRAs raise the targets for senior management every year.

Setting up a rating agency required a net worth of just ₹5 crore until June 2018 when this was raised to ₹25 crore. Before the market for bank loan ratings exploded, around 2008, the raters' universe had been the same 800–900 companies for decades. The bank loan rating was a booster dose but the profile of many of the companies raising large loans between 2010 and 2015 would make one believe that the rating agencies were riding a tiger.

Does India have too many CRAs? Is competition responsible for the mess? Not really. The SEBI has given just three new licences for rating agencies since 1994, while the potential market has grown to at least 30,000 companies!

Learning from the West

In the aftermath of the 2008 financial crisis, when everyone including US lawmakers was dissecting the role of S&P and Moody's, a very disturbing instant message exchange between two managers of S&P went viral.

This conversation took place on 4 May 2007 about a mortgage-backed security deal.

> S&P Employee 1: BTW [by the way] that deal is ridiculous.
> S&P Employee 2: I know right... model def [definitely] does not capture half the risk.
> S&P Employee 1: We should not be rating it.
> S&P Employee 2: We rate every deal. It could be structured by cows and we would rate it.

Former MD Jerome Fons, who worked at Moody's until August of 2007, has said Moody's was focused on 'maximising revenues', leading it to make the firm more 'issuer friendly'.

As it would turn out, such conversations were quite commonplace among employees of Indian rating agencies until IL&FS went bust – and that was over a decade after the 2008 financial crisis.

Seventeen Notches at One Go

ICRA Ltd, a Moody's Investors Service company, downgraded

IL&FS from investment grade to junk, AA+ to D – or at least seventeen notches – at one go. The company had been enjoying AAA status since 1997 and three separate CRAs – ICRA, India Ratings and CARE – had all rated it AAA, the highest level of creditworthiness.

Downgrading a company steeply at one shot may not be a regulatory problem per se. But it does clearly highlights the CRA's inability to recognise long-standing underlying concerns, and indicates a failure to spot the tell-tale signs of liquidity problems and asset–liability mismatches. In fact, these were all ignored and the highest rating was justified with vague rationales.

There are ten CRAs in the US but the 'Big Three' – S&P, Moody's, and Fitch Ratings – have a virtual oligopoly there. India has seven CRAs but the three large ones – CRISIL, CARE and ICRA – hold roughly 80 per cent of the rating business and the rest is shared by India Ratings, Brickwork Ratings, Acuité Ratings & Research Ltd (erstwhile SMERA Ratings Ltd) and the newest entrant, Infomerics Valuation and Rating Pvt. Ltd.

Theoretically, one would welcome competition for two reasons – fees will reduce down, and the quality of ratings will improve. However, in credit rating, fees are already low. The floor for bank loan ratings for many CRAs is ₹40,000 and the fees for rating debt instrument is typically a few basis points – which can go up to a maximum of about 10 basis points – of the size of the debt being raised. One basis point is a hundredth of a percentage point.

In rating circles, there are stories aplenty of obscenely low fees. One such example is the NHAI, which paid a fee of ₹1,100 for getting a rating for a ₹75,000 crore bond issue in 2019.

A 25 March 2019 *Economic Times* news report by Reena Zachariah says CRISIL, CARE Ratings and India Ratings had placed their bids at ₹1,100, while ICRA had put in a bid of ₹1,500. The report also says the raters were willing to receive the fee well after the process was complete and not in advance, as in normal practice.

The large banks are known for not paying reasonable fees.

Instead of raising quality, the presence of more rating agencies may also end up diluting standards further if, as many suspect, a few CRAs may compromise on standards to get business. Desperation for getting business in the face of competition could force a CRA to do funny things.

Why is there such desperation?

In the rating business, the client–rater relationship is like a marriage, with no scope for divorce. This means, as a rater, if you do not win a mandate now, you lose the client forever in practical terms. Also, investors typically look at the market share of the CRAs and not at the quality of ratings. In such a scenario, winning every client is important.

For the same reasons, the investors-pay model (where subscribers to the debt issues pay to the rater) may not work. A nexus could easily develop between the investors and the raters. There are many examples where a banker is unhappy about a low rating since this increases the cost of lending. A few PSBs have stopped asking smaller borrowers to get ratings done as typically these borrowers get a low rating and the banks are then compelled to charge higher interest rates.

In the mutual fund business, even in good times, the competition is really for the share of investors' funds. The mutual funds are happy if their investee companies get a higher rating since it makes it easier to sell the fund.

Most investors, particularly the mutual funds, often treat rating as a formality – a 'stamp' that allows them to invest in a particular paper. They hate any downgrade as that affects valuation and erodes the NAV of the investment.

If indeed investors need to spend to be assured of the quality of debt paper, why would they pay the CRAs? They would prefer to spend the money themselves to conduct their own version of the so-called due diligence.

Beyond IL&FS

The raters did not learn anything from the IL&FS saga. They

repeated the same mistakes in DHFL, Altico Capital Ltd and, Cox & Kings. The case of the double-default of commercial debt obligations (on 27 and 29 June 2019) by Cox & Kings, a tour and travels services company, is especially glaring. The CRAs were CARE and Brickwork, who ignored problems that may have been easily identified earlier.

CARE and Brickwork reaffirmed their highest rating of CARE A1+ and BWR A1+, respectively, for a Cox & Kings' CP issue and gave a 'stable' outlook, which indicates a low possibility of rating change over the medium term; this was just days before Cox & Kings defaulted on payments on its CP in June 2019.

After the default, Brickwork downgraded Cox & Kings' CP from BWR A1+ to BWR D and the non-convertible debt issue from BWR AA-(Stable) to BWR C. CARE also downgraded the company's CPs to 'D' rating from A+.

Both raters said they were comfortable with Cox and Kings' 'liquidity position' and 'healthy financial risk profile'.

SEBI's Displeasure

SEBI penalised the CRAs for their role in IL&FS. But the capital market regulator had been glaring at the rating agencies for quite sometime before that debacle.

Rewind to 2015. In August that year, JP Morgan MF restricted withdrawals from two of its funds – JP Morgan India Treasury Fund and JP Morgan India Short-Term Income Fund – as both were facing redemption. The two funds had an exposure of around ₹200 crore to Delhi-based Amtek Auto Group, a large auto-parts maker that supplied almost every car-maker in India and also exported to many manufacturers abroad.

CARE sharply downgraded the bonds of Amtek Auto, which was on the verge of defaulting on ₹800 crore in bond repayments, and it withdrew or suspended ratings.

This was the first time SEBI put the role of rating agencies under the microscope in the case of a credit failure. The ensuing discussions and investigations revealed that CARE failed to place the ratings of Amtek Auto Ltd on credit watch, and had suspended its ratings without first downgrading to 'D'.

CARE had suspended the Amtek Auto rating on 7 August 2015 when the rating was still AA-, signifying a relatively high degree of safety, or very low risk of default.

The fine print of suspension or withdrawal of a rating without first downgrading allows the rating agency to keep the default 'hidden' from its calculation of the probability of default. To the investors, it creates an impression of stability.

Ideally, CARE should have first downgraded its Amtek Auto rating, using already available public information. After that, it could have informed the public about Amtek Auto's refusal to share information.

Instead, CARE chose not to inform the public and then took the rating out of its regular pool by suspending the rating. At that time, when a rating was suspended, it meant it would not be reviewed. It just disappeared from the rating pool.

SEBI also probed the role of CRISIL, which had rated the JP Morgan funds. The investigation revealed that the rating agency did not conduct reviews of JP Morgan Treasury Fund in March–July 2015 which was needed to assess the credit quality of bond funds. These funds invested in debt papers rated by CRISIL as well as other rating agencies. But a few rating agencies such as CRISIL also rate the funds/schemes itself.

Conflict of Interest

Such instances point to a conflict of interest. Theoretically, a rating agency may deliberately delay, or avoid the downgrade of a bond, if the bond constitutes a part of a portfolio of a scheme/fund rated by them as the downgrade of the bond, would also mean a downgrade of the scheme.

The portfolio of a debt fund consists of a collection of the individual bond/debt papers of various companies. So the rater has to look at each of the individual companies periodically to see if the rating of the fund is correct. This was not done when

Amtek Auto was failing. This made the rating remain high and investors continued investing money in the funds until they got a rude shock.

CRISIL assigned the scheme AAA (the highest portfolio credit quality) in May 2015. It was downgraded thrice by eight notches in the next two months. On 15 October 2015, the schemes were placed on 'notice of withdrawal'.

The rater settled the adjudication proceedings in January by paying ₹28 lakh to SEBI 'without admitting or denying the findings of fact and conclusion of law'.

Mutual fund ratings are important for business-hungry rating agencies. If they can forge a cosy relationship with fund houses, it helps in many ways. Some fund houses have enough clout to get the rating they want, of a particular debt issue of a given company, from its rater. The rating of the funds is a very effective marketing tool for the CRAs as distributors and even individual investors rely on these ratings, unaware of the possible conflicts of interest.

In the aftermath of the Amtek Auto fiasco, SEBI called a series of meetings with mutual funds, debenture trustees, and rating agencies to address concerns over suspension of ratings.

What emerged from one of these meetings, held in September 2016, is stunning. CARE analysts claimed they did not have information about the default from the company while it was available with the debenture trustee and bankers!

Following the norms of the Companies Act, every entity that floats debentures must have a debenture trustee for ensuring the protection of the investors' interest. At that time, there was no mechanism to share such information. After SEBI intervened, debenture trustees now share information with the rating agencies. But the RBI's real time bank data is still not openly available to raters.

'The default information was a hot potato, nobody wanted to have it,' a junior SEBI official, who attended the meeting, says.

Even before this, SEBI had stepped in when a few companies moved court against CRAs for making rating downgrades public.

In October 2012, SEBI Chairman U.K. Sinha urged India Inc. not to drag rating agencies to court. Around that time, there were at least two such instances. Videocon Industries Ltd and SREI Infrastructure Finance Ltd both moved Calcutta High Court separately against India Ratings.

While the raters were bound by the SEBI (Credit Rating Agencies) Regulations 1999 to publish the ratings of companies, the companies obviously have reasons to prevent that when the rating reflects poorly on the business.

New Regulations

In November 2016, SEBI reviewed the regulations and came up with a comprehensive regulation to streamline the CRAs' activities. This was the first of a series of eight circulars that the market regulator issued between then and January 2020.

That put a leash on the free-for-all conduct of activities by CRAs. There is no global precedence for any other regulator anywhere taking such actions to enhance the rating standards.

What has SEBI done?

- It has banned the practice of suspension of rating, asked rating agencies to disclose their criteria, process and policies to bring certain standards and transparency in the business of giving an opinion on the future performance of companies.
- It particularly targeted a common practice of rating agencies and issuers: If a rating is not suitable, do not accept it. Such ratings were never put in the public domain, but armed with such a rating, the issuer and his rating advisor would always try to 'buy' a better rating. SEBI has made it mandatory for the rating agency to disclose the rating even if it is not accepted.
- It banned the MD and CEO from being members of the rating committee. The rating committees of CRAs also need to report to a chief rating officer.

Incidentally, two rating agencies – Acuité Ratings and CRISIL – did not allow their CEOs to take part in any rating committees long before the events related to IL&FS unfolded.

SEBI, in a November 2016 circular after the Amtek Auto default, had recommended that rating agencies should not allow their CEOs to participate in rating committees without board approval.

- SEBI has also mandated that one-third of the board of a CRA must consist of independent directors if it is chaired by a non-executive director. In case the board is chaired by an executive director, half the board shall comprise independent directors.
- The board of a CRA shall constitute a rating sub-committee and a nomination and remuneration committee and the latter shall be chaired by an independent director.
- The chief ratings officer has been asked to directly report to the rating sub-committee of the board of the CRA.
- SEBI has also asked the CRAs to meet the audit committee of the rated entity at least once a year to discuss issues, including related-party transactions, internal financial control and other material disclosures made by the management which have a bearing on the rating of listed NCDs.

However, the rating 'advisers' are still not on the SEBI radar. They are still doing well – running their firms after a stint with a CRA, or even deploying their spouses to float such firms.

The RBI Blast

The RBI has also blasted raters for allowing low-rated companies to do 'rating shopping'. Its Financial Stability Report of December 2019 spoke about 'rating shopping' by companies for long-term bank loans based on indicative ratings given by CRAs that are not available to banks or investors.

It also referred to the SEBI finding on rating agencies offering 'indicative ratings' to issuers without entering into written agreements with the issuers.

Admitting that 'since such "indicative ratings" are not disclosed by CRAs on their websites, it becomes difficult to identify instances of possible rating shopping.' The RBI report says, 'Some instances of possible "rating shopping" can still, however, be ascertained by looking at the dynamics around rating withdrawals where outstanding rating issued by a CRA was withdrawn and a new rating was provided by a different CRA within three months of each other; and in more than two-thirds of the cases new ratings were provided before the withdrawal of the old ones since April 2016.'

Long-term loan rating is a primary device for credit screening for banks. It also has regulatory implications as the capital adequacy of banks is directly linked to their exposure to external long-term ratings.

The RBI's concerns about rating shopping stem from the fact that some of the rating agencies have a much greater share in ratings assigned, compared to their share in ratings withdrawn.

Yet, given the fact that the universe of rated obligors consists of around 40,000 businesses and funds, etc., such distortionary movements are seen across only a small fraction of the rated universe. Given the small sample where distortions are noted, it may not make the external ratings based capital adequacy framework of banks infructuous, the report says.

However, the data used for this purpose – financial data on listed companies – do not capture the rating data properly. The rating data is not comprehensive, and, in some cases, not updated.

Also, the RBI is comparing this data with data on defaults at the CRILC which is fairly accurate. Over the past few years, the rating agencies have been asking for access to the CRILC data but the RBI Act comes in the way.

The performance of a rating agency is best judged through the cumulative default rates and stability/transition rates that SEBI mandates them to disclose. A close look at the large highly-rated borrowers could also more clearly reveal the issue of conflict and compromise in quality of rating.

Raters' Handicap

To be fair to the CRAs, one of the factors contributing to the delays in recognising defaults is the lack of live data. The banks are required to furnish data of one-day default by borrowers (with exposures of at least ₹5 crore) to CRILC. But this data is not available with the CRAs.

While this is a handicap, a few CRAs take advantage of this and delay the defaults to look good as that serves the purpose of both the issuers and the investors. The access of live data will equip the CRAs to better appreciate risks but, at the same time, they should also be made to face hefty penalties for negligence.

Both S&P and Moody's were penalised for their failure to control the quality of the ratings of mortgage-backed securities that led to the global financial crisis of 2008. In addition to a $1.37 billion penalty, S&P paid $125 million to the California Public Employees' Retirement System and another $80 million to the Securities & Exchange Commission, the independent US government agency responsible for protecting investors and overseeing securities markets.

Moody's paid a $437.5 million penalty to the justice department and $426.3 million to the states and Washington DC while committing to ensure the integrity of credit ratings.

What is the size of the penalty imposed by SEBI on a CRA in India? Even though the context is different, the amounts are so small that it is a light slap on the wrist. The penalties are insufficient to keep the CRAs on track.

Cure for the Maladies

What needs to be done to cure maladies? Should the salary and stock options of CEOs be clawed back if they are found guilty of unethical practices?

All raters need to go in an internal cleansing process through forensic reviews. They must purge their systems and change their practices, if they want to address the huge trust deficit between the CRAs and investors.

Banks, NBFCs and other lenders have internal rating systems, but they also need the raters' certificates. Even the IBC 2016 stipulates investment-grade rating from two agencies to move ahead with a resolution plan for bad debt of ₹500 crore and more. The onus is on the CRAs to clean up, or face the wrath of the markets.

One solution could be a push to creating depth in the debt markets. Currently, long-term investors such as insurance and provident funds do not invest in relatively inferior papers. This is because the Insurance Regulatory and Development Authority (IRDA), EPFO and Pension Fund Regulatory and Development Authority (PFRDA) allow only a minuscule portion of a fund to be invested in below-AA-rated papers.

Banks, insurance companies, foreign institutional investors and pension and provident funds can be allowed to participate in this market of lower rated papers. As of now, the mutual funds have such a large share that it may not be sustainable.

Banks too are not happy to lend to a borrower without at least BBB-rating (the lowest investment grade) as the risk weightage for such loans is higher. Exposures to papers with higher risk weights force banks to set aside more capital.

The solution could be the creation of a junk-bond market. Investors and banks can price in the risk and take exposures to lesser-rated debt papers and corporations in such markets. Unless such a market exists, and unless the investment norms are relaxed, the CRAs will always be under pressure to give higher ratings because the big lenders must find ways to park their investible funds.

Investors also need to stop using ratings only as a tool to safeguard against accountability issues. Instead, they need to look at factors beyond ratings, and even to start questioning rating agencies.

There are other critical signs to watch out for. The RBI report has pointed out that there are clear indications of investors in debt instruments using additional credit-screening mechanisms, along with ratings given by raters. Rating is necessary but not sufficient. Using a rating should not be an excuse for lax due diligence.

But the basic conflict-of-interest will remain as long as the issuer pays for its ratings.

There are several possible ways to tackle the inherent weaknesses of the CRA governance structure. One is exploring an investor-pays model (now the issuers of debt papers pay for the rating). Another would be the mandatory rotation of CRAs to avoid long association between issuer and the CRA (intimacy blurs perception!).

Then there could be compulsory ratings by at least two, or multiple CRAs when the size of the debt is big. A market with more CRAs and more competition would also be healthy.

The regulators must also take a close look at the sales practices of rating agencies. When a rater is involved in businesses beyond rating, such as advisory and research in a big way, a company may exploit this situation. A company can engage a rater to provide such services and, in exchange, get good ratings.

The only way to stop is banning a CRA from accepting fees in any other form from clients it is rating. If this sounds too harsh, the rater must mandatorily disclose such relationships which have a conflict of interest.

Such conflict of interest could also arise from mutual fund ratings and bond valuations as the mutual fund managers and rating agencies can easily scratch each other's back.

There can also be a floor for fees. Too much competition can break the market and this would force all CRAs into compromises.

Finally, the regulators can also explore peer review of ratings, especially where the rating relationship is more than, say five years old. Long relationships should receive special attention during a regulatory inspection as this inhibits a CRA from being a messenger of bad news.

■ ■ ■

PART II
THE HEART OF THE MATTER

The three chapters in this segment offer a peep into the world of the public sector lenders, who remain the mainstay of Indian banking despite losing market share in loan assets. Few major economies, if any, are this dependent on a banking industry owned by the government. The problem is not so much with the ownership but with the behaviour of the owner.

On paper, steps have been taken to make the banks independent, allow them to take commercial decisions freely and select CEOs in a transparent manner. But most of these measures have been either half-baked, or cosmetic in nature.

PSBs continue to be obsessed with hitting 'targets' set by the owner. They cannot focus on profitability because the government, and the people who run it in their individual capacity, use the PSBs to further political compulsions.

Sans profitability, it is hard for them to raise capital from the market. The government, therefore, has no choice but to continue to pump in capital – taxpayers' money – to keep these banks afloat. But it has no transparent criteria for such infusions, and bank performance has nothing to do with the capital it receives in these periodic infusions.

After investing trillions of rupees over several decades without much to show for it, the government has found a new magic wand – consolidation. Mergers will reduce the number of banks, but not reduce the government's hold on the banking industry.

Is this an effective solution or will it merely weaken the strong banks?

This section of the book attempts to answer some of the key questions about the existential crisis facing some PSBs. It also details the untold, behind-the-scenes stories of bank mergers.

Here is the stark reality: The share of PSBs in new loans has dropped from 73 per cent in 2014 to 24 per cent in 2019. The erosion in new deposits is even sharper – from 76.42 per cent to 20.48 per cent in this period.

Can the government stop this rapid privatisation by stealth? Should it even try?

5

What Ails the Public Sector Banks?

In January 2015, the government organised the first Gyan Sangam, a unique offsite of the CEOs of India's PSBs and financial institutions presided over by Prime Minister Narendra Modi and Finance Minister Arun Jaitley.

Shortly after this conference, the Ministry of Finance addressed a memorandum to the secretaries of all ministries and departments of the Government of India. This was also copied to the CEOs of all PSBs and financial institutions, the sector regulators and investigative agencies.

The memorandum, titled 'Assurance of freedom of non-interference in PSBs on commercial decisions, transfers, and postings, etc.' was signed by Manish Kumar, under-secretary in the ministry's Department of Financial Services (DFS), [F. No.4/9/1/2014-IR(Pt.), dated 13 January 2015]. It said:

> The banks/FIs should take all commercial decisions in the best interest of the organisation without any fear and favour. All decisions should be taken based on the facts of the case and objectivity. No such decision should be taken out of any other

> extraneous considerations such as the influence, or position, the borrower is holding.
>
> Each bank/FI should have their (sic) own objective, well laid out transfer and posting rules which should be followed strictly. No exception should be made in such rules at the behest of any recommendation given by anyone, including anybody from the Ministry of Finance. If for genuine reasons, any exception to the rule is made, it should be done only by CMD by giving proper reasons;
>
> Each bank/FI should have a robust grievance redressal mechanism for borrowers, depositors, as well as staff. The aggrieved person should have an opportunity to represent his case at least at two levels.

The note ended by saying:

> It has also been conveyed to PSBs that the freedom given to banks/FIs by [the] assurance of non-interference will be used in the most objective manner. However, if any complaint comes to this department from anybody informing that exceptions were made in certain cases without any objective basis, and in order to favour somebody, the person taking such decision should be accountable.

The Transformation

Modi described the Gyan Sangam as a 'unique initiative' and 'the first step towards catalysing transformation'.

Jaitley followed it up in August 2015, announcing the Indradhanush Plan. This, among other things, promised to address issues such as high-level appointments, capitalisation, stress in the system, accountability and, most importantly, governance in government-owned banks.

A key component of Indradhanush was the creation of the Banks Board Bureau (BBB), which was touted as the trump card to address governance.

In May 2014, a committee was set up by the RBI to review the governance of bank boards. It was headed by P.J. Nayak, a former chairman and MD of Axis Bank Ltd. This committee suggested the formation of a BBB as the first step in a three-phase process to empower the boards of PSBs.

In the run-up to the incorporation of a bank investment company as an intermediate holding company for banks, the Bureau would advise on all board appointments, including that of the whole-time directors and top bank management. This was to 'professionalise and depoliticise' the appointment process.

The Nayak Committee recommended that the members of the BBB should have a three-year tenure, or tenure until powers are passed on to the investment company, whichever is shorter. Their remuneration should, at the least, be on a par with that of the banks' chiefs.

Legislative changes would be required to set up such an investment company. For instance, the Banking Companies (Acquisition and Transfer of Undertakings) Acts of 1970 and 1980 and the State Bank of India Act, 1955, and the SBI (Subsidiary Banks) Act would need to be repealed, and all banks would need to be incorporated under the Companies Act. This would be a long-drawn process.

For the time being, the BBB has replaced the appointments committee.

In the pre-BBB era, not all bank chiefs were appointed on merit. There were always murmurs about the selection of the bosses. But the murmurs turned into a public outcry after the CBI arrested S.K. Jain, chairman and MD of Syndicate Bank in September 2014 for accepting a bribe. The government was left with no choice but to scrap the selection of heads of quite a few PSBs and overhaul the process.

Three screening committees were constituted of two members each – from among an RBI deputy governor, the DFS secretary and the secretary in the department of public enterprises along with three independent experts. In the second stage, the recommendations of these committees were to be screened by an appointments board, headed by the RBI governor.

Breaking away from tradition, the government also tapped the private sector for people to head five large PSBs – namely, the Bank of Baroda, Canara Bank, Bank of India, PNB and IDBI Bank Ltd. (At that time, IDBI Bank was not owned by LIC.) It even appointed global management consulting firm Hay Group (which was acquired by Korn Ferry in end-2015), to identify candidates for these jobs.

First Meeting

The BBB replaced all these ad hoc arrangements. Its first meeting took place on 8 April 2016, at the fourth floor of the RBI office, at Byculla, South Mumbai. After the meeting, Jaitley's junior, minister of state Jayant Sinha, tweeted: 'Excellent discussions at the Banks Board Bureau meeting today!'

His tweet tagged two photographs. One shows the minister cutting the ribbon, accompanied by Vinod Rai, the former CAG of India, named as the BBB's first head; and veteran bankers H.N. Sinor and A.K. Khandelwal. The other shows all four plus Raghuram Rajan, then RBI governor, and Roopa Kudva, former head of rating agency CRISIL sitting on sofas and deputy governors R. Gandhi and S.S. Mundra standing behind.

Rai was the BBB's chairman and Khandelwal, Sinor and Kudva were members. Gandhi, a deputy governor then, was an ex-officio member; the other two ex-officio members are the secretary DFS and the secretary to the department of public enterprises.

Rai had been a DFS secretary before he went on to become India's chief auditor. Khandelwal, an HR expert, had headed Bank of Baroda; Sinor, a former JMD of ICICI Bank, headed two national lobbies of banks and mutual funds; and Kudva, a former MD of CRISIL, heads Omidyar Network India Advisors, a US-based philanthropic investment firm.

The board's mandate includes the selection and appointment of MDs and CEOs as well as non-executive chairmen of PSBs, helping banks develop a robust leadership succession plan for critical positions as well as develop business strategies and capital raising plans, and advising the government on the formulation and enforcement of a code of conduct and ethics for bank executives, among others.

It does not have the last word on the selection of the bank chiefs. The BBB recommends names; the Appointments Committee of the Cabinet, headed by the prime minister, takes the final call. However, the names need to be cleared by the DFS first.

It has not been easy for the DFS to digest the loss of absolute power.

Take the case of Mukesh Kumar Jain as an example. An executive director of Punjab & Sind Bank, Jain was picked by the BBB to head Indian Overseas Bank sometime in 2016. But he did not get the job even after the Vigilance Commission cleared his name for the post, which is mandatory for any such appointment. Why? The DFS was uncomfortable with the BBB's choice. It is a mystery why the DFS secretary, who was a member of the Board, did not shoot down Jain's name at the initial stage.

The appointment was referred to the Department of Personnel and Training (DoPT); once again, the Vigilance Commission cleared it after a forensic audit, but the DFS did not budge an inch. Ultimately, Jain was appointed chief of Oriental Bank of Commerce in July 2017. But, by then, he had lost a year.

The Conflict

That was the beginning of an open conflict. To avoid another such fiasco, the BBB started releasing the list of candidates on its website immediately after it had made a recommendation. But the DFS would not lick its wounds in silence. It selected the chiefs of SIDBI and IFCI Ltd via a different committee even as BBB was involved in identifying the MD of India Post Payments Bank.

The BBB was also kept in the dark on extension and termination of services of the MDs of banks. When Sushil Muhnot was fired as chairman and MD of Bank of Maharashtra just four days before he was to retire (he was allegedly occupying two houses) in September 2016, the BBB was not consulted.

Similarly, the BBB got to know about the transfer of Usha Ananthasubramian from PNB to Allahabad Bank in May 2017 from the media.

In essence, the BBB is a glorified version of the appointment boards of past eras. Its other mandates are also sufficiently vague. It does not have any role in choosing the independent directors, many of whom are political appointments.

Two leaders of the ruling Bharatiya Janata Party (BJP) – Bharatkumar D. Dangar and Gopal Krishna Agarwal – adorned the board of Bank of Baroda, at a time when the bank picked both the non-executive chairman and the MD and CEO from the private sector to help professionalise it.

Of course, Dangar is not on the board as the 56th mayor of the city of Vadodara and a senior BJP leader. He is there in his capacity as an assistant professor in the faculty of technology and engineering of the M.S. University of Baroda. Similarly, Agarwal, who is national spokesperson of BJP's economic affairs, is a chartered accountant by qualification. Agarwal's term ended in 2019.

The attendance of most non-official directors and even some of the government nominees at bank board meetings is generally poor. Even though all the government-owned banks are listed on bourses, they do not comply with the regulation about one-third of their directors being 'independent', as stipulated by SEBI.

For many PSBs, the boards are probably the biggest area of risk. Not all the directors understand banking. They cannot guide the management as they lack the vision. Few boards hold the CEO accountable, and some board members even indulge in broking loan deals.

The process of getting on the board of a PSB is interesting. The government picks candidates and the RBI supposedly does the vetting. But the RBI does not say either 'yes' or 'no' to any one's candidature – it just lists the pros and cons and leaves it for the government to decide. And, the less said about shareholder directors the better. The banks can in practice, induct any board member they want, by managing secret ballots.

The Bank Nationalisation Act mandates that an expert on banking regulation and supervision must be on the board of all the PSBs. The person has to be recommended by RBI and nominated by the government. The regulator has been planning to amend the law to avoid this but this amendment has not happened as yet. When Y.V. Reddy was the governor, the RBI started appointing former employees as directors on bank boards, but that has not become the regular practice.

The BBB does not have any say on other critical issues such as the resolution of stressed assets, consolidation among the PSBs, their governance and charting out the roadmap for a banking investment company as envisaged by the Nayak Committee. The government selectively picked what it liked from the report and the profile of the members, in the first round, lent credibility to the platform.

After much persuasion, the Bureau could convince the government to agree to compensate the non-executive chairman of PSBs. But the amount is capped at ₹10 lakh, inclusive of fee for attending board meetings. This is way below the compensation of the chairman of any private bank.

In its effort to stay relevant, the Bureau sent a proposal to the finance ministry overhauling the compensation package for executives of PSBs. It included stock options, performance-related bonus and fast-track promotion policy, etc.

This reminds one of an earlier proposal. In June 2010, the finance ministry appointed a Committee on HR Issues of PSBs. This committee made 105 recommendations on performance management, capability building and freedom for banks to increase variable compensation and offer stock options, among other things. The government accepted 56 of these recommendations, leaving out the really key ones.

Khandelwal, who was later a BBB member, headed the committee.

In a letter to the CEOs of PSBs, dated 21 October 2011, Kumar, the finance ministry bureaucrat who asked PSB chiefs to take all commercial decisions without fear or favour in January 2015, had written, 'The other recommendations… are under active consideration of the government and decision on these shall be communicated, in due course for appropriate action.'

As the term of the first set of members was coming to an end, the strained relations between the BBB and the government became the talk of the town.

On 19 March 2018, the Bureau put up on its website a 59-page Compendium of Recommendations. In the foreword, Chairman Rai wrote, 'It is very much possible for the public sector to reach the same levels of efficiency, as the private sector, provided governance regulations, supervision and the developmental agenda are allowed to be ownership neutral.'

The last chapter of the compendium was its unfinished agenda. Called 'Future Role', it referred to a letter the chairman of the Bureau had written on 26 July 2017 to the finance minister.

Let us look at some extracts from the letter:

> The Bureau has made recommendations on various issues in its remit, such as the ones made under the overarching theme of Governance, Reward and Accountability Framework (GRAF) in public sector banks. These recommendations made by the Bureau, seek to address the root cause of the challenges presently faced by the PSBs. *The Bureau is not aware of the progress made in this regard and there has been no further engagement with Government.* (emphasis mine)
>
> The Bureau, as a body of experts on public sector banking, would be able to provide greater utility to the Finance Minister on matters relating to the governance and performance of PSBs, if there were to be greater organic linkage and dialogue with the finance ministry. *At present, the body is merely functioning as an appointment board.* (emphasis mine)

The Footnote

The letter ends: 'To discuss these matters further with the Finance Minister, Government of India, the members of the Bureau would like to schedule a meeting at a time convenient.'

This statement also merited a footnote. On the day this was posted on the Bureau's website, the footnote (30) said: 'The Bureau continues to await a meeting.'

Almost two weeks later, on 2 April 2018, the footnote changed!

It added: 'During the meeting of the Bureau held on March 26, 2018, the chairman, Banks Board Bureau, informed the members that the finance minister had been kind enough to provide the opportunity of engaging with him on various occasions where issues were discussed and taken forward.'

The Rai-led committee that was managing the Bureau stepped down on 31 March 2018. One of the members, Sinor, had quit the Board before his term ended but was persuaded by Rai to withdraw his resignation.

The day the last BBB meeting was held (26 March) under his chairmanship, Rai dismissed reports of a lack of coordination between the BBB and the government, saying the rapport was 'total' and he often met Finance Minister Jaitley and received guidance from him.

The Press Trust of India (PTI) carried an interview with him (26 March 2018), telling the world how cordial was the relationship between the Bureau and the government, which never ever interfered in any appointment process and gave the Bureau a free hand in everything it did.

This interview also explains the mystery surrounding the footnote.

> The BBB in the last two years has done monumental work with support and cooperation of the RBI and the government along with secretaries to the government of India working as members to the BBB, he told PTI.
>
> The former CAG said that the coordination was to

> the extent that the finance minister himself took him into confidence even when there was a change of guard at the two large public sector banks in May 2017.
>
> He said that since the term of the BBB was coming to an end on 31 March, it was decided to collate all the work done by the bureau so that when the new BBB comes into being it would act as a base document for them.
>
> This consolidated set of record or Compendium of Recommendations would come handy for the new BBB. This was created and put on the website but I could not see the finished document as I was away from the country. I have been to Singapore for 10 days. I came back from Singapore only on (last) Saturday, he said.
>
> When it was put on the website, unfortunately, there were some misleading headlines with regard to a letter written to the Finance Minister in July 2017 in which some suggestions were given, he said. Those suggestions were discussed with the finance minister and the financial services secretary many times after that letter, he said.
>
> I must have met finance minister at least half a dozen times. Whenever I sought an appointment, I used to get the appointment to discuss various things. So formally, informally, issues were discussed and taken forward, he said.

Former RBI governor Raghuram Rajan, in his book *I Do What I Do* has written: 'We will have moved significantly towards limiting interference in public sector banks when the Department of Financial Services (which oversees public sector financial firms) is finally closed down, and its banking functions taken over by bank boards and the Banks Board Bureau.'

Under Section 8 of the Bank Nationalisation Act, the government – the majority owner of the PSBs – can issue directives to the banks in the public interest after consulting with the RBI. For the DFS, doing this without keeping RBI in the loop has been a habit.

The BBB is alive and kicking. But there is no real change in the finance ministry's control over the state-owned banking industry that started with bank nationalisation.

Bank Nationalisation

The Banking system commenced in India with Bank of Hindustan in Kolkata (then Calcutta, capital of India) in 1770. The General Bank of India followed in 1786. SBI, the nation's largest lender, originated as the Bank of Calcutta in June 1806 primarily to fund General Wellesley's wars against Tipu Sultan and the Marathas. It was renamed as Bank of Bengal. This, and two other Presidency banks, set up by the East India Company – Bank of Bombay (1842) and Bank of Madras (1843) – were amalgamated into the Imperial Bank of India in January 1921 and became the State Bank of India on 30 April 1955, by an Act of Parliament.

On its first day, SBI had 400 branches. The government asked it to open another 400 branches outside metros immediately to take banking to the hinterland.

There were multiple other banks which were privately owned. Some had been set up by princely states such as the Bank of Baroda (1908). Others like PNB (1894) had been founded by nationalists, or businessmen. The oldest among them, Allahabad Bank, was set up in April 1865, by a group of Europeans.

On 19 July 1969, Prime Minister Indira Gandhi made a public statement, nationalising 14 banks with deposits of at least ₹50 crore each, with effect from midnight on that very day.

The ordinance that paved the path for nationalisation was challenged; an interim stay was granted on a few issues. But after a 34-day trial before an 11-judge bench in the Supreme Court, the ordinance stood and all roadblocks to nationalisation were cleared. Another round of nationalisation of six more commercial banks with deposits of over ₹200 crore each, followed in 1980.

Whatever the other effects, nobody can deny that nationalisation has helped in the spread of banking services. Since 1969, the number of bank branches has grown phenomenally. There were

8,187 branches on June 1969 and 1,20,535 branches as of December 2019.

It is of particular importance to note the rising share of rural branches. Rural branches were just about 17.6 per cent of the total branch network in 1969, whereas rural branches now comprise 29.5 per cent of network, rising from 1,443 in 1969 to 35,649 in 2019.

The share of semi-urban branches, dropped from 40.8 per cent to 28.9 per cent (3,337 to 34,915). The comparable figures for urban branches are 1,911 to 23,774 and metropolitan branches, 1,496 and 26,197.

The banking industry has grown many times in size. Aggregate deposits have risen from ₹4,646 crore to ₹137.5-lakh crore in March 2020. Bank credit has risen from ₹3,599 crore to ₹104.5-lakh crore.

Till the 1990s, the PSBs' assets grew at a pace of around 4 per cent, which was in sync with the average growth rate of GDP in the Indian economy. That growth accelerated dramatically in the first decade of this century. But the pace has slowed considerably and many PSBs have been shrinking balance sheets since 2015 due to the pile up of bad assets.

A Political Thriller

Experts have different views on bank nationalisation. Mrs. Gandhi, in her address at the Bangalore session of the Indian National Congress on 12 July 1969, pitched for it. This was a week before the ordinance was promulgated.

This was not just a milestone event in Indian banking. Bank nationalisation was also a political thriller. The political-economic setting of the late 1960s gave Gandhi enough reason to consider it.

The ruling Indian National Congress won 283 seats out of 520 in the 1967 general elections. This was not a great performance because, in the 1962 elections, it had won 361 of 494 seats. The party also lost power in seven states. There was also an intense power struggle between the old guard and the young leadership within Congress.

To make matters worse, the 1960s also had two severe droughts, leading to negative economic growth and double-digit inflation. The small pile of India's foreign exchange reserves got even smaller and in June 1966, Mrs. Gandhi decided to devalue the rupee sharply against the US dollar and levy export duties on a dozen commodities.

Also, around that time, the growing influence of left-of-centre political forces was setting the stage for possible new political alignments.

Bank nationalisation was a top secret. Apart from the prime minister, only three people were involved in the exercise – P.N. Haksar, principal secretary to the prime minister; A. Bakshi, an RBI deputy governor; and D.N. Ghosh, a junior bureaucrat in the finance ministry, who would later become SBI's chairman.

Neither I.G. Patel, then the economic affairs secretary, nor L.K. Jha, then RBI governor, was taken into confidence. Even Morarji Desai, then deputy prime minister holding the charge of finance ministry, was kept in the dark. He was stripped of the portfolio on 16 July.

The ordinance had to be ready by 19 July, a Saturday, as then president of India, V.V. Giri, was due to step down on 20 July and the Lok Sabha, the lower house of India's Parliament, would begin its monsoon session on 21 July.

By the early morning of 18 July, the trio of Haksar, Bakshi and Ghosh was convinced it could be done. Fifteen major banks operating in India then – including the National & Grindlays Bank – held about 85 per cent of the deposits. The decision was to nationalise all of them, barring Grindlays; by 9 am, the plan got the prime minister's nod.

The private owners were compensated in line with a formula used earlier to convert banks in the erstwhile princely states into subsidiaries of the SBI. The compensation paid for the 14 banks was ₹87.40 crore. The Cabinet meeting was scheduled at 5 pm on 19 July, and Mrs. Gandhi addressed the nation on bank nationalisation at 8.30 pm.

On 21 July, a full bench of the Supreme Court heard a suit challenging the validity of the ordinance and gave an interim stay on three matters, restraining the government from removing the chiefs of those banks, creating advisory boards and doing anything not outlined in the Banking Regulation Act, 1949.

In Parliament, the bill was passed with a minor change that ensured representation of employees, depositors, and agriculture, exporters and small-scale industries on the boards of nationalised banks.

It wasn't smooth sailing in the Supreme Court. The focus of the 34-day trial before an 11-judge bench was on the definition of banking: Can a bank offer guarantees, safe deposits and businesses such as money transfer beyond taking deposits and giving loans?

The argument was that the government should stick to Section 5 of the Banking Regulation Act and allow the private owners of the banks to keep the non-banking activities (outlined in Section 6) with themselves.

Had the private owners won the case, the purpose of nationalisation would have been defeated. The charters of the three presidency banks – the banks of Bengal, Bombay and Madras – which had outlined the scope of banking beyond taking deposits and giving loans came to the government's rescue.

Hindu Undivided Family

After nationalisation, the government created a banking department, signalling its intent to have a say in running the banks. That made sure that the management of PSBs would not remain ownership-neutral.

Former RBI governor Y.V. Reddy calls it a joint family approach – the PSBs, the government and the RBI became part of a 'Hindu undivided family' where nobody was keeping proper accounts of what they were doing. The transactions among the three were governed by 'plan priorities'. They were all serving people, Reddy had said in a November 2000 speech.

Things have not changed – the overarching theme of India's government-owned banking industry remains a lack of governance.

Let us look at some of the issues originating from poor governance.

The Top Job

Till recently, barring a few exceptions, the heads of PSBs typically did not get to spend more than two years at the helm. It could be even one year. The top position often remains vacant for months.

Even after the Bureau clears the names, the government takes time to announce the appointments as it has its own priorities. After P.S. Jayakumar stepped down as Bank of Baroda MD and CEO, his successor Sanjiv Chadha took over 100 days later. This is when Bank of Baroda was handling the merger of two banks with itself, the first of its kind experiment in Indian banking.

Of course, that is not a long gap if we look at what happened at Andhra Bank (now merged with Union Bank of India). After Suresh Patel's term ended in December 2017, J. Packirisamy walked into the corner room after a gap of 264 days. Similarly, Karnam Sekar got the top job in Dena Bank (merged with Bank of Baroda) and S. Harisankar at Punjab & Sind Bank after a gap of 262 days in each case.

Who runs the bank at such times? There is no uniform norm. One executive director could be given the charge or sometimes two could be asked to share charge. When that happens, problems crop up as both are equally powerful. Each fixes his or her own itinerary, leading to delays in conducting committee meetings as both may not be stationed at the same place. If one suggests something, the other vetoes it, thinking there could be some personal interest involved.

Even after a new CEO takes over, if the person is not from the same bank, as is often the case, it takes a long time to get into the groove culturally since every bank is different. Also, size matters. It is not easy for an executive from a small bank to run a large bank.

Apart from all this, who does not want to leave the office on a high note? So, the focus is always on balance sheet growth without being hawk-eyed about risk management and project appraisal.

Typically, a newcomer tears into the balance sheet she inherits, and launches a clean-up drive. This earns the investors' respect. But as the time to say good-bye approaches, she follows in the footsteps of her predecessor, since the intention is to leave with a happy note. This cycle goes on and on.

In a sense, each of the PSBs is run by three to four groups of bankers, as often the executive directors (two or three, depending on the bank's size) and the MD are from different banks and none of them is there for very long. The other way of looking at this could be the bank itself is on probation every two years, trying to adjust to the whims and fancies of new bosses.

Contrast this with some of the well-run and richly valued private banks, where CEOs enjoy long stints.

Another relevant issue is that, until they step into the shoes of a deputy general manager, most PSU bankers just run branches, collect deposits or manage small loans. Most lack exposure to complex credit and treasury operations. This reflects on their career as the boss.

Finally, no PSB chief has ever been sacked for inefficiency. Of course, bank bosses do get removed for corruption, even though such instances are rare. In the worst-case scenario, the inefficient banker does not get a second term if their first term as boss ends before the retirement age of 60.

That is about banking at the top and how the leaders are selected. The promotion and transfer policies across lower layers in many banks are not transparent either.

Executives at different levels are routinely blackmailed to toe the line of their proximate bosses. If they do not look favourably upon certain accounts, they run the risk of being transferred to punishment postings and/or miss the next promotion. Conversely, if they toe the line, the promotion is secured.

Complan Boy

Some CEOs and executive directors carry their associations with corporate clients from previous assignments to the new bank which they head. That helps build the loan book.

Until bad loans started ballooning, most banks were behaving like Complan kids. In the 1980s, the advertisement for health food Complan showed two children (child actors Shahid Kapoor and Ayesha Takia) claiming each was growing faster than the other. 'I am a Complan girl, I am a Complan boy'. And, they loved their 'Complan mummy'.

Complan is all about boosting the growth of children. But the PSBs are hardly children; in fact, many are over 100 years old. They want to become bigger, but not necessarily stronger! This greed for growth is why many banks sanction loans indiscriminately. How long can their Complan mummy (read: the government) support them by using taxpayer's money? (More on this in the chapter 'Bank Recap and Consolidation'.)

The rise in bad loans forced PSBs to shed their obsession with balance sheet growth. Once the RBI ruthlessly exposed the soft underbelly, all of them were interested in big-time project financing, irrespective of size and risk-appetite.

In May 2017, McKinsey & Company released a report on India Financial Institutions Practice. This points out that the smaller the bank, the bigger the appetite for project financing. For the giant SBI, about 49 per cent of loans were corporate loans; for mid-sized PSBs, it was 57 per cent and, for smaller banks, even bigger, 63 per cent! Most banks were not a great believer in project appraisal and risk management – they wanted to grab a piece of the corporate loans cake, which they often could not digest!

Most have no skill in underwriting and hence, intermediaries play a critical role in loan appraisal. So, the 20-page board memorandum for loan sanctions at most banks was often a cut-and-paste job. Only the logo of the bank and the first page were different.

Brotherhood Banking

When the banks do not understand the risks involved in financing a project, 'brotherhood banking' takes place. What's that? Well, there have been many instances of executives of one particular bank becoming chiefs of many public banks around the same time.

There is nothing wrong in this per se as they go through the normal selection process to move to their respective corner rooms. But once they settle down, one who is relatively more qualified than others in appreciating project financing, takes a call on large loan proposals and she influences the former colleagues who now head other banks to take the plunge.

Brokers had also been playing a critical role as intermediaries between loan seekers and banks. Dozens of broking outfits had come up to arrange loans at a commission. They used to thrive on bankers' ignorance of project financing. Such outfits have contributed significantly to the deterioration of assets in the banking system.

Working Capital

While most bankers lack expertise in project financing, working capital loans, or cash credit is also a problem area. Cash credit, a typical Indian practice, is a sort of perpetual loan, in contrast to a term loan, which gets repaid over a finite period. Factoring in inflation, the limit for such a facility keeps on rising even if the quantity of the produce, or the working capital cycle, does not increase.

Cash credit is supposedly secured by the working capital assets of a company in the form of raw materials, finished goods and receivables. They are movable and continuously changing, unlike the security for term loans, which typically are plant and machinery, land and buildings.

The audit can be fudged and the working capital assets keep on fluctuating, depending on various factors such as availability, usage and realisation of sales, etc. The stock audit of companies generally takes place at multiple places and godowns. Simultaneous audit of stocks at all locations can prevent manipulation, but that does not always happen.

It is not difficult for a company to divert funds as bankers rarely have real-time information. Often, borrowers use the cash credit system as a cash management tool. If they have surplus cash, they dump it on the bank for a few days and withdraw it when they need.

Many smart, cash-rich corporations hardly use the cash credit limits and keep the arrangement in place for a rainy day. Whenever the short-term interest rates in the market flare up, they resort to arbitrage by accessing the cash credit system at a low rate, negotiated earlier, and placing the cash borrowed with another bank in the form of deposits, earning higher interest rates.

Sometimes, they even borrow at an old rate (which is low) and keep the money with the same bank at a higher rate! What does the bank gain from this practice? Growth – both the loan book as well as the deposit portfolio swell.

From April 2019, the RBI mandated that for a borrower enjoying a working capital limit of at least ₹150 crore, 40 per cent of the working capital limits must be drawn by way of a short-term loan. Also, the borrowers need to pay commitment charges even if the loan is not drawn. This may reduce the arbitrage opportunities and instil discipline.

Social Banking

Even before nationalisation, 'social control' was introduced in 1967 to force banks to give loans for the economic development of the nation. The concept of priority sector loans was introduced in 1969 – the year the first set of banks was nationalised. All banks, including foreign banks operating in India, are required to ensure that 40 per cent of their loans go to certain segments classified as 'priority sector'.

Within the 40 per cent target, there are sub-targets and the components of priority loans have been changing over the years. But what has not changed is the pressure put on banks to achieve these targets.

Each political regime requires the PSBs to lend for economic development with different packages in line with ideology, or populist fancy. For instance, in October 1980, the government launched the Integrated Rural Development Programme (IRDP),

India's biggest-ever poverty alleviation programme, to promote sustainable self-employment by offering rural people subsidised bank credit. Within the decade – by 1989 – there were some 25 million defaulters, and not even 10 per cent of the borrowers under the IRDP scheme were servicing the bank loans.

In 2015, the government launched the Pradhan Mantri MUDRA Yojana, or the Prime Minister's plan for a Micro Units Development and Refinance Agency, to give loans up to ₹10 lakh to non-corporate, non-farm small and micro-enterprises. These advances are called Mudra loans.

In November 2019, RBI Deputy Governor M.K. Jain said at a seminar that banks need to focus on the borrower's repayment capacity at the appraisal stage and monitor the loans through their lifecycle much more closely. 'Mudra is a case in point. While such a massive push would have lifted many beneficiaries out of poverty, there has been some concern at the growing level of non-performing assets among these borrowers,' he added.

The Wire, a news and opinion website, quoted the reply to an RTI application as saying that the NPAs under the Mudra scheme for the public sector jumped by 126 per cent from ₹7,277 crore in March 2018 to ₹16,481 crore in March 2019.

Mudra's annual report says the level of gross NPAs under the Mudra scheme since its inception up to March 2018 were 5.38 per cent. It had 30.57 lakh bad accounts in the year ending March 2019, up from 17.99 lakh a year ago. Its net NPAs in March 2019 were 2.33 per cent versus zero in the previous year.

Answering a question in Parliament, in December 2019, Anurag Singh Thakur, minister of state in the finance ministry, said that as on 25 October 2019, at least 20.65 crore loans have been given under this scheme. Thakur also said though data on jobs generated under the scheme is not maintained, a sample survey conducted by the Ministry of Labour and Employment estimates that it helped generate 1.12 crore in the way of net additional employment in three years between 2015 and 2018.

All about Targets

Public sector banking is all about targets. These targets are first set by the government and reinforced at different levels in the bank's hierarchy. The quality of lending and recovery is not as important as achieving the loan targets. The market keeps a close watch on the quality of loan assets and punishes the laggards. But markets are more of a headache for private banks. The PSBs are less afraid of the market as capital is on tap from the government.

So, loans given through the Kisan Credit Cards, part of the priority loans segment, never reduce. It is a time bomb, ticking away. Even after the harvesting season, when the farmers are supposed to pay back, outstanding loans get rolled over.

Yet another weak link is the lending to micro, small and medium enterprises (MSMEs). Until the government redefined such enterprises in May 2020, there were about 63.05 million micro industries, 0.33 million small, and about 5,000 medium enterprises – the second biggest employer in the country with a 31 per cent share in India's GDP. A large number do not have access to bank credit. They find it difficult to get bank loans as the bankers continue to follow the Tandon and Chore Committee recommendations while dealing with the MSMEs even though the RBI has freed them up to develop their own policies.

In the initial stage after bank nationalisation, while 40 per cent of credit used to flow to the priority sector, the rest was going to industry – in line with the Tandon and Chore Committee norms – by a credit authorisation scheme.

The Tandon Committee submitted a seminal report in 1975 on working capital lending. The RBI followed it up with another committee in 1979, under the chairmanship of K.B. Chore, for better credit discipline.

Most MSMEs have problems with cash flow and not capital. They are forced to wait to collect bills and quite often, the government is the culprit, holding back payments. The MSMEs do not have the capacity to carry such receivables but the banks continue to follow the three-month payment formula, based on the

Tandon and Chore Committee norms.

Social banking can continue and even become a stronger component if the approach is changed. The burden of social banking needs to be shifted from the banks, which are commercial entities, to the government. While access to banking is a must, the government can subsidise borrowers directly in the same way it does for LPG cylinders.

Dual Control

There are many other issues such as lack of accountability (no bank CEO gets the boot for non-performance), the poor pay packet for senior bankers (the MD and CEO salary is linked to bureaucrats' pay scale; the secretaries in the finance ministry would not like to see bankers getting paid more than them), inability to directly recruit young talent from business schools because of various court judgments, the glare of investigative agencies, the so-called L1 formula that requires the PSBs to buy everything, from a tea to technology, from the lowest bidder, not the best one.

The list goes on. One crucial issue is the system of dual control. The RBI is the regulator but the owner calls the shots. To use a cliché, regulations are not ownership neutral. This is the crux of the problem. The Narasimham Committee on banking reforms in 1991 described it as a virus and asked for a vaccine but nothing has happened.

Until the turn of the twentieth century, it was triple control – the government, the RBI and the all-powerful trade unions. The unions, with political backing, were the shadow management and the banks were sandwiched between overtly authoritative governments and covertly powerful unions. Over time, the unions have lost their clout and become paper tigers.

The dual control makes the RBI a helpless regulator as it cannot do many things. All commercial banks in India are regulated by the RBI under the Banking Regulation Act of 1949. In addition, the PSBs are regulated by the Government of India under the Banking Companies (Acquisition and Transfer of Undertakings) Act, loosely called the Bank Nationalisation Act. It has two versions – 1970 and 1980 – following two sets of bank nationalisation. Then, there is the State Bank of India Act, 1955.

Section 51 of the BR Act lists out provisions applicable to PSBs, effectively limiting RBI's control over PSBs.

- The RBI cannot remove directors and management at PSBs.
- It cannot supersede the board of a bank. (Of course, it can recommend supersession of the board. The RBI did so in 2014. It wrote to the finance ministry recommending the superseding of the board of United Bank of India [it got merged with PNB in April 2020] but the ministry ignored it.)
- It cannot remove the chairman and MD of a PSB.
- It cannot force a merger for PSBs.
- It cannot revoke the licence of a PSB. (As there is no licence issued by RBI!)
- It cannot trigger the liquidation of a PSB.
- It has no say on the compensation of the top management.

The RBI enjoys all these powers over private banks. One can, of course, ask how effectively the RBI uses such powers. But that is a separate story. If the RBI does not have these powers over the PSBs, these banks cannot be made accountable to the regulator.

When it comes to regulations, there is no level playing field for the RBI and when it comes to operations, the playing field is not level for the PSBs.

The government does not treat the PSBs as commercial organisations, as it should. The PSBs need to do everything their majority owner wants – from opening counters to allow citizens to register for their unique identification Aadhaar card to getting officers to sweep the streets on the Swachh Bharat Diwas as part of the Clean India Mission, launched in October 2014.

Similarly, when India decided in November 2016 to demonetise high-denomination notes, the PSBs were saddled with most of the work of collecting the old notes and distributing the new currency.

The Pradhan Mantri Jan Dhan Yojana, the world's most expansive financial inclusion drive, had 40.41 crore new depositors as on 26 August 2020. The PSBs' share is more than 75 per cent of this – 32.04 crore depositors. An industry estimate puts the cost of opening each account at ₹262.

In the 1990s, Tata Steel Ltd ran a TV ad campaign showcasing its corporate philanthropy projects. It did not mention its primary business but signed off with the line: 'We also make steel'.

Alongside pride (for serving the nation) and nostalgia (for building bridges and taking banking to the hinterland), the PSBs could say: 'We also do banking'.

Market Share

An inevitable fallout of this is a sharp erosion in PSBs' market share.

Sometime in March 2018, Nandan Nilekani, co-founder and chairman of Infosys Ltd and founding chairman of the Unique Identification Authority of India, the agency behind the Aadhaar ID project, had said the pace at which PSBs were losing business had increased and that ten years from now, they would hold 10 per cent market share.

Around the same time, Uday Kotak, MD and CEO of Kotak Mahindra Bank Ltd, had said that private sector banks' market share would go up significantly and equal that of PSBs in the next five years. 'The 70–30 ratio of public and private banks will move to a 50-50 ratio in the next five years,' Kotak had said.

Nilekani expected the PSBs' market share to fall to 63 per cent by 2025. Pegging the pace at which the PSBs have been losing their market share at 4 percentage points a year, he had said that in ten years, this share would be very small and eventually be reduced to something like 10 per cent.

In private, many public sector bankers at that time called Nilekani a Cassandra, while a few private bankers dubbed him a soothsayer. Nilekani got it wrong! The PSBs have been losing their market share much faster than what he had estimated.

In the 1990s, before the RBI gave licences to the first set of private banks to open shop, the PSBs held 90 per cent share of the banking market. In 2000, their share was a little over 80 per cent. By 2014, they held around three-fourths of the market share in deposits, advances and total assets.

Since then, there has been a dramatic slide in their market share. This set of banks had a 75.74 per cent share of advances of the banking industry in 2014. It dropped to 74.12 per cent in 2015 and by 2019, it was at 61 per cent.

This is about total stock. The PSBs' share in incremental advances is falling even at a sharper pace. It was 73.45 per cent in 2014 and dropped to 23.75 per cent in 2019.

In sync with this, their share in overall assets has been sliding, from 72.6 per cent in 2014 to 61.22 per cent in 2019. Here, the fall in the incremental market share will look unreal for someone unfamiliar with the industry, from 72.6 per cent in 2014 to 9.51 per cent in 2019.

What about the pie of deposits? In 1980, after the second round of bank nationalisation, PSBs held 90 per cent of deposits. The going was good even until 2014 when PSBs could hold on to 77.2 per cent share of the banking industry's deposit portfolio. This has been progressively coming down.

In 2019, it was 65.85 per cent. Despite enjoying an implicit sovereign guarantee, PSBs have not been able to compete with private banks to garner deposits. In 2014, 76.42 per cent of incremental deposits flowed into the public sector banking industry; in 2019, it was 20.48 per cent.

The December 2019 Report on Trend and Progress of Banking in India, an annual RBI publication, says private banks have attracted 77 per cent of the incremental term deposits in the financial year 2018–19.

The reason attributed to this is higher interest rates offered by them. This could be one reason. The other, and probably more plausible, explanation for this could be that most PSBs are suffering from an existential crisis in the new banking world. They are disrupted by technology.

Large private banks such as HDFC Bank Ltd, ICICI Bank Ltd, Axis Bank Ltd are not offering higher interest rates to woo the depositors. But armed with technology, these banks are offering personalised and structured liability products, scoring over their PSB counterparts.

State-owned enterprises have experienced similar helplessness in the telecom and aviation sectors. In the life insurance industry, LIC is putting up a brave fight but private entities are grabbing incremental market share at a fast pace.

Between 2014 and 2019, the private insurers' share in new business premium rose at a 20 per cent compounded annual growth rate, double that of LIC. In the area of so-called weighted received premium (WRP), the first year's premium and 10 per cent of single premiums, the private life insurers have been outperforming LIC and between 2014 and 2019, their market share in individual WRP has grown from 38 per cent to 58 per cent.

Between 1993 and 2014, India saw the launch of 14 new banks (not all of which survived). Since then, two universal banks, ten small finance banks and a few payments banks have been launched. These have all contributed to the fall in the market share of PSBs.

However, the real reason behind the sudden drop in businesses since 2015 has been the Indian banking regulator's massive clean-up drive. The surge in bad loans is forcing PSBs to provide more for such loans, leading to losses, and they do not have enough capital for healthy balance sheet growth.

One may call this phenomenon privatisation by stealth. Nilekani has pitched for the privatisation of PSBs before their value is eroded by 'creeping privatisation'. Until recently, privatisation of at least some of the PSBs seemed inevitable. But the governance issue in some private banks has queered the pitch.

One of the votaries of privatisation of some of the PSBs is NITI Aayog Vice Chairman Rajiv Kumar, who strongly feels that such a step 'does make for a better, competitive situation in the economy, in the financial sector'.

A Political Animal

Describing the Indradhanush framework for transforming the PSBs as 'the most comprehensive reform effort undertaken since banking nationalisation in 1970,' a government note says, 'Our PSBs are now ready to compete and flourish in a fast-evolving financial services landscape.'

There are not too many takers for this optimism. At the first Gyan Sangam, the bankers' retreat in Pune in January 2015, Prime Minister Modi said banks would be run professionally, and there would be no interference. He is against political interference but not political intervention in the interest of the people.

The political intervention, according to him, will enable the voice of the common man to reach such institutions. This has been the story of India's public sector banking industry all along.

The PSB is a political animal – the government's milch cow, used for everything from funding infrastructure to supporting MSMEs; buying government bonds to bridging the fiscal deficit, and subscribing to electoral bonds to help political parties.

There are many suggestions on the future of the PSBs – in what form and shape should they be allowed to function, and how many of them should exist. While many feel that some PSBs need to be privatised, others say the PSBs should remain in a limited way to address market failures. Their presence is required for financial inclusion and MSME and infrastructure financing. (More on this in the section 'Governorspeak').

A new twist to the fate of PSBs was given by a bureaucrat – Tuhin Kanta Pandey, secretary, Department of Investment and Public Asset Management. In July 2020, Pandey said that the new policy proposed by the Centre to have not more than four public sector undertakings in each 'strategic sector' could be applied to the banking space too. 'We are very closely working with the department of financial services and I think the general framework will be the same as the finance minister announced... it is in the works, and to be out soon,' Pandey said at an event organised by industry body FICCI, when asked about privatisation and consolidation of PSBs.

Former Citibank India head Pramit Jhaveri says that there are two options for the government and the RBI. They can allow 'fit and proper' Indian private entities and foreign institutions, including private equity, to invest and own 26 per cent in banks. Anyway, such entities already own even higher stakes in the shadow banking system.

The second option is the creation of a banking investment fund on the lines of the National Investment and Infrastructure Fund (NIIF), which could invest up to 26 per cent in banks. NIIF is an investment platform that has brought together the Government of India and international investors, looking for opportunities in infrastructure.

For the time being, consolidation is being tried. This reduces the number of banks but not the government share in the banking industry. The problem is not with the ownership actually but with how the owner behaves.

Unlike Air India which flies people, the PSBs deal with public money. They need to be treated differently. The most charitable way of doing this could be keeping a few of them under government control to address possible market failures. Their presence is required for financial inclusion, and financing MSMEs and infrastructure. But let the other PSBs be allowed to behave like commercial organisations.

■ ■ ■

6

Whose Money is it Anyway?

The coffee turned cold as the CEOs of PSBs kept their ears open for one all-important word as Finance Minister Nirmala Sitharaman delivered her budget speech on 1 February 2020. She spoke for an incredible two hours and 43 minutes and the speech was 13,275 words in length.

But that one word, 'Recapitalisation' was missing.

It is a word that has featured routinely in most budget speeches of the past several decades. Between 1985–86 and 2019–20, the government has injected close to ₹4.17-lakh crore into the PSBs. The bulk of this, around ₹3.85-lakh crore, has been pumped in after the 2008 global financial crisis. The single biggest dose, ₹2.11-lakh crore or roughly 1.3 per cent of India's GDP at the time, was announced in October 2017.

That October package was the mother of all recapitalisation packages. In response to the news of a proposed ₹2.11-lakh crore recapitalisation package over two years, the market value of state-owned banks soared by ₹1.2-lakh crore in one session.

While announcing the big fat recapitalisation of banks, the finance minister of the moment, Arun Jaitley, may have harked back to the predicament of Larry Fortensky. On his wedding night at Michael Jackson's Neverland Ranch at Santa Barbara County, California, in October 1991, Fortensky who had just become Elizabeth Taylor's seventh husband from her eighth marriage, knew exactly what he was expected to do. His challenge was to do it better than Taylor's former husbands.

How could Jaitley differentiate himself from his predecessors who had, since thrown so many lifelines to failing PSBs, each time using taxpayers' money?

Jaitley's recapitalisation package had three components – buying bank shares (₹18,000 crore), raising ₹58,000 crore from the market, and issuing ₹1.35-lakh crore worth of recapitalisation bonds to the banks on which the government would pay interest.

The recapitalisation bond is a debt instrument issued by the government, so it comes with an iron-clad guarantee. It is bought by the banks, using depositor funds (meaning borrowed money). The government re-invests the money back into the banks as equity. It also pays interest.

By this clever circular route, bank deposits are used for recap. If the value of the shares held by the government rises more than interest paid on the bonds, the government can actually turn a profit. Meanwhile, the banks look healthier with a higher proportion of equity to debt on the balance sheet.

The IMF says recapitalisation bonds need not be added in the accounting of the fiscal deficit as they are squared off by buying the shares in banks. In India, however, the government had taken such bonds into account in the fiscal deficit since it pays interest and eventually redeems these.

The First Tranche

It was in 1994 that the government had issued India's first-ever recapitalisation bonds. In the 1993–94 Union Budget, then finance minister, Manmohan Singh, announced a 'provision for a large capital contribution of ₹5,700 crore to the nationalised banks' to protect 'the viability and financial health of the Indian banking system'.

In the same budget, Singh announced the government's decision to allow SBI and other nationalised banks to access the capital markets for raising fresh equity, even as the government would 'continue to retain majority ownership, and therefore effective control' in these banks.

The next budget (1994–95) provided ₹5,600 crore as an additional capital contribution for these banks in the form of government bonds. On both occasions, there was no immediate financial burden. But the government bore the interest cost.

Announcing the first bank recapitalisation plan in the 1993–94 budget, Singh had said: 'While undertaking such a large injection of capital into the banks, specific commitments will be required from each bank to ensure that their future management practices ensure a high level of portfolio quality so that the earlier problem does not recur.'

Had the government forced the banks to stick to such commitments, we would not have seen umpteen more bailouts over the next 25 years.

Jaitley wanted to attach strings to the fund infusion, which equalled more than a third of the core or Tier I capital (equity plus reserves consisting of retained profits) of the state-owned banks. The government also committed to use its discretion while allocating capital to banks, and thus interlace it with a series of reforms.

Has the government kept its word?

First, we need to understand why banks need so much capital. Bank are licenced to take money from anyone on the street because central banks take adequate measures to ensure safety of deposit. Capital provides that safety.

Banks have to adhere to limits set by the Basel Committee in terms of how much capital they need for giving loans to the borrowers. Those limits are set as multiples of capital – Tier I as well as Tier II (long-term bonds and certain other reserves) the banks possess. Even if a bank has access to lots of debt in the form of deposits, its ability to lend is limited by the amount of capital it has.

When loans go bad, banks must set aside money to cover losses.

Those provisions come out of their capital and if there are high levels of NPAs, the capital gets eroded.

The PSBs' share of bad loans is far higher than that of private banks. At some point, the RBI restrained 11 of them from carrying out normal banking activities until they mended their ways. They were put under the so-called 'prompt corrective action' framework of the banking regulator – a sort of quarantine. The recapitalisation was meant to help some of the weaker banks to emerge and start lending again. As I write this chapter in August, not every bank is out of the quarantine.

Until the 2020 Union Budget, giving capital to PSBs had been almost an annual ritual. In the current century, there were just five financial years when the government had not given capital – 2000, 2001, 2004, 2005 and 2007.

Despite deep research, I could not unearth any document that explains in a transparent way how capital was distributed among the PSBs since 1994. In the period between 2008–09 and 2016–17, before the ₹2.1-lakh crore package, the money seemed to have been just handed over for the asking.

During this period, the government infused ₹1,18,724 crore in the PSBs and the capital was not linked to either performance or efficiency. It was a classic story of ad-hoc steps taken in the absence of any policy guidelines.

The bureaucrats in the finance ministry just doled out capital, based on the networking ability of the boss of the concerned bank and the thumb-rule of giving most to the weakest ones. Taxpayers' money was pumped in just to keep banks alive.

Ideally, any such capital infusion should be need-based and it should come with strings attached to force better performance. However, the available records tell a different story. The handouts were done via a cocktail of whims and fancies, defying all logic.

Capital is Core

Capital is core for expanding credit, earning interest and growing balance sheets so that banks can drive economic activities. The government is the majority owner of PSBs.

The statutory requirement in the Banking Companies (Acquisition and Transfer of Undertakings) Act, 1970/1980, and the State Bank of India Act, 1955, ensure that the Indian government shall, at all times, hold not less than 51 per cent of the paid-up capital in such banks.

In 2010, the Cabinet Committee on Economic Affairs (CCEA), after noting the economy's trends, had decided to increase the government holding in all PSBs to 58 per cent. The objective was to create some headroom and enable PSBs to raise capital from the market when they need, without compromising their public-sector character.

Subsequently, in December 2014, CCEA decided to allow PSBs to raise capital from the markets through instruments such as follow-on public offer or qualified institutional placement (QIP) by diluting the government holding up to 52 per cent, in phases.

Besides the direct government holding, the wholly-government-owned LIC also holds significant stakes in PSBs. (The February 2020 Union Budget spoke about selling part of the government stake in LIC through an initial public offer.) As on 31 December 2019, LIC's stake varied from 1.04 per cent (in United Bank of India, which was merged with PNB) to 9.13 per cent (in SBI). Over and above this, a few public sector undertakings, including some of the peer banks, also hold and cross-hold PSB shares. This ensures indirect but complete government control over all PSBs.

Incidentally, IDBI Bank Ltd was 'privatised'. The government was not willing to infuse fresh capital and allowed LIC to step in to IDBI Bank's rescue. In January 2019, it became the majority owner of the bank, completing acquisition of its 51 per cent – a process that had started in June 2018. In August 2018, the Cabinet had approved LIC's acquisition of controlling stake and becoming a promoter of IDBI Bank through a combination of preferential allotment and open offer of equity.

Drivers of Bank Recapitalisation

The regulatory requirements of capital adequacy and credit growth are the two main drivers for bank recapitalisation. The Basel Committee on Banking Supervision – a committee of bank supervisors with members from representative countries – frames the global regulatory architecture.

The mandate of the Basel Committee, headquartered at the Bank for International Settlements in Basel, Switzerland, is to strengthen the regulation, supervision and practices of banks and enhance financial stability.

So far, three sets of Basel norms have been issued. The Basel I norms were issued in 1988 to provide, for the first time, a global regulatory standard on the capital requirements of banks.

The Basel II norms, introduced in 2004, strengthened the guidelines for risk management and disclosure requirements. This called for a minimum capital adequacy ratio (CAR) – or, capital to risk-weighted assets ratio (CRAR) as it is the ratio of regulatory capital funds to risk-weighted assets – which all banks with an international presence were supposed to maintain.

Following the sub-prime crisis and large-scale bank failures in the US and Europe in 2008, these were revisited in 2010, leading to the Basel III regulations. They were evolved essentially to regulate banks in the developed markets from taking wanton risks that could erode capital.

Basel III emphasised capital adequacy to protect shareholders' and customers' risks and set norms for conserving capital by segregating it into Tier I and Tier II capital.

The Tier I capital, or core capital, consists mainly of share capital and reserves; Tier II capital, also known as supplementary capital, consists of certain designated reserves and specific types of subordinated debt.

The RBI has adopted Basel II and set the norms for all commercial banks, including PSBs, a notch higher in line with its usual cautious approach. It intends to adopt Basel III, although the timelines have been postponed due to the NPA crisis.

The assets of a bank generally carry three categories of risks: Credit risk, market risk and operational risk, apart from other associated risks.

Based on the riskiness of the asset, a specific risk weight is assigned to it and the asset value is adjusted as per the risk weight. The riskier the asset, the higher the risk weightage and the lower its value.

In India, RBI prescribes risk weights for different assets and sectoral/individual industry exposures. For instance, the risk weight on a government bond is zero, but for commercial real estate, it could be over 100 per cent.

India has adopted the various stages of the Basel regulations – but years after they were issued. For instance, Basel I norms (1988) were adopted in 1996 and Basel II norms (2004) were adopted in 2008.

Even though the RBI had in principle adopted Basel III norms (2010) in September 2013, the implementation is not yet through because of rise in bad loans and the government's inability to adequately capitalise them.

The Basel III norms are a comprehensive set of reform measures to strengthen the regulation, supervision, risk management and capital management of the banking sector, which were spurred by the global financial crisis of 2008.

The RBI has always been a conservative central banker, and it has usually been more stringent than the BIS. For instance, the Basel Committee prescribes a minimum CRAR of 8 per cent; RBI calls for 9 per cent. In addition, the RBI requires banks to have a 2.5 per cent capital conservation buffer – mandatory capital that they need to hold in addition to other minimum capital requirements.

In April 2020, the CRAR was 10.875 per cent. Going by the RBI's way of doing things, it should have gone up to 11.5 per cent but the central bank postponed any change by six months as the Indian economy, like the rest of the world, has been reeling under the impact of the Covid-19 pandemic.

Different sets of loan assets carry different risks. Simply put, a bank needs to hold ₹10.875 capital for every ₹100 worth risk-weighted assets. For small finance banks, the requirement is higher – ₹15.

The implementation of Basel III norms has been coinciding with subdued economic growth in India and rising NPAs. Banks do not earn any interest on their NPAs, which is why they are called non-performing assets; on top of that, they must set aside money as provision. The RBI is keeping close tabs on the economic scenario before moving to make Basel III norms mandatory.

Performance Parameters

The PSBs have been bleeding because the provisioning of bad loans has eroded their capital base and restricted their capacity to lend money. Two main indicators of bank performance are return on assets (RoA) and return on equity (RoE).

The RoA indicates how profitable a bank is, relative to its total assets; it measures how efficiently the bank is generating profits out of its assets. This is calculated by dividing the net income by the average total assets, and expressing the result as a percentage.

A higher RoA indicates a better-managed, more efficient bank. The profit can be ploughed back to add to capital, and this also improves a bank's ability to tap the markets for additional funds it can lend.

The RoE, on the other hand, shows how efficiently a bank uses shareholders' funds by measuring net income as a percentage of equity plus reserves. A higher RoE adds to the capital of the bank by pumping up reserves and surpluses. A low or negative RoE reduces the ability of the bank to tap the capital markets to raise additional funds to meet regulatory capital needs.

The RoA of PSBs has been consistently lower than that of other scheduled commercial banks, while the RoE of PSBs has been lower than private banks since 2012–13. In 2015–16, both RoA and RoE for most PSBs were negative, indicating losses to the banks and causing concern to the owner, that is, the government.

There was a period of high credit growth during the expansionary phase of 2004–07. This was in tandem with the Indian economy's high growth rate at that time. The advances of PSBs more than trebled from ₹17.97-lakh crore to ₹55.94-lakh crore between

March 2008 and March 2016 even though the rate of increase in advances has tapered in recent years.

The rise in advances, coupled with the RBI's stringent capital adequacy requirements in the wake of the Basel III norms, has meant requirements for further Tier 1 capital. The high levels of NPAs have also led to significant capital erosion, which has further enhanced the need for capital.

PSBs need capital primarily for two reasons: One is to replenish the base eroded by NPAs and, two, to lend out for new business. The capital can come either from the dominant shareholder (the Government of India), or from the capital markets. But banks that are underperforming and have a pile of bad loans have low book value and low share prices. So, it is not easy for them to attract investors.

There is a significant gap between the book value and market value of PSB shares. Barring SBI, all the PSBs traditionally have lower market value compared with book values.

All this means that the government as the majority stakeholder needs to step in to rescue PSBs. However, the norms followed for capital infusion seem to have been inconsistent, ad hoc and piecemeal.

Historically, the PSBs have always been enjoying the unquestioning protection of its majority owner. However inefficient the CEO may be, no PSB chief has ever been sacked for non-performance. Whenever any bank needed capital, it has been there for the asking.

The government's role as protector of PSBs reminds one of the role played by Lord Krishna to protect the modesty of Draupadi. When Duryodhana ordered Dushasana to disrobe her in public after Yudhishthira lost her to the Kauravas in the game of dice, Krishna made sure her saree would be unending in length and she would not lose her modesty. The PSBs have been protected in much the same fashion.

Need-based Capital?

Over the years, the government has been infusing 'need-based' capital in PSBs to ensure they meet Basel II requirements and are also able to feed credit growth expectations. The capital infusion has generally been through preferential allotment of equity shares to the government.

In September 2011, after the global meltdown, a high-level committee on the capital requirement of financial institutions recommended the creation of a holding company for PSBs that could raise the extra-budgetary resources required. The finance secretary chaired the committee, and the other members included the secretaries of the departments of expenditure, economic affairs and financial services and the government's chief economic adviser.

In January 2015, at the first Gyan Sangam, the banking reforms conclave in Pune, bankers discussed key issues such as NPAs and recapitalisation threadbare. Subsequently, in August that year, Jaitley announced infusion of ₹70,000 crore of capital in PSBs over 2015–16 to 2018–19 under Indradhanush, a plan with seven components like the seven colours of a rainbow (Indradhanush is a Sanskrit word for rainbow).

The Process

The finance ministry's Department of Financial Services (DFS) is the administrative authority for PSBs. Every year, the DFS reviews the performance of each PSB on the basis of a number of parameters. It also reviews their capital requirements.

PSBs seek capital from the government taking into account the credit growth and risk profile of assets, and assessment of internal accruals and other sources of capital generation. The DFS verifies and determines the capital requirement on a 'need-based approach' in consultation with the finance ministry and recommends them to the CCEA.

In the context of Basel II norms, the need-based approach means helping the PSBs achieve minimum capital requirements (of both Tier I and Tier II) in line with the regulatory framework. This includes maintaining a 2.5 per cent additional capital buffer, and planning and strategising for future growth too.

The Cabinet considers the overall budgetary support required while keeping in mind the budgetary constraints; it also decides on apportioning capital support to various PSBs. After this, it gives the green signal to the finance ministry to release the capital.

Ideally, such a process of capitalisation should have been based on a long-term plan and a well-thought-out policy and strategy. However, in reality, between 2008–09 and 2014–15, all decisions to infuse various amounts of capital into PSBs seemed based on ad hoc considerations, varying from year to year. There was no planning as such; the finance ministry decided the allocations as part of the annual Union budget.

Looking at the flow of capital between 2009 and 2017, before the floodgates of capital opened up, out of the total capital infusion of ₹1.19-lakh crore, SBI, the largest and most 'systemically important' bank, received the most capital, ₹26,948 crore, or about 22.7 per cent of the total infusion.

The four worst underperformers with the worst loans – IDBI Bank, Central Bank of India, Indian Overseas Bank and Bank of India – also got significant amounts: 8.83 per cent, 8.07 per cent, 7.94 per cent and 7.86 per cent, respectively.

Punjab & Sind Bank and Indian Bank, which were both considered to be relatively better managed, received the lowest amounts of 0.2 per cent and 0.24 per cent, respectively. Indian Bank received capital only once, in 2014–15, while under-performing banks such as Central Bank and UCO Bank were given capital in eight out of nine years.

The criteria for capital support kept on changing from year to year and efficiency was never a basis for doling out capital. It was based on discretion. Incidentally, sometimes the government had taken interest-bearing loans from multilateral organisations for financing capital requirements.

Chronic Ad Hocism

While capital infusion is expected to follow an independent assessment by DFS, there is documented evidence that at least in one year, 2010–11, the DFS decided the capital infusion solely on the basis of PSBs' projections and information and did not verify these independently. In that year, ₹20,117 crore of capital was infused in three phases (₹7,694 crore in the first phase, ₹6,423 crore in the second phase and ₹6,000 crore in the third phase).

For the second phase, the PSBs had furnished data as late as on 1 January 2011 – just three months before the end of the financial year – with projections of shortfall in Tier I capital, vis-à-vis a target of 8 per cent CRAR as on 31 March 2011. Accordingly, the DFS worked out the requirement of capital for the second phase at ₹6,423 crore.

The capital infusion in the PSBs between 2011–12 and 2014–15 was supposedly based on a series of annual performance evaluations of banks (linked to the incentives of the chairman and MDs and executive directors) for which memorandums of understanding (MoUs) were entered into.

The MoUs the banks had signed with the DFS in February/ March 2012 included various performance parameters such as the share of CASA, or current and savings accounts (the low-cost deposits), return on assets, net profit per employee, employee cost to income ratio, other cost to income ratio, market share of deposits, RBI rating, ratio of staff in branches to total staff and outstanding NPAs over the previous two years as a percentage of total NPAs.

The MoUs are supposed to be the preconditions for capital infusions. In reality, between 2010 and 2014, as NPAs mounted, eroding the core capital of PSBs, the MoU targets became irrelevant. Instead, the regulatory requirements regarding capital adequacy and estimates of credit growth became the basis for capital infusion.

Also, the CCEA approval for 'need-based' capital infusion made the MoUs redundant, even though the DFS insisted that 'only on signing MoUs and achieving quarterly benchmarks, PSBs shall be eligible to be considered for capital infusion'.

The DFS continued with the ritual of signing MoUs after the announcement of Indradhanush on the same set of parameters and entered into MoUs with PSBs as late as in March 2017. However, the performance parameters under MoUs are of purely academic interest, except perhaps as one of the tools used to calculate annual incentives of MDs and executive directors of PSBs.

The Indradhanush plan to infuse ₹70,000 crore in PSBs to adequately capitalise them and keep a buffer assumed the projected credit growth would be 12–15 per cent, against an actual rate of 6–8 per cent. It was announced by Jaitley in August 2015 to revamp the PSBs and make them competitive vis-à-vis the private banks.

Back to the Basics?

In the long history of PSB capitalisation, this was the first time the government embarked on a longer-term strategic plan, in collaboration with the RBI.

According to the Indradhanush plan, for 2015–16, PSBs were to get 20 per cent of the earmarked capital infusion based on their performance during the three quarters in 2015–16, judged on certain parameters.

However, even this was not followed up either in letter or spirit and all funds were released on the basis of need after the RBI did its asset quality review or AQR. Under the AQR scheme, launched in the second half of 2015–16, the central bank's inspectors scanned the lenders' books, identified defaulters and asked the banks to clean up their balance sheets in six quarters, by March 2017.

Even during 2016–17, the DFS linked the release of 25 per cent of the funds with performance, but as most banks fell short of the targets set, performance was not considered as a basis for capital infusion during the year.

In March 2016, the DFS decided that 25 per cent of the capital to be infused in 2016–17 would be disbursed upfront and linked the rest to the PSBs' ability to hit the quantitative targets set for them.

The DFS also made it clear that banks which missed their targets would not receive further funds. However, in July 2016, DFS reversed this decision and decided to disburse 75 per cent upfront and link the release of the rest to targets.

Presumably, the DFS did this to ensure that the PSBs had

enough liquidity to support credit growth and were in a position to raise money from the markets. But the reversal clearly violated the objective of ensuring accountability for efficient and optimal use of capital. In 2016–17, the DFS released the entire capital without checking if the PSBs had met any of the performance criteria.

Inconsistencies in Policy

A close look at the distribution of capital across PSBs throws up interesting data. For instance, in 2011–12, the intent was to infuse capital in PSBs so that they reach Tier I CRAR of 8 per cent. But SBI received much more capital than it required to meet this target.

While the regulatory requirement for SBI in 2011–12 was ₹5,874 crore, DFS gave it ₹7,900 crore during the year, in line with the bank's demand for capital (after the impending Basel III norms, SBI would be required to maintain its Tier I CRAR at approximately 11 per cent).

In fact, among the seven PSBs which were given fresh capital during 2011–12, only SBI got the full amount (and more) than it had requested. Bank of Maharashtra got ₹470 crore, Central Bank ₹676 crore, IDBI Bank ₹810 crore, Indian Overseas Bank ₹1,441 crore, PNB ₹655 crore, and UCO Bank ₹48 crore – all less than what they had asked for.

Apparently, the decision to infuse more than the amount SBI had requested was made primarily to take care of future requirements. But this argument does not hold water as the approval of the CCEA was for maintaining a Tier I CRAR of 8 per cent and the 11 per cent target for Tier I CRAR was not maintained uniformly for SBI in later years.

Similarly, in 2013–14, it was imperative that the basis for capital infusion in PSBs be in line with the CCEA decision that they maintain Tier I CRAR at a level above 8 per cent as on 31 March 2014, and the shareholding of the government stay as close as possible to 58 per cent.

However, of the 20 PSBs whose assessment was done, four

(SBI, Canara Bank, Syndicate Bank, UCO Bank) did not qualify according to the given criteria. They all had Tier I CRAR higher than 8 per cent and government shareholdings above 58 per cent. Other three banks – Bank of Baroda, PNB and Union Bank of India – met the CRAR target but with lower government shareholding.

All 20 banks (including those four banks which did not qualify under the given criteria) were, however, given fresh capital during the year.

The DFS had assessed a requirement of ₹15,703 crore for PSBs to meet the Tier I CRAR target in 2013–14 against an available budget of ₹14,000 crore. But 13 PSBs got only ₹9,550 crore to meet the CRAR goal, while seven PSBs got ₹4,450 crore between them (of which ₹2,900 crore was infused in four banks that did not satisfy the criteria).

No uniform criteria were followed for distributing the ₹9,550 crore capital among the 13 PSBs that fell short of the Tier I CRAR benchmark of 8 per cent. For instance, in the case of Corporation Bank, the capital infusion was ₹450 crore (more than the assessed requirement of ₹416 crore), while in the case of Allahabad Bank, it was ₹400 crore (equal to what it asked for).

Instrumentalities of the State

The PSBs are 'instrumentalities of the state'. Managing them efficiently to promote economic development and further public interest calls for efficient public administration and committed public service with due accountability.

For ensuring 'efficiency', two sets of tools were used by the DFS: MoUs and the statements of intent (SoIs). Both were supposed to play a critical role in monitoring capital infusion in PSBs. But a deeper look into how these instruments were deployed gives us a sense of the quality of governance in PSBs, if nothing else.

The finance ministry had introduced the mechanism of SoI on annual goals to monitor the performance of PSBs in June 2005. Performance parameters were defined and targets were set for PSBs against these parameters. The SoI parameters had been revisited and redrafted on several occasions with amendments on 23 April 2010, 21 October 2011 and 20 May 2012.

Incentivising Tool

Following the May 2012 amendment, the DFS had to monitor 44 SoI parameters. The SoIs were not just a tool to monitor the performance of the PSBs but also to incentivise top management. However, a closer look suggests that such monitoring became a routine affair and one of the many factors that influence the incentives of top management. This was not a meaningful exercise to ensure efficient capital management.

Only in one year (2010–11) out of the nine-year period (2008–17) did the finance ministry specify conditions the PSBs had to meet if they were to get fresh capital. No such conditions were set on record for the other years.

Incidentally, the SoI parameters were used as an instrument for efficient management of PSBs and not for ensuring capital conservation, or capital efficiency. For instance, the targets stipulated against specific parameters at the time of sanction of capital in 2010–11 were significantly different from the targets set for the same parameters in the SoI for the same period in the case of five PSBs.

All about Targets

The SoI targets were less stringent than the targets associated with the sanction orders; records show that there was little follow-up and monitoring when the actual achievements of PSBs lagged compared with the SoI targets.

One wonders whether the DFS monitored the incorporation of the conditions set in the sanction of capital orders. The negotiating skills of senior bank managements ultimately decide on the quantum of money each bank gets.

For the DFS as well as the banks, review of the SoIs has been an annual ritual. Despite good intentions to 'control' the management of PSBs, over the years, the SoIs have just become a routine annual management exercise tool on paper with very little or no relevance to the process of capital infusion.

Almost seven years after the SoIs were put in place, in February–March 2012, DFS introduced the system of MoUs with PSBs to ensure that they draw up a firm plan for long-term business development and performance enhancement, and relate it to their capital requirement. The MoUs consist of a set of agreed targets that the PSBs are expected to achieve, which would form the basis for future capital infusion by the government. The aim of the MoUs was to ensure the optimal use of scarce capital funds.

The practices that the DFS followed in preparing, finalising and monitoring of the MoUs are not the best and, as the record shows, MoUs had never been the basis for capital infusion in PSBs. A look at the MoUs also makes it clear that the targets set against some of these parameters were being eased, year after year. For instance, efficiency goals were being lowered.

One can take the case of the target for CASA, the cheapest source of funds for banks, which boosts profits. SBI's actual CASA was 48.66 per cent of total deposits in 2010–11 but defying all logic the target was set at a lower 45 per cent for all the years from 2011–12 to 2014–15. For Kolkata-based United Bank of India, the CASA targets were reduced progressively each year from 39 per cent in 2011–12 to 37 per cent in 2014–15.

For IDBI Bank, while the actual cost-to-income ratio for 2010–11 was 35.15 per cent, the target for 2011–12 allowed costs to go up substantially as it was pegged at 39.4 per cent. This means the target set for the future was lower than the current achievement. The targeted cost-to-income ratio for PNB was allowed to go up progressively between 2011–12 and 2014–15.

For some PSBs such as Andhra Bank and Allahabad Bank, specific targets were set for all components of the RBI ratings. For some, such targets were waived. For example, in the case of Bank of Maharashtra, Bank of Baroda, Bank of India and Indian Bank, the targets were vague and non-specific ('Shall improve upon existing rating on all parameters, particularly on asset quality, management, systems and control').

The apparent arbitrariness of the targets smacks of biases. Or else, these were set according to the whims and fancies of finance ministry bureaucrats.

Lax Implementation

The MoUs took ages to draw up and sign, making them meaningless. For 2011–12, the DFS had directed that MoUs be finalised by 30 November 2011 but they were finally signed in February–March 2012 – a delay of nearly three months. Those MoUs included the targets to be achieved by 31 March 2012! One can imagine the fate of the targets that year.

Even more absurdly, the MoUs between SBI and its associate banks – State Bank of Bikaner & Jaipur, State Bank of Travancore, State Bank of Mysore, State Bank of Hyderabad and State Bank of Patiala – for 2011–12 were signed after the fiscal year ended, in the first week of April 2012! (The associate banks have been merged with SBI.)

The finance ministry can always defend the delays by claiming that it had started discussions with the banks immediately after the draft MoUs were sent to them and even though the signing was delayed, the targets were known to the ministry. However, the figures in the draft MoUs (circulated to all PSBs in October 2011) were significantly different from the actual MoUs signed (February–March 2012), which again points to rampant use of discretionary powers and ad hocism on policy issues.

Wide Variations

There was also wide variation and discretion in the application of the terms of the MoUs. They were supposed to be valid for five years. However, apart from Central Bank of India (for which targets were fixed from 2012–13 to 2016–17), for all other PSBs, the signed MoUs contained targets to be achieved only until 31 March 2015.

It seems the DFS entered into MoUs initially for three years, supposedly to lay a road map towards the final, or ultimate targets, by

2017. In other words, the targets given to the banks to be achieved by 2015 were interim targets, preparing them for the final target in 2017.

The targets for the three years between 2011–12 and 2014–15 were fixed in the MoUs signed in February–March 2012 but the SoI targets were fixed annually. At the least, one would expect the two monitoring mechanisms to be synchronised!

Of the 44 parameters under the SoI, five were common with those in the MoU. They were CASA, RoA, cost-to-income ratio, net profit per employee and ratio of staff in branches to total staff.

There were significant variations between targets set in the SoIs and MoUs for the same parameter. For instance, in the case of CASA, the maximum difference between the SoI and the MoU was 18 percentage points; for RoA, 1.37 percentage points; cost-to-income ratio, 21.3 percentage points; and for net profit per employee, ₹10.15 lakh.

Poor Monitoring

The banks were to submit a progress report every quarter on the performance of the parameters stipulated in the MoUs. Going by this, 273 progress reports were to be received from 21 PSBs (one from each bank for the fourth quarter of 2011–12, four from each for each fiscal year from 2012–13 to 2014–15). But only 21 progress reports were received from PSBs (for the fourth quarter of 2011–12 only).

Isn't this data point enough to give us an understanding of the quality of PSB monitoring and capital management?

Instead of addressing fundamental pain points such as quality of project appraisal, risk management, monitoring and governance, the periodic recap dole for PSBs is handed out in a manner similar to farm loan waivers. Farmers are just given loan waivers rather than being taught to produce more and aided in ensuring the marketing of their produce. Similarly, recapitalisation sans attempts to change the way the PSBs function, just widens cracks in the edifice of banking.

■ ■ ■

One key question is: What has the government got in return?

Even though recapitalisation had started before the economic liberalisation of 1991, the PSBs started entering the market in the late 1990s. The last PSB to get listed was Punjab & Sind Bank, in December 2010. It followed the United Bank of India which had made its maiden public issue in March 2010. While United Bank of India, along with Oriental Bank of Commerce have been merged with PNB, the Punjab & Sind Bank still remains an independent entity.

The Government of India has injected close to ₹3.12-lakh crore over ten years between 2010 and 2019. What has the government earned on its investments?

During this period, the Sensex, the BSE's 30-share benchmark index, has risen 120 per cent (from 17,527 to 38,672) and the 50-share Nifty of the NSE by 121 per cent (from 5,249 to 11,623).

The Nifty Bank Index, representing the banking industry, rose 221 per cent (from 9,459 to 30,426).

The Nifty Bank Index consists of 12 stocks – nine private banks and three PSBs, as of 2020.

The Nifty Public Sector Bank Index consists of 13 PSB stocks and this is a proxy for the overall performance of the PSBs, while the Nifty Private Bank Index, with 10 stocks, is designed to reflect the behaviour and performance of the private sector banks.

The composition of such indices is dynamic.

Let us estimate the return on the Government of India's investments in the PSBs from 2010 till 2019, on the basis of dividends received and the notional market value of these investments, sourced from publicly available share price data.

How much would the government have made had these investments been done in Nifty Private Sector Bank Index?

What is the quantum of notional loss, or profit forgone?

The government has been injecting capital into PSBs for maintaining their capital adequacy ratios and meeting the credit needs of the economy. Over this period, 22 PSBs have received around ₹3.12-lakh crore capital.

The notional market value of its capital infusions from 2010 to 2019, computed using the Nifty Public Sector Bank total returns index year-on-year movements every financial year, is pegged at ₹3.39-lakh crore as in March 2019.

Had the government invested the same quantum of capital in the Nifty Private Sector Bank Index, the value of its holding (including dividends) would have been ₹5.27-lakh crore.

In other words, the government has missed out on a notional profit of ₹1.88-lakh crore, which is the opportunity cost it has paid on its actual investment.

The Economic Survey 2019–20 has analysed the overall government investment in PSBs and returns earned. Going by the survey, at least ₹4.3-lakh crore of taxpayers' money is invested as the government's equity in PSBs.

In 2019, every rupee of taxpayer money invested in PSBs, on average, lost 23 paise. In contrast, every rupee invested in the so-called new private banks – the banks licensed after the 1991 liberalisation – on average gained 9.6 paise.

The notional opportunity cost loss is therefore 32.6 paise (23 paise plus 9.6 paise) for every rupee invested in the PSBs. For ₹4.3-lakh crore, the amount equates to ₹1.41-lakh crore.

The Survey points out that as PSBs and the new private banks operate in the same market, there is a case for making the PSBs more efficient. The return forgone on the taxpayers' investment in PSBs must rank among the largest subsidies. At around ₹1.4-lakh crore at the least, it is comparable with the amount provided for food subsidy.

The Survey also raises a critical question: What is the overall value that a taxpayer derives from her investment in PSBs? For this purpose, it has used the ratio of stock market to book value of PSBs on average, vis-à-vis that of new private sector banks. As on 20 January 2020, every rupee of taxpayer money invested in PSBs fetched a market value of 71 paise. In contrast, every rupee invested in the private banks fetched five times more – ₹3.70.

Pumping capital in banks is not unique to India but not seeking any return seems to be an India-specific story. How does it compare with other markets?

The US Treasury's Troubled Asset Relief Program, set up to tackle the aftermath of the 2008 financial markets' crisis in the US, had planned to spend $700 billion. It did not actually spend so much but the broader bailout programme of the separate rescue packages for Fannie Mae and Freddie Mac together pumped in $634 billion.

As of 19 March 2020, the US government has realised a $121 billion profit, according to the *Bailout Tracker*, a newsletter published by ProPublica, an independent, non-profit newsroom that tracks the return of every taxpayer dollar that went into the bailout.

Many facts and data used in this chapter are sourced from the 'Report of the Comptroller and Auditor General of India on Recapitalisation of Public Sector Banks'. Union Government. Ministry of Finance. Report No 29 of 2017 (Performance Audit).

■ ■ ■

7

Is Consolidation a Panacea?

> If you recollect, the government had announced in the Budget that consolidation of banks will also be on the agenda of the government. In the first step, we had consolidated the five subsidiaries of the State Bank with the State Bank in order to make a mega global bank.

That is how Finance Minister Arun Jaitley started a press conference in Delhi on 17 September 2018, to announce the consolidation of PSBs. Rajiv Kumar, who was then the secretary, DFS, was standing next to his boss.

Before putting his cards on the table, Jaitley said:

> The LIC has for several years been very keen to have a bank of its own because most of its competitors have banks, or are bank-promoted insurance companies, and there is synergy between the two businesses. So, while we were working out ways of bringing down the government equity in the IDBI [Bank], the LIC considered it appropriate to make an offer because it suited their commercial interests...

While LIC took until January 2019 to complete the acquisition of 51 per cent controlling stake in IDBI Bank Ltd, Jaitley did not want to wait.

At the conference, he announced the merger of Dena Bank and Vijaya Bank with Bank of Baroda. This was the first merger of its kind in the history of this set of banks, all of which were majority-owned by the government.

The merger of SBI's associate banks with the parent was a family affair and much less challenging than the amalgamation of a motley group of PSBs.

There have been many mergers in the private sector for strategic and other reasons. But when it came to the PSB, every merger was driven by the RBI's first priority, which was to protect depositors' funds until the government firmed up the consolidation plan.

The Oriental Bank of Commerce taking over the troubled Global Trust Bank Ltd is one such case of a merger designed to protect depositors. Officially, all such mergers have been voluntary but the RBI has always been the matchmaker behind-the-scenes. Typically, a PSB is identified to rescue a private bank through such mergers and not every such script has a happy ending. The first and only bail-out merger in the government-owned banking space was PNB taking over New Bank of India in 1993 and then, Bharatiya Mahila Bank was merged with SBI in 2017.

What was the rationale behind the triple merger? 'While making this "suggestion", we have borne in mind that we do not want a merger of what are relatively weak banks. You can have two well-performing banks absorbing a third one in the amalgamation process and hopefully creating a mega bank which will be sustainable, whose lending ability will be far higher,' Jaitley answered.

Bank of Baroda and Vijaya were the performers while Dena was the weak link. Since all three banks were listed entities, Jaitley said: 'The government has suggested it (the merger) to the banks to consider this proposal and hopefully… their boards will meet and after adequate consultation, they will take an appropriate decision in this regard.'

He assured the employees that their service conditions would remain unchanged and said the merged entity's 'ability to increase and expand will be inevitable' because of its sheer size.

Another Day, More Mergers

A little less than a year later, on 30 August 2019, Finance Minister Nirmala Sitharaman, who had taken over after Jaitley's death, announced another round of bank mergers.

Kumar, who had by this time moved on to become finance secretary; Atanu Chakraborty, economic affairs secretary; and Ajay Bhushan Pandey, revenue secretary, were among those standing with the finance minister at the Press Information Bureau in the National Media Centre in Delhi, where Sitharaman spoke for almost an hour. She detailed the progress of various steps taken to improve the functioning of the PSBs as a prologue to her announcement of creating four mega NextGen banks.

While Jaitley had been for consolidation to create 'mega banks' with higher lending capability, Sitharaman found consolidation imperative for a $5 trillion economy.

Her speech went this way:

> So, having done two rounds of consolidation along with sustained thrust on recognition, recapitalisation, resolution, process-reform and so on, what is it that we want to do for the next?
>
> I've already said the target is $5 trillion economy that we want to reach, a robust banking system that we want and for which the steps that we want to take is what we want to reveal today before you.
>
> So, we are trying to build the NextGen banks… unlocking the potential through consolidation. We are going to be talking a lot about consolidation… Banks with strong national presence and global reach is what we want.… The blueprint that we are coming up with is going to help us towards building a $5 trillion economy.

The Rationale

Then, she went on to explain which banks would be merged and why.

The large capacity of one bank, the technology-driven capacity of another and the strong deposit franchise of the third would create the first mega bank of this round with the merger of PNB, Oriental Bank of Commerce and United Bank of India.

'What will this give us?' she asked rhetorically and answered: A high CASA [current and savings accounts, low-cost funds for banks] and lending capacity created through large cost reductions, ironing out overlaps of branch network, and creation of income opportunities from their joint ventures and subsidiaries.

She also emphasised the fact that great care has been taken to see that the technology platforms of all three banks were compatible. This would help the banks benefit quickly without disruptions in business.

The second set of banks picked for consolidation were based in South India. This was the merger of Canara Bank with Syndicate Bank. Apart from other incentives, here the glue factor was the culture.

The third set consists of Union Bank of India, Andhra Bank and Corporation Bank and the fourth, Indian Bank and Allahabad Bank, converging banks with strong regional presences in the south, north and east.

Sitharaman repeatedly emphasised the common technology platform of these banks and how they would be strengthened in every parameter, particularly in terms of capital, in sync with international norms.

She said the mega banks born out of the consolidation – these four, Bank of Baroda and SBI – will hold 82 per cent share of the business of PSBs and 56 per cent share of all commercial banks.

Sun Run

On 9 June 2019, a couple of months before Sitharaman's announcement of the merger of 10 PSBs to create four mega

NextGen banks, around 2,000 Bank of Baroda employees participated in a five-kilometre 'Sun Run'. This was flagged off by badminton champion Srikanth Kidambi at Jio Garden in Mumbai's Bandra Kurla Complex where the bank is headquartered. That was one of many team-building exercises that would be replicated in other cities.

Sports is an import from Vijaya Bank which, along with Dena Bank, has been merged with Bank of Baroda. Cricketers Anil Kumble and Javagal Srinath, and athlete Ashwini Nachappa, among others, were on Vijaya's payroll. Vijaya Bank excelled in basketball, kabaddi and cricket.

Bank of Baroda wants to imbibe that sporting culture. To preserve the legacy of Vijaya and Dena, it is also creating museums in Bengaluru and Mumbai, respectively, on the lines of its museum in Baroda.

These are some of the soft aspects of the merger of the 88-year-old Vijaya and 81-year-old Dena with 111-year-old Bank of Baroda. It was done on 1 April 2019. But the merger is not yet dusted as I write in May 2020.

Let us see how the merger was done.

On 16 September 2018, Bank of Baroda MD and CEO P.S. Jayakumar was in Radisson Blue Hotel in Goa for a two-day offsite business performance review meeting with the bank's regional heads, zonal heads and corporate financial services branch heads. He got a call from the Ministry of Finance about a meeting scheduled at the DFS the next day. He was not told the agenda.

Jayakumar took an early morning flight to Delhi to attend that meeting. R.A. Sankara Narayanan, MD and CEO of Vijaya Bank, and Ramesh Singh, executive director of Dena Bank (the bank did not have an MD at that time), also attended the meeting.

All three were told that the Alternative Mechanism (AM) headed by Jaitley had, after consultations with RBI, decided that Bank of Baroda, Vijaya Bank and Dena Bank should consider a merger. The AM had replaced the various GoMs or groups of ministers model of the Congress-led UPA government.

The three banks were told to convene board meetings and send the proposal for amalgamation to the government, along with their boards' assessment and recommendations.

In the evening, Jaitley and Kumar of DFS addressed the press, announcing the decision of the AM. Jayakumar returned to the off-site in Goa the next day. From there, he shot off a letter to 55,000 Bank of Baroda employees. Mayank K. Mehta and Papia Sengupta, two of the executive directors, also signed that letter.

> Dear Fellow Barodians,
> You are aware about the announcement made by Government of India about the amalgamation of our bank, Vijaya Bank and Dena Bank.
>
> It is recognition of the Bank of Baroda's stronger balance sheet which enables us to play a lead role in consolidation. (The) Board of Directors of the Bank would meet shortly to consider the amalgamation which will be subject to applicable approvals.
>
> In the current state where banking industry is fragmented with 21 public sector banks having limited differentiation, sub-optimal scale of operations and unhealthy price competition for similar business, consolidation is inevitable.
>
> For us, the amalgamation will help in scaling up the size and increasing geographical reach. The combined entity will have leadership position in Gujarat and increased net work in South (particularly Karnataka) and Maharashtra. The increased customer base with ability to offer add-on services to customers of amalgamating banks will help combined entity to expand its range of services and ability to grow business.
>
> Each of the amalgamating bank has its strengths and niche relationships which can be pooled. We would leverage upon the same to build a stronger bank.
>
> We would also like to state that Barodians should not have any apprehension on the amalgamation as the service conditions will remain unaffected. The combined entity will

offer more and diverse opportunities to the employees since it would have a broader geographic footprint to operate.

It needs to be emphasised that the above event in no way should affect our pursuit towards business growth. The operating units should continue to focus on the growth of business as hitherto.

Further, our priority on journey of transformation to strengthen our systems and processes to make us more efficient, modern and contemporary would continue as also creating more value for all the stakeholders.

We are sure that all Barodians would make the amalgamation a success and contribute to make the amalgamated entity a premier and modern bank which is competitive in market place.

With greetings to all …

Business Plan in 48 Hours

The work for a merger had started much before the announcement even though Vijaya Bank and Dena Bank were not aware of it. This is why the business plan of the combined entity could be finalised in 48 hours.

In the first week itself, there were 80 meetings across India and a team drawn from all three banks addressed the staff. At least 100 town hall meetings were held with the employees of three banks and a fifth of them were addressed by the chiefs.

Bank of Baroda convened a board meeting on 29 September. The seven-hour meeting discussed each aspect of the merger threadbare before giving an in-principle approval. After the boards of the three banks cleared the proposal, the government approved it on 2 January 2019.

For fair valuation, the three balance sheets were scrutinised to check the provisions made for the retirement benefits of 85,000 employees, bad assets (already identified and/or hidden) and the uniformity of accounting policies.

This was to take care of anomalies. For instance, the same asset could have been good on one bank's book and bad on another; also, one bank could have made provision for non-fund based exposure while another had not. At least ₹6,000 crore extra capital was needed. The government stepped in, first with ₹5,042 crore and followed it up with ₹7,000 crore.

There was a share swap. Dena shareholders received 110 shares of Bank of Baroda for every 1,000 shares they held; Vijaya shareholders received 402 shares for every 1,000 shares. Since the Bank of Baroda share has a face value of ₹2 and the other two, ₹10 each, the discount to face value was steep. But the swap ratios largely reflected the prices of the shares of the three banks in the stock market.

The government finalises the scheme of such mergers in consultation with the RBI. Valuers are appointed to arrive at the swap ratio for such mergers but the minority shareholders have no voice.

This is because mergers of nationalised banks happen under Section 9(2)(C) of The Banking Companies (Acquisition and Transfer of Undertakings) Act, loosely called the Bank Nationalisation Act. The Act, which came into existence in 1970, decades before the banks were listed, has no provision for minority shareholders. However, grievance redressal committees are being set up for every merger to listen to minority shareholders.

The Execution

Apart from the town hall meetings, there was the 'pulse check' exercise. This was a survey of the employees' reaction to the merger, done anonymously. It was devised by the management consulting firm Boston Consulting Group (BCG). The idea was to gauge the employee happiness quotient and note any suggestions on the merger.

'Buddy branches' were created. Following the hub-and-spoke model, one Bank of Baroda branch was linked to two branches of Vijaya and Dena – one each from both banks, or even two from one bank, depending on the locations – to create camaraderie and help the others understand Bank of Baroda's business culture.

This was supplemented by 'utsuk' training. At the Bank of Baroda training centres, its policies and processes were drilled into Vijaya and Dena employees. Until the merger was formally consummated, the three CEOs were jointly signing emails to all employees.

The finance minister did not mention which would be the anchor bank in the merger. It was a sensitive issue as, given a choice, no bank would like to surrender its identity. A series of discussions were held but there was no consensus if there would be an anchor bank, or a separate legal entity should be created with a new name.

So, the three banks decided to focus on the process of the merger, leaving nomenclature up to the majority shareholder. The government designated Bank of Baroda as the transferee bank (the surviving entity) and other two banks transferor banks (amalgamating entities). The AM gave 'in-principle' approval to the amalgamation on 20 December 2018.

Even though they no longer possess much clout, the trade unions were active in opposition to the merger. They filed three writ petitions – two in the Delhi High Court and one in the Rajasthan High Court – against the government, challenging the constitutional validity of the amalgamation and seeking a stay.

Bank of Baroda quickly moved the Supreme Court to club all three petitions. On 28 March 2019, just 72 hours before the scheduled birth of the new entity, the Supreme Court rejected the application of the trade unions.

Handling the human resources was a big challenge. Out of the total of 85,000 employees of three banks, only 240 left the merged entity.

The Scheme of Amalgamation notified by the government on 2 January 2019 directed the Bank of Baroda board, in consultation with the RBI, to determine the placement of the employees of other two banks and their seniority vis-à-vis the employees of Bank of Baroda. Of the 15 chief general managers in the merged entity, three each were chosen from Dena and Vijaya.

Roughly 10 per cent of the 9,500 branches of the new Bank of Baroda have been relocated or merged to avoid overlaps. These were logistics issues. For insights and inputs, many experts were engaged at the board and its various committees; they were not directors but attended such meetings by invitation.

The toughest part in any bank merger is technology. While all three have been using Finacle, a core banking product of Infosys Ltd, Bank of Baroda has Finacle 10 while Vijaya and Dena have been using Finacle 7, that too different versions, customised for each bank.

In the first stage, inter-operability had to be developed for three different tech platforms for six basic banking services – cash withdrawal, deposit, transfer of funds, balance enquiry, mini statement and stop payment instructions.

The corporate business of Dena and Vijaya, about 47 per cent of their loan books, was shifted to the Bank of Baroda platform. After that, the merged entity started following a 'branch in branch' concept. In 1,000 Vijaya and Dena branches, chosen on the basis of the volume of business, there was a Bank of Baroda desk to create all new businesses on its platform.

What are the benefits of the merger? In five states – Rajasthan, Uttar Pradesh, Karnataka, Gujarat and Maharashtra – Bank of Baroda's market share in business has risen 10 per cent. By financial year 2023–24, at least ₹9,500 crore will be generated through the sale of non-productive real estate, besides other benefits arising out of business synergies. The low-cost CASA as a portion of overall deposits has been rising, so has been the provision coverage ratio, while the cost to income ratio is reducing.

The merger took effect on 1 April 2019. That same day, the bank issued a press release and held press conferences in 82 cities and towns across India.

The Spillovers

Of course, the entire process could not be completed on that day. There have been many spillovers.

For instance, the payments systems were integrated a year later, on 31 March 2020. This is a complex process that involved integration/aggregation of multiple payment systems as well as changes in customer initiating channels – CTS, RTGS, NEFT, IMPS, UPI, BBPS, ECS, NACH - MMS, AEPS & BHIM Aadhaar, ATM Switch, ATM DCMS, SWIFT, PFMS, Internet banking and Mobile banking. Each payment system application involved multiple vendors.

The integration of three banks' systems started in March 2020 and this could be completed within a year. Technology integration is always a complex exercise. Bank of Baroda had migrated to Finacle 10 version fairly recently – in August 2017.

Different technology platforms make it difficult for the bank to identify bad assets and understand the whole picture. While NPAs of more than ₹30 crore have been migrated to Bank of Baroda's Finacle 10 system, the bad accounts of less than ₹30 crore each continue to be on the Finacle 7 platform of other two banks. This means, until the CBS (core banking solution) of three banks is integrated, the smaller NPAs would need to be counted manually.

Similarly, until all processes are streamlined and IT systems integrated, the three banks will continue to maintain three different current accounts with the RBI. This will last until September 2020 at least and it may take longer, given the disruption of the pandemic. Through their current accounts, the banks settle various transactions, including treasury and government businesses.

The merged entity will be able to have a cohesive approach vis-à-vis cyber security and accounting only after the IT platform is fully integrated. Under the law to prevent money laundering, each bank is required to submit a cash transaction report (CTR) for movements of ₹10 lakh and above in an account, and a suspicious transaction report (STR) of all accounts to the Financial Intelligence Unit of the Government of India (FIU-IND).

At the time of writing, a consolidated report was being created based on alerts generated from three different anti-money laundering (AML) systems. After the IT integration, there will be one report.

Similarly, the accounting policies of three banks were harmonised in April 2019 but the systems can be made uniform only after the IT integration.

The First to Bite the Bullet

SBI was the first PSB to bite the bullet by merging five of its associate banks with itself. This list included the State Bank of Bikaner & Jaipur, State Bank of Mysore, State Bank of Travancore, State Bank of Patiala and State Bank of Hyderabad. These were all banks set up by various princely states. SBI had already merged the State Bank of Indore with itself in 2010 and before that, in 2008, it had merged the State Bank of Saurashtra.

Two of the five associate banks – namely, State Bank of Patiala and State Bank of Hyderabad – were not listed. Among the listed associates, SBI held a 75 per cent stake in State Bank of Bikaner & Jaipur, 90 per cent in State Bank of Mysore and 79 per cent in State Bank of Travancore.

The last lap of the merger with five associate banks took effect in April 2017. In this round, the Bharatiya Mahila Bank – a ₹1,000 crore misadventure launched by the UPA government – was also merged with SBI.

At its launch in Mumbai on 19 November 2013 – the 96th birth anniversary of former prime minister Indira Gandhi – Finance Minister P. Chidambaram had said the Bharatiya Mahila Bank would break even in three to five years.

However, nowhere in the world has a bank for women become successful and the Indian experiment was no exception. The SBI Chairman Arundhati Bhattacharya got a one-year extension, the first in the bank's history, to oversee these mergers.

Immediately after she took over in October 2013, Bhattacharya had suggested consolidation of the associate banks. The logic was fairly simple: While the parent was responsible for making sure that the associate banks are adequately capitalised, they were competing with each other, wasting resources.

Sometime in October 2016, after Jaitley checked with her

whether this could be done at one go, Bhattacharya took up the challenge. Seven groups were formed, led by an executive from each bank (five associate banks, Bharatiya Mahila Bank and SBI) for different areas of work such as accounting, IT, HR, balance sheets, assets, communications and customers' service. Dinesh Kumar Khara, the current chairman of SBI (then MD) coordinated the exercise. The merger was notified by the government in May 2016 and took effect from April 2017.

SBI and the associates were using different versions of the technology platform of TCS Ltd, BaNCS, but FIS was the technology vendor for Bharatiya Mahila Bank. Some 214 applications needed to be changed to make these uniform. There were 62 mock runs for the tech platform before the unified platform was made operational.

Even though it was a 'family affair', it was by no means an easy task. At any given point, the staff grievances portal, set up for the merger, had to process around 200 queries.

The sudden rise in the NPAs in the merged SBI indicates how poorly the associates were run. In March 2015, SBI's gross NPAs were 4.25 per cent of its advances and net NPAs, 2.12 per cent. These rose to 6.5 per cent and 3.81 per cent, respectively in 2016. In 2017, they rose further – 6.9 per cent gross NPAs and 3.71 per cent net NPAs. Following the merger and RBI's AQR, the figures zoomed in 2018 to 10.91 per cent gross NPAs and 5.73 per cent net NPAs.

The merger of Dena Bank and Vijaya Bank with Bank of Baroda could be a template for the next four mergers. But the hurdles faced in both, the Bank of Baroda merger and the SBI merger indicates this will not, by any means, be an easy task.

The two most difficult aspects of any bank merger are HR and technology. When SBI associates were merged with SBI, the general managers of the associates became deputy general managers in SBI – a rank below, in sync with the hierarchy in the State Bank family. But the executives of PSBs are all on a par. This means, the general manager of a relatively smaller bank holds on to the position in the merged entity, which is many times bigger. This is the case even if the person lacks experience or expertise.

Technology is even trickier. Both Union Bank of India and Corporation Bank use Finacle 10 but they are of different versions, while Andhra Bank uses Finacle 7. Similarly, PNB's technology platform is Finacle 10, but both United Bank of India and Oriental Bank of Commerce use Finacle 7. It will take years to synchronise them. TCS is the technology partner for both Indian Bank and Allahabad Bank and IBM for Canara Bank and Syndicate Bank.

The Warriors of the Government

A common theme for all the mergers is that the CEOs of the banks involved were not in the know, in most cases. For the set of four mergers to create NextGen banks, the DFS had been collecting data from all banks for over a year but none of the senior management at the banks had any clue what would be the combination and who the anchor banks would be.

On the day Sitharaman announced the mergers, the MDs of the ten banks and a few more were called to Delhi for a briefing just ahead of the finance minister's press conference.

The CEOs of a few banks that were not due to be merged were also called in to create a smokescreen and thus, not let people know the exact contours of the mergers until the announcement. This is because the banks are listed and merger is price-sensitive information. Immediately after the announcement, the senior management had to face the media and they did so with aplomb, as warriors for the government.

The RBI and the government had been talking 'consolidation' for years. In fact, around the time then Finance Minister Pranab Mukherjee announced the opening up of the sector for more private banks in his 2010 budget, RBI Governor D. Subbarao was pushing for consolidation.

The sector was opened and applications were sought to set up new banks. India was still hugely unbanked at the time, with only one-third of the adult population having access to formal banking services.

Since then, two new universal banks and ten small finance banks have come up. There are a few payments banks too, on the turf. Also, the Pradhan Mantri Jan Dhan Yojana (PMJDY) – a national mission on financial inclusion – has opened some 40.41 crore new bank accounts (as on 26 August 2020).

The success of the PMJDY is probably one of the reasons for the focus on consolidation – we do not need too many banks since a large proportion of India's population is already under the banking umbrella. The emphasis can now be on creating stronger banks to support the investment needs of corporations and economic growth.

The question is: How does one go about this?

This leads to other questions like the following: Should relatively stronger banks take over weak banks? Can some of the weak banks in different geographies be bundled up? Should uniform technology be the deciding factor?

History of Bank Failures

India has its history of bank failures, but that is in the distant past. In 1930, there were as many as 1,258 banks registered under the Indian Companies Act, including loan companies and the so-called 'nidhis'. These were in the business of borrowing and lending only among their members but they issued pass books and cheque books.

By 1947, the number of scheduled banks had fallen to 82. The partition of the country dealt a blow to banking and West Bengal bore the brunt. Of the 38 banks that failed in 1947, 17 were in West Bengal. By the 1960s, many more banks had gone belly up because of greed, corruption and lack of regulation.

No scheduled commercial bank has been allowed to fail since the economic liberalisation of 1991, although quite a few cooperative banks have fallen by the wayside. Each time cracks surfaced in a bank's balance sheet, RBI threw a protective ring around it and 'found' a suitor with the sole objective of protecting the interest of depositors and avoiding any systemic crisis that could be triggered by bank failure. The latest such instance is that of Yes Bank Ltd. (More on this in the chapter 'The Fallen Angels'.)

The Ball Starts Rolling

The second edition of the bankers' retreat, Gyan Sangam 2.0, was held in March 2016 at the State Bank Academy at Gurgaon. Jayakumar of Bank of Baroda, who headed a task force on restructuring and mergers in banking, made a presentation.

He described how most banking crises have been followed by a consolidation drive. Spain reduced the number of banks by 70 per cent, from 50 to 15 between 2009 and 2013 and Malaysia went for an even sharper reduction – by 80 per cent, from 54 to 10 in just two years, between 1998 and 2000 when bad loans rose to nearly 19 per cent. Between 1997 and 2004, Indonesia also opted for large-scale rationalisation of private banks – from 144 to 74 – and the Bank Mandiri was created by merging four state-owned banks.

The task force said the small banks had two choices. These could either merge with big banks or become niche banks; they could not ape the large banks. The merger was actually imperative given limited differentiation in portfolios across PSBs, leading to price-competition. Besides, the small PSBs had not identified specific niche areas where they could develop expertise. This had also been discussed in the previous Gyan Sangam in 2015.

The MDs and executive directors of eight other banks; external experts such as Leo Puri, MD of UTI Mutual Fund, and Bahram N. Vakil, Senior Partner, AZB & Partners, were among members of the task force.

That started the ball rolling.

The task was completed on 4 March 2020 when the latest round of mergers got the Cabinet's nod.

In this set of ten banks, Union Bank has the most chequered history.

The Union Bank Story

Arun Tiwari, MD of Union Bank of India, who headed a work

group on risk management, at the Gyan Sangam 2.0, sent a presentation to NITI Aayog CEO, Amitabh Kant, suggesting a merger between two Mumbai-based banks – Union Bank of India and Bank of Baroda.

One of the key advantages was their uniform technology platform – both used Finacle 7. The work on the merger started with V.S. Narang, a general manager of Bank of Baroda, camping at his bank's Ballad Estate, Fort, Mumbai office, coordinating the project, in which Union Bank was codenamed 'Zen'.

Tiwari retired in June 2017. His last board meeting passed a resolution on exploring merger with another bank, without naming Bank of Baroda.

When Rajkiran G. Rai, an executive director of Oriental Bank of Commerce, took over as MD of Union Bank in July 2017, he arrived with a mandate of merger from the finance ministry even though informally the work on the merger had already begun in March.

Rai took over in July but his appointment was announced two months ahead of the end of Tiwari's term. Rai used this time to sift through the P&L data of Union Bank at his Oriental Bank of Commerce office at Harsha Bhavan in Connaught Place, preparing himself for the next big job.

Unlike most other PSBs, Union Bank has never posted a loss. It had always been in profit. It could do so only by being very miserly in making provisions for bad loans.

The bank needed to make hefty provisions to actually clean up its balance sheet but where would the money come from? Rai spent most of his first month in the new assignment to crunch the data and create a vision document for Union Bank. On 29 July, he made a two-hour presentation to the top 100 executives of the bank at Delhi's JW Marriot Hotel, holding a mirror to them.

The gist of the presentation was: Union Bank had not provided as much as it should have for bad loans. It would need around ₹25,000 crore for provisioning. From its operating profit, it could plough back about ₹15,000 crore but the rest would need to come in the form of capital infusions.

Until June 2017, Union Bank kept on posting net profit, quarter after quarter. But after Rai took over, its net losses over the next three quarters were ₹1,530.72 crore, ₹1,249.85 crore and ₹2,583.38 crore, respectively, as Rai decided to clean up the balance sheet by setting aside money for bad loans.

After posting small profits for three quarters, again in March 2019 it announced a loss of ₹3,369.23 crore and followed up with another loss of ₹1,193.61 crore in September 2019. Its gross NPAs, which were 12.63 per cent of loans in June 2017, rose to 16 per cent over the next year, and net NPAs, from 7.47 per cent to 8.7 per cent during this period.

The merger idea cropped up when Tiwari was on his way out. Bank of Baroda's Jayakumar, who was a new entrant in public sector banking, was keen to push it forward. A former Citibanker and CEO of VBHC Value Homes, Jayakumar took over as Bank of Baroda boss in October 2015. He was one of the first two recruits inducted from outside the public sector banking industry. (The second executive, Rakesh Sharma [who now heads IDBI Bank], was picked up from Lakshmi Vilas Bank Ltd to head Canara Bank, but he was originally from SBI and had just a 18-month stint at the private bank.)

Rai took his executive director Atul Kumar Goyal (later MD of UCO Bank) and a general manager, Nitesh Rajan, into his confidence and tasked them to do the homework for the merger. Many rounds of discussion later, both Rai and Jayakumar understood the banks were not prepared for the merger.

In August 2017, Bank of Baroda wrote to Anjuly Chib Duggal, the financial services secretary, detailing the benefits and challenges of the merger. While the merged entity would become the second largest bank in the country by assets and have a large base of low-cost deposits, the challenges outweighed the benefits.

Stating that 'research typically reveals that only 30 per cent of mergers become successful and result in realisation of the estimated synergies and benefits,' the note highlighted capital constraints as the biggest challenge.

It said that internal estimates of 'Zen' put the provision requirements for bad assets for fiscal year 2018 at ₹9,500 crore and asked for a capital infusion of at least ₹3,500 crore by the government. That may have put a spoke in the government's wheel.

Merger Always on Union Bank's Plate

A merger has all along been on the plate of Union Bank of India. The media was already talking about the possibility of its merger with Bank of India in 2005. If that had happened, it would have created India's second largest commercial bank after the SBI. It was to be consummated in April 2005 but the plan had started two years before.

Finance Minister P. Chidambaram had flagged off the issue of banking sector consolidation during the IBA's annual general meeting in August 2004.

Even before that, in 2003, Union Bank hit upon the idea of a possible merger. V. Leeladhar was its chairman then and M. Venugopalan was the executive director. Both were on the same page and once Venugopalan moved to head Bank of India, they started discussing it with all seriousness.

Janmejaya Sinha, then India MD of global management consulting firm BCG, got involved and a committee was set up to look into all possible aspects of the merger. Again, the uniform technology platform was a big advantage. Both banks were operating on Finacle CBS of Infosys.

On 22 July 2004, Leeladhar even made a presentation to Chidambaram. He was carrying four slides to sum up the discussion – FM against it, FM has low interest in it, FM is interested but not engaged, and FM is interested and engaged.

Chidambaram picked the fourth one.

BCG was not officially engaged on the merger. It was supposedly working with Bank of India on its business process engineering, and its mandate with Union Bank was to make different products more profitable. Under the guise of these assignments, BCG was quietly working on the merger.

The merged entity would have an asset base of at least ₹1.43-lakh crore and emerge as the second largest commercial bank in the country, overtaking ICICI Bank. It would have a network of 4,582 branches and over 68,000 employees.

According to the plan, around 200 branches of the new entity were to be closed while 500 new ones to be opened to tap new businesses, taking the total number of branches to 4,882, while leading to an annual saving of ₹300 crore for the new entity.

Leeladhar left the bank reluctantly to become a deputy governor at the RBI in September 2004, because he thought pushing the merger through was a much bigger assignment than becoming a central banker. After he left, it was Ratnakar Hegde, the executive director, who was running the Union Bank. Venugopalan retried as Bank of India boss on 31 March 2005. (After this stint, he headed Federal Bank Ltd.)

The minutest details of the merger were overseen and finalised by Vinod Rai, then the additional secretary in the finance ministry's banking division. Union Bank of India's emblem, the sun, was to give away to Bank of India's star.

All these were discussed at the board meetings of both banks. But the merger did not happen because of the fierce opposition put up by A.B. Bardhan, a trade union leader and former general secretary of the Communist Party of India, which supported the UPA-led government, running the country at the time.

The Root

The idea of bank mergers was mooted earlier by the second Narasimham Committee on banking reforms, which was set up in December 1997 by the United Front government to outline a blueprint for the next phase of financial sector reforms.

Apart from Narasimham, a former RBI governor, the nine-member committee included former SBI chairman Dipankar Basu, HDFC Chairman Deepak Parekh, National Bank for Agriculture and Rural Development (NABARD) Chairman P. Kotiah, HCL Corporation Chairman Shiv Nadar, EID Parry Chairman and

MD M.V. Subbiah, Hero Cycles Executive Director Sunil Munjal, former RBI deputy governor S.S. Tarapore, and former economic affairs secretary C.M. Vasudev.

The panel recommended the merger of strong PSBs and selective closure of the weak ones. Suggesting a radical recast of the banking structure, the panel opposed bail-out mergers, where a strong bank takes over a weak one, as that could mean an adverse impact on the asset quality of the stronger bank.

It also said the mergers must be meaningful rather than a mere arithmetical merger of balance sheets and staff. Any merger must be driven by business needs and have a force multiplier effect, the report said, castigating the earlier merger of the ailing New Bank of India with the profit-making PNB.

The blueprint for the recast of the banking structure envisaged the creation of a three-tier banking structure – two or three large international banks, 8-10 national level banks and a large number of local area banks.

The committee favoured the merger of strong banks and suggested that the rehabilitation of weak banks must be dealt with separately. It even provided a working definition of a weak bank as one that has accumulated losses and net NPAs that exceed its capital. In respect of PSU banks, a weak bank is one whose operating results minus the income from recapitalisation bonds reveals losses for three consecutive years.

That was the vision of the Narasimham Committee. What is unfolding now is not what the panel had wanted.

Will consolidation end up making the relatively stronger banks weak, defeating the purpose?

Could a better option be converting the weakest banks into so-called narrow banks?

These are questions many analysts have raised. Narrow banks don't lend but they do invest in government bonds. They can also focus on the recovery of bad loans. The treasury income and interest on performing loans will help narrow banks pay interest to existing depositors and salary to employees even if they are not allowed to take fresh deposits. They can also sell loan assets and deposits to other banks.

Once all deposits are redeemed and loans repaid/recovered/sold, these will turn into shell companies. At this stage, their branches and other physical assets could be auctioned to other public sector, private and foreign banks, making the last rites painless and profitable for the owners.

The analysts' community is also unsure about how serious the government is about consolidation. Consider the facts. Jayakumar, who was spearheading Bank of Baroda, got a one-year extension that ended on 12 October 2019. The BBB, the appointment agency, chose his successor on 12 November 2019 and the new chief finally joined on 20 January 2020. For more than three months, nothing was moving at Bank of Baroda because the three executive directors running the show were from Dena, Vijaya and Allahabad Bank. Is this the way to treat such an experiment?

What Next?

After the mergers, India will have 12 PSBs, down from 27 in 2017. The six PSBs that will remain independent are Bank of India, Central Bank of India, Indian Overseas Bank, UCO Bank, Bank of Maharashtra and Punjab & Sind Bank.

Are these in the pink of health?

Both Indian Overseas Bank and UCO Bank returned to profitability in the March 2020 quarter after a long streak of losses. Since September 2015, when the RBI imposed the AQR, Indian Overseas Bank has made losses for 18 quarters in a row with overall accumulated losses of ₹25,037 crore. UCO Bank got into the red zone, one quarter later, in December 2015. From then until December 2019, in 17 quarters, its accumulated losses have hit ₹16,274 crore.

During this period, the Bank of India's accumulated loss has been ₹16,121 crore, followed by Central Bank (₹13,675 crore) and Bank of Maharashtra (₹7,091 crore).

Punjab & Sind Bank has the smallest accumulated losses which amount to a nevertheless substantial ₹1,743 crore. It also had the lowest gross NPAs in December 2019 quarter (13.58 per cent) while the others' gross NPAs were between 16.3 per cent (Bank of India) and 19.99 per cent (Central Bank). Their net NPAs, after provision, varied between 5.46 per cent (Bank of Maharashtra) and 9.26 per cent (Central Bank) of their loan books. All of them have seen higher levels of bad assets in the recent past.

What should be done with these banks? Should four of them be converted into niche, regional banks while Mumbai-based Bank of India and Central Bank, which have larger balance sheets, maintain their current avatar? Can these fend for themselves without the government's regular largesse? If not, should a few of them be converted into private banks, or even allowed to die?

In the past five years between 2016 and 2020, the government has pumped in ₹1.06-lakh crore into this pack. Bank of India got the maximum ₹35,037 crore, followed by Indian Overseas Bank (₹23,534 crore), UCO Bank (₹20,045 crore) and Central Bank of India (₹17,035 crore). Bank of Maharashtra got ₹8,570 crore and the smallest of them, Punjab & Sind Bank, ₹1,572 crore.

The government as the majority owner needs to find answers to these questions, even as the world closely watches the unique experiment in India's banking industry.

Consolidation reduces the number of banks but not the share of government ownership in banking. Should the government be in the business of banking in such a big way? We examined this question in the chapter 'What Ails the Public Sector Banks?'

■ ■ ■

PART III

EVERYTHING YOU WANT TO KNOW BUT ARE AFRAID TO ASK

This section turns a spotlight on the dark underbelly of Indian banking with all its stories of fraud, poor governance, greed and fear.

'Sensational' is just a bald statement of fact when it comes to describing the way Gokulnath Shetty, a deputy manager in a PNB branch, helped to pull off a fraud of nearly $2 billion. Shetty received just one promotion in his 36-year career, and spent the last seven years at the branch where the fraud took place. He was an unassuming character who commuted by local train and autorickshaw even as he was helping to rake in huge sums by exploiting a flaw in the system.

Then, there is the story of Kingfisher Airlines. The auditors and the regulator emerge in poor light in that sorry episode.

Bankers can and do take wrong business decisions in good faith. But the investigative agencies proceed under the presumption of criminality. This feeds into an apparently endless public craving for vengeance, however misdirected that might be. Social media adds fuel to the fire. Chargesheets are filed; bankers are arrested; even sent to jail. In another case, a PSB's CEO was sacked just eight minutes before her scheduled retirement.

A few retired bank executives spent months at Mumbai's Arthur Road Jail in a barrack for undertrials, sleeping on threadbare rugs laid out on concrete floors and using primitive amenities. They endured this until a court decided whether they (like countless others before and since) were guilty or innocent.

This section also narrates the story of Rana Kapoor, the promoter and CEO of Yes Bank, and Chanda Kochhar, a career ICICI Banker and a Padma award winner. The details of those stories are very different but the moral is the same: Beware of hubris. If you believe you are invincible, the comeuppance can be merciless, whether it is merited or otherwise.

The fate of those two erstwhile stars also rang the death knell for the personality cult in banking. Many staunch believers in bank privatisation also began changing their minds after revelations about the style of functioning in these two large, listed private sector banks and the way their boards functioned.

8

The F Word in Indian Banking

As every Indian channel-surfer knows, a men's deodorant brand called Fogg has carpet-bombed TV with ads. The settings are varied. One commercial is shot in a grocery store, another in a hospital, a third in a café and there is even one filmed on the India–Pakistan border.

But the dialogue between two characters remains unchanged:

'Kya chal raha hai?' (What's new?)

'Fogg chal raha hai.' (Fogg is new.)

Replace the F word above – just change 'Fogg' to 'fraud'. This conversation would then accurately sum up the state of Indian banking and finance.

Indeed, fraud seems to be part of a historical tradition. In his political treatise, the *Arthashastra*, the great fourth-century BC economist and statesman, Chanakya (aka Kautilya), noted that detecting corruption among revenue officials is as hard as knowing when a fish is drinking water.

The same story holds when it comes to detecting fraud among bankers. Given an industry where money is the raw material, it is easy and tempting to misuse official positions for self-enrichment.

Of course, the levels of corruption in some other professions including law enforcement, income tax and revenue authorities and even bureaucracy may be as much as is prevalent among bankers, if not more.

When it comes to banking frauds, we need to differentiate between frauds committed on banks, where banks and/or bankers are the victims, and frauds where bankers themselves are complicit. The Nirav Modi case would fall in the latter category, while the Kingfisher case can perhaps be categorised as a fraud committed by the borrower on the bankers, though even that is not quite clear at this stage.

In the first week of November 2019, the CBI searched around 200 locations across 16 Indian states and Union Territories. The CBI deployed at least a thousand officers, making it one of the largest coordinated searches, a PTI report said. This was after registering 42 cases, involving at least ₹7,000 crore worth of fraudulent transactions. In at least four of these cases, the funds involved exceeded ₹1,000 crore.

The Association of Certified Fraud Examiners, the world's largest anti-fraud organisation, which offers training to detect frauds, observed Fraud Week between 17 and 23 November 2019, to create anti-fraud awareness.

For the record, in financial year 2018–19, government agencies detected 6,801 cases of fraud involving a total of ₹71,543 crore. This was more than the Union government was prepared to spend on the proposed merger of telecom majors Bharat Sanchar Nigam Ltd and Mahanagar Telephone Nigam Ltd, or the ₹70,000 crore recapitalisation package for PSBs. In value terms, 90.2 per cent of these frauds involved PSBs. In terms of the number of cases, the share of PSBs was 55.4 per cent.

The value of money involved in banking-related frauds rose more than two and half times to ₹1.9-lakh crore in financial year 2019–20. In terms of number of fraud cases, however, the jump was a modest 28 per cent to nearly 8,700 cases from 7,000.

The number of cases in 2018–19 was 14.9 per cent more than that in the previous year but in value terms, 2019's tally was 73.7

per cent higher. About 86 per cent of these cases were so called 'large value corporate frauds' worth over ₹50 crore each.

It is clear that incidences of frauds have been rising.

For instance, in financial year 2015, banks detected 4,639 frauds, involving a total of ₹19,455 crore, or almost double that in the previous year (₹10,170 crore). The trend continued the next year with 4,693 cases for ₹18,699 crore. In 2017, the comparable figures were 5,076 cases and ₹23,934 crore. This rose to 5,916 cases and ₹41,167 crore in 2018; 6,801 cases and ₹71,543 crore in 2019; and 8,700 cases and ₹1.9-lakh crore in 2020.

These figures refer to the frauds of at least ₹1 lakh. They are dynamic as banks keep on revising them. Banks do not always lose all the money involved in frauds; recovery depends on at what stage a particular fraud comes to light and the profile of the fraudsters.

Vintage Frauds

Not all the frauds detected in each year happened in that particular year. Like so many other financial sector occurrences, there has been a lag effect. The average fraud tends to be detected two years after it is committed. The RBI estimates that large frauds, worth over ₹100 crore each, run for an average of 54 months before being detected.

One of the large frauds involved designer jeweller Modi, and his uncle Mehul Choksi, who siphoned off ₹13,000 crore with the help of Gokulnath Shetty, a deputy manager of PNB's foreign exchange department at the Brady House branch in Fort, Mumbai. The PNB fraud ran for at least 84 months and it would have probably continued undetected had it not been for a 'breach' in the system when a new officer came in to replace Shetty.

The RBI's Financial Stability Report of December 2019, a biannual health check of the banking sector, mentioned 4,412 cases of fraud worth little over ₹1.13-lakh crore in the first half of the year compared with 6,801 cases adding up to ₹71,543 crore in 2018–19. About 97 per cent of the frauds reported, in value terms, occurred in previous financial years. The PSBs' were damaged to the tune of ₹95,748 crore.

For the first time, the June 2017 Financial Stability Report spoke about the growing volume and value of frauds in the banking sector and described it as 'one of the emerging risks to the financial sector'. It highlighted the 'general credit governance issues' and referred to serious gaps in credit underwriting, alongside the lack of continuous monitoring of cash flows and cash profits, the diversion of funds and double financing.

Two years later, the June 2019 Financial Stability Report blamed delayed detection for the rise in frauds and pointed out that 90.6 per cent of the frauds reported in financial year 2018–19 were related to cases that happened between 2000 and 2018.

In December 2018, the RBI flagged frauds as the 'most serious concern' in managing risk in the Indian banking system. The 72 per cent jump in the value of frauds in 2017–18 was largely on account of the ₹13,000 crore PNB scam, involving the nephew–uncle duo of Modi and Choksi, in the diamond business. Since the money involved was dollar-denominated, the size of the fraud depends on the value of the rupee vis-à-vis the dollar, at any given point of time.

It Takes Just One

Just one employee supposedly enabled the biggest fraud in India's banking history and almost toppled one of India's biggest banks. And that man was a relatively lowly deputy manager.

Gokulnath Shetty was a deputy manager in the foreign exchange department of PNB's Brady House branch in Fort, Mumbai, while the Nirav Modi fraud was up and running. The cabin of the general manager of the branch is on the ground floor while the forex department is located on the mezzanine floor and reached by a flight of stairs near the loan desk.

To empty the cash vault of a bank, two persons have to collude. In most public sector branches in India, the strong-room keys are with the cash officer and the accountant; if they collude, they can empty the vault.

But to carry out a fraud and topple a bank in Nirav Modi style, a much larger number need to conspire because this is a complex set of cross-border transactions with many checks and balances.

Banks keep what is known as a Nostro account in foreign currency in another bank overseas for use of foreign exchange and trade transactions.

Let us say Bank A in India needs to transfer money to another bank, Bank B, where the exporter who has shipped goods to Bank A's customer in India (the importer) keeps the Nostro account. The transfer of money happens through a sequence of carefully verified messages. The international banking system uses SWIFT, a messaging network run by the Society for Worldwide Interbank Financial Telecommunications. The SWIFT network is supposed to securely transmit information and instructions for all financial transactions through a standardised system of codes.

At least four persons are involved in bank A when making a SWIFT transaction. The 'maker' keys a message into the SWIFT system, the 'checker' checks it and, at the third stage, the verifier transmits it after she is convinced of its genuineness. So these three – the maker, checker and verifier, or authoriser of SWIFT messages – all definitely need to be involved in the fraud.

But these three are not enough. After the SWIFT message is sent to Bank B for a financial transaction, it transfers money to the Nostro account overseas. A SWIFT message is then sent back to Bank A in India confirming the creation of the loan and transfer to the Nostro account.

The person who receives this message is not supposed to be any of the first three – maker, checker or verifier. The message comes to a secured room and is supposedly printed on a separate printer; everybody does not have access to this secured room.

The credit in the Nostro account (payment made by the overseas Bank B) and the subsequent debit (for making payment to the overseas exporter) are then checked, tallying all entries.

This is what is called Nostro reconciliation, and it is done by a separate group. This group is not involved in the process of such transactions but it has responsibility for oversight.

All these individuals – maker, checker, verifier, 'printer', 'reconciliatory person' – must be involved to enable a fraud involving SWIFT transactions. Or else, the bank has bypassed all the checks and balances designed to prevent fraud.

This was the largest fraud in Indian banking history. It cost $1.77 billion and it ran for over seven years. During that period, Shetty would have had to play the role of all four – maker, checker, verifier and receiver of messages – confirming the creation of loans.

Could Shetty really have been the only banker to be involved in this gigantic fraud? Was there no control system in what was then India's second-largest government-owned bank by assets? Or, was it a failure at the operational level? How many executives were involved in perpetrating the fraud for more than seven years?

The CBI chargesheet was filed on 14 May 2018, by Police Superintendent Sushil Prasad Singh, who was the chief investigating officer of the CBI's Bank Security and Frauds Cell in Mumbai. It named 12 bankers as well as Nirav Modi, his brother Neeshal Modi (a citizen of Belgium) and others of his group companies. All the bank officers named had worked at the Brady House branch at various points in time.

The chargesheet also named PNB's MD and CEO and two executive directors. (More on this in the chapter 'Fear Psychosis'.)

The allegedly accused bankers:

- Shetty was a deputy manager of the Brady House Mid Corporate Branch. He retired in May 2017 after 36 years of service. He received only one promotion in his career and worked in this branch for the last seven years. Born in May 1957 and a resident of Goregaon, a western suburb of Mumbai, Shetty hails from Udupi in Karnataka. A native Kannada speaker, Shetty grew up in Mangalore and came to Mumbai for studies.
- Manoj Hanumant Kharat, a clerk who used to operate as the so-called single-window at Brady House Mid Corporate Branch, clearing cheques and drafts and giving cash payments and receipts to the customers.

- Bansi Tiwari, chief manager, Brady House Mid Corporate Branch.
- Yashwant Trimbak Joshi, manager, Brady House Mid Corporate Branch.
- Praful Prakash Sawant, officer, Brady House Mid Corporate Branch.
- Rajesh Krishan Jindal, assistant general manager, Brady House Mid Corporate Branch. (At the time of filing the chargesheet, he was general manager, credit, at the PNB head office at Dwarka, New Delhi.)
- Mohinder Kumar Sharma, chief manager and internal auditor, Brady House Mid Corporate Branch.
- Bishnubrata Mishra, who retired as the internal chief auditor, Brady House Mid Corporate Branch.
- Nehal Ahad, general manager, PNB.

The chargesheet was filed under Section 120-B of the Indian Penal Code read with Sections 420 and 409 of the same code, and Section 13(2) read with Section 13(1)(C) and (D) of the Prevention of Corruption Act. These sections refer to criminal conspiracy, cheating, criminal breach of trust as a banker and abuse of power by a public servant, among others.

Stock Market Filings

What happened?

On 5 February 2018, PNB, a listed PSB, informed India's stock exchanges of a ₹280-crore fraud. The bank followed up on 14 February, informing the stock exchanges once again that it had discovered fraudulent transactions, dating back to 2011, 'for the benefit of a few select account holders'.

The note did not name designer jeweller Modi, but media learnt that some of the bank's employees at a Mumbai branch allegedly issued letters of undertakings, or LoUs, to Modi's companies, which enabled them to raise money from international branches of other Indian banks in the form of buyer's credit.

The PNB note said, 'These transactions are contingent in nature and liability arising out of these on the bank shall be decided based on the law and genuineness of underlying transactions.' The money involved is '$1,771.69 million'.

The very next day, in yet another detailed clarification to the stock exchanges, the bank said that when Modi's employees approached the Mumbai branch on 16 January 2018 seeking an LoU, the bank asked for 100 per cent cash margin; but they refused to pay any margin, claiming the group had been enjoying the facility for years without any cash margin. That led to the discovery of the fraud – namely the issuances of LoUs through SWIFT without official sanction.

On 25 January, for the first time, a set of LoUs devolved, leading to a $44.2 million liability for PNB. Subsequently, more LoUs started devolving. Apart from Modi Group firms, the involvement of Gitanjali Group firms of Modi's uncle Choksi surfaced. Critically, their point-man Shetty had retired by then.

By 12 February, PNB discovered some ₹11,304.02 crore (at the exchange value of that time) of unauthorised issuances of LoUs and other trade finance instruments to the Modi firms, Gitanjali Group companies, and Chandri Paper and Allied Products Pvt. Ltd, which was owned by Aditya Ishwardas Rasiwasia and Ishwardas Agarwal. The third company is not related to Modi.

What is an LoU?

A letter of undertaking is an explicit undertaking offered by a bank to another bank on behalf of a customer who is importing goods from a company in another country. Backed by the LoU, the overseas bank gives buyer's credit to the importer.

The earlier avatar of LoU was the LoC, or a letter of comfort, which was issued by the importer's bank for a buyer's credit (to the extent of the value of the invoice for goods being imported). In the LoC regime, the importer was supposed to pay to the overseas bank and, in case of a default by the importer in paying the debt, the LoC-issuing bank would step in.

Unlike an LoC, the LoU is unambiguous about the issuing bank's responsibility. It is a direct exposure of the importer's bank to the overseas bank that is extending the buyer's credit.

Buyer's credit is a short-term credit available to a buyer (importer) from overseas lenders such as banks and other financial institutions for goods being imported. The overseas banks usually lend to the importer against an LoU issued by the importer's bank.

The bank that gives the LoU earns a fee, typically 0.20–0.25 per cent of the amount; the bank that gives the buyer's credit earns interest (Libor, or London Interbank Offered Rate plus a spread, depending on the customer profile); and the importer gets a cheap line of foreign credit.

The maturity of an LoU could be between 30 days and one year, depending on the working capital cycle – that is, the time taken for conversion of the imported material into finished goods and the realisation of funds after sales for the importer. For instance, a diamond merchant may need two-to-three months to cut, polish and re-export raw diamonds imported from South Africa, while an entity that imports crude palm oil from Malaysia may need much less time to process it into RBD palm oil.

In the RBI's lexicon, such facilities are short-term external commercial borrowing and these cannot be rolled over. The idea behind having such a scheme is to enable an importer to get low-cost foreign currency funds overseas, especially when they will realise income from exports to pay up. In banking parlance, the exporter who uses an LoU has a natural hedge against any depreciation in the value of the rupee via-a-vis the foreign currency (usually the US dollar).

Under the RBI guidelines, buyer's credit for import of platinum, palladium, rhodium and silver and rough, cut and polished diamonds, precious and semi-precious stones should not exceed 90 days from the date of shipment. This list, however, does not include pearls. Media reports suggest Modi was importing cultured pearls.

The Beginnings

Let us try to reconstruct the story of this massive fraud.

Nirav Modi wanted to import pearls and diamonds, design exquisite world-class jewellery and sell them. He needed money to buy pearls and diamonds. He did not want to opt for a rupee loan, and rightly so, as this is expensive and there is a foreign currency risk. He wanted foreign currency loans, which are cheaper. He had a natural hedge against currency fluctuations as he was earning in foreign currency by exporting jewellery.

So far, so good. The twist came when he decided to take bank loans without having any loan account and other attendant paraphernalia, such as sanctioned limits, collaterals, etc. To circumvent all this, he arranged a guarantee from PNB in the form of an LoU for the cheap short-term foreign currency loans which are meant for importers.

Ideally, the LoU-issuing bank asks for a margin, which could be as much as 100 per cent or more. Why would an importer agree to pay such a high margin? Typically this is kept with the LoU-issuing bank in the form of a fixed deposit, upon which the bank pays interest. The return from the fixed deposit is far higher than the interest paid on the foreign currency loan.

Simply put, this facility allows an importer to arbitrage high domestic deposit rates and low foreign credit rates and if there are export earnings, the currency risk is also covered. But for some reason, PNB did not ask for a margin. And, this is where we see a deviation from normal procedure. This gave birth to the $1.77 billion fraud that shook the Indian banking system in 2018.

MT 799

One morning in 2011, a SWIFT message (code: MT 799) was sent from PNB's Mumbai branch to some Indian banks abroad offering LoUs, committing to pay them principal plus interest on behalf of Modi companies. After checking with the originating bank branch, without batting an eyelid, a few Indian banks extended buyer's credit.

The money flowed into PNB's Nostro account. PNB debited the money by paying the exporter selling diamonds to Modi. Theoretically, Modi should have sold the polished diamonds and jewellery and paid back PNB on every due date for each LoU, and PNB would have paid back the banks overseas for their buyer's credit.

Had this been the case, it would have been a normal set of transactions and there would have been no fraud. What actually happened is that Modi never paid back PNB! He used the money for other purposes. Perhaps he created assets overseas, or played the stock market, or maybe even bought books from Amazon and just enjoyed a good life, partying, reading poetry and listening to music.

How could he and others just continue to do this for seven long years? Well, instead of repaying, he may have asked PNB (read Shetty) to open another LoU, which could cover the principal, plus interest of the previous LoU. Backed by new LoUs, he would get fresh and higher buyer's credit, which would enable him to clear the previous loans. And then, another LoU. And, yet another... The chain continued.

Kite Flying

Paying off a loan by taking another loan and then taking yet another loan, is called kiting or kite flying in banking parlance. If you use one or more credit cards to withdraw cash at the ATM to pay off the dues on another credit card, you are essentially doing the same thing. This way, Modi (and his uncle Choksi) spawned hundreds of LoUs and PNB's liability to the issuers of buyer's credit just ballooned.

It is the sort of Ponzi scheme which is loved by chit funds. They can continue to pay high interest rates to depositors as long as the flow of new money continues. Once the flow stops, their operations come to a halt. Here, too, Modi kept getting fresh LoUs opened to repay old facilities. The game came to a sudden halt only when Shetty retired and his successor at the branch refused to play ball – that is, open a new LoU without margin.

Shetty's absence broke the chain. While at the branch, he had ensured that the scheme operated smoothly. Typically, before a particular LoU would be due for redemption, Shetty would get hold of another bank to replace the existing bank through a broker.

Most Indian banks with overseas operations and a few foreign banks were in the chain. It was not difficult to get banks to agree to fund LoUs because they were taking an exposure to PNB, a large respected member of the banking system, and not to any corporate client. The capital requirement of LoUs is also far lower than a normal loan because it is a bank-to-bank transaction.

In due course, it is possible we will discover the LoUs were opened, based on inflated or even non-existent imports, leading to siphoning of funds.

Shetty, who had been at PNB's foreign exchange department in Mumbai since 31 March 2010, and a few of his colleagues were using SWIFT messages for the LoUs and no one else in the bank seemed to be aware of this. This is because such transactions never showed up in the core banking system of PNB.

Shetty apparently used his personal email – and not the bank's email – to keep all records. He used to send mails at midnight for reconciliation of transactions. He refused promotions and stayed put as a scale II officer (deputy manager) for decades. In 1986, he was promoted from being a clerk to the manager level. Since then, Shetty never opted for a promotion. Also, he made himself so indispensable that he was never transferred after he joined this branch in April 2010.

When he retired in 2017 and his successor refused to entertain Modi's companies unless they paid the mandated margin, Modi claimed that he had all along been enjoying the facility. However, the new officer could not trace the past transactions, and that let the cat out of the bag.

There would not have been any problem if PNB had securities or other collateral to back its LoUs. It would then have sold the securities/collaterals and paid the banks overseas. This has not happened because Modi never enjoyed any credit facility. He probably just had a current account with the bank, and Shetty and company were playing along with him.

Removing the Paper Trail

How did these dealings remain undetected for such a long time?

Shetty removed the paper trail of messages. The unauthorised messages could not be detected as the SWIFT system in PNB is not integrated with its core banking solution or CBS – a software for recording transactions, storing customer information, calculating interest and completing the process of passing entries in a single database.

In fact, this was the case with most banks in India at that time. (More on this in the chapter 'Fear Psychosis'.) As the system was stand-alone, no confirmation from the CBS or any other system that originates the transaction was received.

Before SWIFT, telex was the only means of message confirmation for global funds transfer. It was hampered by low speed and security concerns. Telex senders had to describe every transaction in sentences, which were then interpreted and executed by the receiver. This led to many human errors.

The SWIFT system was born in 1974 when seven major international banks formed a cooperative society to operate a global network to transfer financial messages in a secure and timely manner. For any cross-border financial transaction, SWIFT is the only secured messaging platform available and acceptable to all banks worldwide.

Those who understand banking technology will say integrating SWIFT with CBS is quite a task. Indeed it has a cost but that is much less than a $1.77 billion fraud!

The lack of integration between CBS and SWIFT was not the only loophole in PNB's operations. It was a window for misuse which was complemented and exploited at different levels with the complicity of many employees.

For instance, backed by the LoUs issued by the Brady House branch in Mumbai (bypassing its CBS), overseas branches of Indian banks sent money (buyer's credit) to PNB's Nostro account in Citibank, New York (111 Wall Street, Indian Service Mgmt Centre New York, NY 11043, USA Account No. 36003588 [UID 033086] Swift Code: CITIUS33).

How could such remittances remain outside CBS? Standard

banking practice demands each credit and debit in a bank's Nostro account should have a mirror entry in CBS. The SWIFT system cannot be blamed for this lack of audit control.

Also, what happened to the commission paid for availing the LoUs over the years? Here, too, SWIFT has no role to play. Did a gang of employees, allegedly led by Shetty, pocket it, and share it out?

Key Questions

As of April 2020 while the CBI probe is still on, there are a few questions that need to be answered.

- Indian banks overseas offered buyer's credit by remitting funds through inter-bank transfer in the Nostro account of PNB. How could PNB's CBS not capture such fund transfers?
- As a standard banking practice, Nostro reconciliation for each entry (credit and debit) is done by the treasury back-office of a bank with mirror entry in CBS. How and why were funds pertaining to the buyer's credit loan routed through PNB's Nostro account not reconciled for seven years?
- The SWIFT entries might have been generated without the knowledge of the senior management. But how could the fund entries – payments of principal and interest for seven years – in the Nostro account in PNB remain undetected?
- Overseas lenders sent loan confirmation to PNB via authenticated SWIFT, after the buyer's credit is disbursed. On receipt of such notification from overseas lenders, why was reconciliation not done with CBS to cross-check physically the loan details and book the actual liability for principal and interest?
- Modi continued to pay PNB until January 2018 and the lenders had received these funds from PNB. What was the basis of such repayments for PNB if buyer's credit did not exist in their CBS? How were these Nostro entries reconciled?

- Finally, RBI is very particular about keeping tabs on all transactions in banks' Nostro accounts and it always insists on timely reconciliation of such accounts. How could the rapid rise in transactions in PNB's Nostro account escape the regulator's eye?

A Multi-layered Failure

Can a deputy manager alone create a $1.77 billion hole in a large bank's balance sheet? PNB has suffered a multi-layered failure, surely accompanied by the complicity of its executives at different levels – the branch, circle, zone and treasury. The branch kept its eyes closed to both, to the rise in fee income as well as the regular visitors at Shetty's table from Modi's office.

A 21 June 2018 Reuters report, written by Abhirup Roy, Aditya Kalra and Euan Rocha talks about a 162-page internal report, which the PNB officials presented to the bank's fraud risk management arm on 5 April.

The report, produced by PNB officials tasked with probing the fraud, lays bare lapses that go far beyond a few branch officers. It lays out how failings by 54 PNB officials – ranging from clerks to foreign exchange managers, and auditors to heads of regional offices, allowed the fraud to be perpetrated.

Eight of the 54 are among those who have been charged by the CBI for their roles in the scandal.

> The Brady House branch was a star performer, largely because of its dealings with Modi firms, the PNB report said.
>
> Its import and export transactions in the 12 months to March 2017 stood at $3.3 billion, 50 per cent higher than recorded two years prior. "The exceptional growth should have been noticed," the report said.
>
> In March 2011, the branch issued the first fake credit guarantees of $15.5 million to Modi's firms through SWIFT messages, bypassing the internal banking system, the PNB investigators said.

> Over the coming years, Shetty authorised more than 1200 fraudulent credit guarantees, the report said.
>
> As a mid-level employee, Shetty should only have been able to approve transactions of up to 2.5 million rupees ($37,000) without sign-off from more senior officials. But he had been given unlimited approval powers, the investigators said without explaining how this happened
>
> In the few weeks before his retirement in May last year, Shetty used his personal Yahoo e-mail address to send 22 e-mails – 18 at around midnight – to reconcile large forex transactions involving the Modi Group. The use of personal e-mail was "overlooked" by the bank's treasury department, the report said.
>
> Under PNB policy, no officer should remain in the same office for more than three years, but Shetty retired after serving in Brady House for seven years. Three transfer orders were issued for him during his tenure, but he was never moved, the investigators found.

The report said that it is 'incomprehensible' that branch staff did not notice the fraud being committed.

Incidentally, this is not the first time that PNB's vulnerability to fraud has been exposed. Not so long ago, in 2013, the bank, along with a few others, had been involved in a similar fraud.

A consortium of banks lent ₹6,800 crore to Jatin Mehta's Winsome Diamond Group. Instead of LoUs, this was done through the issue of standby letters of credit to overseas banks which devolved on them. PNB had the maximum exposure – ₹1,800 crore. It did come under RBI scrutiny, which found related-party transactions, among other things.

PNB's Shetty will always be compared with R. Sitaraman, a small-time officer in SBI's treasury department in Mumbai. Sitaraman handheld Harshad Mehta during his inroads into the coffers of India's largest lender, leading to the ₹4,999-crore stock market scam of 1992.

After 25 years, in 2019, an Indian court acquitted both Sitaraman, an assistant manager of SBI, and his wife Meera Sitaraman, a clerk in Canara Bank. They had been booked under the Foreign Exchange Regulation Act and the Indian Penal Code. The ED filed the case in 1994 for an allegedly illegal transaction that took place on 29 January 1992.

How long it will take to punish Shetty, or acquit him, is anybody's guess.

Shetty had led a rather unremarkable life. He bought a 1,482 sq. ft. flat at Rustomjee's plush Ozone complex in Goregaon West, Mumbai, in 2005 for around ₹45 lakh. He owned a Wagon-R and only towards the end of his career bought a Honda City. He used to travel to office by Mumbai's suburban train and from the Goregaon station he would typically take an autorickshaw to reach his residence.

Kingfisher Airlines

Now and then, the RBI penalises a bank for failing to report a fraud or delaying doing so. One such case was the failure of 11 banks to comply with the regulations and classify the now-defunct Kingfisher Airlines account as a fraud, and report it to the regulator immediately after the CBI began criminal proceedings.

Should a case be classified as a fraud simply because an enforcement agency has initiated criminal proceedings against those who cleared the loan?

In the Kingfisher case, for quite sometime after the account went bad, there was nothing on record with the banks to indicate that any fraudulent transactions had taken place in their dealings with the company. In fact, the banks had initially hesitated to use the 'wilful defaulter' tag as the airline was making losses.

How could any bank blindly send a fraud report to the regulator, without any basis to do so?

Banks normally hesitate to talk about fraud, fearing reputational risks. There are also odd cases when they are caught between different agencies and regulators. The Kingfisher episode is one such. The fear of being dragged into fraud cases and being punished also slows down the decision-making process and credit flows.

Ideally, instead of simply putting emphasis on the timely 'reporting' of frauds, should there not be more attention paid to early detection and timely recoveries in fraud cases?

In almost every fraud, the complicity of the concerned bankers is taken for granted by the investigators. This is why there has always been inordinate delay in fraud reporting, especially if the case, going by the prevailing rules, is going to land on the CBI's table.

In late July 2019, the RBI said it had penalised 11 banks for not complying with the norms to classify an account as fraud and report to the regulator. Despite being advised by the RBI to report fraud in an account 'immediately' after the CBI initiated criminal proceedings, the banks had either delayed or did not report the fraud to the central bank.

The RBI release did not mention the account in question but it was that of the now-defunct Kingfisher Airlines. One wonders why RBI acted in 2019 when the so-called fraud was required to be reported in 2015–16, or earlier? Is this delayed action on delayed reporting?

Before imposing the penalty, the RBI had met representatives of these banks, which had been asked to explain why they should not be penalised for failing to comply with its directions on reporting of fraud.

The total penalty on the 11 banks was ₹8.5 crore. The Oriental Bank of Commerce had to pay the highest penalty (₹1.5 crore) followed by Indian Overseas Bank, Punjab & Sind Bank, UCO Bank and United Bank of India with penalties of ₹1 crore each, and then SBI, PNB, Bank of Baroda, Corporation Bank, Federal Bank, Jammu & Kashmir Bank with ₹50 lakh each.

So many banks together, including SBI, the lead bank itself, failed to report the Kingfisher loan as fraud. Did they eventually report the account as fraud?

'This action is based on the deficiencies in regulatory compliance and is not intended to pronounce upon the validity of any transaction or agreement entered into by the banks with their customers,' the RBI release said.

A penalty of ₹50 lakh or even ₹1.5 crore is peanuts for the banks, but such penalties are not good for their reputation. So, why did they delay taking action? It is an interesting story that involves the finance ministry (representing the majority owner of these banks), the CBI, the regulator and the banks themselves.

First, let us rewind to the Kingfisher Airlines nightmare.

In March 2016, UB Group Chairman Vijay Mallya, left for the UK quietly, just six days before the banks were planning to petition the Supreme Court to prevent him leaving the country. By then, his grounded airline owed some ₹9,100 crore to a consortium of banks, led by the SBI.

Since its inception in 2005, Kingfisher had never posted a profit. Its losses zoomed after it acquired low-cost airline Deccan Aviation Ltd in 2007. Of course, losses in the initial years of operation are quite normal in the aviation business. Most airlines, including Jet Airways Ltd and Air India, also incurred losses, for different reasons though.

Between fiscal 2008–09 and September 2012 – when it was grounded – Kingfisher Airlines' accumulated losses reached ₹8,015.8 crore. By 31 March 2013, the losses doubled to ₹16,023.46 crore, taking its net worth a negative ₹12,919.82 crore.

Ministers and Politicians

Why did the banks end up taking such a large exposure to Kingfisher? How did Mallya, a member of the Rajya Sabha, the Upper House of India's Parliament, convince the bankers to keep coming up with loans? It's been said that he was supported by some influential politicians and ministers.

At its peak, Kingfisher Airlines was flying 66 aircraft to 68 locations, including eight international destinations, with 374 flights a day. It held a fifth of the Indian aviation market.

It is easy to construct theories with the benefit of hindsight. I do not know if there was pressure from the politicians and administration. But the bankers did evaluate loan proposals and sanctioned them, with multiple safeguards which they believed could mitigate risks. The assessment of the bankers was not foolproof and a substantial amount turned bad.

The Kingfisher debt was first restructured in November 2010 under an RBI-approved scheme, based on an assessment of SBI Caps. The bankers' consortium converted ₹1,355 crore of debt into equity, at 61.6 per cent premium to the market price of the airline's stock price, based on the market regulator's valuation method for conversion of debt to equity.

As the losses mounted after the sanction of loans in 2009, why was the airline still considered worthy of support and restructuring? Why did the restructuring package fail? Was it because the bankers did not play their part? Or, did Mallya fail to keep his commitments in terms of equity infusion, despite raising funds through the sale of United Spirits Ltd, a group company, to Diageo Plc?

Following this restructuring, the banks owned 23.21 per cent of its equity. The promoter also converted ₹648 crore of unsecured debt into equity. Apart from this, the bankers also stretched the period for the repayment of loans to nine years with a two-year moratorium, cut interest rates and sanctioned a fresh loan.

But by end-2012, it was curtains for Kingfisher Airlines. Rating agency CRISIL downgraded its credit rating to its lowest 'D' grade, denoting default. Incidentally, even in 2008, Kingfisher's gearing ratio, or the ratio of its long-term debt to its equity capital, was 3.54 times, against the industry average of 2.06 times.

While restructuring, the banks seized a couple of Mallya's properties in Mumbai and Goa, his helicopters and the shares of group companies, United Spirits Ltd and Mangalore Chemicals and Fertilizers Ltd as collateral. They also took first-charge on fixed assets such as airport coaches that ferry passengers on the tarmac, and tractors for towing aircraft, besides a corporate guarantee from United Breweries (Holdings) Ltd, the group holding company, and the Kingfisher brand.

It is not appropriate to compare the securitisation structure for airline companies with other firms in different sectors. Ideally, the comparison should be made with companies in the same line of business.

Due to the nature of the airline business, it is not feasible for a lender to obtain a security cover in the same way as it is done for manufacturing or real estate. Since the tangible securities are limited, reliance is typically placed on cash flows and other assets which are considered valuable, including intangibles such as brands, any rights and claims the company may have, over future aircraft deliveries, etc.

The audit firm Grant Thornton India valued the Kingfisher Airlines brand at ₹3,000 crore. The sale of properties and shares generated some money for the banks – a little over ₹2,000 crore at the time of writing – but this covers only a part of the banks' exposure.

The CBI first initiated the so-called preliminary enquiry against the airline and IDBI Bank in August 2014 and later, in 2015, the first information report was filed for irregularities in sanctions and disbursements of short-term loans. It also found that a significant portion of the money raised from IDBI Bank was either diverted to other group companies or parked overseas. (More on this in the chapter 'Fear Psychosis'.)

It was against this backdrop in January 2016, that DFS in the Ministry of Finance stepped in. It wrote to the banks that had lent to Kingfisher Airlines, asking them to scrutinise the accounts in details, and prepare a note for each of their audit committees.

The banks were also told to check whether they had deviated from their credit policy while giving the loans to Kingfisher Airlines; if they had taken steps to monitor the end-use of the funds; and if any deviation/irregularities were found after the fund was disbursed.

Finally, the banks were told, 'directions of the audit committee may be sought on whether to declare the account as fraud'. Essentially, the banks did not need to rush to declare the account fraudulent, following the CBI action.

There are more twists and turns to this story. Since the

preliminary forensic audit was a bit sketchy, the joint lenders' forum could not take a call on the status of the exposure based on this.

In a meeting of the consortium of lenders held on 22 September 2016, it was decided that as directed by the CBI, a detailed forensic audit would be conducted. SBI selected E&Y for the job for a fee of ₹2.5 crore. However, SBI, the consortium leader, never shared the report with the other lenders, apparently at the behest of the CBI. Why did the CBI have reservations about this? Was there nothing to prove allegations of fraud?

There were, in fact, two forensic audits done on Kingfisher Airlines. The first was by PricewaterhouseCoopers (PwC) and the second, by E&Y. The E&Y audit found that Kingfisher diverted funds to its sporting company, Force India that participates in Formula 1 racing. The United Bank of India (merged with PNB in April 2020) was the first bank to declare the company, its promoter and three directors, wilful defaulters.

The penalty hardly pulls the curtain down on the Kingfisher case. It remains shrouded in mystery and too many questions remain unanswered.

- Why did the finance ministry (and not the RBI) direct banks to take the matter to their audit committees?
- Why did the CBI step in the way of the banks' accessing the detailed forensic report?
- Did politicians and ministers influence banks in giving loans to Kingfisher?
- Or, did the forensic report have no incriminating evidence?

Finance Minister Steps In

The fears of the bankers centred on the three Cs – CVC, CBI and the CAG. Finance Minister Nirmala Sitharaman met them in Delhi in the last week of December 2019 with CBI Director R. Shukla in tow. She assured the bankers that a distinction would be made between genuine commercial decisions that go bad, and culpability, in order to allay the bankers' fear.

At that meeting, the bankers were asked to set up a committee, headed by general managers, to decide on pursuing pending cases or closing them. It was also decided that the CBI would issue only computer-generated notices and summons bearing registration numbers and banks would be able to file the cases of frauds through e-filing of FIRs on a designated email address of the CBI.

Yet another decision was that no banking case would go to the CBI directly unless a bank seeks its intervention.

The finance ministry asked the banks to set up internal vigilance committees to look at frauds committed by their employees and to see whether existing cases merit investigation. The committee was to examine frauds worth ₹3 crore and more.

To strengthen the process of empanelling forensic auditors, the ministry urged the IBA to put in a framework to ensure that forensic auditors stick to defined standards, and to tie up with the CBI for training.

The government did not stop there. In January 2020, it constituted a five-member Advisory Board for Banking and Financial Frauds to vet all alleged frauds of at least ₹50 crore in state-run banks and public financial institutions before these are referred to investigative agencies. T.M. Bhasin, former chairman and MD of Indian Bank, and a former vigilance commissioner, is the chairman of this board.

The list of members includes Madhusudan Prasad, former urban development secretary; D.K. Pathak, former director-general of the Border Security Force; Suresh N. Patel, former CMD of Andhra Bank and A.D.M. Chavali, a former executive director of Indian Overseas Bank.

The board will conduct the first level of examination – before any bank initiates action – of executives of the rank of general manager and above, for any alleged role in any frauds involving more than ₹50 crore. The PSBs and public financial institutions are to refer all suspected high-value frauds to this board. It is expected to take a call on any such cases within a month of the reference.

Old Wine in a New Bottle

The board is a classic example of old wine in a new bottle. In February 1999, the CVC had put in place the Central Advisory Board on Bank Frauds for the 'first level of examination' of all large fraud cases in PSBs before they are referred to investigative agencies.

In August 2000, this was renamed as the Advisory Board for Banking, Commercial and Financial Frauds. As an organisation, it was considered part of the CBI, even while the RBI was picking up the tab for its expenses.

Two decades later, in August 2019, in consultation with the RBI and based on the recommendations of an expert committee on bad loans and frauds (chaired by Y.H. Malegam), the CVC constituted the Advisory Board for Banking Frauds. The CBI could also refer cases to that board, which had four members. All of them were co-opted in the reconstituted board in 2020.

The Malegam committee was set up in February 2018 in the wake of the PNB fraud to look at the 'increasing incidence of frauds in banks and measures (including IT interventions) to prevent it'. It also assessed the efficacy of various types of bank audits in mitigating such frauds and divergence in asset classification between what the central bank asks for and what commercial banks end up doing.

Forensic Audit

The bankers' experience with the investigative agencies and the government, the majority owner, has not been a pleasant one.

For instance, a DFS letter (dated 27 February 2018) to the PSB chiefs says, 'all accounts exceeding ₹50 crore, if classified as NPAs, shall simultaneously be examined by banks from the angle of possible fraud.' This means the banks must do a forensic audit of all bad accounts worth ₹50 crore or more.

The letter, which has the subject line: 'Framework for timely detection, reporting, investigation, etc. relating to large value bank frauds', says, 'In case, an account turns NPA, [the] banks shall be required to seek a report on the borrower from CEIB [Central Economic Intelligence Bureau] and such report would be furnished by CEIB within one week of receipt of request from the bank.' This particular letter refers to an earlier DFS letter, written on 13 May 2015, which puts the 'overall responsibility for ensuring compliance' on all these criteria with the chief of a PSB.

The IBA, which represents the managements of banks in India, has been engaging with the finance ministry on these issues.

It took exception to a DFS letter, dated 20 August 2019, which allows CBI investigation against any employee, without a reference to the bank, if the employee has already been named in an internal investigation of the bank. This is against the spirit of Section 17A of the Prevention of Corruption Act, which makes prior approval of the bank necessary for initiating such an action.

Even after all modifications and repeated pronouncements by the finance minister, the assumption continues to be that if a loan turns bad, something wrong must have been done by the concerned bank officers. Once a case goes out of a bank either into DFS or CBI or any other government agency, there is no established procedure to determine whether a genuine error of judgment has taken place, or certain rules have been bent, or omitted due to business compulsions, or there is really some malfeasance or mala fide intent.

The investigative agencies typically proceed on the assumption of wrongdoing as their training and methodology is geared to presuppose 'a suspect guilty until proven innocent'. Besides this, their understanding of banking is quite superficial and not too many police officials can appreciate the nuances and thus identify deliberate wrongdoing.

The Role of Auditors

An audit is the trigger for detecting any wrongdoings. Concurrent auditors in bank branches are assigned the job of periodic on-the-spot verification of transactions. Though they are the first line of defence, they often fail.

The statutory auditors oversee overall compliance with all regulatory aspects and sign off on the balance sheet. They are supposed to check the customer-wise transaction register, along with sanctions/approvals for authenticating the true state of the books of accounts and thus try to establish the bank's contingent liabilities on the date of book closure.

Similarly, a bank's internal auditors are supposed to keep tabs on the front, middle and back offices. They check client files, outstanding transactions, approvals and transaction registers. Besides this, RBI auditors conduct the annual financial review.

For about a decade now, the RBI has been conducting a systemic risk survey to capture the risks in the financial system through the views of market participants. There are different kinds of risks such as global risk, macroeconomic risk, financial market risk, institutional risk and general risk. The PNB fraud is an offshoot of operational risk, which is considered part of institutional risk in the survey.

The October 2017 survey, for the first time, ranked operational risk in banks as 'medium'. Since then, until the October 2019 survey, 17th in the series, operational risk has remained in the same level. It had been 'very low' in April 2015 and 'low' in October 2015; moved up to 'medium' in October 2016. The rise in operational risks indicated gradual deterioration within the system.

Risk-based Supervision

One of the reasons for this uptick in risks could be changes in the way the RBI supervision is now being conducted. The current regime of risk-based supervision is an extremely data-intensive exercise where banks are expected to report automated data seamlessly to the regulator. So, if an entity does not give the data or offers incorrect data, the regulator cannot catch them. This is the story of both PNB and the Punjab & Maharashtra Cooperative Bank.

The new supervision architecture replaced the CAMELS-based supervision. CAMELS stands for capital adequacy, asset quality, management, earnings, liquidity, and system and control. Originally it was called CAMEL and 'S' was added in 1997. Internationally, the 'S' stands for sensitivity (for market risks).

Since the focus of CAMELS inspection was on earnings, among other things, it could have encouraged a bank to show high profitability, earned at the cost of higher business risks, to get a higher rating. Also, the CAMELS approach seemed to be backward-looking rather than being proactive and forward-looking in supervisory risk assessment. That is why the RBI shifted its focus to risk-based supervision.

Describing the move towards risk-based supervision as a step in the right direction for the banking industry, a January 2014 Deloitte paper titled, 'Navigating the risk-based supervision process', listed the challenges for the supervisor and the banks as the industry grappled with wide-ranging issues, including quality of data, scalability of regulatory reporting processes, the efficacy of risk management systems and cost of compliance.

The report says, this supervisory process places significant focus on the continuous collection of data from banks and it relies on the bank's audit and compliance functions to provide transactional assurance to the supervisor. The impetus is on corporate governance and regular dialogue between the bank and supervisor.

An IMF report on India's Financial Sector Assessment Program (released on 19 January 2018) commended the RBI for the 'remarkable progress in strengthening banking supervision'. Stating that supervision and regulation by RBI remain strong and have improved in recent years, it lists the implementation of a risk-based supervisory approach as a key achievement.

'The system-wide asset quality review and the strengthening of prudential regulations in 2015 testify to the authorities' commitment to transparency and a more accurate recognition of banking risks,' the IMF report says.

The way forward could be random transaction testing even in risk-based supervision and what is popularly known as ABC analysis in inventory management.

How could this be done?

The banks can be divided into three categories, A, B and C – 'A' being the most valuable bank (in terms of size and systemic importance, but fewest in number) and 'C' being the least valuable ones (but most in number). The RBI can give the maximum attention to the critical few ('A' banks) and follow the routine for the more trivial many 'C' banks. (More on this in the chapter 'Does RBI Need New Clothes?')

The Fraud Basket

Amount wise, most frauds are related to credit but there have been instances of the misuse of credit cards and the Internet. In some cases but not all, 'insiders' (read bank managers) play a role. Finally, the corporate–banker nexus may not be rampant but it does exist.

Here is how frauds happen:

- **Fund transfer through Real Time Gross Settlement (RTGS) and other clearing platforms**: Typically, money is taken out of a customer's account through fake/cloned cheques. This can also involve the fraudulent collections of demand drafts, issued by a third party.
- **Dormant accounts:** The branch bankers play a key role to make such accounts active by issuing new ATM cards and cheque books to perpetrate withdrawal of money from such accounts.
- **Home loans**: There are multiple ways of defrauding banks. For instance, the builder can sell one flat to many customers; the borrower can take a loan for a property already sold to another person; a person can be given loans higher than he can service, either by forging earnings statement, or with the help of branch bankers; the property value can also be inflated.
- **Advance against bills:** Forged export bills and letters of credit help such frauds. The borrowers can also route their export proceeds through other banks.
- **Gold loans:** The borrowers can get higher loans by inflating the value of gold pledged to the lender or even against spurious gold with the 'help' of the valuer and branch bankers.

- **Kisan credit cards or KCCs:** Such loans can be sanctioned without checking the Know Your Customer (KYC) of the borrowers and the authenticity of the land records. Often the borrowers are untraceable.
- **ATM:** Money is withdrawn using cloned ATM cards.
- **Cash credit:** Frauds involve falsification of the books of accounts and the removal of goods and property hypothecated to the banks.
- **Term loan:** This is the biggest contributor to frauds. Borrowers raise more money than they should, by forging financial statements; they divert funds; they route the sales proceeds of their companies through banks outside of the consortium which has lent to them, and raise export credit through fake export orders. Non-existent collaterals complete this list of ways in which loans can be used to perpetrate fraud.

Abusing an Official Position

There are compromised bankers.

The CBI registered a case of corruption on 15 September 2016 against Archana Bhargava, the former chairperson and managing director (CMD) of United Bank of India (UBI). Before filing the case, the agency carried out raids across multiple cities and recovered cash, jewellery and investment of over ₹13.5 crore.

Allegedly, Bhargava had abused her official position, first as an executive director of Canara Bank, and later as the boss of UBI for making money for herself and/or a company based in New Delhi, which is owned by her husband and son.

The agency also found large sums kept in the bank accounts of Bhargava and her family members. The retired banker, a post-graduate gold-medallist in biochemistry from Delhi's Miranda House and a National Science Talent Scholarship holder, may also have to explain her possession of properties in Delhi and Mumbai.

Bhargava had started her banking career with PNB as a management trainee in 1977. In February 2014, she sought voluntary retirement, citing health reasons, 10 months after she took charge of the Kolkata-based bank and a year before her scheduled retirement.

Sudhir Kumar Jain, CMD of Syndicate Bank is another banker with a dubious record. The CBI arrested him in August 2014 for allegedly taking a bribe of ₹50 lakh. His brothers-in-law were allegedly involved in the mechanics of the pay-off.

Is Gokul Shetty India's Nick Leeson?

In 1995, the discovery of a secret file – 'Error Account 88888' – brought to light the fact that a Barings Bank derivatives trader, Nick Leeson, had gambled away £827 million of the bank's money. The rogue trader, who was based in Singapore, single-handedly bankrupted the 200-year-old bank.

Leeson held the world title for losses due to unrestricted trades for over a decade. Then on 25 January 2008, Societe Generale announced that it had uncovered a $7.14 billion fraud, involving a futures trader, Jerome Kerviel.

Let us hope that it takes many years to eclipse the record set by PNB's Shetty. Of course, there is a big difference between what happened at Barings, and Society Generale and PNB.

Both Leeson and Kerviel were traders who had a record of making profits and earning fat bonuses, in speculative trades, until greed overtook them and they dug themselves deeper into holes in desperate attempts to recover losses. Shetty and his colleagues were not making any profits for PNB. They just worked in tandem with a few rogue promoters to rob their bank.

■ ■ ■

9

Fear Psychosis

Early morning yoga class was a sacrosanct ritual for Ravindra Prabhakar Marathe, 59, the MD and CEO of the Pune-headquartered Bank of Maharashtra. Marathe lived in his official residence on Prabhat Road, in an elite neighbourhood in the heart of the city, a stone's throw away from the Film and Television Institute of India (FTII).

On Wednesday, 20 June 2018, at around 6.30 am his neighbours saw him getting on his old bicycle as usual and heading for the Lele Guruji Yoga Kendra at Erandwane, just two lanes away. Others who attended the yoga session that day say there was no physical activity. Instead, the class was asked to listen to an audiotape on how to keep cool under adverse circumstances.

That may have helped Marathe remain calm when he was greeted by four police officers, including a woman, who were waiting at the gate of his residence when he returned after the class, and some vegetable shopping at the weekly farmers' market on the playground near the Bal Ranjan Kendra.

The police officers allowed him to drop off the bag of vegetables at his bungalow and change out his trackpants into formal trousers and shirt before 'whisking' him away (as they say) to the office of the Economic Offences Wing of Pune Police at Shivajinagar in a police car. He was not allowed to take his mobile phones or his laptop.

The police also picked up the picked up Rajendra Gupta, the bank's executive director; Nityanand Deshpande, the zonal manager; and Sushil Muhnot, former CMD of the bank. They were accused of misusing their authority in making loans to a local property developer, D.S. Kulkarni Developers Ltd (DSKDL).

On that same day, the police also arrested Sunil Ghatpande, the real estate and property developer's chartered accountant and the engineering section's vice president, Rajeev Newaskar. It was the third round of arrests targeting people in the construction company. The Pune police had already arrested the promoter D.S. Kulkarni and his wife from Delhi in February 2018, and some of their close relatives later.

DSKDL is a household name in Pune. Banks and non-banking financial companies had been giving loans to this company; its associate and group companies were raising deposits from small investors by offering high interest rates.

In 2017, DSKDL started facing problems and its associate and group companies started defaulting in paying back individual depositors, many of whom were senior citizens. A group of depositors filed an FIR with police against the company for cheating, forgery and breach of trust, among other things. The Economic Offences Wing was investigating the case. The investigating officer was Nilesh More, a young assistant commissioner of police. Reshmi Shukla was then the commissioner of Pune Police, the first woman police chief of the city.

A 37,000 page chargesheet was filed under the Maharashtra Protection of Interest of Depositors (in Financial Establishments) Act (MPID), 1999.

The chargesheet, filed in May 2018, put the scam's value at ₹2,043.18 crore and said the accused had floated nine firms to siphon off funds collected from 33,000 investors and fixed-deposit holders, who were promised good returns.

As the depositors piled on the pressure to get back their money, the police, sought to implicate Bank of Maharashtra officials for lending to the company, allegedly in violation of RBI norms. The depositors as well as the bank gave money to the company and both were running the risks of losing it.

What purpose would the arrest of the bank officials serve? The police probably had the answer. The Act under which they were arrested has nothing to do with a bank's lending activities.

Marathe and other bankers were questioned at the police station. Before being produced in court, they were taken to Sassoon Hospital for the mandatory medical check-up.

Soon the news of the arrests was flashing on all TV channels. It was a shock to fellow bankers who had met Marathe the previous day at the SBI's local head office at Connaught Place in New Delhi. They had been summoned there by Piyush Goyal, the railway minister holding additional charge of the finance ministry as Arun Jaitley was seriously ill.

Around 4.30 pm, Marathe and his colleagues were produced at the Special Court handling offences under the MPID, as accused in the fraud case of DSKDL against small depositors.

In Police Custody

The court granted the police custody of the bankers for seven days. When lawyers for Marathe and his colleagues in Bank of Maharashtra moved bail applications on their behalf on 23 June, the judge converted the police custody into judicial custody.

Marathe was to be shifted to the Yerawada Central Jail but, as he complained of chest pain, he was taken first to the Sassoon Hospital and later to a private hospital.

For part of the first night, until he was taken to hospital, Marathe was put in a 10ft x 10ft lock up at the police station with a *durrie* to sleep on and a blanket that could double as a pillow. His companion for the night was a hardcore criminal, booked for the alleged murder of a builder.

On 27 June, a special Pune court granted bail to Marathe on a surety bond of ₹50,000 but the others were remanded in judicial custody for 14 days. While granting relief, the court barred Marathe from leaving the country without the court's permission and he was ordered to cooperate with the police. He was also warned against trying to tamper with evidence, or influence witnesses.

A day after Marathe got bail, the board of directors of Bank of Maharashtra resolved to divest him of all functional responsibilities with immediate effect.

Marathe's responsibilities were restored four months later, on 2 November, just weeks before his term as MD and CEO was to expire. The executive director, Gupta, too, was reinstated with his powers.

This followed a closure report filed by the police under Section 169 of the Code of Criminal Procedure (CrPC) as they did not find any evidence against him and other bank officials. Marathe retired on 30 November; Gupta's term ended on 31 December.

On the same day, just ahead of the board's decision to restore his powers, Marathe was seen, along with the CEOs of other PSBs, at the Union government's Vigyan Bhawan convention centre in New Delhi. Prime Minister Narendra Modi addressed public sector bankers there on Mudra loans.

The board meeting was convened at the bank's zonal office at Bhikaji Cama Place in New Delhi where Marathe, Gupta and the government nominee on the board were present. The other board members joined on call from Mumbai, Jaipur and Chennai.

The case was finally closed on 21 January 2019. The special judge of the court handling MPID cases, D.G. Murumkar, accepted the closure report of the investigating officer and discharged Marathe, Gupta and Muhnot from their alleged offences and cancelled the bail bonds.

Restless Bankers

While passing the order, the judge said:

> It is necessary to mention that the investigating officer, without making proper inquiry and investigation, pithily and hastily

> arrested the present accused, who were holding key posts in Bank of Maharashtra, which he should not have done… By his action, banking sector became restless.

Restless was an understatement. This is one of the many such cases that have created an acute fear psychosis among PSBs.

Flashback to 23 January 2017.

Neighbours of B.K. Batra, 61, a former deputy managing director of IDBI Bank, saw him walking briskly in Sheila Raheja Park at Mumbai's western suburb of Malad East, as he did every morning.

By the time he returned to his apartment at Raheja Residency on General AK Vaidya Marg, a few minutes' walk from the park, a posse of CBI officers had already entered the complex.

They pressed the bell at Batra's third-floor apartment and presented him with a search warrant. The reason was IDBI Bank's exposure to the defunct Kingfisher Airlines of Vijay Mallya.

Around the same time, different teams of CBI officers were going through the same exercise at the apartments of four retired IDBI Bank executives at Oshiwara and Santacruz West in Mumbai, Hiranandani in Thane and Exotica Housing Complex on Golf Course Road at Gurgaon, Haryana.

Like Marathe, all of them were asked to keep their mobile phones, laptop and iPad on a table and not allowed to make any calls. But unlike at Marathe's house in Pune, a thorough search was conducted at every place. At the end of it, inventories were made listing the fixed deposit receipts of banks and bank account details, locker keys, jewellery, etc. – a normal practice. The duration of the search was different at different houses.

The CBI SP in Mumbai, Jagroop S. Gusinha – who was to later get the police medal for meritorious service – was overseeing the entire operation. By late evening, when the searches were complete, the officers asked Batra to accompany them to the CBI office at Plot No C-35A, Block G, Bandra Kurla Complex in Mumbai. A colleague of Batra says the CBI officers did ask him whether he would like to take his medicines along, but Batra did not catch the hint.

When Batra reached the CBI office around 10 pm, three of his former colleagues – O.V. Bundellu (retired deputy managing director), S.K.V. Srinivasan (retired executive director) and R.S. Sridhar (a retired general manager from the bank's project appraisal department) – greeted him at the third-floor office. Batra, who had retired as a deputy managing director, was an executive director in the bank when he was handling the Kingfisher loan proposal.

The CBI had picked them up from their homes in the Mumbai suburbs and brought them to its office at different times and arrested them. In the same hall, A. Raghunathan, former CFO of Kingfisher Airlines, and three other former executives of the defunct airline – Shailesh Borker, A.C. Shah and Amit Nadkarni – were also present. They all exchanged glances and nervous smiles.

You are Under Arrest

The office of Suman Kumar, the CBI's additional SP, is on the fourth floor. Bundellu, Srinivasan and Sridhar had already met him. Batra too had to undergo the ritual of being formally placed under arrest.

Why?

None of them was told the reason. They were not allowed to contact any lawyer but could call up their families and inform them of their arrest. All of them did so, using the CBI officers' mobile phones.

That was not needed though since their wives and children already knew. The TV channels had been flashing the news of the arrests and searches non-stop. The raids had been conducted at 11 different locations including Mallya's residence in New Delhi, three floors of UB Towers in Bengaluru and the residences of bankers and Kingfisher Airlines officials.

By late night, they had to leave all their belongings – wallets, credit and debit cards and even belts – in the CBI's custody. One constable was assigned to each of the four senior bankers and four Kingfisher officials. All eight were asked to sleep in a room on a *durrie*. There was no pillow or blanket.

There were no mosquitoes but none of the men could sleep through the long night. In the morning, the bankers repeated their request to the CBI officers to permit them to make calls for legal help but it was denied. They were, however, allowed to call up their family from the office landline.

They had to skip their morning ritual of brushing their teeth as they had not brought toothbrushes. Sipping their morning cup of tea, the IDBI Bank officials were surprised to see their former boss, Yogesh Agarwal join them.

Like them, Agarwal had been picked up from his residence in Gurgaon, Haryana, and flown in from Delhi the previous night. He had been kept in another room.

Agarwal, a former MD of SBI, took over as chairman and MD of IDBI Bank, in July 2007. After a three-year stint, he became the chairman of the Pension Fund Regulatory & Development Authority (PFRDA) in June 2010 and resigned in November 2013 before completing his five-year term.

All of them were taken for a routine medical check-up at a nearby hospital and then brought back to the canteen at the CBI office for lunch. Then they were taken to the Sessions Court at the Old Secretariat Building, Kala Ghoda, beside Mumbai University at Fort, Mumbai.

It transpired the bank had arranged for their legal support. As the chargesheet had already been filed, the investigation should have been completed. But the court refused to grant them bail and they were sent to judicial custody.

In the same bus, accompanied by the same set of constables, the five bankers and the four airline executives were ferried to the Mumbai Central Prison, also referred to as the Arthur Road Jail, on JR Boricha Marg, Lower Parel, Mumbai.

Arthur Road Jail

What unfolded at the jail was surreal – very different from what we typically see in Bollywood movies. All nine were put into a large hall, called a barrack, which housed at least a couple of hundred others. There were three rows of bare *durries* on the floor to sleep on but that night there was no pillow or bedsheet.

There was virtually no space between the sleeping inmates, making it difficult for anyone to turn over without touching somebody. Since they were all undertrial prisoners, there were no jail uniforms for them.

This was a barrack for the undertrials – the senior citizens (without any special facilities for them) and the underage (juvenile) and those who were in transit, returning from court hearings. Pillows and blankets were in short supply and prisoners would just need to grab what they could.

A big blackboard in the hall lists the entitlement of each undertrial – a dish for meals, a glass, two *katories* and a teacup. In real life, they were given none of these; they had to get the utensils from the common pool, wash them after use and put them back in the common pool.

In the initial days, plastic mineral water bottles were cut up to make cups for drinking tea. *Upma*, *poha* or *halwa* was the staple breakfast; lunch and dinner consisted of rice, *chapatti*, dal and vegetable. The less said about the quality of food, the better, but there was no choice but to gulp it down for sustenance. On festival days, the kitchen served non-vegetarian food.

There were four toilets within the barrack, shared by the 200-plus occupants. The senior citizens found the Indian-style squat toilets extremely difficult to use but there was no alternative. There were a few more toilets outside the barrack, in the compound, but those were also squat latrines and prisoners could use them only at certain hours of the day.

There was only one bathroom where they could take baths; in the open compound, there was provision to wash their clothes with soap provided by the jail authorities. The meals were served outside the barrack but one could carry their plates indoors to eat.

'The Kingfisher Gang'

In the barrack, these nine people were called the 'Kingfisher Gang'.

They could meet a relative once a week, from behind a glass wall and talk for a few minutes on the intercom. The lawyers could come and meet them more frequently in the mornings. But all meetings were in the presence of jail staff.

Daily newspapers, a few for the entire barrack, were their only other window to the outside world.

Judicial custody is always for two weeks. This means, every two weeks, the undertrials were taken to the court where a judge would hear their bail petition. Bundellu, Srinivasan and Sridhar were released on bail in the second week of February, after 18 days. But Agarwal and Batra were not so lucky. They had to move an appeal at the high court and spend many more days in this hellish environment.

Those who had seen them in the barrack say Agarwal used to lose his cool over trivial things like the tea being lukewarm or somebody sneezing near him. The two bankers were treated in the same way other undertrials were, many of whom were criminals, but at least the bankers were spared the slaps and abusive heckling faced by the others.

The bankers would eagerly look forward to bail-hearing day in court when they could meet their family and get some home-cooked food.

Finally, on 17 March 2017, the Bombay High Court granted bail to Agarwal and Batra after they had spent 54 days in judicial custody. Justice Sadhana S. Jadhav granted the bail on sureties of ₹1 lakh each.

The judgment says:

> In the present case, (the) respondent (CBI) is unable to substantiate the contention as to why further incarceration of the applicants is imperative after filing of the charge-sheet. At the time when they were presented before the magistrate also, respondent-investigating agency had sought for judicial custody and therefore, it cannot be said that the interrogation of the present applicants would be necessary. In any case,

> after initial 15 days of judicial custody, (the) CBI cannot pray for police custody for the purpose of interrogation... The case rests upon documentary evidence and there would be no question of tampering of evidence more so when both applicants have retired on superannuation. It is in these circumstances that this court is of the opinion that applicants deserve to be enlarged on bail.

The 183-page chargesheet alleges that IDBI Bank sanctioned and disbursed ₹150 crore on 7 October 2009, ₹200 crore on 4 November 2009 and ₹750 crore on 27 November 2009 despite weak financials, negative net worth and low credit rating of the borrower. This was in violation of the corporate loan policy of the bank.

The chargesheet also refers to meetings held between Vijay Mallya and Agarwal on a holiday.

It alleges that a significant portion (₹263.48 crore) of the funds was transferred by Kingfisher Airlines to other accounts through Axis Bank, ICICI Bank and Bank of Baroda. Part of the money was used to service the company's debt to different banks and non-banking financial companies, including IDBI Bank.

The Kingfisher Loan

The proposal for the sanction of a corporate loan of ₹950 crore was submitted by Kingfisher Airlines' CFO Raghunathan and marked for the attention of Batra. The chargesheet also mentions Raghunathan referred to a meeting between Mallya and Agarwal in a letter dated 6 October 2009, and requested the bank to lend the airline ₹150 crore for six months to pay overseas vendors.

Mallya's meeting with Agarwal took place in the last week of September 2009. The application for ₹950 crore loan was submitted a few days after the meeting, on 1 October. Realising that the detailed appraisal of the main loan application was likely to take time, Kingfisher asked for a ₹150 crore short-term loan to meet its urgent and critical requirements. This request was processed by the bank on priority and approved on 7 October 2009.

Raghunathan, again referring to Mallya's meeting with Agarwal, sought an ad hoc release of ₹200 crore and, on 4 November, IDBI sanctioned a short-term loan of ₹200 crore.

This ad hoc release was against the main loan of ₹750 crore already under process and it was to be adjusted against the sanction of ₹750 crore. This was done.

After the sanction of ₹750 crore loan, the ₹200 crore ad hoc loan was extinguished. Only two loans remained on IDBI Bank's book. One was a short-term ₹150 crore loan and the other, a long-term loan of ₹750 crore.

The short-term loans were disbursed while the original proposal for a corporate loan of ₹950 crore was being processed. The proposal was placed first before the credit committee on 19 November 2009 and later, on 27 November 2009, the bank's executive committee of the board of directors approved a corporate loan of ₹750 crore.

The total requirement of funds for Kingfisher was ₹2,000 crore as assessed by SBI in its detailed appraisal note. SBI and three other banks had already sanctioned and also disbursed ₹1,050 crore when the airline approached IDBI Bank for the balance ₹950 crore.

S. Ananthakrishnan, executive director, in charge of large corporate groups, who was overseeing the Kingfisher account, died in 2016. There were a few others involved in the loan process but the investigative agency picked up only the retired bankers.

Agarwal and Bundellu had retired from the bank in 2010. Batra and Srinivasan retired in July 2016. The last of them, Sridhar, who was reporting to Ananthakrishnan, retired in December 2016. They were all arrested in January 2017.

The CBI needs the government's permission to act against serving officers.

Agarwal's meeting with Mallya had not been a clandestine affair. It was on his calendar and the meeting took place in his chamber in the presence of other officers of the bank and of the airline. His secretariat staff was also present in the office. In IDBI Bank and even other banks the chairman coming to office on a holiday is not rare.

It is debatable if this is the right approach or not, but the bank's loan policy permitted it to give 10 per cent of loans to companies with lower than investment-grade rating, provided sufficient security cover was offered.

For security, the bank took a corporate guarantee from the group's flagship United Breweries, the Kingfisher brand and the personal guarantee of Mallya. Since the fleet of aircraft was hypothecated to other lenders, IDBI Bank opened an escrow account to capture the entire cash flow of the company. According to their April 2010 report, Grant Thornton attached a value of around ₹3,000 crore to the Kingfisher Airlines brand.

Before IDBI Bank disbursed the ₹900 crore loan (₹150 crore of short-term loan and ₹750 crore of long-term corporate loan) to Kingfisher Airlines in 2009, the airline had sought ₹2,000 crore support from the banking industry.

The SBI carried out the detailed appraisal of the company's fund requirement. SBI, Bank of India, Bank of Baroda and Union Bank of India had already sanctioned and disbursed ₹1,050 crore and another ₹200 crore was sanctioned by UCO Bank.

IDBI Bank sanctioned the balance ₹750 crore as corporate loan, which is typically used for multiple purposes ranging from paying salary to employees to lease rentals. Such loans are given to companies to tide over cash flow mismatches.

IDBI Bank managed to recover the short-term loan of ₹150 crore, along with interest, albeit with a small delay in its maturity period of six months.

Since Kingfisher did not come forward for timely compliance of certain material conditions of release of the main loan of ₹750 crore, IDBI Bank decided to recall the entire loan well before even its first instalment of principal fell due for repayment. Later, in order to fall in line with the restructuring of Kingfisher loans by the entire banking sector, IDBI Bank had to backtrack and withdraw its loan recall decision.

A close look at the Kingfisher–IDBI Bank saga reveals that there were deviations from some parameters while sanctioning the loan.

But there was no violation of the corporate loan policy of the bank. The deviations were permissible within the policy.

Loan Restructuring

In 2010, the loan was restructured in line with the RBI-approved guidelines and SBI-led consortium decision. The new structure saw the corporate loan split into three parts. A sum of ₹525 crore was rescheduled to be paid over nine years with a two-year moratorium, beginning October 2010. The interest rate on the loan was also reduced. The rest of the loan – about 30 per cent – was converted into two equal components of cumulative redeemable preference shares and compulsorily convertible preference shares.

This restructuring was in line with the RBI's decision to ease the conditions for the distressed airline sector in general. The RBI did not issue any notification on the relaxations, but it did write to SBI, the leader of the consortium of lenders to Kingfisher Airlines, and Jet Airways, on 18 August 2010.

Another letter, written by M.P. Baliga, an RBI general manager, in response to certain queries of State Bank says, 'The restructuring exercise has to be based entirely on the viability parameters... in a holistic manner...' and 'the banks should convince themselves on the viability and sustainability of the cash flows.'

Since the airline industry was 'at a critical juncture', Baliga wrote, the banks must make it clear to the airline that it had to cut costs and rationalise routes if it wanted 'one-time' restructuring of the loan. It also asked banks to look for tangible securities for hypothecation and mortgage, and not opt for intangibles such as brand value and personal guarantees.

Whatever tangible securities were available with the airline were brought into the consortium security pool.

Typically, the airline companies carry limited tangible assets; the aircraft are generally leased, and not owned (it is easier for an airline to pay leases out of their cash flows than to buy aircraft outright). The ground assets do not incur heavy capex.

Apart from aviation fuel costs, which can amount to as much as

35–40 per cent of operating costs, the major expenditures of airlines include large overheads in terms of compensations for highly skilled staff, such as pilots, and in renting parking slots. Apart from this, marketing and brand building cost a lot. Occupancy is the key – a flight costs the same whether the plane flies full or empty.

Airlines make losses in the initial years of operation while capacity builds up to reach the breakeven level. Most commercial airlines the world over go through losses in the first five to eight years, depending on the funding pattern of their specific business.

In June 2010, 18 banks, including IDBI Bank, had a total exposure of ₹6,573 crore to Kingfisher Airlines, inclusive of working capital and term loans. The SBI led the list with ₹1,902 crore, followed by IDBI Bank (₹750 crore). PNB, ICICI Bank and Bank of India had an exposure of at least ₹500 crore each.

Money Laundering

A month after Agarwal and Batra emerged from Arthur Road Jail on bail, the ED stepped in to explore the money laundering angle in the case. The directorate served a summons to all five bankers and, by July 2017, it filed a fresh complaint.

In November 2017, after several hearings of the case in the Special Court that deals with cases related to the Prevention of Money Laundering Act, bail was granted to all the five.

As I write this chapter in May 2020, they need to appear before the court every month and they cannot leave India without the permission of the court. This may continue indefinitely. But another shock was also in store for these hapless retired bankers: IDBI Bank stopped extending legal support and asked them to refund the money that it had already spent on their behalf.

While the executives have written to the bank to reconsider its decision, those who have fixed deposits with IDBI Bank or taken home loans have not been able to liquidate their fixed deposits, and claim title deeds of their apartments even after clearing the loan. They will have to wait until the bank takes a final call on this.

IDBI Bank has a board-approved policy for extending legal and financial support to the directors and officers, including those who have retired. When the Kingfisher Airlines account turned bad, the bank's internal staff accountability committee probed it but found nothing wrong.

In sync with the CVC's norms (based on an office memorandum, dated 28 August 2015), once again a two-member panel examined staff accountability and found that all aspects of credit delivery were followed.

The report of the committee was yet again examined in April 2016 and gave the credit decision a clean chit. Which is why, the legal support extended to the retired officers in the Kingfisher case was in line the board-approved policy of the bank.

However, the finance ministry's DFS wing 'advised' IDBI Bank through a letter dated 8 January 2019 not to extend legal and financial assistance to these retired executives and to recover the money already released. A copy of this 'advisory' was sent to all PSBs.

Certain questions have been troubling the banking community ever since the arrest of this set of bankers. The publicity given to the CBI action against the officers, whose guilt has not been proved, has destroyed their reputations and turned them into social pariahs.

- Was the arrest and detention of all these retired bankers warranted, particularly when they fully cooperated with CBI at every stage during investigation and when the chargesheet had already been finalised and was later filed with the court?
- What was their crime? Did they receive any favour, pecuniary or otherwise, from Mallya for sanctioning the loan? The CBI chargesheet does not seem to make any such allegation.
- Was sanction of a loan with deviation of certain norms an unusual phenomenon in Indian banking? Can such a sanction be defined as a criminal offence?
- Was IDBI Bank the only bank to have sanctioned loans to Kingfisher with a deviation of its parameters?

- Finally, should these retired bankers, dependent on their meagre pension, be made to cough up hefty legal expenses to defend themselves in court, especially when their bank's policy permits such legal expenses to be met by the bank?

Sacked, Eight Minutes before Retirement

The list of public sector bankers under the scanner of the investigative agencies does not end here. Usha Ananthasubramanian, former MD of PNB, is another one.

Ananthasubramanian was removed from PNB in the first week of May 2017 for her alleged involvement in the ₹14,300 crore Nirav Modi fraud. Her next assignment was at Allahabad Bank. She was sacked on 13 August 2018, eight minutes before the end of her last day in office.

Just minutes before her planned farewell function at the board room of Allahabad Bank's headquarters on 2 NS Bose Road in the Kolkata's central business district, a mail arrived from Jnanatosh Roy, under secretary in the DFS. That ended her career.

She left the bank premises abruptly as news of her dismissal broke for 'failing to exercise proper control over the functioning of PNB while serving as its MD and CEO'. She was removed after the CBI sought the government clearance for her prosecution in the fraud case.

Three months before the removal, Ananthasubramanian, a gold medallist in school for general proficiency and topper in every subject, had been divested of her functional powers on 15 May 2018 after CBI named her in its chargesheet.

The CBI filed its chargesheet on 14 May 2018 in Mumbai. Rajiv Ranjan, the joint secretary in Ministry of Finance's Department of Expenditure who was the government nominee on the Allahabad Bank board, called an emergency board meeting in Delhi after he was informed about the CBI action by the finance ministry.

The agenda was to pass a resolution stripping her of the powers. Those who could not physically attend the board meeting joined in through video conferencing. N.K. Sahoo, an executive director of the bank, called up Ananthasubramanian to convey the board's decision.

Ananthasubramanian was MD and CEO of PNB between August 2015 and May 2017, before being shifted to the much smaller Allahabad Bank. No reason was cited for this. Typically, the MD of a smaller bank moves into a bigger one. One of her predecessors in PNB, K.R. Kamath, had headed Allahabad Bank before moving to Delhi.

Incidentally, Ananthasubramanian had headed a far smaller bank in her career – Bharatiya Mahila Bank – before becoming the PNB boss. After starting her career at Bank of Baroda as a specialist planning officer in 1982, she rose to become a general manager and later moved to PNB as executive director.

The CBI, armed with government sanction to prosecute her, issued summons to her in Mumbai. Unlike some of her peers, Ananthasubramanian was not arrested, and nor was her residence, a two-bedroom flat in Paridhi Society in Thane West, Mumbai, searched. CBI had recorded her statements twice at its BKC office in Mumbai – once in February and later in March 2018.

The special court in Mumbai handling CBI cases granted bail to her and to Sanjiv Sharan, former executive director of PNB, on 20 August 2018.

The bail order says:

> In the present case, there is no specific evidence against the applicant/accused and there are no peculiar circumstances pertaining to applicant/accused except that she was holding high position in the management of complainant bank. Moreover, the Ld. SPP [learned special public prosecutor] for CBI has specifically stated that applicant/accused had co-operated with the investigating agency during investigation. Further, the applicant/accused had appeared on service of summons. Therefore, the Ld. SPP for CBI has not opposed the bail application.

SC Sets Aside NCLAT Order

One and a half years down the line, in February 2020, the Supreme Court set aside an order of the National Company Law Appellate Tribunal (NCLAT) that had directed the freezing of her assets.

India's highest court accepted the stand of senior counsel C.S. Vaidyanathan, appearing for Ananthasubramanian, that the powers to freeze assets can be exercised only against a company in which acts of mismanagement have been alleged – which, in this case, is Gitanjali Gems Ltd – and not imposed on other entities like PNB.

A bench led by Justice R.F. Nariman rejected the government's stand that the jurisdiction under Section 339 of the Companies Act is wide enough to include freezing the assets of any person who was 'knowingly a party to the carrying on of the fraudulent conduct of business'. However, the apex court clarified that the judgment would not have any effect on the probe of CBI, or the Serious Fraud Investigation Office (SFIO), in the case.

On 31 January 2019, the Mumbai bench of the National Company Law Tribunal (NCLT) had made her a party, along with 18 others, after the Ministry of Corporate Affairs sought to make them respondents in the PNB fraud. The tribunal also directed that the assets of all accused be frozen, and they be restrained from disposing of movable and immovable assets.

The ministry had moved the tribunal under various provisions of the Companies Act, 2013, pertaining to freezing of assets of a company on inquiry and investigation, and also related to the imposition of restrictions upon securities. Ananthasubramanian had challenged this order first in the NCLAT, and then in the Supreme Court.

Gokulnath Shetty, the retired deputy manager of PNB, remains the chief villain of the piece in terms of being the bank insider. Shetty ensured that designer jeweller Nirav Modi's companies could receive LoUs and raise money from international branches of other Indian banks in the form of buyer's credit.

The fraud involved the issue of LoUs through SWIFT without any official sanction. Globally, banks use the messaging network SWIFT, or Society for Worldwide Interbank Financial Telecommunications. The network ensures that banks transmit information and instructions for all financial transactions through a standardised system of codes. Apart from Modi's firms, his uncle Mehul Choksi's companies too were involved in the fraud. (More on this in the chapter 'The F Word in Indian Banking'.)

Along with a few of his colleagues, Shetty, who had been stationed at the foreign exchange department of PNB's Fort branch in Mumbai, since 31 March 2010, was using SWIFT messages to create LoUs. No one else in PNB seemed to be aware of this because such transactions never showed up in the CBS of the bank.

The RBI first wrote to all banks on 3 August 2016 to link SWIFT with CBS. In banking parlance, that was an 'advisory' note. A 'caution' note was issued on 10 August. The banking regulator followed it up with another communication in November 2016.

> A 21 June 2018 *Business Standard* report, by Somesh Jha, says PNB has claimed that the lender did not receive a crucial directive sent by the RBI in November 2016 asking all commercial banks to strengthen their risk mechanism to avert fraud.
>
> The report quoted PNB General Manager Ashwini Vats, saying "The referred letter (dated 25 November 2016) is not received".
>
> The central bank again wrote to PNB Managing Director and Chief Executive Officer Sunil Mehta on March 7 attaching a copy of the e-mail delivery notification of the November 2016 directive. "You are advised to examine the reason for non-availability of the circular at your end and report to us," said Deepan Dey, assistant general manager, banking supervision, RBI.
>
> PNB reverted saying though the bank received an e-mail with a password to open the November 2016 circular, it did not receive the e-mail containing the circular.
>
> "Both the e-mails were sent on November 30, 2016, to

md@pnb.co.in within 11 minutes gap," RBI General Manager (banking supervision) Pankaj Ekka told the CBI during the investigation.

As a practice, the RBI sends passwords of its confidential circulars to banks through e-mails in advance.

After conducting a thorough probe, the bank's chief compliance officer confirmed to the RBI again on March 19 that it had received no such e-mail. Among all banks, only PNB did not receive the RBI's e-mail containing the November 2016 circular.

"Notwithstanding the bank's claim of not having received the e-mail containing the November 25, 2016 circular, the controls enumerated in the first two circulars (August 3, 2016 and August 10, 2016) were not implemented by the bank... Had the control mechanism prescribed in the above circulars been implemented by PNB in letter and spirit, the fraud could have been averted or detected early," Ekka said in his submission.

On 20 February 2018, RBI again mandated that all banks integrate SWIFT and CBS latest by 30 April 2018.

On that day, the central bank issued a press release which said:

> The risks arising from the potential malicious use of the SWIFT infrastructure, created by banks for their genuine business needs, have always been a component of their operational risk profile. RBI had, therefore, confidentially cautioned and alerted banks of such possible misuse, at least on three occasions since August 2016, advising them to implement the safeguards detailed in the RBI's communications, for pre-empting such occurrences. Banks have, however, been at varying levels in implementation of such measures.
>
> In the wake of SWIFT-related fraud involving significant amount, reported recently by PNB, RBI has today reiterated its confidential instructions and mandated the banks to

implement, within the stipulated deadlines, the prescribed measures for strengthening the SWIFT operating environment in banks.

A year down the line, on 8 March 2019, RBI said in a release that it had slapped penalties on 36 banks (the amount varies between ₹4 crore and ₹1 crore) in two phases, on 21 January and 25 February, 'for non-compliance with various directions issued by RBI on time-bound implementation and strengthening of SWIFT-related operational controls.'

The RBI release says it had asked 49 banks to explain why they should not be penalised for not complying with the central bank's directions. The RBI said it had imposed the penalty after considering their replies and giving them personal hearings and it would continue to closely monitor compliance with these controls.

The list includes large public sector, private and foreign banks such as SBI, Bank of Baroda, ICICI Bank, IndusInd Bank, Citibank, Standard Chartered, HSBC, Union Bank and Canara Bank.

The Chargesheet

Going by the CBI chargesheet, the RBI directive was brought to the notice of Ananthasubramanian and other senior PNB executives, including two executive directors, Brahmaji Rao and Sanjiv Sharan. But it was marked 'downward' without taking any meaningful corrective measures, follow-up measures, and necessary reconciliation of SWIFT–CBS system by these accused persons.

It also alleges that these persons were aware of the fraud but chose to remain 'silent spectators' and 'thereby facilitated continuance of the fraud' leading to 'wrongful loss to PNB'.

The CBI investigation 'revealed' that Ananthasubramanian and others, through their acts and omissions, facilitated the use of fraudulent LoUs. The chargesheet mentions Shetty continuing with the issuances of LoUs because of the 'patronage' he was enjoying from the senior bankers working at the Brady House branch of PNB and accuses Ananthasubramanian of 'criminal misconduct' and 'conspiracy' for 'omitting to take any precautions or preventive steps to prevent the fraud'.

A foreign exchange branch (technically called 'authorised dealer') such as the Brady House is subjected to several audits and inspections like concurrent audit, quarterly audit by statutory auditors, regular inspection by the bank and Foreign Exchange Management Act (FEMA) audit beside the RBI inspection, but Shetty's misdeeds never came out in the open.

The finance ministry's show-cause notice issued to a few senior PNB executives spoke about the fraud going on for several years, snowballing into a large amount.

An RBI letter to the ministry also indicated that the fraud had been happening since March 2011 at the branch.

PNB insiders say the bank took the August 2016 RBI communication seriously and set up a committee with close to a dozen executives from the relevant departments such as technology, international business, treasury, information security, etc. The committee held three meetings. But, like many others, PNB too, did not integrate its CBS with the SWIFT system.

No Criminal Offence

Is it a criminal offence? Ananthasubramanian could probably be blamed for alleged negligence. But there was no criminal intent on her part, says the bank's board. Under the instruction of the finance ministry, the board discussed the MD's role and passed a resolution blaming her for not adhering to the RBI directive. The punishment for this is a penalty on the bank.

In the PNB hierarchy, Shetty, the villain of the piece, was eight layers below the MD. He was working at a branch overseen by a circle office/divisional office/regional office, generally headed by deputy general managers. The supervision of circles rests with the zonal managers/field general managers (headed by general managers).

The operational lapses have been overlooked by the agencies. PNB had 7,000 branches and at least 70,000 employees on its payroll, before United Bank of India and Oriental Bank of

Commerce was merged with it in April 2020.

The branch manager was named in the supplementary chargesheet, not the first one which named the MD, two executive directors and two general managers.

How does the legal community view this case? A well-known lawyer asked me: Will you sack the railway minister, or, for that matter, the Railway Board chairman or even the divisional general manager for a train accident at a rail gate, killing some people? The responsibility ends with the engine driver, linesman and perhaps the guard.

Winsome Diamonds

Quite a few Indian bankers have become familiar with CBI chargesheets in the past few years. Apart from the individuals mentioned above, two former CMDs of Canara Bank – Avinash Chander Mahajan and Sunder Rajan Raman – have been named for their alleged role in a loan default of ₹146 crore by Jatin Mehta of Winsome Diamonds.

The agency filed a chargesheet in June 2018 against 21 accused, including Mehta, his wife, 15 public servants such as Mahajan, Raman and a former executive director of the bank, Archana Bhargava. The chargesheet was filed on 8 June 2018 under Section 120B, 420 & 409 of the Indian Penal Code and 13(2) and 13(1)(d) of the Prevention of Corruption Act in the Special Court handling CBI cases.

Raman, who had a five-year stint with the markets regulator, SEBI, at a senior position (whole-time member) after his Canara Bank days, lives in Kandivali in the western Mumbai suburbs in an austere two-bedroom flat.

He started his career as a clerk in SBI at 19, when he was not even a graduate. On completing his graduation, he was selected as a direct recruit probationary officer in Bank of India in the 1970s. From there, he moved to Union Bank of India, as an executive director, and then went as chairman and MD at Canara Bank, where his father had worked as a stenographer.

Months before the chargesheet was filed, Canara Bank wrote to Raman, requesting his presence at the CBI's BKC office to answer certain questions relating to the case registered against Forever Precious Jewellery and Diamonds, a company of the Winsome Diamonds Group.

He did go to the CBI office for recording his statement. A look-out circular has been issued to ensure that he does not leave India during the investigation for interrogation or enquiry.

Even Central Bankers not Spared

Even former central bankers have not been spared from being questioned by the investigative agencies. A look-out notice has been issued for at least one of them. Armed with a look-out notice, also known as a look-out circular, the immigration officials at airports prevent an accused from leaving the country.

Central bankers have been called into the CBI's Mumbai and Delhi offices for questioning on subjects ranging from the government's gold import policy (notified through the central bank) to the Kingfisher Airlines loan restructuring, alleged irregularities in the Foreign Investment Promotion Board's clearance granted to a media group for receiving overseas funds and a loan given by a PSB to a travel agency.

In one case, while a central banker was engaged in conversation with CBI officials at their BKC office, the TV channels were running his photograph with the ticker saying he was being grilled by the CBI in the Nirav Modi case. Another central banker, now a non-resident, was barred from leaving India following a look-out circular even though he has not been an 'accused' in any banking fraud.

A Joke

In September 2008, just after the collapse of Lehman Brothers, at a parent-teacher meeting at a Brooklyn middle school, a teacher asked the students to talk about their fathers. Many spoke glowingly about their fathers – engineers, scientists, retailers, accountants... When one boy said his father was a pole dancer, there was pin-drop silence in the classroom. Even if your dad is a pole dancer, it takes a brave child to admit this publicly.

At the end of the meeting, when everybody left, the teacher hugged the student and said how proud she was of his courage and honesty. Sheepishly, the student whispered into the teacher's ears, 'Ma'am, actually I lied. I was too embarrassed to say my dad is a banker.'

I do not know about the bankers' children, but public sector bankers in India, including the retired ones, are now an embarrassed and much-harassed lot. The investigative agencies are hounding them, both for loans that have gone bad, and for outright frauds. Are we replicating the Chinese banking system where many borrowers are dishonest, many bankers corrupt, risk assessment is poor and the legal system weak, leading to a large number of loans not being backed by genuine collateral?

The arrests of Syndicate Bank's Sudhir Kumar Jain, CMD for allegedly accepting a bribe to enhance the credit limit of private companies, and of United Bank of India's Archana Bhargava for alleged corruption did not shake the industry. In both cases, there was apparent criminal conduct by a banker.

But the other instances of arrests and harassment have had a chilling effect. That is reality.

Writing on the Wall

The banking community saw the writing on the wall in January 2017 when former IDBI Bank chief Agarwal and deputy managing director Batra were arrested. That is when the nightmare started.

A group of bankers, led by Arundhati Bhattacharya, then SBI chairman, rushed to meet Finance Minister Arun Jaitley after Agarwal's arrest. They tried to impress on the finance minister the impact of such arrests could have on the banking system.

But that did not stop the CBI. After the CBI named three top bankers in its first chargesheet in the PNB fraud case, these three were stripped of their powers. The agency also booked the MDs of Syndicate Bank and Indian Bank, Melwyn Rego and Kishor Kharat.

Another person who came under the CBI scanner was the former UCO Bank chairman Arun Kaul. I may have missed out a few names!

The IBA has strongly protested the arrest of Marathe, but there have been no mass protests against such actions. Probably, the poor customer service by most banks has isolated the banking community from the masses. Traditionally, the big borrowers get all the respect from the bankers; retail borrowers are tolerated; and savers whose money banks lend out, get the least attention.

Should bankers be booked, sacked, divested of powers and arrested indiscriminately? There is a clear difference between giving a loan that goes bad, and giving a loan in return for a favour. Can inefficiency, poor risk management and even negligence be interpreted as criminal offences?

Since the Prevention of Corruption Act applies to both the so-called public servants as well as private bankers, shouldn't private bankers also be booked for alleged graft? What about the role of politicians, bureaucrats and even ministers in influencing, or forcing bankers, to lend to particular companies?

In private, many bankers talk about such 'influences' from these quarters for the loans to Kingfisher Airlines. What about the board members who often broker loan deals? And the promoters who entice the bankers with goodies to give loans that are not recoverable?

The Demonstrative Effect

The investigative agencies are quick to file chargesheets and arrest bankers, but in how many cases have they been able to prove their charges? The focus seems to be more on managing the optics.

There is a cascading effect. The impact is first felt on the next rung of leadership. Not only do they refrain from taking loan decisions; they also prevent the next level of employees from doing so.

The lesson bankers learn from such incidents is: 'If you take decisions, there will be some mistakes; if you don't take decisions, there can't be any mistake.'

In PSBs, there is now a distinction between a clean record (one who took decisions but did not face trouble) and blank record (one who did not take any decisions, and hence did not face any trouble).

In the first week of December 2019, Prime Minister Narendra Modi told the 17th Hindustan Times Leadership Summit that India's banking sector has emerged from the crises of the past and urged bankers to take 'genuine business decisions' without fear. 'The government cannot have him (a banker) helpless… I will take responsibility. That is how the country will progress,' he said.

Weeks later, Finance Minister Sitharaman, at a bankers' meeting in Delhi, addressed concerns over genuine decisions being questioned by the three Cs – the CBI, CVC and the CAG. CBI Director R.K. Shukla was also present at that meeting.

Banking is a business of risk assessment. If a banker is blamed when a loan turns bad, the same banker must also be praised for loans that fetch profits.

Dishonesty by bankers should be taken very seriously as they deal with public money; corruption in banking is as bad as deaths in police custody. Nobody should be spared. But a better way to clean up banking could be to select cases of high-value corruption and criminal connivance and prosecute these to the logical end, making optimum use of the limited resources investigative agencies possess.

The investigative agencies also need to see a pattern: Is the banker involved in just one fraud, or bad loan, or many?

The Indian economy has become the biggest loser from this practice of subjecting bankers to public humiliation, unending investigations and the tarring of the entire banking community with the same brush.

Tardy credit growth tells a story – bankers are a harassed and scared lot. They know if they do not lend, they will not be chargesheeted or arrested and no one loses his or her job for not lending. But if a loan turns bad, they may end up spending sleepless nights on a *durrie* and rubbing shoulders with hardened criminals in an over-crowded jail barrack.

■ ■ ■

10

The Fallen Angels

PART 1

There have been fallen angels in every decade.

Take M. Gopalakrishnan, for instance. He was CMD of the Chennai-based Indian Bank for a seven-year stint until 1995, with seven extensions. He was a darling of the media, liberal in his advertisement support to newspapers and Doordarshan, and happy to be involved in all sorts of public events, including inauguration of public urinals. Post-retirement, he has been sentenced to rigorous imprisonment in multiple cases for sanctioning big money to shell companies run by politicians.

A year after he stepped down, Indian Bank posted a loss of ₹1,336.40 crore for 1995–96. This was the highest loss ever posted by any bank in India until that time. It wiped out the bank's entire net worth. Prior to his retirement, the bank had simply kept on declaring profits, by refusing to recognise its bad assets and setting aside money. The RBI forced it to recast the balance sheet for the year ending March 1996.

Ramesh Gelli was the fallen angel of the first decade of the twenty-first century. He was 37 when he became the boss of Vysya Bank in 1983, which made him the youngest chairman in Indian banking. In 1990, he was awarded the Padma Shri.

In 1994, he promoted Global Trust Bank Ltd when the RBI allowed the first set of new private banks. But in the next decade, Global Trust Bank went belly up after betting big on the stock market, leading to a forced merger with a PSB.

By that time, Gelli was non-executive chairman. In an interview with *Business Standard* in July 2004, Gelli blamed his experimentation: 'complete delegation of power and full dependence on the senior management team' for the fall of the bank. Those familiar with the case say his claim was very far from the truth. 'My career as a banker is over. I may pursue academics or be a mentor to new entrepreneurs,' Gelli, then 58, had said.

The current decade has seen two angels falling from grace: Rana Kapoor and Chanda Kochhar.

Rana, the Warrior

I am a Rana – a warrior, always ready to battle my way to victory.

That was Rana Kapoor's attitude and persona from his formative years at Bank of America. He joined the bank as a management trainee in 1980. After completing his MBA from Rutgers, the State University of New Jersey, commonly referred to as Rutgers University, Kapoor applied to three banks – Citibank NA, ANZ Grindlays and BankAm.

He was among the three candidates shortlisted by ANZ Grindlays. It is said he could not get the job as the other two were sons of senior bureaucrats. It may or may not be true as Kapoor was also well-connected. His father, an Indian Airlines pilot for 37 years, was a mentor pilot to the young Rajiv Gandhi, and a close associate of Congress leader, Satish Sharma.

His BankAm colleagues recall how Kapoor would come up the winner from all sorts of adverse situations. He rose to head the corporate banking business at BankAm in 16 years, reporting to country head Vikram Talwar. He was eventually forced to resign by Ambi Venkateswaran, who replaced Talwar. The reason? The banking community says he had not followed norms when sanctioning a huge credit-line to one of India's largest corporate houses.

The two-year run that followed at ANZ Grindlays Investment Bank, as general manager and country head of corporate finance, was phenomenal. By 1998, Kapoor had raised funds for Jet Airways' fleet acquisition and Airtel's rollout of cellular services in Delhi. Airtel's promoter, Sunil Mittal, was an old friend. They used to play snooker at Panchsheel Club, South Delhi, when they were both in their teens.

Kapoor's brother-in-law Ashok Kapur was the first Asian to be appointed ABN Amro's country manager for India. Kapoor and Kapur teamed up with Harkirat Singh, the Deutsche Bank India boss, to set up Rabo India, a non-banking financial company (NBFC). The parent was Rabobank, a Dutch multinational banking and financial services company, headquartered in Utrecht, the Netherlands.

It is not that well-publicised that the NBFC was Singh's idea. He had first approached Kapur who, in turn, brought Kapoor on board. When a Rabobank team arrived in India in February 1995, scouting for opportunities, Singh proposed a joint venture to the visiting team. Since it would take time to get the banking licence from the RBI, another joint venture was planned for an NBFC, until such time as the bank licence was issued.

The NBFC was set up in February 1998. According to media reports, each of the three chipped in with equity capital of ₹9 crore and collectively held 25 per cent stake, but this could not be confirmed. Media reports also indicate Kapoor contributed ₹40 lakh for his stake, with the rest being a joining bonus from Rabobank.

Kapoor, Kapur and Hans Hannaart and Anton Nillesen (both on deputation from Rabobank), formed the management team of Rabo India Finance Ltd while Singh was made a special adviser to the managing board of Rabobank International in London, supervising projects on capital and risk management and international strategy.

His role later changed, from general manager, UK operations, to co-head of the global capital markets business.

In India, Kapoor looked after financial services such as trade and commodity finance, corporate banking and advisory services. Kapur, a director, along with a Rabobank executive, were driving other parts of the business.

In no time, Rabo India turned into the best boutique investment bank in India. And, Rabobank started eating out of Kapoor's hand after he engineered Tata Tea's takeover of Tetley in 2000, which was the biggest cross-border acquisition made until then.

Birth of Yes Bank

In 2002, Yes Bank Ltd, a greenfield project, and another NBFC, Kotak Mahindra Finance Ltd, got the RBI nod to set up a bank each. The initial capital required for a new bank was ₹200 crore. The trio sold their stakes in the NBFC to generate the seed funding.

The three of them were to hold 17 per cent each in the bank. Rabobank looked at several options of holding between 20 per cent and 49 per cent. Finally, it settled for 26 per cent, which gave Rabobank the power to veto any special resolution. That made up 77 per cent equity. The plan was to offer around 5 per cent of the residual 23 per cent to the employees, and the rest would be raised from a set of private equity investors.

Yes Bank's launch was even more dramatic than its near-collapse in 2020. According to the original plan, Singh was to be the CEO of the bank; Kapur, the non-executive chairman; and Kapoor would play a dual role as a non-executive director of the bank as well as CEO of the NBFC.

But Singh withdrew from the venture, following serious differences of opinion with his two partners. An April 2003 *Economic Times* report quoted Singh saying, 'There is no longer a complete alignment with the vision, going forward.'

Singh's exit was triggered by Rabobank's proposal to appoint Kapur (who was by then, an executive vice president and regional manager with ABN Amro, Singapore) executive chairman.

Singh was not consulted on the proposal, the report says. 'This decision is further evidence of a lack of mutuality of the objectives of the bank as envisioned by me. I have therefore decided to withdraw as a promoter of this new banking company… I value my reputation above everything else,' Singh said to the paper.

Singh also found the profile of the bank's proposed business very different from what he had envisaged. That also contributed to his decision to exit.

Kapoor seized this opportunity with both hands. He flew to Utrecht and met senior executives of Rabo, convincing them to stay put after Singh's exit, and thus, bagged the top job. Two Rabobank personnel – Hans ten Cate, chairman of the managing board of Rabobank International, and Wouter Kolff, vice chairman, managing board, Rabobank International – joined the Yes Bank board as directors.

The rift emerged in the open after the RBI's deadline for setting up the bank expired. By that time, the regulator had already given a three-month extension and the roll out was scheduled for August 2003.

Following Singh's exit, instead of holding 17 per cent stake each, Kapoor and Kapur needed to hike their stake to 25.5 per cent each (by splitting Singh's 17 per cent between the two). Rabobank gave them a bridge loan to arrange the additional equity but also decided to reduce its own equity contribution from 26 per cent to 20 per cent, locking this down for three years.

(In April 2010, Rabobank got the RBI nod to open its own India operations, after paring its stake in Yes Bank below 5 per cent.)

Kapoor wooed three private equity funds, which came on board. Quite a few other funds had shown interest but they walked out after Singh quit. Citicorp International Finance Corporation, ChrysCapital II, LLC and AIF Capital Inc. contributed a total of 25 per cent. ChrysCapital chipped in 10 per cent, and the other two picked up 7.5 per cent each. The remaining 4 per cent was reserved for the top management.

The bank was incorporated as a public limited company on 21 November 2003.

The RBI cleared the entry of the three private equity investors on 26 February 2004 after extending its 'in principle' approval yet again, for a period up to 29 February 2004 through a letter dated 29 December 2003.

Yes Bank obtained its certificate of commencement of business on 21 January 2004. By March, it could mobilise the initial minimum paid-up capital of ₹200 crore and, finally, on 24 May 2004, RBI granted it the licence to commence operations.

Meanwhile, Singh had filed an arbitration case in London against Rabobank for removing him as the proposed bank's designated CEO without assigning any reason. A *Times of India* news report, dated 15 March 2005, says Singh won the case against Rabobank for 'breach of contract and loss of profits' from the International Arbitration Panel in London.

There was another interesting sideshow many missed at the time.

Yes Bank had impressed the regulator with its plan for financing agriculture and allied activities. In the original business plan, Yes Bank was to mirror Rabobank with interests in agri-tech, pharma, telecom, education, green-power and financing technology solutions.

However, Kapoor turned it into a corporate bank. Of course, he had set up the Food and Agribusiness Strategic Advisory and Research group within the bank to reinforce his commitment to agriculture sector. But this division never went beyond writing a few reports. This, of course, does not prevent Yes Bank claiming the group to be India's premier food and agribusiness knowledge unit with several prestigious advisories, and research mandates to its credentials!

Kapoor Vs Kapur

The popular perception is Kapoor changed his style of functioning after Kapur's unfortunate death in the 26 November 2008 terrorist attacks on Mumbai. But those who knew the duo say they were never close to each other even when Kapur was chairman of the bank. At best, they shared a love-hate relationship. At public meetings, they put up a show of camaraderie but in private, one never missed a chance to bitch about the other.

People who witnessed their interactions claim Kapoor walked all over Kapur. He used to make fun of his chairman even in front of the junior employees of the bank, saying, 'He is good enough to be the chairman of Bombay Gymkhana (which he was). We pay him ₹48 lakh (a year) to read newspapers in the office for two hours every morning.'

The last act of the Kapoor Vs Kapur drama was pretty long. It started in 2013 when Madhu Kapur, widow of Ashok Kapur, moved court claiming that, after her husband's death, her daughter Shagun Gogia should have been given a seat on the bank's board. Kapoor and the board said no to her proposal as Gogia did not have the requisite experience.

After a long legal battle and Kapoor's exit from the saddle, Gogia got a berth on the board in April 2019. A little over a year later, in May 2020, the Kapur family relinquished their status as a promoter and turned into ordinary public shareholders ahead of the bank's plan to raise capital in June. Madhu Kapur also withdrew the case filed against the bank.

Many Yes Bank employees say the turning point for Kapoor was the 2013 court case. Until that time, he was focused on building an institution. But Madhu Kapur's challenge changed him. He started seeking power, money and self-glorification. And, he was in tearing hurry to get all that. That was the beginning of the game of manipulating industry bodies, regulators and bureaucracy.

'I, Me, Myself'

People in Kapoor's inner circles had seen him losing his cool every so often. He could get furious if anyone else had an opinion that was even remotely related to banking. On strategy, he would always have the last word – others were meant to execute his vision. If anyone ever breached this *Lakshman Rekha*, Kapoor's standard reaction was: 'Don't teach me banking.'

During the bank's IPO in 2005, his slogan was 'Nothing can come between me and the IPO.'

Nobody knows the 'I, me, myself' syndrome better than Yes Bank's head of direct banking in the early days when every bank needed RBI clearance for setting up offsite ATMs.

This executive was looking after all banking channels barring the branches. Once the RBI gave the go-ahead to Yes Bank to put up 200 ATMs, he could not control his excitement and sent a mail to all employees at headquarters breaking the news.

The mail triggered an earthquake. A furious Kapoor blasted the channel banking head – how dare he make such an announcement! It was the CEO's prerogative. Kapoor, feared by most and respected by a few, was a firm believer in the demonstrative effect of a dressing-down in public. His usual demeanor towards his executives was: 'You exist because I "allow" you to exist.'

As a leader, Kapoor was a strong believer in the 'divide and rule' policy. No business head was allowed to feel secure. He always 'cultivated' the No 2 in any business division when he got the feeling that the business head was getting powerful and 'independent'.

He also did not take kindly to employees quitting the bank. Once anyone expressed her intention to move on, Kapoor would ask that person to leave immediately, at times even ordering her to leave the company car behind in the office parking lot and 'walk back home'. There were instances when people were asked to sign exit letters with non-disclosure agreements that bound them not to speak about the bank and its activities.

Some of his colleagues also say he would not allow them to sell shares of the bank that they received in the form of stock options. Kapoor would often send his emissaries from the bank's HR team to 'subtly' persuade employees not to sell shares.

A handful who worked closely with Kapoor and his family office were disproportionately rewarded. But the majority of Yes Bank employees, arguably a fine pool of talent, were not well looked after. After the can of worms opened, many felt they were working for a 'Don'!

Going by one account, one of the management committee meetings of the bank in 2005 lasted for two days with a six-hour break. It started on a Thursday morning and continued till Friday early morning, and, after the break, went on till Saturday morning.

The meeting had started with eight executives but, by the time it ended, there were around 30 people in the room. That was typical of Kapoor's style. As the meeting progressed, he asked more and more people to join in.

Booze flowed in the evenings. Kapoor's preferred drink is Johnnie Walker Black Label. To keep him happy, colleagues would keep topping up his glass. He could reputedly drink half a bottle neat without getting drunk. But people around him would hardly remain sober, and that created an ideal opportunity to get his message across.

In the early days, there were many parties at Kapoor's residence at Grand Paradi behind the Shalimar Hotel, Babulnath, Kemps Corner, Mumbai. The party would start at around 9 pm and continue till early the next morning. The choicest alcohol would be served and senior bankers would listen to· Kapoor spellbound while Bindu (Kapoor's wife) would engage their spouses separately. Kapoor could mesmerise his colleagues when he was in full flow.

He is known for being a driven and extremely ambitious man. Kapoor could make plans looking 15–20 years ahead. In his scheme of things, there were two phases of business development – the first phase was meant for the bank, and the second, for himself.

■ ■ ■

PHASE 1

After Ashok Kapur's death, the quality of the board deteriorated fast as many of Kapoor's yes men moved in. Kapoor, too, changed his role from being the key man running the show to becoming the bank itself as he had to migrate to the second phase of his vision.

So, Yes Bank started positioning itself as the lender of last resort as Kapoor bet on his inherent belief in the high-risk, high-return business model.

How were loans sanctioned?

Kapoor believed in 'phone banking'. He was in direct contact with the borrowers on the one hand and his top executives from the business verticals, on the other, to get things done. It was a 'direct dealing' methodology.

The first round of discussions would typically happen at his residence. Then proposals would be presented to the credit committees brilliantly, dissecting all aspects of the borrowers – positive and negative. But the loans would actually be sanctioned by tweaking the weightage on different aspects.

The bank was aware that such loans would turn bad but Kapoor was confident that the said loans could be parked with another bank or an NBFC and bought back later. It was a 'sharp' practice within the banking norms which permit the sale of loans. If Kapoor was selling something, it was understood within the industry that he would buy it back. But there was nothing in writing.

He was arbitraging between the banks and NBFCs, using the letter of the law on bad loan norms of two sets of financial intermediaries. For banks, a loan turns bad after the borrower fails to pay interest on it or the principal for 90 days. For NBFCs, in those days, this limit was 180 days.

Banks had safety valves for such rotten loans. One of them was an exorbitant processing fee for sanctioning such loans. Beside fee income, that was the first tool of recovery.

The second was a very high interest rate. In its heydays, Yes Bank was enjoying much higher returns than any other bank as it was not only earning interest on the amount lent, but also extracting huge processing fees. As a result of this, the actual cash inflow could be as high as 80 per cent of the principal. This is why the bank could take risks and write it off, if and when a loan turned bad after a few years.

This is how it worked. Let us assume Yes Bank sanctioned a loan of ₹1 crore to a borrower for 15 per cent processing fees and 15 per cent interest. In three years, the bank would get ₹60 lakh (₹15 lakh processing fee and ₹45 lakh in interest). At this time, even if the borrower defaulted, the bank could afford to settle for a sizeable haircut and still make a profit from this account.

The Junk Bond Approach

Given his insatiable risk appetite, Kapoor was looking for high returns and creating a junk credit market in India. He is the pioneer in this space. There is nothing fundamentally wrong in this approach. But Kapoor began misusing this business model at every stage.

Also, all the large exposures were not plain vanilla loans – many were bonds and debentures issued without any collateral. When such exposures turn bad, virtually nothing is recoverable.

Kapoor resorted to evergreening the bad accounts by giving them fresh loans. He also parked some of the bad accounts with other obliging lenders (mostly NBFCs) and bought them back, in a circular process.

Kapoor could generally get his money back from the promoters ahead of other creditors. However, in this high-risk, high-return model, the excesses of the past catches up when the economic cycle turns down.

In addition, of course, there was the involvement of his family offices, and the alleged triangular relationship among Yes Bank, some of its borrowers and Kapoor's family offices. Kapoor and his family ran a labyrinthine network of companies as described later in this narrative. Those firms were deeply involved in many Yes Bank deals. It was not money alone; real estate was also involved in such deals.

The bank's board never questioned or dared to question Kapoor. Everybody in the bank was happy and dancing, or made to dance, until the music finally stopped.

The Red Flag

Kapoor had his own explanation of how the bad loans were being kept low. In an interview with CNBC-TV 18 in April 2016, he spoke about his famous three-eyes principle: Relationship managers, product managers and risk managers – all looking at a relationship from all angles. 'That makes sure that when you have a problem, the red flag surfaces early enough,' Kapoor said.

One research analyst who flagged off the bad loan problem in Yes Bank ahead of others is Vishal Goyal of UBS. His 7 July 2015 report (written along with Ishank Kumar and Stephen Andrews) found the bank 'most vulnerable to a prolonged weak credit cycle' and downgraded it from buy to sell, with a ₹740 price target (from ₹1,000).

The report said:

> Yes has reported strong asset quality so far, with its impaired loans ratio the lowest among its peers at 1.2 per cent. However, according to our study, it is most vulnerable to a large corporate default. Estimated loans to potentially stressed companies recorded a 60 per cent CAGR over F12-15E and would be 125 per cent of the net worth of Yes Bank.

UBS conducted a 'proprietary survey' of at least 7,000 collateral documents (used to secure loans) filed at the Registrar of Companies (RoC) linked to a sample of 100 potentially-stressed companies (covering around $100 billion in loans) to understand exposure and lending practices of Indian banks.

Kapoor's tolerance level about any criticism of the bank was pretty low. Yes Bank rushed to complain to the market regulator SEBI against the UBS report. It found the report had an exaggerated sense of its exposure to the stressed companies, given the RoC filings were dated and did not reflect the actual disbursement. In its filings with the stock exchanges, Yes Bank said UBS did not seek its views before coming out with the report.

■ ■ ■

PHASE 2

Once Yes Bank achieved the targets he wanted, Kapoor entered the next phase of focussing on his personal growth, by monetising his investment in the bank. That was the genesis of the problem. 'I, me, myself' became 'I, me, myself and mine' in this phase.

The 49-page provisional attachment order of the Directorate of Enforcement, signed by Kapil Raj, deputy director Mumbai Zonal Office 1, dated 5 May 2020, alleges Kapoor and his family ran a labyrinth of at least 101 companies.

This was an inverted pyramid structure based on three holding firms – Morgan Credits Pvt Ltd (MCPL), Yes Capital (India) Pvt Ltd (YCPL) and RAB Enterprises (India) Pvt Ltd, and their subsidiaries and step-down subsidiaries. Many of the subsidiaries have equity capital of just ₹1 lakh.

MCPL, the oldest among them, was incorporated in 1991. YCPL (originally DOIT Capital (I) Pvt Ltd) was incorporated in May 2003. Both are RBI-licensed investment companies. MCPL has 59 subsidiaries, YCPL 24 and RAB Enterprises, which is wholly owned by Kapoor's wife Bindu, has 15 subsidiaries. RAB was incorporated in May 2005, for investing in properties. Kapoor's wife and his three daughters – Radha, Rakhee and Roshni – share ownership of these all.

The dominant themes that run through the names of Kapoor's family firms illustrate his aggression and passion – 'DOIT', 'Bliss' and 'Art'.

The businesses managed by these companies are very diverse.

Let me put the business activities in alphabetical order: Art (Art Arc [India] Pvt Ltd and a dozen more firms), affordable housing (Art Housing Finance (India) Ltd), dry cleaning (Press2 Drycleaning and Laundry Pvt Ltd), eco-tourism (Alibaug Eco Tourism [India] Pvt Ltd and DOIT Eco Tourism [India] Pvt Ltd), milk products (Ravi Milk Products [India] Pvt Ltd), movie production (Azure Entertainment Pvt Ltd), Omni channel grocery supply (Freshlee Retail Pvt Ltd), real estate (DOIT Smart Housing [India] Pvt Ltd), renewable energy

(Ravi Renewable Energy & Lightning [India] Pvt Ltd), sports such as cricket and kabbadi (Dabang Mumbai Sports Management Pvt Ltd, DOIT Sports Management India Pvt Ltd and Dabang Delhi Sports Management Pvt Ltd), talent management (DOIT Talent Ventures (I) Pvt Ltd) and venture finance in start-ups (Art Venture Finance (I) Pvt Ltd).

The family also owns quite a few foreign subsidiaries. These include DOIT Creations Jersey Ltd, DOIT Hospitality Delaware LLC, Conduit Holdco, which runs a club in London, and Audley Grosvenor Ltd, which is setting up a boutique hotel on Grosvenor Street, London.

People, who know Kapoor well, say urban infrastructure business, design and art are all close to Kapoor's heart. The Indian School of Design and Innovation (ISDI), which was set up by his daughter Radha, has partnered with Parsons School of Design, the only American art and design school within a comprehensive university. The ISDI has a sprawling facility at Tower 2 of One Indiabulls Centre on Senapati Bapat Marg in Mumbai's Lower Parel.

Then there is the Indian School of Management and Entrepreneurship Pvt Ltd (ISME). Radha is the co-founder of The Three Sisters: Institutional Office, which manages ISDI and ISME through a holding company.

Too Long a Rope?

Yes Bank, as most readers will be aware, ended up in a downwards spiral. Even as the investigative agencies probe Kapoor's role in the downfall of the bank, many questions arise.

Did the RBI give Kapoor too long a rope?

Was the regulator caught napping?

Shouldn't he have been caught out much earlier?

Let us try to dig deeper.

RBI was aware of the promoter-CEO aggressively pursuing growth, with high-risk exposure to real estate borrowers. Kapoor was also lending to those who were generally not entertained by other banks, or borrowers who had already turned defaulters on others' books. The bad loans were taken over by Yes Bank with a 'standard' tag.

How was this done? Suppose a real estate developer is working on a project in Mumbai. It is cash-strapped and its loan has gone bad. Yes Bank would step in. But it would not give money to the developer for this particular project. Instead, it would lend to another project of the same developer. The amount would be much more than that particular project required. The extra cash was actually meant for the first project.

This 'over-financing' helped Yes Bank grow its balance sheet, earn profits, pay good dividends and keep the shareholders – which include Kapoor and his family – happy.

The RBI was watching this game on its radar for sometime but it waited until 2016 to intensify supervision. The speed with which the NPAs were getting resolved made the regulator suspicious. Every time the RBI inspection team found a bad loan, Kapoor's standard response was: 'I will take care of it.'

True to his promise, Kapoor was indeed taking care of these bad loans. The troubled loans would be out of the bank's book before the next inspection but the next year, new bad loans would surface. That had been the pattern.

This phenomenon and something else – what in RBI's parlance is 'quick mortality accounts' – made RBI inspectors suspicious. Quick mortality accounts are defined as ones that become NPA within a year of the first sanction or disbursement.

How could Yes Bank resolve bad loans so fast compared with other banks? The RBI probed deeper. It found that many accounts were turning bad but the bank was smartly covering them up or evergreening them between two annual inspections. The regulator was not getting a whiff of the real picture.

Evergreening is a process of showing loans as standard or performing by crediting the loan accounts with monies from seemingly unknown sources.

Initially it was believed that Kapoor had to go because of the under-reporting of bad loans by the bank for two consecutive years. However, the real reason behind Kapoor's ouster was very different.

But first let us take a look at the under-reporting of bad loans.

Its annual report for the financial year 2015–16 showed that the lender's assessment of bad loans in the previous fiscal year was very different from that of the RBI. For 2016, Yes Bank had disclosed gross NPAs of ₹748.9 crore, but the RBI's assessment of the correct level of gross NPAs was over six times higher at ₹4,925.6 crore.

As far as the net NPAs were concerned, there was a divergence of ₹3,319 crore between Yes Bank's reported figure and the RBI's assessment. Had Yes Bank assessed the quality of its loan assets the RBI way, its 0.8 per cent gross NPAs would actually have been 6 per cent.

The next year, in 2016–17, the divergence was even greater at ₹6,355 crore. The bank declared gross NPAs to the tune of ₹2,018 crore while, going by the regulator's yardstick, it should have been ₹8,373.8 crore.

The Anonymous Letter

Sometime in September 2018, an anonymous letter reached RBI Governor Urjit Patel's table, alleging various violations by Kapoor. It made a string of allegations about poor governance and cast aspersions on Kapoor's integrity.

> Allegation No 1: Kapoor's family purchased a villa in Lutyens' Delhi from Avantha Group chairman Gautam Thapar to settle a bad loan. Yes Bank had given ₹300 crore in an all-purpose corporate loan to the group.
>
> Allegation No 2: Yes Bank had written off a loan of ₹150 crore given to Nathella Sampathu Chetty Trust of Chennai.
>
> Allegation No 3: Kapoor was paying huge compensation to some employees – much more than what should have been given to them – and they were primarily working for his family offices.

At the RBI, supervision and regulation, two key departments that oversee how banks are run, are typically handled by two deputy governors. After Deputy Governor S.S. Mundra stepped down in July 2017, N.S. Vishwanathan, the senior-most deputy governor, who was handling regulation, took over the supervision portfolio of Mundra. He ran it until M.K. Jain, a commercial banker like Mundra, succeeded him in June 2018.

By that time, the anonymous letter had already reached the governor's office and an investigation was on. Vishwanathan told his colleagues that Kapoor was running a very high-risk bank for high returns and the business model could not be sustained. Very few loans were going bad at that time but Vishwanathan was sure that Kapoor was 'managing' the show.

RBI Gets into Action

The RBI got into action. But it was not an easy task as Kapoor had many moles in the central bank. Every move that RBI was contemplating was relayed to Kapoor in no time. It took a while for the central bank to identify the suspects and isolate them from the investigative process.

The Thapar property at 40, Amrita Shergill Marg, New Delhi, was acquired in partial settlement of dues, and the account was still alive. What intrigued the RBI team was that the property was not offered as security, while taking the loan. Had that been the case, the security could have been attached.

When the property offered as security does not cover the entire loan that has turned bad, the bank can attach more properties. But the CEO's family cannot buy it by floating a company. It must be auctioned and there must be a transparent and open bidding process, starting with advertisements in newspapers.

Avantha Holdings, the holding company of the Thapar Group, was given a general-purpose corporate loan, an unsecured facility. The loan and the sale of property by the company were two separate deals.

Kapoor's wife and family bought the property through Bliss

Abode Pvt Ltd, incorporated a few months before this, with nominal capital.

The loan given to the trust in Chennai was sanctioned by Kapoor himself and written off by him. Typically, a write-off should be done by a higher authority – in this case, the bank's board. But this was not referred to the board.

None knows who wrote the letter to the RBI.

Varun Sood, a writer at the Morning Context, a news website, put up a report on this deal at LinkedIn in March 2020. He claimed this was written in December 2018 but never published. It says:

> Avantha Realty, the privately-owned firm which owned the 40, Amrita Shergill Marg property, had borrowed ₹400 crore at an 11 per cent interest. The bank's in-house experts had valued the property at ₹330 crore. Six months later, in October 2016, property consultants, Cushman and Wakefield, hired by Yes Bank, put a market value of ₹357 crore.
>
> In June 2017, Thapar expressed its interest to sell this property and asked Yes Bank to remove the charge on the property. The bank removed the charge, claiming that it is normal practice. Three months later, in August 2017, Rahul Bhatia, owner of IndiGo Airlines, expressed his interest to buy the property for ₹375 crore. For some reason, the deal fell through. Finally, towards the end of August, Bliss Abode emerged as the winner, when it agreed to pay ₹378 crore to buy the property.
>
> ...A spokesperson for IndiGo declined to offer a comment, saying it does not comment on personal matters. An email sent to Bliss Abode went unanswered.

Referring to the same property deal, an *Outlook Business* story by Krishna Gopalan in October 2019 says:

> The default on the loan meant that it went on the block and was picked up by Rahul Bhatia, co-founder of Interglobe Aviation,

the company behind IndiGo Airline, at a price significantly more than what was quoted. Kapoor managed to quietly scuttle that sale and bought it for himself. A livid Bhatia wrote to the government complaining about the inappropriateness of the process and a government, already uncomfortable with the running of Yes Bank, began to push for Kapoor's removal.

The Delhi property was not the only deal. There were quite a few, including Khursheedabad building, a residential apartment block, jointly owned by Citibank and healthcare major GlaxoSmithKline on Altamount Road in Mumbai, which was put on the block in March 2018. The Kapoor family bought this property for ₹128 crore to build their home. The building was located next to Mukesh Ambani's 27-storey home, Antilla.

There were other gross irregularities. The RBI followed the money trail and found that money was travelling through seven-eight-nine banks on the same day – either before entering Yes Bank's accounts or after leaving Yes Bank.

Detecting this was not easy. Money can be electronically transferred by the press of a button and flow through banks, NBFCs, real estate developers and other entities. It is extremely difficult to do simultaneous scrutiny as not all the entities are regulated by the RBI.

The RBI investigations found many skeletons in Yes Bank's closet. For instance, there were many employees on the bank's payroll who were also working for Kapoor's family offices.

The bank was also charging exorbitant processing fees – in some cases as much as 25 per cent of the loan amount. Kapoor was picking up borrowers other banks would not touch with a bargepole. The RBI found this a highly 'unnatural' banking practice.

There was no proper appraisal of loan proposals, no checks on sanctions. Aided by a few lieutenants, Kapoor was running the bank like his fiefdom. None of the board members ever raised questions about his style of functioning.

The RBI also found that one Suraksha Asset Reconstruction

Ltd (formerly known as Suraksha Asset Reconstruction Pvt Ltd), promoted by Sudhir Valia and Vijay Parekh, purchased most of the bad loans of the bank. There was no due diligence, and no bids for price discovery when Yes Bank sold its bad loans.

Valia, brother-in-law of Sun Pharma's MD Dilip Shanghvi, a director on the central board of RBI, was an executive director of Sun Pharmaceutical Industries Ltd and director of Sun Pharmaceutical Advanced Research Company Ltd. He changed his role in Sun Pharma from a whole-time director to a non-executive, non-independent director from 29 May 2019.

When the investigation and the database of the CRILC confirmed RBI's worst suspicions, it decided that Kapoor had to go.

When the RBI decides to remove a bank's CEO, the regulator typically doesn't allow the incumbent to continue once the term ends. It can also sack private bank chiefs, a power it lacks in the case of PSBs.

But it needs to have proof of wrongdoings. Sacking the CEO of the apparently profit-making, well-capitalised Yes Bank, was not an easy task.

Kapoor had to Go

Kapoor's term was to end on 1 September 2018. Predictably, at the 12 June annual general meeting, the bank's shareholders had approved his reappointment for another term of three years and the bank sent the proposal to RBI for approval.

When Yes Bank informed exchanges on 30 August that RBI had approved Kapoor's reappointment 'till further notice' (instead of offering another three-year term), it was clear that the regulator was not in favour of allowing him to continue at the helm.

A little over a fortnight later, in an exchange filing, on 19 September 2018, Yes Bank said: 'The Reserve Bank of India has vide letter dated 17 September 2018 received on Wednesday, intimated that Rana Kapoor may continue as the MD & CEO till 31 January 2019,' adding that the board of the bank will meet on 25 September to decide on the 'future course of action'.

The RBI wrote to the Yes Bank board, headed by Ashok Chawla, former finance secretary, to look for Kapoor's successor.

There was hard lobbying with the regulator to allow Kapoor to remain in the saddle as 'the bank could not run without him'. In one such meeting at RBI, Kapoor called the bank his son – his only son beside his three biological daughters – tears rolling down his eyes. But the regulator was not impressed.

The RBI letter was extremely critical of the 'persistent governance and compliance failure reflected by the bank's highly irregular credit management practices, serious deficiencies in governance and a poor compliance culture'.

It said:

> The serious lapses in the functioning of and governance in the bank and, in particular, the poor compliance culture, other serious violations of statutory and regulatory guidelines during the past three financial years, notwithstanding the subsequent corrective actions stated to have been initiated by the bank, reinforce our grave concern and regulatory discomfort with the role of the incumbent MD & CEO in the governance, management and superintendence of the affairs of the bank.

Chawla was then also the chairman of National Stock Exchange. He saw merit in the RBI's directive but he stepped down from the Yes Bank Board in November 2018 after being named in the chargesheet filed by the CBI. Brahm Dutt, a board member, replaced him.

The bank cancelled the first round of interviews to pick Kapoor's successor but at RBI's insistence, it had to continue the process. Management consulting firm Korn Ferry identified close to a dozen persons as a prospective successor. One of them was Ravneet Gill, then CEO and MD of Deutsche Bank in India.

My Bank

Kapoor and his family-run firms YCPL and MCPL exited from Yes

Bank in December 2019, losing all control and voting rights. This was some ten weeks after Kapoor tweeted 'Diamonds are Forever: My promoter shares of @YesBank are invaluable to me.'

Three other tweets of Kapoor on 18 October 2019 read:

- I will eventually bequeath my @YESBANK Promoter shares to my 3 daughters and subsequently to their children, with a request in my Will stating not to sell a single share, as Diamonds are Forever!!
- Even after I demit office as MD & CEO of YES BANK, I will never ever sell my @YESBANK Shares.
- In this leadership transition at @YESBANK, I continue to remain fully committed to the interests of the Bank and all its stakeholders. I will be fully guided by the Board of Directors of YES BANK and the Reserve Bank of India.

However, after selling almost the entire promoter group stakes of the two family-run firms in September 2019, Kapoor was left with 3.92 per cent and YCPL 0.8 per cent. MCPL had exited before that.

Kapoor, in his personal capacity, sold a part of his direct stake between August and October 2019, primarily to repay debts taken by the promoter group firms. In a stock exchange filing on 9 January 2020, Yes Bank said that Kapoor and Yes Capital were left with no stake at end-December.

Kapoor was never a commercial banker. As a corporate banker, he was great in raising money and a relationship manager par excellence but how could he have the last word on everything in a bank, including HR and technology?

Bharat Patel, former chairman, Procter & Gamble India, a part of the first board of the bank, was instrumental in choosing the name Yes Bank from the shortlisted five names. The other four were Gateway Bank, Octra Bank, Mint Bank and My Bank.

From Yes Bank to No Bank

In 2004, the RBI granted a licence for the bank; in 2008 after Kapur's death, Kapoor got the licence to run it his way. He changed the name from Yes Bank to My Bank and, by the end of his tenure, it became No Bank for him.

The bank retracted his performance bonus of ₹1.44 crore, clawing back 100 per cent of the performance bonus paid to Kapoor for 2015 and 2016. It had not paid any bonus to Kapoor for 2017 and 2018.

For the record, Kapoor was arrested by the ED on 8 March, a day after the CBI Economic Offences Wing registered an FIR against him in Delhi, for alleged money laundering.

Among many other allegations, the ED has found that in April–June 2018 Yes Bank invested ₹3,700 crore in the short-term debentures of Dewan Housing Finance Corporation Ltd (DHFL) whose promoter Kapil Wadhawan paid a ₹600 crore kickback to the Kapoor family in the form of loan given to DOIT Urban Ventures (India) Pvt Ltd. Kapoor's three daughters own this company through MCPL.

'It was also apprehended that Mr. Rana Kapoor had similarly misused his official position in several other transactions and had obtained illegal kickbacks directly or indirectly…'

The CBI on 25 June 2020 filed a chargesheet against Kapoor, his daughter Roshni and DHFL promoters Kapil and Dheeraj Wadhawan, alleging that the Kapoors and Wadhawans conspired with each other to siphon off public money and benefit themselves.

Kapoor, his wife, and three daughters held 168 bank accounts – 69 of them with HSBC, 79 with HDFC Bank, eight with DCB Bank Ltd, five with Yes Bank, four with Axis Bank, and one each with Central Bank of India, IDBI Bank and PNB.

The ED attached the 168 accounts which had ₹59.4 crore in the form of deposits. It also attached 15 mutual fund accounts and 58 paintings of Aslam Shaik and one each of Arpana Caur and M.F. Husain.

The London-based Shaik's paintings are known for the 'kinetic energy of his bold strokes and daring impasto work.' That mirrors Kapoor's life and career.

Yes Bank's Second Life

Yes Bank has a new lease of life after Kapoor. What has that been like?

Typically, a bank gives the RBI a list of names to pick from for the CEO's post. The regulator's primary focus is on the so-called fit and proper criteria. This means, unless the person who tops the list is unfit, it does not look at the second person even if the second person is more competent than the first.

Two names were sent to RBI for approval for the top post – Gill and Rajat Monga, the senior group president of Yes Bank, and believed to be Kapoor's Man Friday. Actually, Monga had been sidelined by Kapoor when he started objecting to many loan proposals Kapoor was pushing for approval. However, he was an insider and arguably, close to Kapoor.

Naturally, the RBI chose Gill. Gill (and probably a few others) did have rounds of discussions with senior RBI officials before meeting Kapoor at his Samudra Mahal residence, along with a Korn Ferry executive. Half a dozen directors of Yes Bank board interviewed Gill in the first week of January 2019. They wanted to know how he would run the bank differently.

Could the regulator pick the MD unilaterally? Yes, it could. In the past, on rare occasions, it has chosen the MDs for banks. At least on two occasions, the RBI has chosen the boss of one private bank, Tamilnad Mercantile Bank Ltd: M. Jesudasan (1992–96) and S. Krishnamurthy (1997–2002). Both of them were RBI executives.

Even after Gill was appointed, Kapoor wanted to remain associated with the bank as an adviser, occupying his room on the 9th floor at Nehru Centre, Dr Annie Besant Road, Worli, Mumbai. He suggested the new CEO be given another room.

As an adviser, he wanted to inspire the confidence of the prospective investors. The Board for Financial Supervision, a committee of the central board of directors at RBI, put its foot down. Kapoor was politely told that as a promoter his wholehearted support to the new management would inspire sufficient confidence; he would not need to be an adviser!

Gill Takes Over

When Gill took over in March 2019, the so-called CET1 or Common Equity Tier 1 ratio of Yes Bank – a measure of the ratio of a bank's capital against its assets – was just 8.4 per cent, the lowest in the industry and just 40 basis points (or 0.4 per cent) higher than the minimum regulatory requirement.

Gill also reportedly found massive under-provisioning of bad assets. Just three stressed exposures – ADAG Group, Essel Group and DHFL – could have wiped out the bank's entire net worth of ₹26,000 crore. Yet, not a paisa was provisioned against any of them.

Yes Bank had the single-largest exposure to Cox & Kings Ltd, after taking over Axis Bank's exposure to the tours and travels agency, which went bankrupt. After SBI, it was the second-largest lender to the now-defunct Jet Airways. Its exposure to IL&FS was around ₹2,500 crore.

Apart from this, there was a string of real estate developers to which Yes Bank had lent – Omkar Realtors & Developers Ltd, Radius Developers Ltd, Sahana Builders & Developers Pvt Ltd, Suman Developers Pvt Ltd, Skill Infrastructure Ltd… You name it.

Every bad loan that surfaced in the Indian financial system seemed to have a link with the bank. Yes Bank had probably lent to every Indian company that went belly up between 2018 and 2019.

There have been many stories about the relationship between Yes Bank and Indiabulls Housing Finance Ltd as well. But as a borrower, Indiabulls had an impeccable record, not missing a single instalment for its ₹6,000 crore loan.

According to a board member, on 16 May 2019, two-and-a-half months after taking over, Gill made a presentation to the board on all stressed assets. A month later, he got the board approval for preferential allotment to private equity funds.

Advent International Corporation of the US, under the

guidance of its adviser P.J. Nayak, conducted due diligence for a possible investment. Once it was done, Nayak, former chairman of Axis Bank met Yes Bank Chairman Dutt and said the stressed asset book could be as much as ₹80,000 crore, one-third of the total loan book.

A bank cannot grow without capital. But for Yes Bank, it was an existential crisis. It could not survive without capital infusion as the bad loans had to be provided for.

So, capital was Gill's priority number one.

At the first analysts' call on 26 April 2019, he outlined his task:

- Build a better revenue mix between wholesale and retail loans.
- Ramp up retail liabilities to cut down the cost of money.
- Strengthen governance by empowering the board on risk and HR matters and delegating authority to the respective business heads – something unheard of in Yes Bank's history.
- De-risk the corporate book.

After Advent refused to invest, there was no choice but to go for a QIP or a qualified institutional placement, the fastest route to raise money. In August 2019, Yes Bank raised ₹1,930 crore at ₹83.55 a share of the face value of ₹2. The QIP opened on 8 August and closed on 14 August.

This is what Gill said in a release after raising the equity:

> We are delighted with how our fund raise has been supported by marquee global and domestic investors... The success of the QIP is extremely satisfying given the strong global and domestic headwinds and a credit environment beset with challenges. We see this as a strong endorsement by the investor community of the inherent strengths of the Yes Bank franchise and its future growth prospects.

Gill also started selling off the loan portfolio to bring down the requirement for capital. The problem is, there were takers only for good loans. So, when the loan book shrank from ₹2.4-lakh crore to ₹2.05-lakh crore over 9 months, it turned even uglier.

There were other issues. Gill had taken the assignment presuming that, like all listed companies, Yes Bank would be a board-managed entity. The problem started fairly early when the board wanted to appoint Kapoor as an adviser with sweeping powers. When Gill refused to play ball, the battle lines were drawn between him and some board members.

An Obstructionist Board

Insiders mention that there were frequent run-ins with the board on matters of hiring new talent, credit, audit, staff accountability – everything, in short. That probably led to the RBI nominating R. Gandhi, former deputy governor on the board.

The way the board functioned was quite bizarre. Kapoor's stake in the bank came down to zero in October. But his nominee director (his daughter's father-in-law, Ravi Khanna) was allowed to be on the board until March 2020, when SBI was ordered to carry out a rescue. There were only two bankers on the board among its dozen-odd directors – Anil Jaggia and Subhash Chander Kalia.

As if an obstructionist board was not enough, the RBI and finance ministry started getting anonymous letters that made wild allegations about Gill's style of functioning and his alleged purchases of artwork at exorbitant prices.

When the third such letter reached the RBI and the ministry, apparently Monga told Gill that from the tone and language of the letters, he was sure that Kapoor himself was writing them. Monga was qualified to make this judgment since he had worked with Kapoor for over a decade. He went on to add that if the promoter of the bank was hell-bent on destroying it, nothing could save it from going under, before himself resigning.

Monga's observations were discussed at the board and the RBI was kept informed as, by that time, the bank had already sought the regulator's clearance for making Monga an executive director. Ashish Agarwal, chief risk officer of the bank, was to be promoted to the board level. But the RBI rejected this.

The regulator was extremely unhappy with the bank's risk management and credit appraisal culture. The regulator's Risk Assessment Report for three successive years from 2017 to 2019 – based on the annual inspection of the bank – was scathing on governance and the overall functioning of the board. They highlighted very poor credit discipline and compliance and too much centralisation of powers. They were also very critical of the role of the board.

Was a turnaround too daunting a task?

Gill had arrived from Deutsche Bank so it makes sense to compare the institutions. Yes Bank was 1.7 times Deutsche Bank in size. It had 22,000 employees against 12,000 of Deutsche Bank. The business mix of the banks is fairly similar – ranging from retail to wealth management, structured finance, transaction banking, investment banking and corporate banking. Deutsche Bank had the lowest net NPAs in the industry and one of the highest post-tax returns on equity. And, India was the most profitable location for Deutsche Bank in the entire Asian region, including China, Japan, Australia, Hong Kong and Singapore.

More than the enormity or the complexity of the role, the real challenge for Gill was the balance sheet, which had been dressed up through creative accounting.

When he took over, Gill got two pieces of advice from the regulator:

- Kapoor has lots of external business interests which he synergises through the bank and they must be stopped.
- Yes Bank has a lot of veneer. Typically, under veneer there is teak, but in this case, there is a lot of rot. 'We want you to clean it up,' RBI told Gill. For any bank CEO, it was a nightmare assignment.

If insiders are to be believed, Gill kept on stumbling across clients who talked about what they had been made to do in the past. Even these issues, vexing as they were, could possibly have been addressed.

What really broke the back of the bank was Nippon Life Asset Management selling Kapoor's shares as the loan to value had spiked due to a decline in the share price and Kapoor was not able to top up the collateral.

Kapoor had pledged his shares to the Anil Ambani's ADAG Group-owned Reliance Nippon Life Asset Management and Franklin Templeton. As soon as Nippon Life Insurance Company bought ADAG out, allowing the ADAG Group company Reliance Capital Ltd to exit the mutual fund business, it took a call to sell the pledged shares as the loan to value had breached all covenants.

On 31 September and 1 October 2019, Nippon Life sold 100 million shares of Kapoor, leading to a 37 per cent drop in the bank's share price. This made the investors and the depositors anxious.

The problem was exacerbated by two contributing factors.

The Punjab & Maharashtra Cooperative Bank had just gone under and it had severely jolted confidence in the banking system.

The annual bargain sales of e-commerce majors Amazon and Flipkart, which were running at that time, put a lot of pressure on MTNL and BSNL telephone lines. As a result, net banking services were down for a few banks, including Yes Bank. That made Yes Bank depositors apprehensive about the state of affairs in the bank. In the next two weeks, Yes Bank saw an outflow of nearly 20 per cent of its deposit base.

A Run on the Bank

The sudden drop in deposits and the rise in provision for bad assets led to successive rating downgrades and that, in turn, undermined depositor confidence further. There was very nearly a run on the bank and its solvency was under growing pressure.

Stemming the tide became virtually impossible. In September, the bank's CET1 dropped to 8.7 per cent.

In late October 2019, Gill led a team to the office of S.C. Murmu, executive director in charge of supervision at RBI, to make a presentation on the bank's liquidity and asset quality. He also submitted projections on every aspect of the bank's financials along with the likely earnings of December 2019 and March 2020 quarters. From then on, Yes Bank started sending a daily report to the regulator on the liquidity management.

As things got worse, both the RBI and the finance ministry were monitoring Yes Bank in real time as it could not be allowed to fail. To maintain the private character of the bank, the initial plan was for SBI and HDFC to pick up a minority stake each and get a string of foreign investors on board for the balance. However, SBI was not willing to play ball as it wanted to buy the share at its face value of ₹2. And, if it was given to SBI at face value, others too would have got it at the same price.

The plan had to be changed as nobody was comfortable offering the shares to foreign funds at face value. The foreign funds were ready to invest at a higher price but not as much as called for by SEBI norms. Going by the SEBI norms, the price per share was about ₹37 – roughly four times the intrinsic value.

Under SEBI's Substantial Acquisition of Shares & Takeovers Regulations, 2011, anyone acquiring a 25 per cent stake in a listed entity also has to make an open offer to the existing shareholders. It also has its norms on how to price a share when it is sold this way.

SEBI Norms Stumbling Block

These norms had also come in the way of the revival of Jet Airways. Abu Dhabi-based Etihad Airways, which owns 24 per cent in Jet Airways, was willing to put in money and increase its stake, had SEBI waived the norm but the market regulator did not budge.

An open offer is made to the existing shareholders to buy their shares if they are willing to sell. How does it help a company which needs the money? If a company dies, what happens to its minority (and majority) shareholders?

SEBI waives such norms only when a company is insolvent and is being revived through the bankruptcy law. But the catch is the moment a company goes through this route, its value gets eroded and investors lose interest as it is no more a 'going concern' – an accounting term for a firm that has the resources needed to continue operating. It denotes a company's ability to make enough money to stay afloat and avoid bankruptcy.

There was another issue too. When a share is bought below market price, the difference in pricing is treated as income for the buyer and income tax needs to be paid on that.

Under the SEBI pricing formula, if a group of entities – termed as 'persons acting in concert' – is buying a stake in a listed entity such as Yes Bank, the price for the acquisition is determined by its takeover code.

The pricing formula under the takeover code says it has to be the highest among the following three criteria. The average market price of the share in the past 52 weeks before the public announcement, the highest price in the immediately preceding 26 weeks, and the average market price of the past 60 trading days.

If the shares are not traded, merchant bankers can step in for valuation.

Anshu Jain, former co-CEO of Deutsche Bank AG, and now president of Cantor Fitzgerald, a New York-headquartered investment bank and brokerage firm, who is also a mentor for Gill, was helping him in arranging equity along with two domestic investment banks – Ambit Pvt Ltd and IDFC Securities Ltd.

JC Flowers & Co., Tilden Capital, Oak Hill Advisors and Silver Point Capital were willing to put in money but time was running out. Yes Bank would have to announce its December quarter earnings by 14 March and the money had to come before that or otherwise its deteriorating legacy asset book could trigger a run on the bank.

Not too Little but too Late

But the RBI could not afford to wait until then. It had already informed the finance ministry of Plan B led by SBI, which was in the making since January. The ministry was to brief Prime Minister Narendra Modi on the evening of 5 March.

The plan was to reconstruct the bank, first putting it under a moratorium, under Section 45 of the Banking Regulations Act. The government announces this, not the central bank.

Gill camped at the RBI office for the most part of 4 March. Jain's colleague at Cantor Fitzgerald, Ashwini Mathur, flew down from London to rush through the deal. The RBI wanted to see money on the table. That was also done. Tilden Capital put in $500 million in an escrow account in Bank of New York. The amount was not too little, but it was too late.

After market hours on 5 March, the government clamped a moratorium effective 6 pm that day until 3 April 2020, freezing all activities of Yes Bank and capping withdrawal of deposits at ₹50,000 per account. Higher withdrawal was allowed for meeting expenses of medical treatment, education, wedding and other emergency needs.

The reconstruction scheme was announced the next day, expanding the bank's equity base and making the SBI 49 per cent owner.

The last time a new private bank was put under a moratorium was in July 2004. Global Trust Bank, the bank in question, was merged with the public sector Oriental Bank of Commerce within 72 hours. This time, SBI stepped in as the white knight. But SBI did not merge Yes Bank with itself; instead, it put in 49 per cent equity and may continue to hold at least 26 per cent stake for the next three years.

Two weeks later, the moratorium was lifted with a consortium of lenders putting in ₹10,000 crore as capital. SBI apart, the investors were HDFC, ICICI Bank, Kotak Mahindra Bank, Axis Bank, IDFC First Bank, Federal Bank and Bandhan Bank.

On 6 March, a day after the moratorium was clamped, the Yes Bank stock closed at ₹16.20 after slipping to ₹5.55 in the early hours of trade. On 18 March, when it resumed operations, the stock closed at ₹60.8, after hitting a high of ₹88, giving near four-fold returns to the new investors.

The regulator explored a market-led solution first but the SEBI norms did not permit it. In April 2009, the Mahindra Group could rescue the scam-hit Satyam Computer Services Ltd after SEBI waived the norms. Under the current takeover code, the market regulator does not have any discretion to do that.

The only losers in the deal are those who invested in the bank's additional tier-I or AT-1 bonds, of ₹8,400 crore. These are mostly mutual funds. Such bonds are quasi-debt instruments and carry higher risks. A few bond-holders moved court against the reconstruction plan.

Yes Bank had issued two tranches of AT-1 bonds – ₹5,400 crore and ₹3,000 crore. Going by the agreement between the bank and the bondholders, Yes Bank had the option of completely writing down the bonds and converting them into equity, in case it is reconstructed through the moratorium route.

But this was for one tranche of the bonds. Another tranche envisaged writing it down. Even the tranche of bonds, which had the option of both, did not spell out the conversion formula of calculating how it could be converted into equity and when. The bank chose to write these bonds down permanently.

RBI's Challenge

In March 2009, Yes Bank had a loan book of ₹12,403 crore. A decade later, in March 2019, its loan book had increased by 20 times to ₹2.42-lakh crore. Had the RBI waited for a few more years, at this pace, Yes Bank would have become too big to fail.

Since it was a well-capitalised and profit-making bank, it was not easy to get rid of Kapoor. Couldn't RBI have imposed the moratorium immediately after Kapoor's exit? That would have probably created a bigger problem as it was already grappling with the multi-state Punjab & Maharashtra Cooperative Bank fraud, which shook the depositors' trust in a big way.

Besides, in March 2019, Yes Bank had a deposit portfolio of ₹2.28-lakh crore. It came down to ₹1.66-lakh crore in December 2019 and ₹1.05-lakh crore in March 2020. Had the moratorium been imposed earlier, it would have caused a far larger crisis for the depositors.

■ ■ ■

PART 2

Kochhar Gate

On 23 November 2019, a Delhi court stayed the release of a biopic on former ICICI Bank MD and CEO Chanda Kochhar. The producers of the movie – *Chanda: A Signature that Ruined a Career* – were restrained from screening the movie online, or offline.

Kochhar could stay the screening of the film, an alleged attempt to 'vilify' her. But she could not prevent the crashlanding of her high-profile career as a Padma awardee banker, or the drama that followed the crash.

One of the acts of that drama was played out in the first week of March 2020 at the Bombay High Court when a Division bench of Justices N.M. Jamdar and M.S. Karnik dismissed her petition challenging the termination of her employment by ICICI Bank, calling it 'illegal, untenable, and unsustainable in law'.

The bank also denied her remuneration and clawed back all the bonuses and stock options between April 2009 and March 2018 for her alleged role in granting out-of-turn loans worth ₹3,250 crore to the Videocon Group, which benefited her husband Deepak Kochhar.

Flashback to February 2017. Kochhar was addressing a group of investors at a Singapore hotel at the bank's in-house merchant banking outfit's annual roadshow. Much to her embarrassment and annoyance, one global investor asked her with a straight face: 'Wouldn't a bank chief in any other geography have lost the job after the kind of performance ICICI Bank has put up over the years under your stewardship?'

An awkward smile laced with silence was her answer. After all, ICICI Bank had underperformed its peers as well as the Bankex, the BSE's banking index, by yards. She could scarcely blame the investors for losing patience.

Kochhar's Renewable Empire

By that time, the Infra Live magazine's 'Kochhar's Renewable Empire' was almost eight months old. Most people in the financial sector had read the story (issue dated 15 July 2016). It alleged that her husband Deepak Kochhar (his smiling mugshot was on the magazine cover) had a dubious business relationship with Dhoot's Videocon Group, a borrower from ICICI Bank.

The story was being discussed on the cocktail circuit and many wondered why Kochhar or her bank wasn't filing a defamation suit against Live Media & Publishers Pvt Ltd, the publisher of the magazine. Interestingly, the story has since been removed from the magazine's web archive.

Two years down the line, Kochhar got the boot. This was not because of her poor performance, but for violation of the bank's code of conduct. Three months after she resigned, in January 2019, the bank's board terminated her services for her failure to deal with a conflict of interest (not recusing herself from credit committee meetings that took a call on giving loans to Videocon) and lack of disclosure (of her husband's business links with Videocon).

Kochhar was 'disappointed, hurt and shocked' for being treated this way after serving India's second-largest private bank by assets for 34 years with 'dedication and hard work'. Proud of her 'honesty, dignity and integrity', she was certain that 'truth will ultimately prevail'.

This was Kochhar's first reaction after the bank sacked her and asked her to return her bonuses earned (around ₹8 crore as the 2018 bonus has not yet been cleared by the regulator) and denied her at least ₹125 crore in the form of stock options. She moved court in November 2019.

What went wrong? Why had the bank's board rushed to deny all allegations against her while Kochhar kept quiet initially? Why had it then taken this extreme step?

Kumarakom Lake Resort Offsite

In the first week of March 2010, the top brass of ICICI camped out at Kumarakom Lake Resort in the backwaters of Kerala. This was their first offsite after Kochhar took over as boss in May 2009, succeeding the legendary K.V. Kamath, India's king of retail loans.

Ahead of the offsite, consulting firm McKinsey & Company made a presentation to senior executives of the bank, pointing out that ICICI Bank had not been growing and was losing market share. From around ₹4-lakh crore in 2008, ICICI Bank's asset base declined to ₹3.8-lakh crore in 2009 and further in 2010 when its loan book declined by 17 per cent and deposits by 7.5 per cent.

The analyst community was happy when Kochhar shrank the balance sheet. This was anathema for her mentor Kamath whose model was the big fat Chinese banks. But after the consolidation phase, she grew the balance sheet again and that included plenty of bad assets.

Most analysts thought that she had read the economic trends wrong; lent money to corporations liberally as she was convinced about the India growth story. None could anticipate that an intelligent and articulate Kochhar who had every possible award in her cupboard – from the Woodrow Wilson Award for Global Citizenship to Padma Bhusan, the third-highest civilian award in India – would compromise on her integrity, as the Justice B.N. Srikrishna Committee found.

Arvind Gupta

The Infra Live report was based on a letter written by Arvind Gupta, a shareholder activist and the founder and trustee of the Indian Investors Protection Council. He was a shareholder of both Videocon and ICICI Bank. The letter raised many questions about the financial links between Kochhar's husband and Videocon's V.N. Dhoot, and her role in the bank giving loans to the Videocon Group.

The chairman of the ICICI Bank board at the time was M.K. Sharma. He appointed law firm Cyril Amarchand Mangaldas (CAM) to advise him on this matter. The law firm gave her a clean chit.

The RBI also conducted a probe. It did not find anything wrong in the process of the loan disbursements, but pointed out that the business relations between Deepak and Dhoot spread beyond the shores of India. While the RBI could not go beyond India's shores, it could have requested the appropriate investigative authorities to follow up. But the banking regulator did not do that.

By January 2018, the CBI got into the act. The *Indian Express* front-paged the story of the Deepak–Videocon relationship in March.

There was extensive media coverage of how Kochhar allegedly used her position to favour her husband and brother-in-law and how several investigating agencies were following the trail. The ICICI Bank board, led by its chairman, M.K. Sharma, backed her to the hilt. N. Vaghul, former chairman of development institution ICICI Ltd, the earlier avatar of the bank, also rushed to support Kochhar. Vaghul had been the non-executive chairman of ICICI Bank until April 2009.

The bank's communication division got busy sending denials of the 'misleading' reports and clarifying that 'the brother of a husband does not fall within the definition of a "relative" under the Companies Act… and, hence, there is no requirement of any disclosure of such a relationship…'

In contrast, after the *Wall Street Journal* reported the alleged misuse of company assets by WPP Plc CEO Martin Sorrell, the board of the world's largest advertising company hired a law firm to look into the allegations; Sorrell rejected the allegations, but recognised that the company had to investigate.

On 14 April 2018, the WPP board announced that after 33 years as CEO, Sorrell had resigned even as the law firm hired by the board was investigating allegations of his 'personal misconduct'.

This is ideally the way a corporation should function. But ICICI Bank chose not to go down this path initially, probably giving the benefit of doubt to a star CEO. Incidentally, Vaghul, while saying that Kochhar was not one to be involved in nepotism, agreed that the bank's board could have considered a deeper external inquiry into the matter in the interest of good governance.

Anonymous Whistle-Blower

The scenario dramatically changed when an anonymous whistle-blower wrote a much more elaborate letter, listing many more alleged misdoings of Kochhar and her family, which Gupta's letter had not mentioned.

That brought SEBI into action and, for the first time, Kochhar was forced to disclose her husband's business relations with the Videocon Group. These developments probably made Sharma realise his mistake. He appointed retired Justice of Supreme Court B.N. Srikrishna to conduct a comprehensive probe for the period between April 2009 (a month before Kochhar took over the mantle from Kamath) and March 2018.

CAM immediately withdrew its report as it was based on an assumption that no relationship between Deepak and Dhoot ever existed, as Kochhar had never mentioned this before.

The Srikrishna panel did not have any deadline. This was odd. However, allowing the Srikrishna panel to have as much time as it wanted to complete the probe was a masterstroke by the bank's board. By doing this, it more or less forced Kochhar to put in her papers.

A Bloodless Coup

India's banking law does not allow the boss of a bank to stay away from office for four months or more. Kochhar, who went on her annual leave in June 2018 and later had to stay away for the completion of the probe, had no choice but to quit as the probe took its own time. It was a sort of bloodless coup which did not allow her to come back to the bank as CEO.

Under Section 10B(9) of the Banking Regulation Act, if the MD of a bank is on long leave, then an alternative arrangement must be put in place for running the bank but that cannot continue for more than four months. Kochhar resigned voluntarily and was later sacked.

On 1 June, Kochhar went on indefinite leave until a probe into her conduct by an independent agency was complete. A little over a fortnight later, on the late evening of 18 June, ICICI Bank issued a release saying it had appointed Sandeep Bakhshi, MD of ICICI

Prudential Life Insurance Co. Ltd, as whole-time director and chief operating officer (COO, a new position created for Bakhshi) of ICICI Bank for five years, with immediate effect, subject to regulatory approval.

All business heads would report to Bakhshi, who, in turn, would report to Kochhar, who 'has decided to go on leave till the completion of the enquiry'.

Kochhar's decision to go on leave is 'in line with the highest levels of governance and corporate standards', as the bank's release says, but why did she take so long to decide on this?

By delaying her leave inordinately, both Kochhar and ICICI Bank pushed themselves into a corner and finally were left with no choice but to demonstrate to the world that they cared for corporate governance.

Except for a brief appearance at a public function in Mumbai, in the few months since the controversy flared up, Kochhar focused on her daily chores with meticulous care and confidence, until the day she went on leave.

Even during her leave, she dropped by at ICICI Bank's headquarters in Mumbai's Bandra Kurla Complex on 13 June 2018 to attend a board meeting, which took the call on selling a 2 per cent stake in the life insurance outfit to raise ₹1,100 crore.

In her interaction with analysts, after announcing the March quarter earnings, she gave a two-year guidance. Did she underestimate the gravity of the charges? Or, was she highly confident about her ability to tide over this crisis?

CBI FIR

A few days before the board sacked her, on 22 January 2019, the CBI filed its FIR (FIR No: RCBD1/2019/E/0001), alleging criminal conspiracy, cheating, a public servant taking illegal gratification, criminal misconduct and abuse of official position.

The CBI alleged a quid pro quo. It said ICICI Bank sanctioned ₹3,250 crore to Dhoot's group companies and Dhoot, in turn, invested ₹64 crore in Deepak's NuPower Renewables Ltd.

Going by the FIR, the bank sanctioned six high-value loans to the Videocon Group between June 2009 and October 2011, violating the norms of loan sanction. Damningly, Kochhar was one of the members of the sanctioning committee.

The FIR also named other senior bankers who were directors on the board of ICICI Bank then. They are prominent names in Indian finance, heading foreign and local banks, a foreign investment bank, an insurance company, a non-banking financial company and even a multilateral development bank.

Of course, the CBI will have to probe these allegations. Investigating complex financial misdeeds is not something which the country's premier investigative agency is very good at. Both Arun Jaitley and Piyush Goyal had, in the past, come down heavily on CBI's 'investigative adventurism'.

What is Kochhar side of the story?

Barring issuing a statement expressing shock, she kept mum until she moved court against the bank.

Those who know her well wonder why would the Videocon Group do a favour to Kochhar's husband as a quid pro quo to get a loan? After all, it has taken money from the entire banking industry and ICICI Bank's share in the pie is not even 10 per cent. So, if it had a quid pro quo with Kochhar to get the money, it must have had similar arrangements with other banks as well. If this is not the case, one must accept that it had got money from all banks, including ICICI Bank, without any under the table conditions.

They also claim that Kochhar all along made statutory disclosures about her husband's companies. But she did not disclose Videocon's investments as she was not aware of them.

They say that a particular corporate house was baying for Kochhar's blood because she stopped giving it fresh loans and had been hounding it to recover money already lent.

How would she recuse herself from the credit committee when she was not aware of her husband's dealings, they ask, pointing out that out of the six loans mentioned in the CBI's FIR, she was involved in sanctioning only two.

Those who trust her judgment and swear by her intelligence, integrity and articulation also say it is unfair to drag her into such a controversy. They ask: Can't a successful woman professional have an equally successful husband?

Finally, Dhoot's ₹64 crore investment in Kochhar's husband's company is not gratification for her; it is an investment by Dhoot, which he can liquidate after 2021.

Srikrishna Committee Report

There were takers for many such arguments defending Kochhar. That was until the Srikrishna Committee report, submitted on 27 January 2019, called her bluff.

It found that Kochhar had not made several mandatory and appropriate disclosures which she should have done to avoid conflict of interest. By not making the disclosures, she had violated the provisions of Companies Act, 2013, the listing obligation and disclosure requirement of SEBI and the Prevention of Money Laundering Act of 2002.

Let us look at some of these violations:

> Deepak Kochhar and his brother, along with the Videocon Group, had substantial shareholdings in Credential Finance Ltd from 1996 to 2001. Deepak was also a director of the company in 2007–09 and later became MD. Chanda Kochhar herself held shares of the company until 2001. Still, she claimed to be unaware of any business dealings between her husband and the Videocon Group until 2018, when SEBI launched its investigation.
>
> The residence of Kochhar at CCI Chambers in South Mumbai between 2009 and 2016 (including the period when she was the MD and CEO of the bank) was owned by a Videocon Group company, Quality Techno Advisors Pvt Ltd.
>
> In October 2016, the company effectively gifted the apartment to a Kochhar family trust as the ownership was

transferred at a cost much lower than its market value. Her husband was a director of the company.

Sometime in 2009, when Kochhar was the boss of the bank, NuPower Renewables Pvt Ltd, of which her husband was the co-founder and CEO, entered "non-arm's length" transactions with the Videocon Group. It received multi-crore investments from the Videocon Group, which did not earn anything from such investments until 2016 when it got 3.99 per cent return.

Her husband also had extensive business dealings with another Mumbai-headquartered industrial group – the Essar Group. A relative of the Essar Group promoters made multi-crore investments in NuPower Renewables. Kochhar attended various meetings of the bank at which loans were sanctioned to the Essar Group.

Incidentally, Neelam Advani, wife of Kochhar's brother Mahesh, was working with the Essar Group. Even before the Srikrishna report was submitted, the bank wrote to SEBI requesting it to 'decouple' the bank from Kochhar's case. This was ICICI Bank's first attempt to insulate itself from its CEO's activities.

Kochhar's fall from grace has dealt a blow to the personality cult which is so common within India's banking sector. In many cases, CEOs don a larger-than-the-institution persona.

Many saw the seeds of Kochhar's downfall in November 2014 when Shah Rukh Khan danced at the sangeet ceremony of her daughter's wedding in a Mumbai hotel, attended by many celebrities, including Amitabh Bachchan.

At the 60th anniversary of the ICICI Group in January 2015, she shared the stage with Prime Minister Narendra Modi, who graced the occasion to dedicate to the nation the first digital village adopted by the bank – Akodara in Gujarat.

But when it came to the crunch, brushing shoulders with the high and mighty and her penchant for glitz and glamour did not come to her aid.

On 27 September 2019, yet another *Indian Express* report spoke about an alleged break-in at the office of Alka Tyagi, one of the chief commissioners of Income Tax. At the time, Tyagi was the supervisory head of units that assess taxes of all companies and banks located in Fort, Ballard Estate, Colaba and Nariman Point in Mumbai's premier business districts.

The break-in was discovered after the Ganesh Chaturthi holiday on 2 September. The security staff found locked cupboards broken and ransacked in Tyagi's office on the fourth floor of Aayakar Bhavan, the headquarters of the Income Tax department in Mumbai. The seven-storied building is secured by at least 100 closed-circuit TV cameras. Tyagi was handling the Deepak Kochhar–ICICI Bank case, among many other sensitive matters.

The Kochhars are being probed by multiple revenue and law enforcement agencies, including the income-tax department, the CBI and the SFIO, and of course, the ED.

In January 2020, the ED seized the South Mumbai residence of Kochhar as well as some assets of companies owned by her husband. The provisional attachments, pegged at ₹78 crore, were made in a case of alleged money laundering being investigated by the agency.

The key lessons from 'Kochhargate' are:

The boards of all private banks are not necessarily efficient and independent. The directors, including the chairman, could be hand-in-glove with the CEO. The ICICI Board first rushed to give Kochhar a clean chit and later did an about-turn.

In ICICI Bank, close to 20 per cent of the shares are held in American Depositary Receipts or ADRs. The ADR holders are entitled to a dividend but they do not have any board representation, neither can they vote. The 'independent' directors handpicked by the MD are as independent as the boss permits them to be. Should the government and the RBI take a fresh look at the current policy that leaves a large part of the foreign stakeholders voiceless, allowing any power-hungry CEO a free run?

All along, the RBI maintained a stony silence. Shouldn't the banking regulator review its perceived 'hands-off' approach for a systemically important entity such as ICICI Bank?

The larger-than-life image of a CEO in a company (not necessarily only banks) sows seeds of misgovernance, particularly when the leader's tenure is long.

The personality cult in Indian banking is past its sell-by date. Banking is a boring business. Bankers need to spend more time bringing down the cost of funds, pushing up the quality of assets and concentrating on good governance.

If one spices up this boring set of tasks the Kochhar way, there should be a price to pay. In sync with the feudal style that she adopted after moving to the corner office, Kochhar never waited for the lift at the bank's headquarters. Someone would always be there to press the button and hold the lift, when her blue Mercedes-Benz E-Class E 350 d entered the premises.

She could always say that was a legacy. But the rest is not. We do not know how long she will have to wait for redemption, or downfall and atonement.

The Directorate of Enforcement arrested Deepak Kochhar in Delhi on 7 September 2020, after hours of questioning, and 18 months after filing the money laundering case.

■ ■ ■

There is one thread joining all the fallen angels – Gopalakrishnan, Gelli, Kapoor, Kochhar and many more: A dictatorial style of leadership. The boss grows in the role and becomes invincible or, so the person thinks, till hubris ends the career. At the end, the leader may or may not be in jail but he or she stands alone, disowned by politicians who encouraged him to lend (Gopalakrishnan), industry bodies to whom he was a darling (Kapoor), or the bank itself (Kochhar).

I am sure the regulator regrets giving banking licences to Gelli and Kapoor. It is time to review the so-called fit and proper criteria for the banking licence, particularly with reference to the individuals applying for it. Ditto for choosing the boss of a bank – regardless of whether that person is a promoter or a professional. At the least, psychometric tests should be mandatory to gauge the personality traits and aptitude of prospective CEOs.

■ ■ ■

PART 3

The Role of the Bank Boards

Both ICICI Bank and Yes Bank spotlight the role of the board of banks, the CEO, corporate governance and the so-called conflict of interest. And, these cases also highlight the regulator's abject failure in keeping a tab on how bank boards function.

Eliminating conflict of interest is at the heart of provisions in the Banking Regulation Act of 1949, which governs the banking companies in India. Bimal Jalan was the first RBI governor to make a formal policy announcement on corporate governance in the mid-term review of the monetary and credit policy on 21 October 2001.

A consultative group was set up the following month. It was headed by A.S. Ganguly, a former chairman of Hindustan Unilever Ltd.

Before that, in March 2001, an advisory group on corporate governance, headed by R.H. Patil, founder of NSE Ltd, had examined the relevant issues in the Indian banking industry and made recommendations to raise governance standards.

Yet another advisory group on banking supervision, chaired by former SBI chairman M.S. Verma, submitted its report in January 2003.

The mid-term review of the monetary and credit policy in November 2003 introduced the concept of 'fit and proper' criteria for directors of banks, following the recommendations of the Ganguly Committee.

The exercise dealt with the process of collecting information, doing due diligence and the constitution of a nomination committee of the board to scrutinise declarations made by the bank directors.

An RBI circular, dated 24 June 2004, lays down norms for selection of directors on boards of private banks, based on their qualification, expertise, record and integrity. At least 51 per cent of the directors need to have special knowledge or practical experience in areas such as accountancy, agriculture and rural economy, banking, cooperation, economics, finance, law and small-scale industry. This requirement arises out of Section 10A(2)(a) of the Banking Regulation Act.

Where does the Buck Stop?

The board plays a critical role in running a bank, but the buck stops at the MD and CEO. Section 10B of the Banking Regulation Act makes it abundantly clear that the management of the affairs of a private bank is 'entrusted' to an MD, who exercises her powers, 'subject to the superintendence, control and direction of the board of directors'.

For governance, the various committees of a bank board oversee different aspects of the business. For instance, the credit committee of a large private bank once had three members. There was its chairman, who is a legal expert; its MD and CEO; and an independent director who was a public policy specialist with expertise in water management.

Apart from the MD and CEO of the bank, did others have the expertise to clear high-value loans? Were they there to challenge and question the decisions of the MD and CEO, or endorse them? How many credit proposals were rejected by such a panel?

Section 36ACA of the Banking Regulation Act empowers RBI to supersede the board of directors of banks – 'in public interest or for preventing the affairs of any banking company being conducted in a manner detrimental to the interest of the depositors'. But this is only for a period not exceeding six months. The supersession of the board can be extended, but not beyond 12 months.

During this period, an administrator with experience in law, finance, banking, economics or accountancy needs to be appointed, but the person cannot be an officer of the central government or any state government. RBI can constitute a committee of at least three people to help the administrator run the bank.

The Punishment

Under Section 46 of the Act, if any bank official furnishes a false statement or suppresses facts in 'any return, balance-sheet or other document', the punishment can be imprisonment up to three years or a penalty of ₹1 crore, or both. Depending on the nature of the offence, the penalty varies, and there is a provision of imposing a fine of ₹50,000 for every day during which the offence continues.

In all these cases, there is a legal process involved. But for certain offences, the courts have no role to play. Section 47A of the Act, which defines RBI's power to impose a penalty, says the central bank needs to issue a show-cause notice to a bank before imposing a penalty for certain offences and must offer a 'reasonable opportunity of being heard' and 'no complaint can be filed against any bank in any court of law in respect of any contravention or default in respect of which any penalty has been imposed'. A bank needs to pay the penalty within two weeks of receiving the RBI notice.

CEO's Appointment

Under the Banking Regulation Act, RBI's 'prior' approval is a must for appointment and reappointment of the CEO; the central bank could seek the CEO's removal also. Apart from solvency, it does not specify what qualities a CEO should possess. But it does point out disqualifying characteristics.

An individual being appointed as CEO should be solvent, should not have suspended payment to creditors or settled for payment of a lesser amount and must not be convicted by a criminal court of an offence involving moral turpitude.

In the application form for RBI approval of a CEO's appointment or reappointment, a private bank needs to explain whether the person to be appointed as CEO is subject to any of the disqualifications mentioned in Section 10B(4) of the Banking Regulation Act.

This particular section deals with 'substantial interest' that a prospective CEO *should not have* in any other company or a partnership firm.

What is substantial interest? It is 'direct' or 'beneficial interest' held by the individual or spouse of such an individual, or minor child of such an individual, whether singly or taken together, in the shares of a company which exceeds ₹5 lakh or 10 per cent of the paid-up capital of the company – whichever is less. 'Substantial interest' in partnership firms does not specify any value but says the holding should not be more than 10 per cent of the total capital subscribed by all the partners.

Who is a Relative?

Against the backdrop of recent developments, the definition of 'relative' takes the centre stage. Going by the provision of the Companies Act, 1956, a person is a relative of another person if they are members of the same Hindu undivided family, or they are husband and wife.

Besides this, Schedule 1A of the Act lists 22 relations. They are: Father, mother (including step), son (stepson), son's wife, daughter (stepdaughter), father's father, father's mother, mother's father, mother's mother, son's son, son's wife's son, son's daughter, son's daughter's husband, daughter's husband, daughter's son, daughter's son's wife, daughter's daughter, daughter's daughter's husband, brothers (stepbrothers), brother's wife, sister (stepsister) and sister's husband.

The Companies Act, 2013, which replaced the old Act, compressed the list; now, only eight relationships feature there. They are: Father (including stepfather), mother (stepmother), son, son's wife, daughter, daughter's husband, brother (stepbrother) and sister (stepsister).

The new Act got the assent of the President of India on 29 August 2013 and was notified on 30 August. Various provisions of the Act were enforced on different dates. The definition of relative was enforced on 12 September 2013. This means, until then, the old definition as outlined in the earlier Act continued.

Section 184(1) of the new Companies Act says every director at the first meeting of the board in which she participates and, subsequently, at the first board meeting in every financial year, or whenever there is any change in the disclosures already made and at the first board meeting held after such change, should disclose her interest in any company. If a director violates this provision, the punishment is imprisonment for up to one year, or ₹50,000–₹1 lakh penalty or both.

Also, the rules that define the meetings of a board and its powers dictate that the companies that are required to set up an audit committee (banks fall in this category) must ensure that if any of the members of the committee has a conflict of interest in a given case, the person should recuse herself. Also, every director must disclose an interest in any company by giving notice.

Finally, even where the director herself has no personal interest in any contract or arrangement but any of her relatives has, the director is deemed to be indirectly interested.

Anomalies and Absurdities

All provisions of the law, as well as definitions, need to be seen in the context of developments. If we take them literally, there will be many anomalies and absurdities. For instance, in 1949, when the Banking Regulation Act was framed, ₹5 lakh had a different meaning as personal income above ₹1.5 lakh a year was subjected to 'super tax' then.

Over time, many parts of the law have become archaic. Sections 5 and 6 of the Act list the businesses that a bank can undertake. But the list does not include many contemporary business opportunities. For instance, insurance, mutual funds, management of pension funds, hire purchase, among many other businesses, do not feature in the list. The banks could get into these sectors only after the government gave permissions through special notifications.

Do the bank CEOs make all the disclosures they need to do? Most CEOs in private banks have long innings and, often, they are home-bred, rising from the ranks. This means they join the board as a director even before becoming the boss. Do they make the disclosures all through their career? After all, perception of governance is as important as governance itself.

There are many ways to restore the perceived erosion of standards about governance in Indian banks – both private and public. One such option could be the appointment of governance officers.

Their task is very different from that of ethics officers, which some of the Indian companies, including banks, have started appointing. But then, the company secretary of a bank, to a large extent, is the governance officer in a bank. Are they doing their jobs properly?

Post Script: In June 2020, the RBI released a discussion paper on governance in commercial banks. The objective was to align the current regulatory framework with global best practices while being mindful of the context of the domestic financial system. The RBI also constituted an internal working group to review the ownership guidelines and corporate structure of private banks.

■ ■ ■

PART IV
GOVERNORSPEAK

In this section, four men who had a ringside view of Indian banking and the economy explain why bad loans ballooned. C. Rangarajan, Y.V. Reddy, D. Subbarao and Raghuram Rajan served as governors of the Reserve Bank of India between 1992 and 2016.

In a series of candid interviews, conducted between December 2019 and January 2020, the four former central bankers have taken a 360-degree view of Indian banking, warts and all.

They touched upon diverse issues, ranging from the creation of bad loans to the need for corporate governance; the state of affairs in PSBs; the fear among government-owned bank officers of facing an inquiry even for commercial credit decisions; the nexus between crony capitalists and bankers; government ownership; the crisis in the NBFCs; the progress of insolvency law and even why the central bank needs reforms.

While they differ on how the pile of bad loans came to be created and what needs to be done to prevent a recurrence, all four are on the same page when it comes to consolidation, governance and government ownership.

All agree that consolidation is no panacea for the banking sector's ills, that governance is the elephant in the room and the government must pare down its stake in PSBs.

Raghuram Rajan (4 September 2013 to 4 September 2016), who waged the battle against bad loans, identifies excessive investments by corporations and exuberance by banks coupled with the economic slowdown as the prime cause of bad loans and says the inability to act fast also contributed to the problem.

The solution, according to him, is to speed up the process of recognising bad loans, recapitalise banks where necessary and focus on governance.

D. Subbarao (5 September 2008 to 4 September 2013) says the problem started in the high-growth years before the 2008 global financial crisis, continued through it and even afterwards. At least one of the causes of the bad loan problem is the extraordinary liquidity infusion after the collapse of Lehman Brothers, and he readily shares the blame for this. He is also liberal in giving credit to Rajan and Urjit Patel for arresting the problem and preventing it from exploding into a crisis.

Subbarao bats for privatisation of PSBs. It requires a lot of political capital but Prime Minister Narendra Modi has that in abundance. 'Modi arguably has more political capital than any other prime minister in decades. He has to be prepared to invest that capital to do politically difficult things. And one of those politically difficult things has to be the denationalisation of PSBs,' Subbarao says.

Y.V. Reddy (6 September 2003 to 5 September 2008) says when the pressure on the banks increased – both for social banking and infrastructure banking – credit growth for working capital was choked. Bank credit has not been expanding after the 2015–16 AQR but the economy has been expanding.

Adding a new dimension to the debate, he says someone was providing money to replace bank credit. In the first round, it was mutual funds; in the next round, the NBFCs. In a way, the problem of stressed assets spilled over from the banking system to the mutual funds and, finally, the NBFCs.

Reddy raises a question on the objective of public ownership in banks but does not find any problem with the government ownership per se. His concern is: How does the owner behave?

C. Rangarajan (22 December 1992 to 21 November 1997) feels the closing down of the development finance institutions was premature, and wants them to return in some form to provide medium- and long-term credit to manufacturing and infrastructure sectors.

He says India's response to the global crisis following the collapse of Lehman Brothers was exaggerated and blames the government for not recapitalising banks aggressively. The government, according to him, should own a smaller number of banks which can be adequately capitalised.

The government should always have a majority stake in SBI, the nation's largest lender, but the number of other banks it controls should be derived from its capacity to provide capital.

Finally, he sees the banking mess spilling over into economy, making it an economic crisis. His diagnosis is that an unsustainable credit boom accompanied by real sector's problems in completing projects had led to a slowdown, precipitating a banking crisis.

11

'It is an economic crisis'

C.R. Rangarajan

Before becoming the governor of the RBI in December 1992, Chakravarthi Rangarajan had a long stint as a deputy governor (1982 to 1991). After the RBI stint, Rangarajan – who holds a PhD in economics from the University of Pennsylvania – served as the governor of Andhra Pradesh, chaired the 12th Finance Commission and also the Prime Minister's Economic Advisory Council.

He laid the foundation for a modern banking system in India – introducing capital adequacy and prudential norms in phases, deregulating interest rates, pulling down the wall between banks and development finance institutions and ending the government's practice of issuing ad hoc treasury bills to the RBI – an instrument of automatic monetisation of central government's fiscal deficit. He also opened the doors for the first set of new-generation private banks.

Edited Excerpts

Who is responsible for the banking mess?

It is difficult to pinpoint 'who' but one can look at the set of circumstances that led to the current situation. It is almost a crisis. The banking system is under great stress and this is making the economic situation more difficult.

The irony is that normally the banking system can help to get the economy to come out of a difficult situation like the one we are passing through. Had the banking system been in a very strong position, it could have been effectively used to provide better support and get the growth rate moving, but that option is not open to us as the banking system is under even greater stress than the economy.

A series of developments over a period led to this situation. We had the extraordinary boom in the banking system in the period between 2004–05 and 2009–10.

When the economy grew at over 9 per cent and the credit growth was three times more...

The non-food credit almost trebled during that period. The exuberance of the economy was visible and many – not the bankers alone – felt that we were on a new growth path, which would lead to a sustained rate of growth of 8–9 per cent for a fairly long time.

There is an old saying that bad loans are sown in good times. That was the time when everything looked rosy and as a result many projects were approved. One may not call it irrational exuberance but at least part of it was irrational. Largely, it was a reflection of what was happening in the economy at that time. The bankers had a party.

The economy boomed and as more and more new projects were being sanctioned, problems started emerging in terms of land acquisition, environmental requirements and then the global crisis happened in 2008–09 and the economy started slowing down.

Already there were problems in the completion of projects

and the slowdown in growth led to a fall in demand and affected investment. In economics, this is called 'acceleration principle' – investment in any particular period is a function of the change in the output in the previous periods. Once a slowdown happens, it has its consequences leading to a further decline in demand.

All capitalist economies have gone through this – the boom and the bust and again the boom cycle. In India, probably for the first time, we are witnessing this in a significant way. The banks were slow in providing for bad assets, as it affected their profitability and that led to the RBI's AQR in 2015–16. It was well motivated and the clean up was necessary but it came out at a time when the banking system started experiencing difficulties.

For PSBs, the non-performing assets ratio almost doubled.

They needed capital to provide for that. The whole problem with the economy is that once something starts declining, it has its own dynamics. It happens in the boom and the bust phases. A combination of the general decline in the economic situation and the drive to clean up the banking system at that particular time led to what we see today – the banking system is in real trouble.

If you look at the NPAs, you will find more than 80 per cent emanated from six sectors – iron and steel, mining, aviation, roads, power and telecom. All of these were the booming areas but they were affected for different reasons. The steel sector was affected because of the Chinese imports, telecom was affected because of court decisions, road projects had problems because of environmental issues. An extraordinary growth in credit combined with a huge concentration in certain areas led to the current mess.

As RBI governor you pulled down the barriers between DFIs and banks, and created the road map for universal banking. Were the seeds sown at that time? The banks were forced to get into project financing but they never learnt the art...

There are two clarifications. One, during my period – 1992 to 1997 – the development banks continued to exist but certain concessions which the RBI had been giving were withdrawn. The real problem cropped up when they were allowed reverse mergers with banks they set up. It did not happen when I was the governor. I allowed IDBI and ICICI to set up banks. Later the DFIs merged with the banks and that is where the problem started.

Second, the banking system was given a long time to learn the art of project financing. This is a talent that the banks can easily acquire. Also, there is not enough evidence to show that the problems were only with respect to projects; there have been problems in working capital also.

The DFIs were envisaged to provide medium- and long-term credit supplementing the commercial banks, which provided short-term credit for working capital. DFIs grew rapidly – the combined asset base of DFIs was ₹6,143 crore in 1981, which increased to ₹52,054 crore in 1990–91 and ₹158,379 crore in 1998–99.

The DFIs had access to cheap funds, which was vital as it enabled them to lend directly or indirectly (through banks and other financial intermediaries by way of refinancing) to enterprises at an affordable cost.

As banking reform gathered pace, the role of DFIs diminished. Now, with the growing NPAs, the flow of long-term credit has been choked and this has affected corporate investment.

Is it the time to revive DFIs?

I think so. It is time to rewind and accept that the closing down of the DFIs was premature and allow the setting up of term-lending institutions. A Long-Term Credit Bank or by whatever name it may be called, must be set up by the government to provide medium- and long-term credit to manufacturing and infrastructure, barring the power sector, which is well served currently by DFIs such as PFC, REC and IREDA.

Also, when we started nudging the banks to do project financing, it was felt that the corporate bond market would develop. It was part of the scheme. A sort of American model where long-term capital requirements are met essentially by the corporate bond market.

All these links got broken – the insurance companies continue to invest the bulk of their funds only in the government paper because that rule has not changed. The handicap of a thriving corporate bond market in India is that everybody is on the demand side and only a few are on the supply side.

In the absence of a deep corporate bond market, an arrangement for long-term funding by institutions could be appropriate. The time is ripe for that with a caveat that the institutions are able to attract funding. You cannot once again make them deposit-taking institutions. If you do that, you are creating a wholesale bank. We need to figure out whether such institutions will sell bonds or get a subsidy from the government or RBI. This is a question that will have to be resolved first.

The banking sector had even higher NPAs in 2002–03 but it was resolved relatively quietly. Why is there so much noise this time around?

The intensity of the problem now is much more than in the earlier periods. But basically, these are different periods. For example, in the mid-1990s, we had NPAs accumulated over several decades. We sorted out by tightening norms gently. We finally got where we were in 1997 but it took us five years to tighten the norms. We recognised the fact that prudential norms were necessary but we could not do it overnight and we must do it step by step.

In the current phase, the pile of NPAs was a shock. The question was whether adequate recapitalisation was available or not for the PSBs. That is something that the government and the RBI should have thought through. While the recapitalisation has been happening in phases, the tightening happened at one go – that is a mismatch.

Had the government been prepared for recapitalising the banks at one go, much of the problem would have been solved. Some understanding between the government and the RBI would have softened the situation. If you are going to tighten it, you should have been ready with recapitalisation simultaneously.

Did India overestimate the impact of the Lehman collapse and go for monetary and fiscal easing much more than what was required?

I have always taken the view that the 2008 crisis would not have affected India. Look at the countries that got affected by the global crisis. I remember the governor of Bangladesh Bank telling me that they had managed well. Even South Korea was not affected. It is a world crisis because its secondary effects were on all countries but the primary effects were only on countries that actually invested in the toxic securities. As these were the richest countries in the world, when they contracted, all the other countries got affected.

Even though we were not a closed economy, we did not allow our banks to invest in any of the foreign securities. That had been the policy for a long time.

We overreacted to the secondary impact, as we got scared that our exports would shrink when the economies contracted in the Western Europe and the United States. Remember, at that time we had a surplus in the current account. We thought we must do something, we increased our fiscal deficit and there was monetary easing.

I was in the Rajya Sabha at that time and I criticised these moves heavily. The extraordinary increase in fiscal deficit – almost double the mandated level – was the villain responsible for the subsequent mess.

And we were slow in unwinding...

Well, the question is how much tightening we should have done, even earlier. Dr. Reddy did tighten but in spite of that, we had the 30 per cent credit growth annually. There may be difficulties in putting the brakes at that time but the fact of the matter is we were slow in tightening and the injection of fiscal stimulus was far in excess. As a result of that, we faced very high inflation. Very high fiscal deficits for two successive years contributed to the problem.

Is it a banking crisis? Or, a larger financial crisis? Or, an economic crisis?

It is an economic crisis – the increasing stress in the banking system combined with real sector problems led to a very sharp decline in the rate of growth of the economy. The credit boom could not be sustained. The slowdown in real sector made the banking crisis worse as the borrowers found it difficult to repay. NPAs accumulated. In short, unsustainable credit boom accompanied by real sector problems in completing projects led to a slowdown, which precipitated a banking crisis. The continuance of real sector problems partly policy-driven in the most recent period such as demonetisation has aggravated the banking situation.

Bank credit is growing at a snail's pace...

If the banks expand credit without looking at the merit (of the loan proposals), the system could be in deeper trouble. The expansion in credit is probably needed in order to bring down the NPA ratio, but that should be done in a very reasonable way.

Where does the government stand in the banking crisis?

Well, there is a difference between government dominance and fiscal dominance. Fiscal dominance arises when the government incurs a higher deficit and part of it is converted into monetised deficit. The government dominance in banking occurs when the government intervenes in the banking system almost directly and makes the banks do what it wants them to do. This happens when there is large public ownership of banks. When the government and even some part of the Reserve Bank nudge the banks to expand credit, it leads to a problem. The government's role in the current banking crisis will be two-fold. First, it must recapitalise PSBs not only to offset the additional provision requirement but also have the ability to expand credit. Second, it must help to quicken the process of resolving the debts owed to banks.

Do you hold the government responsible for the rapid expansion of credit?

Yes, partly. The government is always keen that banks should expand credit. Even the expression 'lazy banking' was coined. We need to have clarity on the desired rate of growth in credit. Monitoring of the macro prudential indicators is a function of the Reserve Bank. The overall rate of growth of the economy, the degree of concentration in terms of sectors and borrowers, the extent of credit to vulnerable sectors – all these are macro prudential indicators. Each bank might not know how much credit was going to a particular sector but the central bank should have kept a vigil and cautioned the banking system.

You gave licences to the first set of private banks in 1994. Shouldn't we have more private banks?

The point is whether the private segment of the banking system has fared better than the public segment, even in terms of the crisis that we are witnessing. Some of the private banks have also had NPA ratio as high as the PSU banks even though, on the whole, they have done better.

The distinction between the private and the public banks and their role in the current economic situation is not very clear but none can deny the fact that more competition is required. The number of banks that is required at any particular time is conditional not upon the situation that prevails at that time, but what you want the economy to be in the next few decades.

It takes almost 10 to 20 years for a bank to grow to a meaningful size. Rightly, the licensing of banks should be put on tap rather than making it at periodic intervals. There is scope for a larger number of private banks. As more private banks make their presence, the role of RBI as a regulator assumes greater importance.

Should the government remain the majority stakeholder in PSU banks?

The government must decide on how much of the banking system does it need to hold in order to steer the banking system in a particular direction. It is not necessary for the government to hold nearly the whole of the system, even under the old theory of 'commanding heights'. We should look at it from a non-ideological angle.

As long as the government has to hold 51 per cent of the capital, the extent to which they can take care of these banks so that they can play a role in expanding the economy becomes limited by the ability to provide capital. The fiscal capability becomes an important consideration. The method of recapitalisation that we are following is not the most appropriate. We are giving the banks long-term bonds and are not really infusing funds into the banking system. If the government infuses ₹70,000 crore of cash into the banking system, the strength of the banking system will be very different from giving it ₹70,000 crore of bonds. In the case of bonds, the gain for the banks is only the interest they earn on the bonds. It does not add to the banks' capability to lend more except through a higher nominal capital. This way, we are defeating the very purpose of recapitalisation.

I must admit that I am also responsible for this because we did this in the early '90s but the situation was very different at that time. We had certain compulsions and the fiscal situation was very tough. We must move away from this. If we want to recapitalise the banks, we should recapitalise them by giving them adequate funds. This will really pinch the government and will set a limit on the government's share of the banking system.

The government should own smaller number of banks which can be adequately capitalised. The SBI should always remain with its majority owned by the government. Beyond SBI, how many more banks are needed should be derived from the fiscal capability of the government to provide capital.

Your take on bank consolidation...

Whether the weak banks can be rescued this way is not clear because we do not have too many banks strong enough to take care of all the weak banks. The merger question arises from the advantages of what they call scale and scope but it should not be imposed on the banks on the ground of combining the weak and the strong. This cannot be the idea behind a merger.

If a bank with a large spread in the north wants to merge with a bank with a wide spread in the south, there is an economic rationale for it. There should be clear advantages that can be derived from scale and scope.

Also, the manner in which this decision has been taken violates the fact that in some of these banks there are private shareholders. The government completely overlooked their interest. If this has been done in the private segment, the corporate affairs ministry could take objection because it is not taking into account the interest of the minority shareholders. They have been completely ignored. When there is private shareholding in the PSBs, it should be governed by the Companies Act and not the Bank Nationalisation Act.

Would you rather like the government to follow the PJ Nayak Committee recommendations which envisaged setting up of a bank holding company?

I do not agree with the idea of a holding company. The basic question is on the relationship between government as the owner and the management of the bank, what is the 'arm's length' between the banks and their owner. You can have a holding company but it can still reflect the government's views and implement them. The arm's length concept needs to be discussed not only in relation to the PSBs but all public sector enterprises. For banks, it is even more important and unless the government decides that it will restrict its role to nominating the chairman or MD and the board and allow the board to take all decisions, the problems will continue.

Should we privatise the PSU banks, at least some of them?

In 2018, the SBI's gross NPA was 10.9 per cent of advances. This was not much higher than that of the second-largest private bank, ICICI Bank, 9.9 per cent. The ratio at a foreign bank, Standard Chartered Bank, 11.7 per cent, was higher than that of SBI. Moreover, private and foreign banks were part of the same consortia that have fared badly.

The problem lies elsewhere. The PSU banks had higher exposure to the five most affected sectors – mining, iron and steel, textiles, infrastructure and aviation. These sectors accounted for

29 per cent of advances and 53 per cent of stressed advances at PSBs in December 2014. For private sector banks, the comparable figures were 13.9 per cent and 34.1 per cent. The PSU banks accounted for 86 per cent of advances in these five sectors and by an interesting coincidence, this number is exactly the same as their share in total NPAs. In any case as I mentioned earlier, given the limited fiscal capacity to capitalise banks, government should decide on its total holding in the banking system.

Are you happy with the new bad-loan resolution infrastructure?

If a loan has gone bad, banks will have to accept a haircut. If the banks expect that all the money will come back and if they hold on to the loans, they will hold them forever. There is no choice but to accept the haircut but if the banks do that, the investigative agencies may step in. So, we need an arrangement under which any decision of the bank on haircuts gets shielded from the investigating agencies. And therefore it is necessary to evolve a system in which such decisions are made by an independent set of people. We had done that even in the early 1990s.

The passing of the IBC is an important innovation. But our experience so far is limited. The Supreme Court has not said that the central bank of the country does not have powers to direct the banks on bad loan resolution; it has said the RBI does not have the blanket power and it can do so only on a case-by-case basis.

For the first time the promoters now feel that when the chips are down, they can lose everything. This threat was not there earlier.

A defaulter is a defaulter. Why do we say wilful defaulter? It is a unique Indian concept.

What the Reserve Bank could have done is to find out how much of the NPAs were due to external factors and how much due to internal factors. For instance, dumping had caused problems. Some of the road projects have become unviable because of certain judgments. So, bad assets can arise due to external factors. It can also be the result of bad judgment or even mala fide. Is the default due to the machinations of the borrower or is it because there are genuine reasons? The distinction between the two is important. A wilful defaulter is a borrower who has the ability but who refuses to repay her obligations to the bank.

While China and Japan keep the bad loans problem alive and allow it to fester the US takes the bull by the horns. What is happening in India?

We are not going the China–Japan way. The idea behind the AQR was to clean it up, irrespective of the fallout of such a decision. From time to time we have been doing this. We did it in 1992–93. We did it early this century and again in 2015–16. The underlying philosophy is to clean up and not to cover up.

But the problem comes from evergreening. Banks offer more and more credit to keep a loan good. It is primarily a bank's responsibility to end such a practice; the regulator comes in later. The RBI keeps warning the banks against evergreening but they do not listen.

I asked a banker why there is a difference between what you say and what RBI says, and she told me sometimes banks take a lenient view. For instance, in the power sector, the state governments have delayed payments, and after 90 days if the banker were to classify the exposure as NPA it cannot provide fresh credit to the borrower. So, the banker takes a lenient view. What we really have to guard against in India is evergreening of loans.

What needs to be done to get over the current impasse?

There are reforms that are needed to be done. Our ability to use the banking system more effectively depends on how quickly we resolve the problem faced by banks. If the recapitalisation of the PSBs is required, then we must make a complete assessment and go ahead, at one go. The government must give the capital and solve the problem.

The task becomes difficult because of the tight fiscal situation.

Maybe the suggestion to give cash is difficult. There can be some combination of bonds and cash. The next task is to speed up the resolution process and both banks and government must exert their best to recover payments from borrowers. Whatever changes in IBC are required must be undertaken quickly. A 'bad bank' is not a good idea. Banks which granted the loans regularly must take the responsibility. Asset reconstruction companies have not been that successful.

What are the lessons the Reserve Bank has learnt from this crisis? What are the lessons for the banking system? And, what are the lessons for the government?

As far as RBI is concerned, some of the lessons are:

The regulator has the responsibility to monitor macro prudential indicators such as overall credit growth and also to spot excesses, if any, to certain sectors, and groups. This has implications when the RBI tightens or loosens monetary policy. The RBI's concerns must be communicated to the government/owners and made public. Regulation is no substitute for good governance. The regulatory design needs to reckon with financial and business cycles and take remedial measures in time. This is not to deny the challenges faced by the RBI on account of external factors like the global financial crisis (2008–09) and the Taper tantrum (2013).

Notwithstanding several measures taken by the RBI including the 2016 guidelines, the performance of the resolution process has been slow and needs to be reviewed and remedial measures taken. The IBC is an important innovation. But glitches need to be ironed out.

As international experience shows, increase in compliance cost does not automatically translate to better regulation. The regulatory regime needs to pinpoint parameters that need special attention.

The lessons for the government are:

The government certainly has the responsibility for overall management of the economy and being owner of the banks, it may push the banks in certain directions. This may have immediate benefits but may cause problems in the medium term. The government may ensure that banks are run in larger national interest but commercial decisions are best left to bank boards. Improvement in governance of the boards has been talked for long, but much needs to be done. The relationship between the government and the boards/CEO is still an unresolved question. There is no clear definition of 'arm's length'.

The government and regulators need to promote specialised institutions for project finance. This is a throwback in time but worth considering. The promotion of corporate debt markets both for performing loans as well as distressed loans needs special attention. Reliance on a project appraisal by just one single institution has entailed loses to a number of small and medium banks. These banks should not piggyback on project appraisal of other agencies.

The boards of the banks must be empowered to decide on capital raising plans from the market within a well-defined framework. It is a well-accepted axiom that organisations raise capital when they do not need it immediately.

Recapitalisation may be done in cash rather than through bonds or in some combination.

And, the lessons for the banks?

They need to take responsibility for the soundness of credit decisions. They need to define their own risk appetite rather than lean on the big lenders' appraisal. Project appraisal and working capital assessment are quite distinct, though related. Banks need to significantly upgrade their appraisal and monitoring skills and invest heavily in training. These cannot be sporadic and one off but well planned for the long term. Risk management must improve at all levels.

And, the assurance systems (internal and external audits and credit rating) need to be strengthened. Given the reported large-scale siphoning of funds and round-tripping of debt as equity through dozens of shell companies need to be checked through forensic audits at annual reviews.

Do you find fault with RBI's supervision and regulations?

Regulation is obviously important but how much regulation is required is also a critical question. Paul Krugman has said 'Make banking boring'. Essentially this means a limited role to banking and no complicated products like derivative products. Essentially, this denies an extensive role to banking. In that case, what will be the impact on the growth of the economy?

The other extreme view is tightening the regulations. There is a need to strike balance. Excessive regulation can also impede innovation. The regulator must determine a select number of parameters that need to be regulated and keep a very close watch of them.

In pre-1991 days, we used to say 'we have too many controls and too little control'. This should not happen with the regulatory system.

In Western Europe, they have calculated the cost of compliance – at one per cent of GDP. Many banks tell me they now have a separate compliance department. It is important that the regulators need to identify the key parameters that must be monitored.

How do you regulate the NBFCs?

There was a time when we were very strict about the NBFCs. Then there was a period when it was felt we should not be too tight and the NBFCs had an important role to play in the economy and the major distinction that should be made was between deposit-taking and non-deposit-taking NBFCs. The deposit-taking NBFCs had to be controlled tightly. Over a period of time a close link between the NBFCs and the banks had been established and monitoring of the functioning of the NBFCs had slackened. That the NBFCs are borrowing from the banks by itself is not a problem. The problem is the failure on the part of banks to monitor what the borrowing NBFCs were doing with the bank credit. The end-use of credit needs to be monitored by banks.

The NBFCs have a role to play as they are able to reach out to sectors of the economy which the banking system finds difficult to reach but the failure of the banks to monitor the activities of the NBFCs has created the problem.

Do you agree with the idea of an inflation-targeting central bank?
Since 1990 when it was first adopted by the Reserve Bank of New Zealand there has been a widespread adoption of inflation targets by several central banks. Some 28 central banks since then have adopted inflation targeting. Many regarded such a system to be quite durable, until the 2008 international financial crisis. Writing before the crisis, Marvin Goodfriend had titled his essay 'How the World Achieved Consensus on Monetary Policy'.

The adoption of inflation targeting by India has given rise to many doubts and concerns. The new monetary policy framework requires Reserve Bank to maintain consumer price inflation at 4 per cent with a margin of + or – 2 per cent. Thus in a sense, it is flexible targeting.

Does the focus on inflation targeting by monetary authorities mean neglect of other objectives such as growth and financial stability? Hardly so. What inflation targeting demands is that when inflation goes beyond the comfort zone, the exclusive concern of monetary policy must be to bring it back to the target level. When inflation is within the comfort zone, authorities can look to other objectives.

This at least is my interpretation of inflation targeting. It is sometimes said that the crisis of 2008 has sounded the 'death knell' of inflation targeting. It is not so. Many monetary authorities in the West failed to grasp the true meaning of inflation targeting. The rise in asset prices which happened prior to 2008 should have alerted monetary authorities and they should have taken action to raise the interest rate even though consumer prices were low.

It is also important to observe that the objective of control of inflation is not independent of the objective of growth. For example, the amendment Act of 2016 relating to RBI says 'whereas the primary objective of monetary policy is to maintain price stability while keeping in mind the objective of growth'. This is more or less the statement in almost all countries that had adopted inflation targeting. It is interesting to see the minutes of the Monetary Policy Committee of RBI. Before taking a decision on price rates, discussions have centred around output gap, the extent of liquidity, likely trends in GDP and possible supply shocks on prices. Without taking away the importance of price stability as a prime objective, there is no exclusion of considerations of growth.

And RBI often gets its inflation projection wrong...

That can happen in any regime of monetary policy. If they ignore the growth prospects, you can question them but that has not happened. As mentioned earlier, every policy statement keeps hammering at the importance of growth. What the monetary policy statement does not mention is the money supply. This is my concern – money supply has gone out of monetary policy.

A central bank cannot act like King Canute. It cannot order interest rates. To get to the desired interest rate, it must act on liquidity. And it is durable liquidity – another name for it is money supply. To bring about significant changes in the system, the RBI must pay attention to durable liquidity.

Finally, what do you say about RBI's autonomy?

A perennial question with respect to central banking is how much independence should a central bank enjoy. In the history of central banks, almost all of them until recently were treated, in the final analysis, as subject to the control of the government. Central banks did enjoy the freedom to state their views. Most governments respected their views because of the credibility enjoyed by the heads of central banks. Particularly in the parliamentary form of government, the finance minister, who is responsible for economic policy claims that the last word on major decisions is hers.

The argument in favour of independent central banks rests on the premise that monetary stability, which is essential for the efficient functioning of the modern economic system, can be best achieved only if the task is entrusted to professional central bankers who can take a long-term view of the monetary policy stance. Too much concern with the short term can result in 'stop-go' policies. Implicit in this kind of reasoning is the assumption that the political leadership normally tends to take too short term a view and such an approach is not conducive to ensuring stability. This is what is referred to the problem of 'dynamic inconsistency'.

In India, there has always been the dominance of government over the central bank...

Yes, it has been implicit all through. Jawaharlal Nehru in his letter to Governor Rama Rau at the time of his resignation said, 'You have laid stress on the autonomy of the Reserve Bank. Certainly it is autonomous, but is also subject to the Central Government's directions... Monetary policies must necessarily depend upon the larger policies which a government pursues. It is in the ambit of those larger policies that the Reserve Bank can advise.'

In fact, Nehru's letter was harsh in its tone. The then finance minister sounded even more aggressive. Unfortunately, this exchange of letters sealed the relationship between government and RBI for several decades.

In India, persons who were appointed as governors were men of erudition, scholarship and rich administrative experience. Governments listened to them. However, when the chips were down, the government had its way. It was not just a matter of 'fiscal dominance'. The government wanted the Reserve Bank to consult it before any decision was taken. If the government differed, it had its way.

Section 7 of the RBI Act says, 'The Central Government may from time to time give such directions to the Bank as it may, after consultation with the Governor of the Bank, consider necessary in the public interest.' Government of India has never used this section. It also acted always through other channels.

What exactly you are hinting at?

Monetary policy is part of the overall economic policy. Monetary policy and fiscal policy running in different directions can impose a burden on the economy. There has to be a close dialogue and coordination between RBI and the government. At the same time, there is an advantage in specifying the areas in which RBI has a clear mandate. The system of the issue of ad hoc treasury bills to replenish the cash balances of the central government implicitly amounted to automatic monetisation of fiscal deficit. It certainly weakened the role of RBI. It was good that this system was abolished in early 1990s.

The then government and finance minister saw the rationale for the abolition of the practice and were willing to go along with RBI. This was an act of great statesmanship on the part of the finance minister. The FRBM Act later took it forward by preventing the entry of RBI in the primary market in government securities. In fact, the new monetary policy framework is a major step forward in enhancing the autonomy of RBI. It not only establishes the primacy of price stability as the objective of monetary policy, but also gives the power to set the rate of interest rate exclusively to Monetary Policy Committee. As of now, the finance minister gets to know of the decision on interest rate along with others.

Central banks like the RBI perform multiple functions. They are not only monetary authorities but also regulators of the banking system. This in some ways complicates the autonomy question. As a regulator, they have only the freedom other regulators enjoy.

In determining the mandate to the Reserve Bank, the government has complete authority. Once the mandate is given, RBI must be given the freedom to take such actions as it deems fit. This is sometimes called 'instrument independence' as distinguished from 'goal independence'. It is important to make the distinction between 'autonomy' and 'independence'. It is in the best interests of the government itself to cede certain areas to the central bank and let the Reserve Bank act in those areas according to its best judgment.

■ ■ ■

12

'The problem is how the owner behaves'

Y.V. Reddy

An economist and a 1964-batch officer of the Indian Administrative Service, Yaga Venugopal Reddy, like Rangarajan, had served as a deputy governor before becoming the RBI governor. In between the two stints, he worked with the IMF as executive director and later chaired the 14th Finance Commission.

Reddy carried on the financial sector reforms that Rangarajan had initiated and is credited with ring-fencing the Indian banking system from the 2008 subprime crisis in the US by taking tough decisions to curb bank lending. In one of his interviews, Nobel Laureate Joseph E. Stiglitz, professor of Economics at Columbia University, has said, 'If America had a central bank chief like Y.V. Reddy, the US economy would not have been in such a mess.'

Reddy coined the term 'financial inclusion' in 2005 which is now a buzzword in the Indian financial system.

Edited Excerpts

Who is responsible for the ₹10-lakh crore bad loan pile? How did this happen?

The bad loan profile that we witness now is predominantly a public sector phenomenon. In PSBs, the bad loan profile is of significant public interest because fiscal support in the form of recapitalisation [by the government] is needed. That has to come from the taxpayers. In the case of private sector banks, the burden has to be borne essentially by the private shareholders, barring a few exceptions where there are bail-outs.

In both cases, the primary responsibility for bad-loan profile rests with the owners; the government in the case of PSBs and private shareholders in the case of private sector banks. The management is accountable to the owners. Frauds also are the responsibility of the owners since they are the losers.

It is possible that there can be macroeconomic factors or regulatory failures, but they generally cause system-wide problems.

Bad-loan profile in PSBs is of significant public interest since substantial fiscal support in the form of recapitalisation is needed. Recapitalisation of PSBs happened in two phases. The first one was in the 1990s. This reflected partly the effect of introducing global standards of regulation and partly social banking in the past. The second phase of recapitalisation happened after 2015–16. This is mainly on account of NPAs arising out of large accounts, in particular infrastructure and housing sectors, and also frauds.

In brief, we should distinguish different phases of the bad-loan profile warranting recapitalisation and treat the public sector and private sector separately in terms of public interest.

Earlier this century, in 2002–03 or so, the bad loans of banks were pretty high, but they were brought down by several actions: effective prompt corrective action including the merger of Global Trust Bank, consolidation in private sector banks, expansion of credit in PSBs, etc. The banking system was made healthy in five years by all accounts.

This is when you were at the helm, just before the fall of Lehman. In the five years in the run-up to the Lehman crisis, the fundamental macroeconomic factors in India and global conditions facilitated the growth. It was not a bubble created through the infusion of liquidity by RBI. In fact, we resorted to monetary tightening and regulatory tightening. At the same time, there was an increase in household financial savings and a reduction in the government's revenue deficit. So, the situation was conducive to genuine growth. Of course, interspersed in that, there were elements of a bubble, particularly in the housing and infrastructure sectors, to begin with.

You did tighten sector-specific regulations, ask for more capital... Yes. Though we had sound macro-economic fundamentals which facilitated credit growth, the RBI policy recognised over-heating elements. To what extent you can tighten the policy, up to what point you can go without dampening growth is a matter of judgment. But from the macroeconomic and regulatory point of view, the policy recognised the problem promptly and tried to fight it to the extent possible, despite resistance from political and financial markets. The gross and net NPAs of both public and private sectors reached low levels because of tight regulatory standards and supervision.

That is up to 2008. What happened after that? The global financial crisis happened in 2008 and, of course, the Indian economy was impacted though our financial sector was less affected, for many reasons. Globally, there were coordinated fiscal stimulus, monetary stimulus and regulatory forbearance. The issue is whether in India those were more than necessary and lasted longer than required. Notably, though we were affected by the global crisis, our growth was extraordinarily high immediately after the crisis. Why was that? Further, financial savings started coming down.

In brief, the aggregates of bad loans cannot be viewed in the context of individual projects or individual banks only. You have to view them in the broader policy context and macroeconomic conditions also.

Do we miss the DFIs or development finance institutions?

We have to see what the DFIs were doing in the past... Were they funding infrastructure? How much of infra-funding did IDBI and IFCI do? Did ICICI – which was not a public sector infrastructure financing entity – do much on infra? What was the private sector's involvement in infrastructure prior to the reforms in the 1990s?

There are a lot more DFIs continuing than those who were wound up. You have Small Industries Development Bank of India but what is happening to the small industries? What has happened to housing with National Housing Bank? How is National Bank for Agriculture and Rural Development doing in terms of agriculture?

The RBI gave licences to banks to be promoted by IDBI and ICICI, which they did. After a few years, they both decided to merge the DFIs with the respective promoted banks since DFIs were not commercially viable. The DFIs could succeed only if there was government support. The government was not willing to extend that support at that time.

So, you don't agree with the theory that the abolition of the DFIs contributed to the problems as our banks did not learn the tricks of project financing?

We did not have experience in infrastructure funding outside the government. DFIs like IDBI and ICICI had the experience but mainly in project funding. So, there was a need for a specialised institution to finance private sector or public-private sector partnership in infrastructure. Infrastructure Development Finance Company (IDFC), predominantly funded by RBI and the government, was established in the late 1990s.

What happened to it? Then IIFCL was started.

Exactly, what difference did they make? In fact, we also have long-standing specialised DFIs in the power sector, like PFC and REC. How did they perform?

The issue is that whoever has to do infrastructure financing, it needs long-term savings. You do not have enough long-term savings in India and, in any case, 60 to 70 per cent of our household savings are cornered by the government.

Is it a banking mess that spilled over to the economy?

When the pressure on the banks increased – both for social banking and infrastructure banking – the credit growth for working capital was choked. Bank credit, as a whole, has not been expanding after the AQR, but the economy has been expanding for a few years. Someone was providing money to replace bank credit. In the first round, it was mutual funds; in the next round, the NBFCs. In a way, the problem of stressed assets spilled over from the banking system to the mutual funds and the NBFCs.

At a broad level, fiscal laxity and financial repression left little room for financial intermediation. In financial intermediation banks dominate and PSBs have diffused objectives. In a way, fiscal problem spills over into banking and then financial sector problem with a feedback loop into the real economy. In brief, NPAs are not only a problem but a consequence of other problems.

That is my question: How were the NPAs created?

The RBI should make an internal analysis of the NPAs. You just take the large NPAs – and find out: How did they happen?

How much is due to courts, government clearances, mismanagement, macro-economic environment, and how much of these are under a bank's control? Or, for that matter, promoter control?

The notion that the NPA problem reflects entirely or significantly on the bankers may not be exactly right.

In banks, the NPAs are measured but in other sectors where we have state-owned enterprises, there is no clear yardstick to measure performance. For instance, let us take the government schools. How do we measure performance? Looking at the students' attendance?

So, you are saying that the government has no business to be in the business of banking?

No, I am not saying that. How can the PSBs perform like private banks if the government wants these banks to cater to the public interest as defined by the government? And, if the government manages PSBs like private sector banks, then why lock up taxpayers' money in banks?

The real question is: What is the objective of public ownership in banks and, if so, whether public ownership is the best or least-cost way of achieving those objectives?

Because it is taxpayer's money…

Yes. The taxpayer's money is locked up in banks. Then, they are recapitalised once; and now again.

In fact, the private shareholders of PSBs are not sharing the burden of recapitalisation now. Why? Of course, the taxpayer's money is involved, directly or indirectly, in case of private banks also when there is a bail-out. In terms of magnitudes of the burden on the taxpayer, which is less costly?

What is your take on the so-called corporate–banker nexus?

That is partly true; and they are mutually dependent.

My opinion is that the PSBs provide a bridge between politics and the business… In recent years, most of the politicians (or their families) are in business and many businessmen (or their allies) are in politics. It is politics–business nexus with PSBs as bridges. That does not rule out corporate–bank nexus.

Let us not be on a fault-finding mission as finding fault only erodes the trust and confidence of the public in banks. What is more important is what do we learn from the past and do things to improve trust and contribute to improving the system? The emphasis should be more on how to learn from the past than on how to punish the suspected faults of corporates, bankers and their nexus.

Between 2007 and 2009 when you were the governor, India recorded 9 per cent-plus economic growth and the credit growth was more than three times the GDP growth rate. Was that the beginning of over-leveraging by corporate India?
I had already said that the data should be analysed. Just take the largest 1,500 NPAs and find out when they became NPAs. You will get the answer.

Why was the RBI so inhibited about opening up the banking sector? Competition would have changed life both, for the industry as well as the customers.
We had proposed amendments to the Banking Regulation Act to empower the RBI to monitor and regulate fit and proper criteria. We in RBI were waiting for legal changes. In the meantime, we concentrated on consolidating smaller private sector bank segments.

Can you explain this?
We wanted the voting share [to be] in proportion to the ownership, but we wanted the regulatory regime governing fit and proper criteria on a par with the global standards.

That was a time when the foreign banks wanted to take over some of the old private banks. We wanted to ensure an appropriate regulatory regime before we open up. I did not consider any licences during my regime. My request to the government was pending for amendment of the Banking Regulation Act and it happened later, after I left RBI.

Do you agree that we have a repressive financial system?
Yes, undoubtedly.

Why do you say so?
One, of course, is the parallel administered interest rates, including small savings rates. Second, you have the high reserve requirements and the government-bond-buying by the banks. Third, the banks have the priority sector lending obligations. All in all, relative to the

other forms of financial intermediation, there is a burden on the banking system.

Now increasingly there is a competition between banks and non-banks which are not subject to such norms. You have to take an integrated view of banks, non-banks and mutual funds, and address the issue of competition and financial repression, in addition to directed/or behest lending.

Do you think that the government ownership in PSBs is too high?

The problem is not with the extent of government ownership. The question is fairly simple: How does the owner behave, and whether the owner, being a sovereign, creates a non-level playing field?

Further, if the government's controlling powers in PSBs are not linked to the extent of ownership, how does too much or too little matter?

What is your take on consolidation in public sector banking, which the government is pushing for?

Consolidation by itself does not solve the problem of governance. Look at the market share of PSBs – outstanding deposits and credit and also their share in incremental business. Take a look at the figures of the last five years and within that the captive market of public sector enterprises. The government has been putting more capital but is losing market share. Recapitalisation burden is only on government and not private shareholders in public sector banking. If the trend continues, Indian banking sector will be dominated by private banks, especially foreign-owned and incorporated in India.

Are you happy with the way the new insolvency platform is working?

One needs to take a holistic look at the complete judicial process. We need to solve the systemic processes, systemic contractual enforcements, starting with the government. Is the government honouring the contracts? The whole system of the relationship between government and public is built on the practice of government not honouring a contract and getting away with it.

The first step should be to prove the credentials of the government and the public enterprises that they honour the contracts. The standards of contracts, respect for contracts and enforcement of contracts should be set by the government, observed by it, and [they should] insist on others following them. That is how the eco-system for finance can be improved.

Do you think the RBI during the Rajan and Patel regime was over-aggressive in the bad-loan clean-up drive?

Historically, from 1998 to 2008 is a continuous period of tightening of the regulatory standards. After 2008, post the global financial crisis, there was loosening. I think the divergence between the NPA estimates of the banks and the revised NPA estimates of the RBI also increased until the correction took place on both counts (regulatory forbearance and laxity in supervision) through the AQR by Governor Rajan. The bad loans were accumulated over a period of time, and divergences between what banks accounted for and what the regulator found subsequently increased. When an accumulated problem is announced in one go, there is an effect of the announcement.

The RBI wanted the banks to make even one-day non-payment of dues public.

The fact remains that in handling finance one has to take into account the impact of the way you state the problem and how you resolve a problem. Recognition and identification of a problem is just the beginning. The disclosure of the problem, its handling and the timing of when you want to take measures to tackle the problem are very important. That is critical for maintaining trust in the banking system.

The NPAs in the banking system were even higher in the past but the clean up happened without much noise. How?

We recognised the problem, disclosed it but simultaneously projected and acted upon solutions. The emphasis was on a solution and not so much problems of NPAs alone.

Are you happy with the mandate for inflation targeting?

It is very difficult to say. There are two ways of looking at it. Raghuram Rajan said he only formalised what Dr. Reddy indicated in his monetary policy statements. I had indicated that informal self-imposed inflation target was desirable. He says he has formalised what was informal. And the formalisation is also is in the form of formal flexible inflation targeting. How much flexibility you have is the issue. The law offers a reasonably good range of 2 to 6 per cent inflation target.

So, you have a range. And, you have the MPC (Monetary Policy Committee) to decide on this. It is no more a policy of the governor or the RBI; it is a policy of the MPC. So, do not call it RBI's inflation targeting. The MPC's interpretation of the tolerance level, the balance between financial stability and external stability, growth and inflation need to be seen. If the inflation targeting did not work, the RBI cannot be blamed.

I am not blaming the RBI. My question is on the timing...

Those who favour inflation targeting can take the view that inflation targeting is good, but the way it was handled was not right. Those who are opposed can take a stance that the very fact that you are imposing inflation targeting, means there is a huge bias in favour of price stability. In reality the system in India gives flexibility to the MPC and to RBI. Much depends on how the two exercise flexibilities and interact with each other on inflation, growth and stability, including the external sector.

You favoured inflation targeting...

My record shows that I did not exactly favour formal inflation targeting. My stance was that the focus should be on maintaining inflation expectations and convincing the people that we are keeping price stability uppermost in our mind.

India has certain unique features in banking such as technical write-off and 'wilful defaulters'.

My recollection is that at one stage the RBI wanted the banks to write off loans whenever the recovery was not likely. But if a bank writes off, its right to recover may be gone when the case is pursued in the courts. Therefore, to keep the right to recover, banks do not write off – just do technical write-off where the loans are out of the balance sheet but not out of the bank's rights. This unusual system is, perhaps, necessitated by the unique time horizon and effectiveness of a judicial process.

Globally, a default is a matter between bank and borrower. In India, partly because the banking system was mostly owned by the government, there was pressure to put the list of defaulters in the public domain. The problem is that in any business, there can be a default for several reasons. So, a distinction was made between wilful defaulters or others. Generally, those instances where banks file cases before courts are declared as wilful defaulters. The concept of 'promoter' is also somewhat unique in India. In practice, nothing much happened after the naming and shaming of the defaulters in respect of those where cases have been filed before courts.

That is how the banking system works...

It is a reflection of the state institutions; it cannot be judged in isolation. This problem cannot be understood fully or assessed unless it is recognised that it is a bigger problem of the government and governance. The contracts entered into by the government are not honoured by the government and they cannot be enforced easily and in a timely manner. And, if a contractor is doing a shoddy job, government is not taking any action. He is not blacklisted. The government is a party to the majority of the cases being fought in courts.

My point is that the banking problem is a reflection of the totality of the system. NPAs are everywhere, not only in banking but in our government departments also. But, because of regulations, we measure NPAs in banks and not in other government departments.

We have to assess the capacity of the state institutions, their performance and their interface. More importantly, the problem is not only how the public sector performs vis-a-vis the private sector; it also lies in the relations between the public and private sectors.

Can this be solved by a periodic infusion of capital in PSBs?

Of course, not. But, there is a fiscal cost in recapitalisation and we have to see the benefits. Perhaps, that needs to be answered.

In India now we have different kinds of banks – small finance banks, payments banks, PSU and private banks – and we also want a club of big banks through consolidation of PSBs.

Many countries, including the USA, have different kinds of banks – wholesale banks, small banks and big banks. In the USA, there are banks confined to just one town. We need to make a note of what we want, study international practices and our circumstances. My limited point is that what ails the banking system does not lie only in the banking system; it is, to some extent, a reflection of the economic, political and social system, in particular, government departments and public enterprises.

Should we take the bull by the horn and clean up the banking mess overnight or allow the wound to fester for long? Post-Lehman crisis, the US government did not waste time to step in ...

In the USA, it was a banking sector mess, and banks were almost wholly private; so that government cleaned up. In India, the mess is in the government-owned banks: internal to it.

The fiscal strength of China can support the banking system. Japan too can afford to bail out any bank. What do you do when both the banking and fiscal situation are weak, as in India?

How do you see the governance problems in some of the private banks?

It depends on what you mean by governance problems. As a regulator, there is scope for a regulator to define and enforce fit and proper criteria for ownership and senior management.

Finally, is the creation of a bad bank the solution?

If the banking problem is generalised, then a systemic solution like a bad bank may be needed. If it is select bank's problem, then bank-specific solutions are needed. In any case, solution should be prompt and effective. We cannot afford a delay between the identification of a problem and completion of correction action – to bank on our banks!

■ ■ ■

13

'PSBs have served a purpose... It is now time to move on'

D. Subbarao

Duvvuri Subbarao, a 1972 batch officer of the Indian Administrative Service (he topped the civil service examination), did his graduation and post-graduation in physics from the Indian Institute of Technology and got a master's and a PhD in economics while in service.

Ten days after the finance ministry parachuted Subbarao into the RBI in September 2008, the iconic US investment bank Lehman Brothers collapsed, plunging the world into its biggest financial crisis. (Many finance ministry bureaucrats were later appointed the RBI governor but Subbarao was the first serving finance secretary to be given the job.)

Subbarao followed an ultra-loose monetary policy to insulate India from the impact of the global financial crisis. It paid off as the economy was back to the growth path quickly but the seeds for high inflation were sown. While he was fighting hard to contain inflation, the rupee started depreciating against the dollar – an inevitable fallout of a record high current account deficit.

In his five-year stint, Subbarao raised the policy rate 13 times and cut it 10 times, making it a record 23 changes in interest rates – the most by any governor in RBI's history. The Subbarao regime will also be remembered for his relentless fight with the finance ministry for the central bank's independence.

Edited Excerpts

What is the origin of the bad loan pile? The abolition of DFIs? The high growth period of 2007–09? Or, the deluge of money and easy credit after the collapse of Lehman when you were the governor?

You are asking two interrelated questions: When did the problem start and what caused it?

I do not think the bad loan problem has got anything to do with the abolition of DFIs. The DFIs were creatures of the pre-reform regime when capital markets were underdeveloped and we needed institutional mechanisms for supply of subsidised risk capital to private investors. An important component of the 1991 reforms was to develop financial markets. Once capital markets took root, the rationale for DFIs eroded and they were wound down. Your implication that there would have been no bad loan problem had the DFIs continued is I think misplaced.

To return to the question of when the problem started, I think the answer straddles the two periods you suggest. The problem started in the high growth years before the global financial crisis, continued through the crisis and even beyond, up until about 2010.

Tell me more on this...

To understand the root cause of the bad loan problem, it is necessary at first to throw the mind back to the turn of the century when an extraordinary investment boom accompanied by an extraordinary credit boom set India off on an unprecedented growth trajectory.

An important consequence of India's momentous economic reforms in 1991 – lifting controls on production and liberalising markets – was to unleash the huge reservoir of entrepreneurism that remained pent up for decades. As the economy gradually but surely broke out of the stranglehold of the proverbial 'Hindu rate of growth', entrepreneurs were hungrily scouting for investment opportunities. Meanwhile, a significant, although silent, consequence of the reforms was to remove the urban bias that ruled economic management until then and shift the terms of trade toward the rural sector. Rural incomes went up, pushing up demand for consumption goods, which in turn pushed up the demand for investment.

This matching of supply and demand for investment was fortuitous. What made it even more so was that it came about at a time when India also entered the world's consciousness as a software powerhouse. Thousands of Indian engineers were at the frontlines in resolving the much-feared Y2K glitch in computer systems around the world as the calendar turned to a new century.

In short order, India emerged as the world's back office as a counterpart to China becoming the world's factory. Foreign investors looking to hedge their investments started seeing India as an attractive alternative to China. In a much-coveted nod to India, the *Economist* at that time commented that India scores over China because of 'English, democracy and a decent legal system'.

As investment boomed, going up from 24 per cent of GDP in 2000–01 to an unprecedented high of 38 per cent by 2007–08, the India growth story started unfolding with the economy expanding at an average annual rate of over 7 per cent during the decade 2001–10, notwithstanding the global financial crisis. Our country of a billion people, it seemed, had at long last discovered the holy grail to rapid growth, triggering tantalising speculation about it being India's turn to be the next growth miracle.

But that was not to be...

Things started unravelling around 2010 when investments started crumbling, bad loans mounted and the financial sector came under stress. In popular perception, this was all a result of crony capitalism.

There may have been some of that, but there were several other – and bigger – factors at play.

Importantly, much of the investment went into infrastructure which was an uncharted territory both for the corporates making the investments and for the banks lending to them. There was irrational exuberance too, with investors making demand projections, unrealistically assuming that the good times would roll on forever. Supreme Court orders cancelling government allocations of wireless spectrum and coal blocks, and restraining some mining projects added to the uncertainty and delays. Having to fight on several fronts in this general milieu of corruption and scandals, the government went into what was derisively called 'policy paralysis'.

Meanwhile, as projects got delayed or derailed, bad loans piled on, stressing the balance sheets of both corporates which borrowed and banks which lent to them, brewing the notoriously complex 'twin balance sheet' problem.

One could well ask what were the banks doing as they were getting saddled with bad loans. After all, banks had access to coercive mechanisms for recovery such as the DRT and the SARFAESI process. The point is even though these mechanisms seemed speedy and effective on paper, in practice they were neither; there were enough loopholes for borrowers to game them.

More importantly, senior bank management personnel operated under a perverse incentive system. They had no incentive to recognise bad loans as it would spoil their record. On the other hand, there was a strong incentive for them to kick the can down the road by evergreening the loans. The net result was bad loans festered, piled up and reached explosive proportions.

You were at the helm at RBI just before the Lehman collapse. You flooded the system with money. Cheap monetary policy was supplemented by expansionary fiscal policy. When it was time to tighten the policy, you were slow in action. Do you share the blame for this?

Oh, absolutely. I take full responsibility for all the measures we took to contain the impact of the crisis and their consequences. To the extent that at least one of the causes of the bad loan problem traces its origins to the extraordinary liquidity infusion we had done to mitigate the impact of the crisis, I share the blame for it.

To appreciate my response in its context, I want you to throw your mind back to 2008 when Lehman Brothers collapsed and the global financial sector came to a near-death experience. Financial markets were gripped with fear and anxiety, and in advanced economies, trading was hurtling towards a total stop. Policy makers in governments and in central banks were bewildered, uncertain and anxious. The pre-emptive priority was to restore calm and confidence to the markets, and towards this end, central banks pumped in massive amounts of liquidity into the markets and cut rates. The received wisdom was that it was better to err on doing too much, rather than too little.

Yes, that was the milieu in which you were operating. What were the challenges?

Our most pressing challenge was to ensure that our markets continued to operate and that credit continued to flow to productive sectors. Pumping in excess liquidity seemed the right thing to do, and it can well be argued that had we not done that, the situation would have been much worse. If that massive liquidity caused problems down the line, it was an inevitable by-product and has to be seen as the price we have had to pay for restoring stability in the aftermath of the crisis. Note that we were operating in real-time whereas critics evaluating our policies and actions are doing so with the benefit of hindsight.

The same logic applies to why we did not reverse the crisis measures, or 'tighten the policy' to use your words, in good time. With the benefit of hindsight, we now know that had we tightened sooner and faster, inflation would have been contained that much sooner. But again, throw your mind back to that period. The global financial crisis segued into the eurozone sovereign debt crisis giving policymakers no respite at all. Virtually all advanced economies and most emerging economies were still in an accommodative policy mode and there were persisting concerns about the contagion of financial instability and market upheaval. It was in this setting that we had to calibrate our exit from the crisis-driven expansionary stance. Erring on the side of maintaining the easy money stance seemed the wise thing to do.

I am elaborating at length not so much to defend my action or inaction, but to give you a realistic appreciation of the global uncertainty at that time and the universe of knowledge in which we were operating.

But where do bad loans come into all this?

They come in because one of our policy priorities during the crisis, as I said earlier, was that credit must continue to flow to support production. We were, therefore, encouraging banks to restructure loans that were having liquidity problems. It turned out that as the message passed through the bank operational hierarchies, not just illiquid loans, but many insolvent loans too were restructured. I am not suggesting there was corruption but there certainly was looseness. This restructuring of insolvent loans was one of the early causes of the bad loan problem. As the supervisor, the RBI was responsible for guarding against such looseness, and since this lapse occurred on my watch, I am to that extent responsible.

I must add though in this connection that pressure in the financial system is difficult to detect in real-time. Stan Fischer, possibly the most authoritative macroeconomist of our time, says that the financial sector can withstand pressure for much longer than we believe possible with the result that when the inevitable implosion takes place, it is not just disruptive, but even catastrophic. This, in fact, is the root cause of all financial crises. You must evaluate our inability to see the problem in real-time in this context.

As regards my responsibility for the bad loan problem, Tamal, you may have forgotten but when you interviewed me after the release of my book back in 2016, I had admitted my responsibility for my inaction. Please feel free to quote from there.

I moderated the discussion at the release of Subbarao's book *Who Moved My Interest Rate?* at the RBI headquarters in Mumbai, along with Lata Venkatesh of CNBC TV-18.

A PTI news report, dated 5 August 2016, says:

Admitting that the "action or inaction" of RBI during his tenure could have been among reasons for the present bad loan crisis, former governor D. Subbarao on Friday said he should have addressed those issues.

"NPA problem is getting bigger than any of us has thought it might be. Looking back at the benefit of hindsight, I believe I should have addressed the problem of NPA. Even as when I was writing my book, I was not very sure that I have anything to add to public discourse except to say that some of the causes of present (banking) crisis owe to action or inaction of RBI on my watch.

"...now looking back I should have addressed some of those issues," Subbarao said Subbarao's comments come days after outgoing RBI governor Raghuram Rajan, who has mandated a "deep surgery" of banks' balance sheets to cleanse them of bad loans, said that the central bank should have done the clean up job earlier.

Replying to a question, whether the world will again face a crisis like the collapse of Lehman Brothers, the former bureaucrat-turned-governor, who recently wrote a tell-all memoir, *Who Moved My Interest Rate?*, said, "I think Lehman crisis like moment is unlikely but another crisis is certainly possible." Subbarao said his world-view changed after he shifted to RBI from the finance ministry.

In hindsight, do you think India's response to the Lehman crisis was a bit exaggerated?

With the benefit of hindsight, it might look like our response was exaggerated, but in real-time, it seemed to be an appropriate and measured response to the fear and uncertainty of that time. We are not alone in thinking so. If you go back and look at the commentary of that period, you will find that economists, analysts, media pundits and retired policy makers were all arguing for an extraordinary easy monetary policy stance. Indeed, many had criticised the RBI for not being even more accommodative. It was a very uncertain situation and the logic at that time was to err on the side of doing much rather than too little.

Do you see there is a corporate–banker nexus?
As I said earlier, crony capitalism is one of the factors, but certainly not the only factor, responsible for the bad loan problem. However, I have no first-hand knowledge of any nexus that you are suggesting.

Earlier in the late '90s and early 2000s, when we had NPA in percentage terms even higher than the current numbers, the situation was handled quietly. There is a perception that the new administration – both the government and the RBI – seems to be happy in red-flagging the problems without having the solution on the table. Do you think so?
I think your characterisation of 'red-flagging the problems without having the solution on the table' is too simplistic and does not factor in the changed times. It is possible, as you say, that the bad loan problems of the late 1990s and early 2000s were resolved 'quietly'. But in today's situation and context, it is neither possible nor even advisable to opt for 'quiet' solutions. Not possible because there is such intense public scrutiny of the government and the RBI in part because of the move towards a culture of transparency and the right to information. Not advisable because by suppressing information, you are depriving the stakeholders of the time they need to make the adjustment to manage the problem.

Do you think that the regime under RBI after you left – under Raghuram Rajan and Urjit Patel was too aggressive in the clean-up drive?
No. On the contrary, both Dr. Rajan and Dr. Patel deserve credit for arresting the problem and preventing it from exploding into a

crisis. I completely reject your suggestion that they had magnified the problem by not giving enough time. We did not have the luxury of time. We know from experience that if a banking crisis is allowed to fester unattended, it would quickly snowball into a financial crisis.

Contrary to your suggestion, I think the actions started by Dr. Rajan and continued by Dr. Patel arrested the problem and prevented a bigger crisis. Go back to Dr. Rajan's tenure: He started with building an information base and launched several schemes such as the joint lenders' forum, 5/25, S4A, SDR, etc. As the bankruptcy code was still in discussion, he engineered a resolution mechanism that mimicked the bankruptcy process, without of course the legal backing. I think he gave the banks enough time to recognise and resolve bad loans before launching the AQR.

And, mind you, the AQR was not a penal measure; it was just a diagnostic measure. I do not see how it could have hurt anyone.

You are an economist first and then a central banker. Is it a case of a banking crisis engulfing the economy?

The bad loan problem has been long and deep. The economy has paid a heavy price for it. Private investment which had gone to as high as 38 per cent of GDP before the global financial crisis fell to 28 per cent. It is this collapse of investment that is at the heart of our growth slump. It follows that reviving investment is key to reviving growth. Presently, the investment sentiment is negative for a number of reasons; the twin balance sheet problem is one of the reasons but not the only one. So, I would not agree with the characterisation of 'the banking crisis engulfing the economy'. But I believe that resolving the bad loan problem is a necessary – although not a sufficient – condition for reviving investment and hence growth.

Do you think the delay in infusing capital into the banks led to this problem?

Your question does not admit a binary answer. I need to qualify my response.

I call questions of this type silo questions – looking at a problem through a tunnel ignoring the larger context.

The picture you are painting is this: There is this huge bad loan problem that is crying out for a solution. It is evident that the solution is for the government to pump in capital into troubled PSBs. Instead of doing that, the government is twiddling its thumbs even as the problem is hurtling towards a crisis.

The reality is far from that. Yes, the bad loan problem is big and real. But, what is also big and real is the fiscal constraints of the government.

I have spent many years as a finance secretary at the state and central government levels. I have first-hand experience of making budgets which call for managing the tension between huge expenditure demands and limited funds. The challenge for the finance minister is to prioritise expenditures. Put yourself in the shoes of the finance minister. Her thinking would be somewhat like this. We have already allocated a significant sum to recapitalise PSBs. Also, there is a plan under way to merge PSBs to make them fewer and larger. Let us wait and see the results before committing more funds.

From this perspective, your suggestion that there was a delay in infusing capital into banks is true in a literal sense, but only in a literal sense.

So, fisc is the issue?

Yes, absolutely. The government is not wooden-headed. They know the nature and size of the problem. They know too that recapitalising banks is necessary. The challenge for them is to find the resources and invest them optimally.

When I asked you about recapitalisation of banks, you say I am not fair and I am seeing it in silos. Public sector banks still have a little over 60 per cent market share of banking assets. Are they inefficient? Are they not allowed to work? Does the government play an active role in directing them?

The government putting pressure on PSBs to favour some borrowers is the essence of crony capitalism. I have heard about it but have had no first-hand exposure. Having been in the government for nearly 40 years, it seems quite plausible.

But I must also add that how the CEO of a PSB responds to pressure is a function of the individual. Some people resist, some cave in and some are even eager to do the bidding of the government. You cannot paint all of them with the same brush.

To get a perspective on this, let us look at all the charges against the government.

- First, that the government indulges in crony capitalism. The PSB top brass has no choice but to succumb to pressure unless they are resigned to compromising their careers.
- Second, the government did not recapitalise the PSBs in good time and in adequate quantity.
- Third, not only did the government not do its bit, but it even resisted measures by the RBI to clean up bad loans. For example, the government put pressure on RBI to relax or even withdraw the 12 February 2018 circular regarding (bad loan) recognition. The government sought special dispensation for the power sector even as it was this sector that accounted for a big chunk of the bad loans.
- Finally, the government uses the PSBs as its extended arm by asking them to implement its socio-political agenda even if that means eroding credit quality and credit standards. It is this vested interest that is behind its lack of enthusiasm to implement the Naik Committee recommendations.

These, in a nutshell, are the charges against the government. None of them can be brushed away. On the other hand, there is also some exaggeration. Also, it is not the case that all politicians are alike. There certainly are some who were/are sensitive to the PSB autonomy and have even taken measures to further it.

Would you blame the fear psychosis among bankers responsible for low credit offtake?

There are many factors responsible for the low credit offtake. We cannot rule out fear psychosis as one of them. The government, of course, makes pronouncements that top PSB management will not be penalised or victimised for decisions taken in good faith. But I get a feeling that this assurance fails to inspire confidence.

Having been part of both the government and central bank, do you think it is time to bring down the government's stake in PSBs?

Absolutely. Where is the doubt? I think the best option is for the government to divest completely.

Bank nationalisation happened 50 years ago. That was in a different era and a different context. Undoubtedly, nationalisation delivered some very positive results. Most importantly, it was because of nationalisation that we have achieved deep penetration of banks into villages, to the envy and admiration of many developing countries. There are many factors behind the sharp decline in poverty over the last several decades; at least one of the reasons is the opportunities provided by rural credit flow from PSBs.

But we have to recognise that in these changed times, confronting different challenges, the rationale for government ownership of banks has ebbed away. The financial sector is wide enough and deep enough to take care of financial intermediation without the government at the driving seat. It is time to move on.

But public sector banks have become a holy cow; they cannot be touched.

Yes, privatising them requires, therefore, a lot of political capital. That Prime Minister Modi has in abundance. In fact, Modi arguably has more political capital than any other prime minister in decades. He has to be prepared to invest that capital to do politically difficult things. And one of those politically difficult things has to be the denationalisation of PSBs.

Sure, it cannot be done overnight. It has to be done over time in accordance with an agreed and openly shared time plan. But as Mao said, even a 1000-mile journey has to start with a first step and the time to take that first step is NOW.

You are not worried about the governance structure in some of the private sector banks?
I am by no means suggesting that there are no problems with the governance structures of private banks. Neither am I arguing that if you have only private banks, you will not have any problems. But problems with governance structures in private banks can't be an argument for persisting with PSBs. As I said earlier, PSBs have served a purpose; that task is done. It is now time to move on.

What is the right way of the government withdrawing from them?
In the literature on economic reforms, there are two models. One is the *blitzkrieg* reform model which says that you cannot cross a chasm in two leaps; you have to take one big leap to the other end. That is what we did in 1991. The other is the gradualist model – crossing the river by feeling the stones.

For government withdrawal from PSBs, I think the latter model is more advisable since there are many stakeholders. But it is important to start now, prepare a road map, indicate milestones and a definite end point. I think a ten-year plan with all PSBs privatised by 2030 will be optimal.

The government is pushing for consolidation. Does it serve any purpose?
If you want a one-word answer, my answer is 'no'. If you recall, the finance minister made the statement about bank mergers shortly, I believe a week after, growth had plunged to 5 per cent.

Actually, it was announced, I mean making ten banks into four, the second phase of consolidation, just an hour before the GDP grown data was released...
Maybe she had advance information about the growth slump and

timed the bank merger announcement accordingly. It was meant to be seen as a measure to arrest the growth slowdown. In my view, it is a distraction. Because, to revive growth and resolve the twin balance sheet problem we require all banks, particularly PSBs, to give their undivided attention to resolving the NPA problem and scouting for fresh lending opportunities. Instead, they will now be saddled with resolving the nitty-gritty of mergers and worrying about their career progressions. In the short term, bank mergers will not help revive growth. If anything, they take away attention from more pressing challenges.

You might well ask, even if bank mergers are net negative in the short term as you say, will they be positive in the medium term. I believe the answer is 'no'.

In support of mergers, it could be argued that the initiative is in line with the Narasimham Committee recommendation that India should have a few large banks, many medium-size banks and many small banks. But that should be an organic process – more efficient banks should grow in size through mergers and acquisitions in a competitive market, not through marriages arranged by the government.

It is not as if large banks are a completely benign solution. Experience has shown that they pose 'too big to fail' type of problems. Which means they should be subjected to tighter regulation and closer supervision. Furthermore, large banks are inefficient in providing last-mile connectivity. We need small and medium banks to do that.

The short point is inorganic mergers of PSBs of the type the government is organising is net negative both in the short term and the medium term and distracts from addressing the underlying problems.

What is your take on the progress of the insolvency process?
I have read somewhere that everywhere around the world, especially in emerging economies, IBC has taken at least a couple of years to stabilise. What has been happening in India fits that pattern. We

perhaps had unrealistic expectations from the IBC because of the special circumstances we were in. There was this huge and festering NPA problem, growing in size by the day, and we saw the IBC was the magic bullet that would set things in short order. We are disappointed that it did not actually turn out that way.

It took sometime for the legal issues under the IBC to be settled, and hopefully, that is all done now and IBC will now roll out in a streamlined fashion and deliver some quick results.

In order to get optimal results from the IBC on the way forward, we must keep in view some broad guidelines. First, a timely resolution is at the heart of the IBC process. For that to happen, we must exercise discretion to ensure that the system is not overloaded. It means, among other things, invoking the IBC has to be the last resort – not the first. It cannot be that every bad loan case is referred to the IBC. Much of the IBC has to happen under the threat of the IBC rather than under the IBC itself.

Finally, all stakeholders – the government, the banks, the regulators (both RBI and SEBI) – must be on a vigil to ensure that the system does not get gamed as happened with other supposedly pre-emptive recovery measures over the years.

Was creation of a bad bank ideal to clean the system?

I do not believe so. It is not unambiguously clear that a bad bank option is better than having individual banks address their own bad loans.

A bad bank typically has two objectives: First, allow banks to clean their balance sheets by selling their assets to the bad bank; and two, discover and recover the steady-state economic value of assets that may be currently depressed. And for these objectives to be met, the bad bank has to be sufficiently capitalised to meet its under-recovery risk. Where will that come from? If PSBs have to meet that, we are back to square one. If private investors have to meet that, they will demand a huge haircut which will totally cripple some banks. If the government has to meet that, they may as well use that money to give to individual banks.

No matter how you look at it, a bad bank does not seem to be the magic bullet that it is made out to be.

During your stint at RBI, you did not give a single licence to a new bank. Don't you think that the Indian banking system is repressive and anti-competition. And, when the government does not have the capital, why not allow corporations with deep pockets to set up banks? Also, do you think larger skin in the game actually ensures governance?

It is true that during my regime at the RBI, no new bank licence was given. But please note that it was during my regime at the RBI that we, in fact, reopened the dormant issue of new bank licences in a systematic way and set about drafting the guidelines consistent with the credit needs of the underserved and the demands of the changed economy.

One of the big issues we had to determine was whether or not to allow corporates, with 'deep pockets' as you say, to set up banks. In order to crystallise opinion on this, we generated a public debate, consulted all stakeholders, sought the views of experts including media personnel such as yourself and studied international experience.

Historically, there has been and there still is some wariness about allowing corporates to promote banks for fear of self-dealing. That threat is even more acute in a poor country like India where a bank failure and loss of deposits can mean loss of life savings and even destitution for millions of households. On the other hand, if we did not allow corporates, there weren't any credible groups or parties with track record or experience to set up banks.

After extensive consultations and internal debates, we determined that the balance of advantage lay in allowing corporates to promote banks, albeit with extensive safeguards.

And capping the promoters' stake at a certain level?

Oh yes, that will have to be an important component of the safeguards. After all, depositors have to trust a bank, and they won't do so unless the safeguards are credibly, and are transparently tight.

On the issue of depositors' trust in the bank, I must raise an issue that at first may seem unrelated to new bank licences, but is in fact connected. It is the issue of whether depositors must bear part of the risk in the event of a bank failure. A few years ago, there was a proposed amendment, I think, to the Banking Regulation Act which proposed that in the event of a bank failure, depositors must bear the risk beyond deposit insurance. There was outrage and protest and some people even branded it as draconian. But what was missed in this protest was that if the depositors do not bear the risk, the cost passes on to the government, which means the government will be bailing out the sinking bank using funds that could have used for some development or anti-poverty scheme. Saving a sinking bank has an opportunity cost and that needs to be taken into account in deciding whether or not a sinking bank should be saved at all.

A bank failure is a sad thing. As the regulator, RBI should prevent failures. But should it happen, the cost must be borne by the direct stakeholders rather than all the people.

What has this to do with corporates promoting banks? It is relevant in the sense that if we are allowing corporates to promote banks, we give minute attention to their track record and build in safeguards against their abuse of the trust and confidence of depositors placed in the promoters.

I have digressed. Let me return to your original question about why no new licences were given during my tenure. The reason was that we drafted the guidelines, and in order to build in the safeguards, the RBI Act had to be amended giving additional powers to the RBI. This took time and the whole process of scrutinising the applications and awarding of the licences could not be completed before my time ran out.

What went wrong in the NBFC sector?

The NBFC sector implosion, as we know, was triggered by big defaults by IL&FS and a few other large NBFCs. I must say that in the event, things turned out to be better than what we feared at the height of the problem.

Was it, to use your phrase, a Lehman moment for India? I do not think so because there was no domino effect. The NBFC sector did not collapse, there was no shakeout, all liabilities are now in the open and the lenders, I understand, are reopening lending to some NBFCs. So, it certainly was not a Lehman moment of rapid contagion and systemic collapse.

Why did it turn out to be better than we feared? Again, my understanding comes entirely from what I have read. IL&FS is a very untypical NBFC, a conglomerate with several NBFCs under it, and unlike other NBFCs, with relatively low exposure to mutual funds.

We must also recognise that RBI's quick action of pumping in liquidity prevented the problem from snowballing into a systemic crisis.

What caused the problem? I think there were two factors: One general and the other more specific to IL&FS.

The general cause traces its origins to demonetisation; all the money that was invalidated flowed back into the banking system. Banks were swamped with unexpectedly huge deposits. However, battling as they were with bad loans, they were unprepared to lend this money directly to clients and found it safer to lend to NBFCs which in turn lent to consumers. In other words, NBFCs took over the lending space vacated by the banks and in the event some NBFCs went overboard which sowed the problem in the sector.

The specific cause was there must have been some irresponsible risk-taking by IL&FS.

What are the key takeaways from the NBFC crisis?

There are several takeaways.

First, we have to remember that NBFCs serve a very useful purpose. In our anxiety to keep the sector safe, we should not overreact and tighten regulation so much that the sector chokes to death. The task is to ensure that inherently strong NBFCs are revived and remain strong.

Second, we must recognise that the NBFC model is inherently risky. Their sources of funding are costlier and narrower than those of banks and their assets are riskier. Like all financial intermediaries, they do maturity transformation, but the degree to which they do so is much higher than banks. The regulation and supervision mechanism has to recognise this riskiness, yet allow sufficient freedom to NBFCs to function since they add value to the economy.

Third, the government decision to subject the NBFCs to the bankruptcy process is a good one. As our financial sector expands and diversifies, we must get used to the idea of some financial entities dying because of business failures. The notion that every financial sector entity should or will somehow be resurrected no matter what the cost, should be wiped out. Those NBFCs which are not sound or solvent must be allowed to die. That will be a deterrent to the entire sector and push them into more responsible behaviour.

Fourth, as much as we criticise bad decisions and actions, we must also appreciate good decisions and actions. In the event of the NBFC crisis, I think the RBI acted with wisdom and alacrity and we must acknowledge that.

Finally, as someone said after the Lehman collapse, we should not waste a good crisis. Notwithstanding the timely action by the RBI, the crisis pointed to some loopholes, gaps and lapses in our system of regulation and supervision. It is important to recognise here that as a nation, we are good at drafting good laws and sound rules, but are awfully inept at implementing them. That is true of RBI's supervision as well. What this means is that the focus has to be more on making supervision more effective rather than writing new regulations.

The RBI gets a lot of flak when it comes to supervision. Does RBI need to change itself?

The short answer is yes.

As I said earlier, the bank NPA problem and the NBFC sector

implosion were at their heart failures of supervision and point to the need for RBI to learn from experience and improve its supervision capability.

I must add here that RBI is a knowledge institution and has a culture of learning from experience. I am sure that within RBI there must have been a lot of introspection to identify what went wrong, where and when. I am also sure they have taken corrective action to fix the gaps and loopholes.

The question is this. Is that internal exercise enough or does something more needs to be done? My view is that an internal exercise is good but not good enough. In order to inspire public confidence, RBI must be more transparent and subject itself to a more open scrutiny.

The model here is what the US Federal Reserve and the Bank of England had done after the global financial crisis. The Anglo-Saxon central banks were at the receiving end of a lot of criticism for sleeping at the wheel even as a deadly crisis was brewing in the underbelly of the financial system.

After some calm was restored in the financial markets, they went through an introspection, but they also did something more. They both appointed external committees to inquire into where lapses occurred and whether the corrective action taken was adequate and effective. By doing so, they demonstrated that they were prepared to admit to mistakes and render accountability. There is a need for the RBI to do something similar.

When Dr. Rajan was stepping down in September 2016, he invited all former governors for an informal lunch. The NPA problem was at its peak then. I am sure it figured prominently in the conversation. What was your suggestion?

I suggested that the RBI must appoint an external committee on the model of the Fed and the BoE to inquire into its supervisory lapses, and to evaluate the corrective action taken. I argued that such humility will demonstrate RBI's intellectual integrity and act as a catharsis too. I also suggested that we should draw some leading international experts who will bring credibility to the whole exercise. I felt confident in making that suggestion since it is highly probable that the lapses would point to my regime and nobody could accuse me of trying to find a scapegoat.

Nevertheless, that suggestion did not get support from other past governors. They suggested instead that RBI should first appoint an internal committee and think of an external committee depending on the findings of the internal committee. Raghu perhaps felt, rightly in my view, that any such decision must be taken by his successor. Nothing came of that during the later regimes.

Even now, I do not think it is too late to appoint an external committee as I suggested. It will set a model for responsible behaviour by a public institution.

Is inflation targeting in the current economic scenario in India a mistake?

I think it will be somewhat rash to write off inflation targeting just three years after embracing it. We must give it more time before making a judgment on whether inflation targeting is an appropriate framework for India.

In order to give a more informed response, let me start with some perspective. Inflation targeting acquired a halo in the years before the global financial crisis. It was credited with sustainably delivering low inflation and steady growth in advanced economies. With inflation targeting, it seemed like central banks had at long last discovered the holy grail to macroeconomic stability.

That view crumbled after the crisis when it was found that in their undivided pursuit of an inflation target, central banks lost track of other concerns and allowed the cancer of financial instability brew in the underbelly of the global financial system. The received wisdom post-crisis was of flexible inflation targeting – that is target inflation but with growth and financial stability too on the radar.

It is this flexible inflation targeting approach that we adopted in India. Flexibility is built in by allowing a wide tolerance band for inflation and by enjoining the Monetary Policy committee to keep growth concerns in view as it calibrates monetary policy to target inflation.

I have long had reservations about the appropriateness of an inflation-targeting framework for an economy like ours.

What are your concerns?

First, inflation in India is driven more often by supply shocks rather than demand pressures. For example, if there is a flare-up in Syria, global crude price will go up and put upward pressure on inflation. Similarly, if food distribution is impaired because of floods in a part of the country, food prices will go up pressuring inflation. This sort of inflation is less amenable to control by monetary policy.

Second, as experience has shown, we are vulnerable to volatile capital flows which can destabilise the exchange rate and impair inflation targeting. Third, there is fiscal dominance – huge borrowing by not just the centre but all the state governments, which can undermine RBI's ability to control inflation through monetary policy action. Finally, even after some dismantling, we still have a significant administered interest rate regime – for example, on small saving instruments – which can inhibit monetary policy transmission and erode the effectiveness of inflation targeting.

You have devoted an entire chapter in your book* Who Moved My Interest Rate? *to give your views on inflation targeting.

Since I left the RBI, some of these impediments to inflation targeting that I pointed out earlier have been eased. Nevertheless, I believe inflation targeting has yet to be fully tested in India. True, much of the past three years since we embraced inflation targeting, inflation has largely been on target. But it is not clear how much of that was due to benign supply conditions rather than the efficacy of inflation targeting.

So, as I said at the beginning, we must give inflation targeting a little more time before embarking on any revisions to the framework.

Talking about clean up – should India clean up the system in a very aggressive way a la US, or should it follow the Japan way, delay the inevitable, allow it to fester and lose a decade?

The answer is implicit in your question itself. Given Japan's bitter experience, the Anglo-Saxon model seems better. Indeed we have already lost a lot of time. There were delays in acknowledging the problem and getting to grips with its magnitude. And as we discussed earlier, resolution was hampered by a flawed incentive system and the absence of a bankruptcy process. And even after the IBC had been enacted, we had to move up a steep learning curve. There were also legal challenges to the IBC. Hopefully, all these problems are behind us and resolution will go on stream effectively henceforth.

What is the way forward for the Indian banking system?

That is an omnibus question and perhaps the right way to wind up this long and exhaustive interview. Some important directions for the way forward.

First, we must have an action plan for deepening and diversifying our financial sector consistent with our deepening and diversifying economy. It will still be a bank dominated system but with a much reduced dependence on large commercial banks. In particular, we need to develop the corporate bond market; and create a conducive environment for a variety of financial entities like small finance banks, payments banks, NBFCs including microfinance institutions. By not putting the entire burden of financial intermediation on large commercial banks, we will allow them to operate to their comparative advantage.

Second, we must acknowledge that the historical dominance of PSBs will ebb away as future expansion will be almost entirely in the private banking space.

Third, we must plan for total privatisation of PSBs. Consolidation is not a solution. The way forward is for total divestment. Sure, this cannot be done overnight but we must prepare a 10-year road map so that the banking sector will be entirely private within a decade.

Fourth, all financial sector regulators, RBI included, should recognise that going forward they will be on a steep learning curve. The financial sector will evolve and change at a pace and in ways that we have not seen before. New technologies will be transformative, but they will also expand the scope for cybercrime. The markets will design new instruments and products. Globalisation will pose new and often forbidding challenges. Regulators will have to be on constant vigil, be on a self-improvement drive, learn from international best practices but adapt them to the Indian context.

Fifth, we must recognise that the financial sector is prone to crises. This, in fact, is the thesis of the much-celebrated book *This Time is Different* by Kenneth Rogoff and Carmen M. Reinhart. After every crisis, there is an extensive effort to learn from the mistakes and take corrective action. Yet, there comes another crisis in unexpected places, at unexpected times and in unexpected ways. What Rogoff and Reinhart say is that governments and regulators believe that 'this time is different', but it is not. All financial crises over the last 800 years trace their origins to the same fundamental causes. Regulators, in particular, must recognise this and be on constant vigil.

Finally?

Let me wind up on a philosophical note that is applicable everywhere, not just India. Over the last seven decades or so since the end of the Second World War, the world has come to see the financial sector as a solution to all real sector problems. The view was that for every real sector problem, no matter how complex, there is a financial sector solution. The crisis has debunked that notion. The post-crisis world view is that for every real sector problem, no matter how complex, there is a financial sector solution, *which is wrong*.

As countries, as economies and as people, we must recognise that the growth and development of the financial sector is not an end itself. The financial sector has meaning and indeed *a raison d'être* only if it helps solve real sector problems such as growth and equity.

■ ■ ■

14

'I do not see a sense of urgency or clear agenda in this government'

Raghuram Rajan

Among the four governors being interviewed in this section, Raghuram Rajan had the shortest stint in RBI – three years. The speed at which he had led the central bank in different areas – ranging from internal reorganisation to inflation-fighting, stabilising the currency, taking on rogue corporations, getting banks to clean up their balance sheets and opening up the sector for different sets of new banks – makes one wonder whether Rajan had known that he had only three years to do his job!

While Subbarao took over just a week before the subprime crisis hit the world, Rajan's task was no less daunting. The Katherine Dusak Miller Distinguished Service Professor of Finance at the University of Chicago Booth School of Business, who had served as chief economist and director of research at the IMF and as the chief economic advisor to the finance ministry, Rajan walked into this assignment when India's current account deficit as a percentage of GDP was the largest in history, inflation was in double digits and the local currency was depreciating every day.

Beside bottling up the inflation genie, stabilizing the rupee and forcing banks to start cleaning up their balance sheets, Rajan was also instrumental in institutionalising decision-making on interest rates with flexible inflation targeting.

Edited Excerpts

What is the origin of bad loans? How did it happen?

I think there are many reasons but what happened can really be attributed to quite a few things. One, what Alan Greenspan referred to as irrational exuberance. We were coming after a time in 2007–08 when lots of investments had been made and they had paid off; they had been completed; they were repaying and it was a time of lot of optimism in India about its growth prospects. That is the time when generally banks make mistakes.

One promoter once told me that they (the banks) were running after him at this time with cheque books, asking him how much he wanted and promising him the money. It was also the time when the private banks were under some stress because they had gone the whole hog into retail lending and had made mistakes there. If you remember during the 2008 crisis there were talks of fragility at ICICI Bank. The PSBs sensed an opportunity to gain market share and, around the same time, the government wanted to expand infrastructure investment and was pushing these banks to lend.

It was basically a story of more lending as well as less equity. I think the promoters saw an opportunity to essentially reduce their equity stake by sometimes even borrowing the equity they were putting in. These were very thinly capitalised ventures. And, there was a lot of exuberance.

The second issue was the slowdown – both in terms of the economic slowdown (the years after 2007–08 were much worse in terms of economic growth) as well as the slowdown in government clearances. The investigation of corruption scandals led to the reversal of certain kinds of permissions that were given – for instance, the coal blocks. So, there were a bunch of reversals coupled with an extreme degree of risk aversion among the bureaucracy in doing what they used to do earlier – facilitating the way for the promoters. There was a whole lot of apprehensions about what this would mean for their future, given the focus on corruption. Even legitimate door opening became a lot more difficult.

Put all this together and you have the beginnings of the crisis. Now add to that, we really did not have good mechanisms to restructure some of these entities and especially get the promoters to part with the assets they could not manage anymore. We did not have a good restructuring process. The net effect was that the promoter himself lost interest but still would not let go as there was a chance a miracle could occur and the asset would come back to life.

So there was a lot of extending and pretending on the banks' side and hoping and praying on the promoters' side. The problems did not get better; they got worse. The prime cause was excessive investments and exuberance coupled with the slowdown but the inability to act fast was also part of the problem.

During your tenure as governor of the Reserve Bank, you have spoken about the banker–promoter nexus. Do you still stand by that?
I won't deny that to some extent there was corruption but I do not think you can put all the weight on that and ignore some of the traditional sources of risk that built up. It happens even in advanced countries. The optimism, the exuberance... all contributed to the mess. I do not think we can blame only corruption for the kind of systemic crisis we had with non-performing loans hitting 10 per cent of assets and more.

Some say you were too aggressive in the clean-up drive. It was like shifting from first gear to fifth gear of a car. The system was not prepared for that. There are others who feel you were too lenient.

You offered a series of restructurings to the banks. How do you describe your actions?

The truth is somewhere in the middle. I did not want a shock therapy for the system when there was no restructuring process in place. So, my first attempt was to create a restructuring process over and above the existing CDR (corporate debt restructuring) platform. CDR was simply not working; lenders were not moving assets from those who could not manage them anymore. Many assets were just stuck and nothing was happening. The companies were accumulating more and more liabilities but there was no movement on the ground partly because the clearances were stuck and the promoters were not pushing hard to get the project done. Some of the projects were so much under the water that they did not feel the need to push. *Theek hai, ho jayega to ho jayega. Nahi hoyega to humara nuksaan nahi hai. Kisi aur ka nuksaan hai*. That was their approach.

In this situation, the first step was to improve the restructuring process to ensure more attempts to clean up and put the assets back on the track. Remember, we did not have the bankruptcy code then. My aim was to get these assets back to work because dead assets – an incomplete road, an unfinished power plant – serve nobody's interest – not the promoters, the banks, the country. So, my idea was to put them back to work. If in some instances, in order to convince the banks to restructure loans some incentives were to be given, I was happy to do that provided they did what we wanted them to do – start restructuring the assets.

We made clear that there would be no more forbearance – no more kicking the can down the road. We were going to end that. We were not going to be lenient on that because that simply avoids recognition. You have to recognise but in the process of recognising if we can help you in some way that is fine. The process has to move towards recognition and restructuring to put the asset back on track. We tried a bunch of things in order to get movement there.

As you pointed out, instead of saying you were too tough, some people told me that I waited too long. We started the AQR in the middle of 2015. Why did we take so long? Well, we were building the structures that would allow the banks to put the assets back on track once they recognised the bad loans.

Is it correct to say that those restructuring schemes actually mimic the insolvency code of different parts of the world?

Well, we were trying to mimic it when we did not have a code. That was precisely the point. We designed it that way – created the shadow of a bankruptcy process or mimicked the bankruptcy out of court.

If you remember, we reached an agreement with SEBI which allowed control over the firm to move away from the promoter. Earlier, we could not get the promoter to give up equity. So, we allowed the bank to take out the promoter and, in that sense, take control. That was a partial way to create an effective bankruptcy system.

We did the AQR in phases. Remember that there were two phases at least. The first phase was recognising up to certain extent and the second phase was to recognise the rest. It took two years to complete the entire recognition process. It was not an order to recognise one fine morning – something what the western system would have done. A lot of people have said that we were bringing in the American system. No, the American system would have required banks to recognise everything immediately.

We said okay, we get together and find out what the size of the problem is so that we know what we have to do and then we chart out the course of action in phases. But the accent has to be on restructuring of the loans and putting them back on track. By the way, Tamal, in terms of whether our action killed the economy which some of my friends have suggested, look at the data. The Indian economy grew at 9 per cent in June 2016 and 8.5 per cent in September 2016. So, this was not killing the economy. In fact, we were doing reasonably well just before the demonetisation happened.

When it comes to regulation and supervision, weren't you a bit harsh and aggressive? You pushed for Basel III norms which was not required at that point of time; even now. The government also feels that way. In retrospect, do you think you were a little more aggressive than what you should have been when it came to capital requirements and Basel III?

No, I do not think so. I do not think they know what they are talking about. We were not aggressive. In fact, in some places we went slower than what the actual requirements were. If you remember, when there was a need to recapitalise the banks, we actually released capital of ₹40,000 crore to the banks by waiving some regulations.

This is why many accuse me of leniency. Since the government was not recapitalising the banks, we decided to look at all the regulations where we thought we might have asked them to hold more capital than was necessary. We rolled those back and announced around ₹40,000 crore of recapitalisation of the banks. We were not weakening some of the regulations but we did so because we thought we were asking them to hold capital which was not needed.

Do you think the government's inability to put on the table the right amount of capital at the right time was also the root of the problem?

Let me put it this way: When we saw the size of the problem – and remember, Arvind Subramanian, chief economic adviser, had also been talking about the twin balance sheet problem – after the AQR, I went to the finance minister and explained to him the size of the problem and the size of capital we needed. There was complete agreement that this would have to be provided.

I think the problem to some extent was that there was not a sense of urgency about this. Yes, in due course, it would happen but the sense of urgency that we must clean up the banks now was not there. It is not just about cleaning-up and recapitalising the banks; it is also to make sure the governance also changes so it does not happen again. There was the initial Gyan Sangam meet in Pune about changing governance, etc. and then the Banks Board

Bureau was brought in. But all that was really stymied. It never went anywhere and you had this period of 10 to 12 months when many banks did not have their CEOs. Some banks were actually run by aggressive CEOs, who effectively made things worse during their term because they had a short horizon.

So, I repeat, the sense of urgency that there is a banking problem which needs to be fixed quickly and we need to do it in multiple steps was missing. We needed to recapitalise, we needed to clean up and we also needed to change the governance structure. One important thing the government did was bringing in the bankruptcy code and we must give it credit for having operationalised it so quickly. But where I think there was effective inaction was in governance and I have said it in my book that I suspect the finance ministry effectively undermined any change.

Did you keep the finance ministry in the loop when you launched the AQR? The impression is the ministry had asked you to do the AQR and RBI was merely implementing it. Is this right?

I do not really mind whatever the government wants to say. After all, it is going to fight the elections and it needs to take the political heat. Let it take the political credit also. What I do worry about is that this was an important time in which PSB reforms could have also been pushed through. That was something on which nothing was done.

The Banks Board Bureau was set up but effectively it became like a government committee to appoint the CEOs of banks. It was disempowered in many ways. We thought perhaps it could appoint the members on commercial banks' boards so that we have professional board members instead of the politically connected chartered accountants of the past. But even that has not been followed through.

My sense is that the DFS (of the Ministry of Finance) simply did not want to let go of its power and, of course, it was catering to a variety of political interests also. The net effect was that nothing really was done to change the governance process. There were a couple of important moves, including bringing in a private sector person to run Bank of Baroda and there the experimentation ended. We missed a golden opportunity to change the governance of the PSBs.

You never pushed for the creation of a bad bank to clean up the system?

This is one place where borrowing from the West is not a great idea. Who will run the bad bank? If it is a private sector entity, why will PSBs sell their bad loans to it at a discount? They will forever fear being subject to investigation if the bad bank recovers much more than the price they bought it at. And since the private entity wants to make money, this will invariably happen.

If the bad bank is a public sector entity, it will suffer from the same lack of initiative, capacity, and fear that plagues PSBs. How will it recover any of the loans it buys? Or is it meant to just sit on them at taxpayer's expense? Put differently, we need to work out how the bad bank will operate and how it will improve on the current system. Nobody really thought this through, they simply said 'Bad Bank, Bad Bank' as if that would solve everything.

As a governor, you have seen the banking system for three years and before that as a CEA also, you had seen it. What ails the public sector banking industry?

In the past, it had been quite effective in attracting good professionals and even today when I look around the PSBs, there are always some very good people. But the question is, by and large, has the rank and file got the capabilities of managing in some of the more advanced areas? Does the capacity exist in evaluation of technical projects and debt structuring in appropriate ways and monitoring it closely so that you do not have the usual gold plating and over-invoicing which is how sometimes money is taken out? What was not clear was how capable the rank and file was and whether the system itself took away any sense of responsibility.

We have got some banks which were ruined in one CEO's term

– absolutely ruined, in terms of the kinds of loans made but nobody felt responsible. We pick one loan and say this loan went bad and you made this loan and some poor loan officer who signed off the documents gets hauled up. That is not the way we should go about it. We should look at it as a business decision gone bad and if 20 business decisions go bad, the CEO should be hauled up. At the very least, an inquiry into why the CEO made these decisions needs to be done and if there is enough evidence, perhaps there can be a criminal investigation.

We do not follow the pattern of what a particular manager does over his lifetime. Instead, we pick one loan where you did not get one document from the borrower and you are accused of being cahoots. We are not doing it on a systematic basis. These people who ruined the banks are living a good life while some poor officer gets hauled off.

Is fear psychosis the main reason for the low credit growth in India?

It is a part of it. I do think that if we had systems that protected reasonable decision making, where a loan officer did not fear accusations if one loan went bad, there might be more confident lending. But if 10 or 15 of your loans go bad, disproportionate to the normal number, the loan officer should fear some consequences. I do not think we are doing the right thing by hauling people up for one or two bad loans. Instead, we should be looking systematically at what the loan officer did. And if she made bad loan after bad loan, more investigation is warranted. That way, a good loan officer feels protected.

Do we have a disproportionately big public sector banking industry? Is it the time to bite the bullet and go for privatisation, at least selectively?

I am not a fan of saying there is only one perfect way. I would not say that the immediate answer is privatising all PSBs. If you privatise them and have poor governance, you will get a worse disaster. Some people say there is no way of improving governance, you have to privatise in order to get better governance. But we have many bad examples of governance in private sector banks. The real question is how do you improve the governance? How do you take off the shackles that inhibit their ability to get talent and acquire capabilities?

It is quite possible as Singapore has demonstrated to have state-linked banks which may have a large ownership by the state but not so much that it completely determines what those banks are allowed to do. Put differently, we need to distance banks from the state. I do not buy the notion that the government is not going to interfere in the lending decisions but it is going to intervene – I mean, the state intervention. State intervention, even with good intent, can be detrimental – as you can see in the examples of growing NPAs in Mudra and MSME loans.

What we need to do is try different experiments. By all means, privatise a couple of PSBs and see how that works but privatise keeping in mind that you want to have good governance – irrespective of whether you have institutional players governing or a variety of promoters. You need to have reasonable governance and you have to be sure that the people who run the private banks are fit and proper in more ways than one.

It also seems to me that you should give the PSBs a chance without tying their hands. One example of how we tie their hands is the National Institute of Bank Management in Pune. That is funded in part by the PSBs, but they are not allowed to recruit from there because campus recruitment by PSBs is disallowed by a Supreme Court order. We really have hamstrung our PSBs – sometimes for idealistic reasons – but the net effect is we have prevented them from being able to attract talent. We have some loopholes like they can hire some people at the lateral level but not for more than three years then their salary or promotion prospects are capped.

But what people are looking for are careers. How can the PSBs provide attractive careers? If they do not, they will never attract the talent they need to compete with private banks. They will have some good people coming through the ranks but not enough. The share of PSBs is shrinking and will continue to shrink. Why do we do that to our public sector system?

Talking about experiments, during your tenure as RBI governor, the central bank gave licences to two universal banking licences, 10 small finance banks and 11 payments banks. The payments bank model has not worked out. Is it the way to go forward? As banks need big capital, should corporations be allowed to get into banking?
Experimentation while controlling the risks is good. You have to be careful to not take too much risks. My thought about the payments banks was, well, if they are unviable, they won't start. Now, when they do not start, somebody says 'oh, this is a failure'. It was not a failure.

The key here is that the commercial banks were not using mobile and fintech technology and the telecom companies were not cooperating with the banks to do it. The only way to get cooperation was to let the telcos into the business. The moment you let them into the business, the banks wanted to do work with them and there was some possibility that the banks would see them as competition and start doing their own thing.

The aim of trying to use mobile banking in a much bigger way has been achieved and also we could bring in some of the new technologies... If I had been around longer, we could have revisited what the payments banks could do. If we could trust them to manage money in a reasonable way and give us clear information, then perhaps, at some point their scope of operations could have been extended. The initial model was the first step; this wasn't the final step.

What about corporations' entry into banking?
I am still very reluctant for that to happen in the Indian context. We know which corporations will typically think that they deserve a banking licence and will surely press to get it. We already have an immense concentration of economic power in India. Do we want

to couple that with banking licences? I do not think we have the separation between corporations and banks that can ensure good lending. I fear that if we open the window, some wrong people will get the licences and we will get over-lending.

Is consolidation the answer? The government has already started this.

In the interest of experimentation, I would have started with one merger and seen if it worked and then taken a view on the rest. I do not think that further consolidation was the most pressing thing that needed to be done; a focus on governance could have paid higher returns. Also, freeing the banks to manage their HR better to keep good talent and attract new talent would be higher on my priority list as this is what the banks sorely need.

Consolidation takes the attention away from the immediate problems of cleaning up their balance sheets and figuring out new ways to lend. Instead, bankers may focus on office politics – which office am I going to get and who is going to be my boss.

How do you see the progress of insolvency law?

There are teething problems. When you bring in a new system, people will try to test it in every possible way – moving courts, making appeals, and so on. Now that we have established certain rules, norms and precedents... Some appeals are necessary but do we have so many levels of appeals when no constitutional or legal issue is involved? My hope is that we have established some of these procedures and can move faster down the line.

It is also important to note that the bankruptcy court is the last resort. It should be the fear of going to the bankruptcy court that straightens out the negotiations between the lender and the borrower and they come to an agreement outside the bankruptcy court. That is how it works in many countries. This will happen and our judges and lawyers will become more experienced and the system will work more smoothly.

The people whom I do not want to become more experienced

are some of our promoters who have figured out how to beat the previous two systems (SARFAESI and DRT) using the courts. I hope they do not figure out a way to beat this one too. The judicial system should be more circumspect this time about entertaining the ruinous number of appeals that entirely defanged the previous two systems. Delay will destroy this system too, and I hope the judicial system understands its responsibility here.

Talking about the NBFC crisis, what has gone wrong? Do you think the NBFCs are relevant in the Indian financial system?

To some extent, we have had a rolling crisis. First, the private sector banks in 2008, then the PSBs, and, finally, the NBFCs... The reality is that there are some risks which are difficult to lend to and when somebody loads up on those risks too quickly assuming they can contain those risks (in the case of NBFCs to construction, developers and so on), eventually they find it hard to manage it.

Some of the ills that the NBFCs are experiencing come from the real estate sector which has really slowed for a variety of reasons and developers themselves have gone bust. There was also some amount of trying to hide the problem a little bit initially but eventually it proved impossible to cover it up. I do not know the details of the nexus between some banks and some of the NBFCs but in my time (as RBI governor) we suspected that all was not well in market practices, and we started scrutinising them more closely. But this was before some of the rapid expansion in 2017–18.

I would say that something like the IL&FS problem has been in the making for long – partly a result of the problems in infrastructure and partly abject failure in governance at every level. Of course, the regulator must also take some responsibility.

Have financial sector problems spilled over to the economy and the slowdown is a result of the banking sector problem? Or, are the economic issues affecting the banking sector? What is your take?

It is not one or the other; they have affected each other. I would say that the project-specific slowdowns did affect economic growth.

We saw so many projects stalled, new projects and investments not taking up… They affected bank balance sheets and additional lending.

Since they feed on each other, you have to work on both sides. You need to try and get the projects going. For example in the real estate sector, the challenge is how to reduce the overhang of flats that are unsold and ensure that some of the half or three quarters finished projects are brought to fruition so that the asset does not deteriorate. How do we complete the buildings? How do we sell down the overhang of flats in a way which does not create a crash in prices but, at the same time, gently pushes it down to a level where the market clears?

That is really what we should be thinking of. Only when they clear, there will be a strong incentive to resume construction at least in the segment of upper-end flats. My sense is affordable housing is possible because there is so much demand for it. But if you have to clear the so-called million flats aimed at richer households, you need to take some pretty serious actions.

You spoke about RBI also owning up some responsibility. Do you think RBI needs new clothes? This is a too inward-looking, non-transparent and, in some cases, an inefficient regulator which must change itself?

It has to be a constant process of revisiting what you did and trying to figure out what your mistakes are and determining to be better. No central bank, including the RBI, assumes that it is perfect. You have to recognise that you have made mistakes in the past and you need to look at those mistakes to understand what went wrong and whether you could have done something differently to avert it. Every time you learn from that, you have to then come up with 'Okay, so what does this imply for us? What does this imply for industry?'

For example, in some cases, you might say the problem was we did not look too closely enough at the books. We did light supervision in this case and we did not go into the details and we took the word of the auditor. Should we have taken the word of the auditor? Should we have done deep checking of the books ourselves? In the case of a bank, should we have gone to a particular branch and done a thorough check of everything?

We used to do this in the past at RBI and over time there were some people who said it does not really add any value. Maybe we need to revisit some of these issues. It is also true that if somebody wants to really play the system, it is very hard to catch them. This is especially if they are in a position that you think, given all the governance in place, that extent of fraud cannot take place. But sometimes, everybody assumes that everybody else is looking at the fraudsters and no one is really taking responsibility for monitoring. Think of Satyam. I think IL&FS is a situation where once we learn what really happened, we have to revisit our systems.

Are you saying that instead of following the risk-based supervision alone, the RBI should opt for transaction-based supervision as well?
I am just saying that we should look at each of these scandals and see what could have been done better. Sometimes when you are looking at a certain level, when you are looking at the information you get electronically, for example, it is at a level that perhaps may not capture some of the details of how the data are generated. The question there is: Should we go further and check the authenticity of the data? Maybe surprise checks are also required.

Sometimes, we do not get to that level of governance assuming that there is a process in place since the management, the board and everyone is looking at it but maybe for systemically important banks we should check. For example, the US Federal Reserve has some people in the systemically important banks every day just to make sure that they hear what is being said, they breathe the same air, they go to the same canteens and find out the gossip. In that sense, they have feet on the ground and people in place. That is something to think about, especially when we will have some mega banks in the future that are really important for the system.

Now we follow a monetary policy with flexible inflation targeting. Certain quarters have reservation on this. They say we are not yet prepared for it.

I am totally unsympathetic to this view. Are we the only country in the world that cannot bring inflation down? Somehow India is magical. We do not obey the laws of economics. When we said we would bring inflation down, people said, 'No, no, we cannot bring it down.' We brought it down. Then they said, 'It's too low, too low.' Now it's high and they are saying, 'Oh, you cannot control it.' Now some learned commentators want to go back to WPI. WPI does not really measure what *aam admi* faces. *Aam admi* is what you should be concerned about.

If commentators believe there are problems with CPI, the response should be to fix CPI. Interestingly, these problems with CPI are raised every time inflation goes up, when the real issue is that the commentators do not want policy to tighten. You rarely hear about problems with CPI when inflation is low. Please do not say we will not do CPI targeting, we will do some other targeting. So as long as that other index is moderately sensible, you will find some reason to dispense with it when the inflation it indicates is high. The reality is that we need more discipline – institutions work when they discipline us, not when we shelve them every time they are inconvenient.

Globally there are two models of cleaning-up the banking mess. One is the USA–UK model which you wanted to do and the other is to allow it to fester – basically, the Japan and China model. Where do you see India?

I think it is a fight between the American model and the Japanese model. At least, we tried to clean up quickly, but the vested interests wanted to go slow. Political and vested interests do not want any pain whatsoever and the net consequence is that pain will persist for a long, long time. We have to decide.

How long? Is it more than a decade?

This process got started in 2015. We are now in 2020 and we still have not cleaned-up and we are creating more NPAs in the system. Shouldn't we reflect at this stage and think what are we doing? Do we have an idea of where we are going? That is my greater worry – we do not have an idea of where we are going.

What is the way forward for Indian banking?

I would just accelerate the recognition process. I would recapitalise where necessary. I would also start focussing on governance. How can I improve the governance? What ideas can we bring in? There are plenty of ideas out there. I do not think we need new ideas. Give the PSBs more freedom but hold them more accountable – freedom from government interference as well as intervention. We should not make a distinction between the two. Give them freedom on the HR front. This, coupled with governance and holding them responsible for the bad loans they make, would be a step in the right direction.

And, what needs to be done to bring back the economy on the growth path?

The whole socio-political division that the government is into is not good for the economy's prospects, our national security and cohesiveness, and our country's image. I also think it takes the attention away from what is most important at this point, which is the economy.

The short-term focus should be on revival: Cleaning up the financial sector and the power sector and encouraging corporate investment. Agriculture has to be revitalised and set on a more sustainable footing. Then we need a more medium-term plan to push growth up to 8 per cent. I have written about this in detail, so let me not offer bromides. I do not yet see, however, a sense of urgency or a clear agenda in this government.

Finance Minister Nirmala Sitharaman has blamed you and former prime minister Dr. Manmohan Singh, for the banking mess. How do you react?

I do not want to get into the politics of it. She has to say what she has to say. What I will say is that I repeatedly told the government if we do not clean it up quickly, you cannot blame the problem on the previous government. It will be your problem. I think now it is the government's problem.

■ ■ ■

PART V
CRYSTAL GAZING

This section looks at what the future holds. Until the Covid-19 pandemic laid waste to much of the economy, the impression was that the banking industry had graduated from 'recognising' bad loans to 'recovering' whatever it could.

The banks have been on a mission to clean up their balance sheets and the insolvency law is helping them resolve bad loans. It has been a slow road to recovery, fraught with many legal twists and turns and smart promoters looking to game the system.

But the biggest achievement of the new law has been the way it has changed the body language of the promoters who, for the first time, fear losing their empires. The bankers are using the law as a tool to instil fear and settle the cases quickly outside the bankruptcy court. Banks can improve the recovery rate and cut down the days it takes to recover their money, and India has caught up with the world in terms of cost of recovery: it is down to 1.5 per cent from 9 per cent before the insolvency law.

This segment also analyses the RBI's role. Should it remain a full-service central bank? Many believe that the shift in the supervisory model – from compliance-based to risk-based – undercuts the RBI's ability to detect big-time frauds. The RBI cannot give up transaction testing entirely. Historically, it hasn't been a reluctant regulator but a reticent one. The RBI needs to strengthen its market intelligence and may have to go in for new clothes; dry cleaning the old robe will not do the trick.

The only prescriptive chapter in this book – 'The Way Forward' – ends this segment. While corporate India kept on leveraging, banks changed their preferred asset classes – from steel to infrastructure to telecom – and the RBI kept on offering forbearance. Treasury profits helped banks clean up their balance sheets periodically.

If this story continues, at some point, there won't be any potentially sound borrower, barring the government. That is the last bastion and it would signal ultimate fiscal dominance and debt stagnation. It is time for both government and the central bank to clean up the mess, once for all.

15

The Great Indian Asset Sale

In August 2016, the chairman of a large PSB celebrated the arrival of the IBC, a new bankruptcy law, by cutting a cake in the boardroom. The bank in question was groaning under a mountain of bad assets. The jubilant boss asked one of his colleagues how many days it would take to settle a bad loan under the new law.

What the chief heard would not have been music to anyone's ears: 1,800 days, which was 10 times what the law stipulated! The banker colleague was perhaps wide of the mark, but there was some merit in that pessimistic estimate.

Looking at the subsequent progress of the single-window insolvency and bankruptcy resolution process, which has been introduced to minimise cost and time for resolution or liquidation of bad assets, the (now retired) chairman would have been tempted to rename the colleague Cassandra.

The IBC was legislated in record time. Based on a two-volume November 2015 report of the Bankruptcy Law Reforms Committee, headed by T.K. Viswanathan, secretary-general of the 15th Lok Sabha, the Bill was introduced in the Lok Sabha, the lower house of India's Parliament, in December 2015 and passed on 5 May 2016.

The Rajya Sabha, the upper house, cleared it ten days later.

President Pranab Mukherjee cleared it on 28 May 2016 and the code was in place by August 2016. The Insolvency & Bankruptcy Board of India (IBBI), the regulatory body, was set up on 1 October 2016. The process kicked off on 1 December 2016.

It is the first week of June 2020, as I write. Almost 1500 days have passed since the law came into force. How has it performed?

The Roll Out

ICICI Bank Ltd, India's second-largest private lender by assets, filed the first insolvency case, against Innoventive Industries Ltd, a Pune-based steel products maker. However, the first case resolved under the IBC was that of Synergies Dooray Automotive Ltd, an auto ancillary company. The creditors got ₹54 crore back out of the total debt of ₹972 crore when the case was resolved on 2 August 2017.

The recovery seemed minuscule – just about 6 per cent of what was owed. But it was six times what the lenders would have got had the company gone into liquidation.

Synergies Dooray had been placed under the Board for Industrial and Financial Reconstruction (BIFR) for over a decade. When it entered the insolvency process, the realisable value of its assets was just ₹9 crore or less than 1 per cent of the lender's claims.

Going by IBBI data which is available until March 2020, the resolution process for 3,774 cases under the IBC have been launched. The National Company Law Tribunal (NCLT), which deals with such cases, had closed 469 cases (312 of them were either settled or reviewed or there have been appeals against them and 157 cases were withdrawn) and approved resolution for 221 cases.

There were 914 cases of liquidation, while hearings have been on for 2,170 cases. Out of these, 738 cases were at least 270 days old, 494 cases were between 180 and 270 days old, 561 cases between 90 and 180 days old while the remaining 377 cases did not spill over 90 days.

The average realisation by the lenders was 45.96 per cent of their claims until March 2020. But this is 183 per cent of the liquidation value. If we include all classes of creditors, then the recovery rate for the resolved cases is 44 per cent.

Close to 11,000 cases were pending with NCLT for the initiation of insolvency resolution when the government announced a six-month holiday in June 2020 (extendable up to one year) on the filing of fresh cases under IBC by anyone. This is to insulate Covid-19-affected borrowers from normal loan defaulters. This covers any default occurring on or after 25 March 2020.

Under the law, any default of at least ₹1 lakh could be dealt with on this platform by financial creditors, operational creditors and even borrowers themselves. The threshold was raised to ₹1 crore in March 2020 to help small and medium enterprises remain out of the insolvency process even if they default during the Covid-19 lockdown period.

Woefully inadequate infrastructure is just one of the many reasons why a case is not settled within 180 days, or even 330 days, as envisaged by the law. As of June 2020, the NCLT had only 16 benches and it also has to handle cases related to the Companies Act and antitrust cases under the Competition Act, apart from the insolvency cases.

The Dirty Dozen

Even though ICICI Bank was in the vanguard of the banking industry for bad asset resolution using the IBC platform, the process gathered steam after the Banking Regulation (Amendment) Ordinance 2017, was issued in May, adding sections 35AA and 35AB to the Banking Regulation Act, 1949. The new sections empower the RBI to push banks hard to deal with bad assets.

The RBI lost no time. In June 2017, it listed 12 defaulters against whom it had wanted immediate bankruptcy proceedings to be invoked. The regulator followed it up in August 2017 with another list, of 28 defaulters. Collectively, these 40 accounts owed over half the value of bad loans of banks at that time.

The first set – 'the dirty dozen' – owed the banks ₹3.45-lakh crore and the second set ₹2.8-lakh crore. Sector-wise, metals accounted for the biggest chunk with a 37 per cent share, followed by engineering, procurement and construction (EPC) 26 per cent and consumer goods, 12 per cent.

Out of the first set of 12 cases against which bankruptcy proceedings were initiated between May and August 2017, eight had been resolved as of May 2020 and two companies were being liquidated. The liquidation value of the 12 accounts is ₹73,223 crore. From these eight resolved cases, banks have recovered ₹1.36-lakh crore or around 57.5 per cent of the principal amount.

The eight cases that were resolved are Essar Steel Ltd, Bhushan Steel Ltd, Electrosteel Steels Ltd, Monnet Ispat & Energy Ltd, Jyoti Structures Ltd, Alok Industries Ltd, Bhushan Power & Steel Ltd and Jaypee Infratech Ltd.

Two cases, Lanco Infratech Ltd and ABG Shipyard Ltd, have gone into liquidation while Amtek Auto Ltd has been brought back to the NCLT, as the top bidder did not honour its commitment. The Era Infra Engineering Ltd case is yet to be resolved.

In terms of recovery, the best case in the dirty dozen is Jaypee Infratech where lenders got 100.2 per cent of their admitted claims (₹23,223 crore versus ₹23,176 crore). The recovery in Jaypee is the highest but most of it is in the form of land parcels and construction undertakings.

In the Essar Steel case, the lenders got back 82.91 per cent (₹41,018 crore) of their ₹49,473 crore claims. Next on the recovery list is Bhushan Steel with ₹35,571 crore recovery against ₹56,022 crore debt which amounts to 63.5 per cent. The others on the list are Jyoti Structures (50.12 per cent), Electrosteel Steels (40.38 per cent), Monnet Ispat (26.26 per cent) and Alok Industries (17.11 per cent).

Of the second set of 28 cases, the two biggest cases are Videocon Industries Ltd (₹59,451 crore) and Jai Prakash Associates Ltd (₹45,080 crore). From this list, only two cases have been resolved – Orchid Pharma Ltd (₹1,309 crore recovered out of ₹3,200 crore owed) and Ruchi Soya Ltd (₹4,350 crore out of about ₹12,000 crore) – and four have gone for liquidation (Shakti Bhog Foods Ltd, Coastal Projects Ltd, IVRCL Ltd and Nagarjuna Oil Corporation Ltd).

A few have been admitted to NCLT but many others are yet to be listed there. On average, the NCLT takes 589 days to deliver an order (from the day the resolution process begins).

Nuts and Bolts of Bankruptcy

Typically, after a case is filed, it takes between a fortnight and a month to be admitted into the NCLT. The platform should find a solution within 180 days; but it can take another 90 days, depending on the complexity of a case. So, a case should ideally be resolved within 270 days.

This timeline does not include the time spent on litigation, which can be long. To cut this short, the Act was amended on 16 August 2019 to ensure completion within 330 days from when a case is admitted, including any intervening litigation period.

However, in practice, if a case still runs over 330 days due to interim litigation, courts are likely to accept such a delay instead of passing a liquidation order.

While admitting the case, the NCLT appoints an interim resolution professional (IRP) whose term lasts till the appointment of a resolution professional (RP) to carry forward the process. The IRP is generally identified by the person filing the application with NCLT. The IRP collates the claims and forms a committee of creditors (this includes only the financial creditors) or CoC. The RP heads the CoC.

At the next stage, the information memorandum is prepared and the so-called expression of interest is sought from the prospective bidders. After checking the eligibility of the bidders and evaluating resolution plans, the CoC takes a view.

The RP then submits the plan approved by the CoC to the NCLT for its approval. A Supreme Court ruling says the CoC's commercial wisdom cannot be challenged in a court.

The Problem

The problem starts here. Even losers can make fresh bids and new bidders can also join the fray. The IBBI amended the regulations to prevent any fresh bids from being entertained after a certain deadline. However, nothing prevents the CoC from extending the deadline for all bidders to allow for better bids.

Allowing new bids after sealing the process hurts the sanctity of the exercise and leads to delays. Why is this allowed? The logic could be, this increases the chances of getting the best price.

It is also true that certain assets may not get any bid at all. There have been cases too where the NCLT allowed fresh bidding, after the original winner cited misrepresentation of facts in the information shared.

Nothing prevents the defaulters from moving first to the appellate body, the National Company Law Appellate Tribunal (NCLAT), and, after that, or at any time, the high courts and even the Supreme Court. For instance, Jai Balaji Industries Ltd and Anrak Aluminium Ltd (both from the RBI's second list), with exposures of ₹3,600 crore and ₹3,500 crore respectively, had moved different high courts.

The Chhattisgarh High Court disallowed Jai Balaji's admission into the NCLT while another high court ruled in favour of the one-time settlement scheme being implemented instead of moving ahead with the NCLT for Anrak Aluminium.

The Supreme Court admitted a petition filed by Soma Enterprises Ltd, another defaulter, which did not want to go through NCLT for resolution.

Court Cases Galore

Since its inception, IBC has been fraught with court cases. The most critical of them centres around Section 29A of the code. This Section was introduced in the IBC in 2017 through an amendment to prevent certain persons from bidding for a company undergoing the corporate insolvency resolution process.

Importantly, the promoters are among them who are being

disbarred from bidding. Under Section 29A, a prospective bidder is barred if it suffers from certain disqualifications such as being the promoter of a company which is a bad asset in banks' book for more than one year, disqualified by SEBI from trading in public markets, convicted of certain criminal offences, etc.

Allowing promoters to bid for their assets would create a moral hazard if they can buyback assets at steep discounts after defaults on servicing the loans. In other words, it benefits them at the cost of the lenders.

More broadly, such buybacks would benefit promoters at the cost of the government and, by extension, the public. Most bad loans are on the books of the state-owned banks. The bad loans lead to repeated capital infusions and that is public money.

The first case where this issue came under the spotlight was Binani Cements Ltd. Its promoter, backed by Ultratech Cement Ltd, offered to pay the lenders substantially more than the amount offered by the highest bidder. The Supreme Court permitted the lenders to consider the promoter's bid, putting a spoke in the sanctity of the resolution process.

It took a different turn with the case of Essar Steel Ltd. The resolution professional found both bidders – NuMetal Ltd and ArcelorMittal India Pvt Ltd – ineligible under Section 29A of the Code.

The Ahmedabad bench of the NCLT, dealing with the case, accepted that for the following reasons. One of the shareholders of NuMetal was Rewant Ruia whose father, Ravi Ruia, was a promoter of Essar Steel. The steel maker's debt was classified for more than one year before the insolvency resolution process began.

ArcelorMittal was held ineligible under Section 29A (c) of the Code. ArcelorMittal Netherlands was found to have been the promoter of two companies – Uttam Galva Steels Ltd and KSS Petron Ltd – that had been NPAs for more than one year before Essar Steel's insolvency resolution process began.

The NCLAT concurred with the disqualification of ArcelorMittal but it had a different view on NuMetal as Rewant Ruia had divested his holding in the company in favour of a third party. ArcelorMittal then moved the Supreme Court against the decision of the NCLAT, which found both disqualified under Section 29A of the Code.

However, the apex court exercised its extraordinary power under Article 142 of the Constitution of India and gave both the companies another opportunity by asking them to clear the dues within two weeks of the verdict.

The promoters of Essar Steel then offered to clear all its dues to be eligible as a resolution applicant under Section 29A, in line with the instructions of the apex court. Its promoters also made the lenders a settlement offer roughly 25 per cent higher than the highest bidder's offer. But they were barred from offering a competing bid due to Section 29A of the IBC.

The lenders of Essar Steel offered to proceed with ArcelorMittal; NuMetal withdrew from the race. A new clause, Section 12A, was inserted into the Code in June 2018, to allow withdrawal of a bidder with the approval of 90 per cent voting share of the CoC.

There have been other interesting fallout from the case law developed around Section 29A. ArcelorMittal had to ensure that Uttam Galva cleared all its dues to the lenders. Uttam Galva, where ArcelorMittal had picked up 29.05 per cent stake, turned into bad asset in 2017.

This is a positive outcome. But there have also been negative outcomes.

NTPC Ltd's bid for the 600-MW power plant of Jhabua Power Ltd in Madhya Pradesh was two-and-a-half times higher than that of the Adani Group. But it could not be allowed as Ratnagiri Gas & Power Pvt Ltd, one of NTPC's joint ventures, which used to be owned by Enron Corporation, is an NPA. NTPC, along with GAIL Ltd, had stepped in to rescue Dabhol Power Company after its promoter Enron went bankrupt.

Promoter's Role

Should the promoters be kept out of the race even if they are willing to offer more than the other bidders? While the government decided to adopt this stance in order to avoid accusations of crony capitalism, this is not fair to all stakeholders.

For one thing, it means that the lenders have to be prepared for bigger haircuts because it takes a potential bidder out of competition. In behavioural terms, it kills entrepreneurship as the provision does not discriminate between genuine business failures and rogue promoters. Any bankruptcy means that the promoters become outcasts.

During a court hearing, a lawyer representing a promoter group, made a passionate plea: 'When do we give capital punishment to someone? For a premeditated murder – a heinous crime. Often a contract killer does this just for money. If the person is hanged, what happens to his family – his innocent wife and school-going children, who are not even aware of the crime? Should we treat them outcasts or rehabilitate them? Can business failure be treated as more heinous than a murder?'

The courtrooms reverberated with similar arguments until the amendment prohibited the relations of a bank defaulter from bidding for such assets.

Abhinav Harlalka and Simone Reis of law firm Nishith Desai Associates in a February 2019 article at Mondaq, a syndication platform, 'The Economics of Morality: The 29A Conundrum', batted for the promoters, suggesting that a promoter may be permitted to bid as long as such a promoter has defaulted only in respect of the corporate debtor, and not any other company. They should be considered only in situations when there are other bidders as this will ensure price discovery. The promoters should not be provided with any waivers such as past non-compliances, non-payment of stamp duties and levies, etc., and they must care for minority shareholders.

Finally, the promoter's resolution should not be misused as 'evergreening' of loans. While the lenders may be permitted to convert loans into equity, no debt should be permitted to be outstanding once the resolution plan is approved and implemented.

Global Scenario

Globally, promoters are allowed to bid for their bankrupt companies by offering revival plans. But the India story is different for several underlying reasons. The insolvency proceedings are based on the concept of a debtor in possession in several jurisdictions.

Under the US Chapter 11 bankruptcy law, the managers have an exclusivity period for submitting a restructuring plan. In other words, the control of the defaulting company remains with the debtor. But in India, creditors are placed in control during the process.

This is because the worldwide concept of promoters is very different from that in India. Most companies overseas are run by investors and there is a clear demarcation between management and ownership. GE and Ford Motor tell the story, for example. Walmart, the American discount department store chain, and 101-year old Hilton Hotels & Resorts and some of the big infotech companies are indeed exceptions to the rule.

In India's corporate world, there is hardly any difference between the management and the ownership in most companies. There is a lurking fear that the promoters can go to any extent to keep their control over the company. So, it is handed over to the RP.

Many companies are family-owned (ownership and management are the same) in India and there is always a shortage of equity. Most promoters are reluctant to put money on the table; they look for innovative ways to 'create' equity. One of these creative methods is the diversion of bank funds, which are round-tripped overseas and brought back as equity.

Many promoters enter the infrastructure space by floating an EPC outfit and making money through that. Another way of creating funds for equity infusions is borrowing through a set of holding companies and using the debt as equity for other group companies. Finally, many promoters also create funds by pledging of shares in listed concerns.

Essar Steel, the Epicentre

Essar Steel has been at the epicentre of the legal battle. It rushed to Ahmedabad High Court challenging the RBI's 13 June 2017 directive asking lenders to initiate action against the steelmaker and 11 others. It contested RBI's statement, which said NCLT would give priority to resolve the Essar Steel case and 11 others, and contended that it was in an advanced stage of loan restructuring and should be given time to complete it.

The high court dismissed Essar Steel's plea against the RBI directive on 17 July. The 83-page order rejected the company's claim that the RBI direction was irrational, unjust, arbitrary or discriminatory but it held that the lender banks could initiate proceedings under the IBC even without RBI direction.

What started in July 2017 in Ahmedabad High Court ended more than two years later at the Supreme Court in November 2019. It took 871 days to accomplish the biggest bad loan resolution so far.

ArcelorMittal's plan was approved by the CoC of Essar Steel in October 2018 but the issue was how the proceeds would be distributed among the lenders, the operational creditors and one particular lender to Essar Steel which was not part of the bankers' consortium – Standard Chartered Bank.

When the dispute reached the apex court through NCLT and NCLAT, the IBC was amended yet again. This time, it modified the payments to operational creditors. By now, the law was more than three and a half years old.

The Supreme Court verdict, delivered on 15 November 2019, settled several issues that had plagued the insolvency resolution process since the inception of the IBC in May 2016.

It set aside the principle of equality of all creditors as laid down in the NCLAT order and unequivocally held that the principle of 'equality' could not be interpreted to mean that all creditors (irrespective of their security interest, or their status as operational or financial creditor) would be entitled to equal recovery under a resolution plan.

It also said that operational creditors are a separate class of creditors – they cannot have equal rights with lenders.

This judgment settled many of the legal controversies as it was made clear that the ultimate discretion of deciding the distribution of funds lies with the CoC. While taking the call, the CoC must ensure that the company concerned should be kept as a going concern during the resolution process, the value of assets should be maximised, and the interests of all stakeholders protected in a balanced way.

If this encouraged lenders to bite the bullet, the bidders' frayed nerves were calmed by yet another amendment to the IBC law, in December 2019, banning enforcement agencies from attaching assets of companies for offences committed by the previous management and/or promoters. This received President Ram Nath Kovind's assent in March 2020.

Supreme Court Intervention

The amendments and court judgments have continuously changed the contours of the insolvency code and trying to fast pace it. But a Supreme Court judgment in March 2019 dealt a blow to the RBI's resolve to clean up the system.

The apex court set aside the 12 February 2018 RBI circular which, among other things, directed banks to take the defaulting power, sugar, shipping companies to the insolvency court. The court also stayed the insolvency proceedings against at least 70 defaulters in the power, sugar, textiles and shipping industries.

These guidelines were issued by the RBI 'in exercise of powers conferred under Section 35A, 35AA and 35AB of the Banking Regulation Act, 1949; and, Section 45(L) of the Reserve Bank of India Act, 1934.'

A bunch of power companies, as well as industry bodies such as the Association of Power Producers and Independent Power Producers Association of India, had moved the Supreme Court in August 2018, challenging the constitutional validity of the circular.

Chevron Deference

The Supreme Court quashed the RBI directive on interesting grounds.

Typically, courts in developed markets do not interfere with policy decisions of the government and the regulatory bodies in 'deference' to their expertise. But a court can always examine possible procedural violations in the implementation of a regulation. And, it can also take a call if it finds that a regulation is violating a constitutional provision.

There was a landmark case of Chevron USA, Inc. Vs Natural Resources Defense Council Inc., in 1984 that led the coinage of the term 'Chevron Deference'.

Chevron deference is a principle of administrative law requiring courts to defer to interpretations of statutes made by those government agencies charged with enforcing them unless such interpretations are considered unreasonable. Under Chevron, even if a court finds that another interpretation is reasonable, or even better than the agency's interpretation, it must defer to the agency's reasonable interpretation.

In this case, a two-judge bench, led by Justice R.F. Nariman, found that the RBI circular violated the spirit of Section 35AA of the Banking Regulation Act, amended in May 2017. Under this Section, directions can be issued for 'a default' but the regulator, in this case, had bunched together many default cases.

The power companies alleged that the RBI had adopted a 'one-size-fits-all' approach without taking into consideration why the power companies could not service debt. They also based their arguments on the issues of supply side (shortage of coal) and demand (inability to raise the tariff).

The RBI, on its part, maintained that those companies were given ample time to resolve issues but failed. A parliamentary panel was also critical about the RBI directive.

The banking regulator won the first round of the court battle when in August 2018 the Allahabad High Court denied any relief to the power companies, represented by the two industry associations. It, however, suggested that the government could use Section 7 of the RBI Act and 'direct' it to modify the order – something which the government threatened to do.

Following the Allahabad High Court judgment, some three-dozen plus companies moved the Supreme Court, which transferred all the cases being fought at different high courts (in Chennai and Delhi) to itself and stayed insolvency proceedings against these companies.

Strike at Midnight

The final order sealed the fate of the RBI circular that had been posted on its website close to midnight of 12 February 2018. Why was it so? The next day, 13 February, was a holiday on account of Maha Shivaratri. By releasing it just ahead of a holiday, the RBI wanted to avoid any knee-jerk reaction from the market.

The bankers had been losing sleep over bad loans; the directive made the promoters lose sleep as they feared losing their empires. The government also needed to go back to the drawing board to calculate how much capital the banks would need to remain operational.

The Supreme Court judgment changed the scene. The government has a soft corner for these power companies. It had tried to convince the central bank not to be harsh on them in the circular and even threatened to 'direct' it and using a clause of the RBI Act, without success. Despite the government's nudge, the central bank did not dilute its stand on taking power sector defaulters to the NCLT.

This was the starting point of the conflict between Urjit Patel, then the RBI governor, and the government. It turned acrimonious in due course. Patel quit in December 2018, citing 'personal reasons'.

The circular had asked banks and other lenders to either execute a resolution plan for big stressed accounts (of ₹2,000 crore or more) or file insolvency petitions against them in the insolvency court. For resolution, 180 days were given, failing which the asset was to be taken to the NCLT for insolvency.

This was only one part of the circular. It had many other directions. For instance, all existing frameworks for addressing stressed assets – such as corporate debt restructuring (CDR), strategic debt restructuring (SDR) and the scheme for sustainable structuring of stressed assets (S4A), among others – were withdrawn and the joint lenders' forum, an institutional mechanism that was overseeing them, was dismantled.

By saying that all bad loans should be resolved within 180 days failing which the account must be referred to the NCLT under IBC, the RBI made it clear that when a borrower fails to pay a bank loan in time, it becomes a defaulter. It also wanted to remove the term 'stressed' account from its lexicon since this was often an excuse for the banks to postpone the inevitable.

The postponement was done, in many cases, by giving fresh loans (evergreening) to help borrowers service an old loan. The banks were typically reluctant to take a hit on their balance sheets and many bankers also enjoyed a cosy relationship with their borrowers.

The Long Road to Recovery

This RBI directive abolished all the existing loan recast schemes. This leads us to ask why these schemes were put in place and how did the process of bad loan recovery evolve?

The recovery laws were designed to shield defaulters in the days before the SARFAESI Security Act of 2002.

The erstwhile individual or partnership insolvency laws (Provincial Insolvency Act/Presidency Towns Insolvency Act) were grossly ineffective and rarely resorted to by lenders, due to being complex and time-consuming.

The Companies Act, 1956 provided for winding up laws, with the primary ground being the inability to pay debts, and remedial action. But the maximum recovery was in the range of 15–20 per cent, that too in a timeframe of at least five or six years and often extending to 20 years.

The BIFR, set up under Sick Industrial Companies (Special Provisions) Act (SICA) in 1987, had a fundamental flaw. It was based on the impossible goal of revitalising and reviving hopelessly sick companies. The prime objective was to protect jobs and industries but this was a non-starter. The kindest description of the BIFR would be it was a misadventure.

The DRTs, set up after the passing of the Recovery of Debts Due to the Banks and Financial Institutions Act (RDDBFI) 1993, were designed as a summary recovery procedure, liberated from the rigidities of the judicial system. As part of the department of financial services of the Ministry of Finance, the DRTs were to expedite recovery of defaulted loans. But they have fared miserably.

The SARFAESI Act, for the first time, did provide a potent tool in the hands of the secured creditors. This Act allowed secured lenders to enforce and realise their security without court intervention.

Put in place at the beginning of the century, it succeeded in reducing the bad loan pile as asset reconstruction companies (ARCs) started buying bad loans at discounts, but the pace could not be sustained.

ARCs issue security receipts or SRs when they buy bad assets. Typically, when they purchase bad assets, they set up a specific trust for managing the assets and the trust issues the SRs. The banks get the SRs, plus some cash up front, when they sell their bad assets to the ARCs. If they are not able to redeem the SRs, the banks are left with no choice but to write off bad loans. The secondary market for SRs has not yet developed.

India has 29 ARCs and collectively they must have issued close to ₹1.5-lakh crore worth of SRs to the banks. About one-fifth of these were redeemed until March 2019.

One of the bones of contention between banks and ARCs is the pricing of bad loans. The ARCs pay less cash and offer more SRs while making bids and often redemption turns out to be a never-ending process. The cash-strapped ARCs have not been able to play an effective role in reducing bad assets.

All these failures and partial successes prompted the RBI to intervene.

Recast Schemes

Since 2001, at regular intervals, the RBI has tried various schemes, offering flexibility to the banking system for restructuring bad debt. Different schemes approached the problem differently.

One idea was to pool all the banking creditors in large accounts for restructuring (CDR, August 2001). Then, there was an attempt to distinguish the sustainable part of the debt from the unsustainable part of the debt (S4A, 2016). In infra projects, the repayment period was stretched beyond 20–25 years (the so-called 5/25 scheme).

There was even the desperate recourse of banks taking over of management of sick companies by resorting to the conversion of debt into equity (SDR in 2015). In this, bankers could either take control of failed companies and sell them on to buyers, or ensure they got a better price for the equity they held by converting their debt in such firms.

The CDR mechanism, the very first loan recast scheme to deal with the menace of bad loans, was ineffective for multiple reasons. Until September 2017, when it was dismantled, 655 accounts were sought to be restructured on the CDR platform but 125 of these (with a cumulative loan value of ₹1,70,988 crore) were rejected.

The total loan value approved under CDR was ₹4,03,004 crore, involving 530 borrowers. Some 291 accounts were withdrawn (₹1,72,463 crore). As of September 2017, there were 130 live accounts (₹1,45,528 crore) under CDR. These cases have been transferred to the NCLT.

Industrial sickness requires prompt corrective actions undertaken in cohesive manner. This has never been the case under CDR. Most resolutions happened by writing off the bank loans which is a classic instance of 'the patient died but operation was successful'.

The restructuring was mostly carried out to rectify the lenders' books of accounts and revive the units. The lenders were rarely united in their approach and, finally, most CDR schemes were advised by the subsidiaries of leading banks, leading to conflict of interest. Such agencies were primarily interested in protecting the interest of their parents and not in resolving the problems.

In nine out of ten cases, the promoters either failed to bring in their contributions as laid down in the approved schemes, or could not actually give personal guarantees and other securities which they had committed. Also, the banks often sanctioned fresh working capital and/or additional term loans just to protect their interests. How? The new money was used to evergreen the debt, temporarily cleaning up the banks' books. In the process, the companies' indebtedness rose but they could not restart operations meaningfully.

It is also the case that many companies did not generate enough earnings to service debt as the promoters had no desire to revive the companies after siphoning off cash. There could also have been cases where debtors colluded with some of the bankers for their gains.

In practice, most CDR cases were from the infrastructure sector which needs long-term support. But the restructuring packages typically prescribed only a two-year moratorium on loan repayments. This mismatch could only delay the inevitable.

Finally, just a recast of an outstanding loan cannot revive a company, unless the specific issues that have caused industry distress are addressed. For instance, the PPAs and the fuel supply agreements are the sore spots in the power sector; road projects have often stalled due to non-payments or delayed payments by the NHAI to EPC contractors, and also due to the NHAI not acting decisively to harmoniously substitute contractors for the BOT (build-operate-transfer) projects when a contract is not able to deliver. A loan recast is useless unless such issues are tackled and this is not within the lenders' powers.

The CDR framework was voluntary and non-statutory, based on debtor-creditor agreements (DCA) and inter-creditor agreements (ICA), leaving the fate of the borrowers to the discretion and wisdom of the lenders.

On 31 March 2015, when the RBI asked lenders to provision restructured loans on a par with non-performing loans, it rang the death knell of the CDR. Prior to that, lenders had to provision for a restructured loan at 5–15 per cent of the loan value, far lower than what they were required to provide for NPAs. Treatment at par meant it took away the incentive for the banks to push for restructuring of stressed loans.

The CDR was replaced by more flexible schemes such as the for infra projects. All these schemes were more flexible, with better features than the CDR. But these also failed primarily because the banks and the corporations were both keen to recast schemes just to prevent big loans turning bad.

The story continued till the RBI withdrew all these schemes on 12 February 2018. When its directive was struck down, the banking regulator had to formulate new policy.

Fresh Guidelines

On 7 June 2019, three months after the Supreme Court struck down the RBI's 12 February 2018 directive, the central bank released fresh guidelines to deal with bad loans. Titled the 'Reserve Bank of India (Prudential Framework for Resolution of Stressed Assets) Directions 2019', it came into force with immediate effect, replacing all the earlier resolution platforms in vogue until February 2018.

Under the new NPA resolution norms that replaced all the previous models, defaults are to be recognised within 30 days, as opposed to the old norm which mandated lenders to start the resolution process even on a one-day default.

At the same time, the RBI sought to accelerate the resolution of stressed assets. It put in place a system of disincentives such as additional provisioning in cases of delayed implementation of the resolution, or slow initiation of insolvency proceedings. The lenders must fix their resolution strategy, including the nature of the resolution plan and the approach for its implementation, within 30 days.

The new directive asked banks to make additional provisions in case of failure to implement a resolution plan within the given timelines. Some of the salient features are:

- All lenders must put in place board-approved policies for resolution of stressed assets.
- They should initiate the process of implementing a resolution plan even before a default.
- They must circulate credit information weekly on all borrowers having aggregate exposure of at least ₹5 crore.
- For credit facilities with more than one lender, all lenders must be on board for the resolution of the stressed asset by signing an inter-creditor agreement for the implementation of the resolution plan.
- The ICA will provide rules for finalisation, implementation of RP for those with credit facilities from more than one lender.

For an aggregate exposure above a certain threshold, the resolution plan is to be implemented within 180 days from the review period. When will the review be done? The lenders must review the borrower account within 30 days from default. The resolution plans must ensure payment of not less than the liquidation value due to dissenting lenders

In case the resolution is not achieved within 180 days, the lenders have to make 20 per cent additional provisioning for the bad debt. If it is not achieved within 365 days, the provisioning requirement goes up by another 15 percentage points. Such provisioning is reversed partially as and when the case is admitted at the insolvency court.

Change in Ownership

The 2019 directions give a relief to the lenders for asset classification in case the ownership of the borrower is changed. Following such a change, the loans of the borrower may be continued or upgraded as 'standard', either under the IBC or this framework.

If the change in ownership is implemented under this framework, then the classification as 'standard' shall be subject to the following conditions:

- The lenders shall conduct necessary due diligence and establish that the acquirer is not a person disqualified in terms of Section 29A of the IBC. The 'new promoter' should not be a person/entity/subsidiary/associate – domestic as well as overseas – from the existing promoter.
- The new promoter needs to acquire at least 26 per cent of the paid-up equity capital as well as the voting rights of the borrowing company and must be the single largest shareholder.
- The new promoter shall be in 'control' of the borrower entity as per the definition of 'control' in the Companies Act, 2013.

Following a change in ownership, all the outstanding loans of the borrower must be regularly serviced during the monitoring period. If the account does not perform satisfactorily at any point of time during the monitoring period, it will trigger a review.

The provisions already made by the lenders for the loan as on the date of the change in ownership of the borrowing company can be reversed only if the loan is performing well until the end of the monitoring period.

Four stressed sectors contributed the most to the pile of banks' bad loans. Read on them in the Appendix. (See page 485)

The Roadblocks

While the amendments and the court rulings have been shaping the resolution process, there are many other issues coming in the way.

Asset Preservation

While the Indian insolvency law is more aggressive than that in most developed markets, the law itself lacks scope for preservation of assets. This is unlike the situation in the US and some other countries. This means that, once the bankers move against, say, a defaulting steelmaker, the machinery of the factory may just disappear.

Theoretically, the IRP/RP is required to take control and possession of the assets of the defaulter as soon as possible after appointment. In practice, this poses many challenges. One way of tackling it could be appointing a 'preservation agent'.

In the absence of such a preservation agent, the value of incomplete projects is fast eroded. Also, lead lenders should be forced to mandatorily invest in keeping projects going by keeping critical people on the payroll and ensuring the supply of essential items to prevent value erosion. The lenders must also renew existing insurance for the assets and operations of the company.

Beef up NCLT Strength

Even if the resolution process has been conducted in an efficient manner, the backlog at NCLT has meant cases are taking longer to close. It would be helpful if the bench strength in the busier NCLTs is increased. There is also a need to have more NCLAT benches to clear the bottlenecks there. Finally, the NCLTs could be made dedicated bankruptcy courts on the line of the US federal bankruptcy courts.

Resolution Professionals

The RP enjoys virtually no immunity although the law offers protection for the RP's actions. In one case, the police filed an FIR against an RP who was overseeing insolvency proceedings of a company in West Bengal, which had not deposited the provident fund of its employees.

At the same time, a possible nexus between the RPs and consultants and lawyers is an issue. It is in the interests of lawyers and consultants to prolong the process to earn more. And, the RP can end up working in tandem with the promoters too! There have been such instances and disciplinary actions have been taken against RPs.

India's insolvency code does not distinguish between asset-light, weak-cash-flow services companies, and asset-heavy, weak cash-flow manufacturing units, which operate very differently in practice.

Thomas Cook in the UK could opt for liquidation but Cox & King in India is referred to the NCLT despite being in the same category of asset-light service firms. This is also true about all EPC contractors. Shouldn't such businesses head straight for liquidation, skipping the tedious and complex resolution process?

Pre-pack

In the US, pre-packaged insolvency or pre-pack, a form of bankruptcy procedure, has been in vogue. A restructuring plan is agreed to before a company declares insolvency. A pre-pack sale cuts down erosion in asset value.

US courts have held that an administrator can sell the company's assets immediately upon appointment, without court approval or the approval of the creditors. This can be done, even if the majority creditor objects.

Typically, the so-called Swiss Challenge method is used in such a process. Under the Swiss Challenge method, the highest bid in the first round of bidding becomes the base price to place counter-bids in the second round of bidding. If no other bidder can better the highest bid, the top bidder in the first round is declared the successful bidder.

A plan to introduce pre-packs has been in the works for sometime. In April 2019, the Ministry of Corporate Affairs sought comments on pre-packaged IBC from various stakeholders. There could be three possible solutions – pre-packaged insolvency, pre-arranged insolvency and pre-arranged sale.

Group Insolvency

A group headed by U.K. Sinha, former chairman of SEBI, has examined the issues relating to group insolvency and made recommendations which were being considered as I am writing this chapter, in June 2020.

Price Discovery

There is a weakness in the price discovery process. No one knows when the bidding for an asset up for sale ends – even the losers can make fresh bids and new bidders can also join the fray. This indeterminate method of allowing new bids after sealing the process helps in price discovery.

But it also leads to inordinate delays and kills the sanctity of the process since it can be gamed by cynical bidders. The judiciary seems to be in favour of value maximisation rather than early resolution. But even more than the judiciary, the CoC is instrumental in delaying the process.

You cannot score a goal after the final whistle in a football match. But the CoC has been known to extend the match time to allow for such goals. The CoC also looks for value maximisation only from the lenders' perspective. Instead, it should be value optimisation for all stakeholders, including critical operational creditors. For instance, if the interests of equipment suppliers to a sick power plant are not taken care of, the new owner cannot run it.

Incidentally, at least one successful bidder for more than one asset has not been able to put money on the table – US hedge fund Deccan Value Partners LP. It was the winning bidder for Amtek Auto and two of its subsidiaries, Castex Technologies Ltd and ARGL.

Competition Law

The competition law also used to come in the way of speedy resolution but this has been taken care of. Under a Competition Commission of India (CCI) rule, no single company can enjoy more than 40 per cent share in any market. This prevented some existing steelmakers from bidding for any distressed steel asset.

To speed up things, the IBC was amended in 2018 allowing CCI clearance before CoC approves the resolution plan. So far, CCI has cleared all eligible cases in record time.

Jury Still Out

The jury is still out on the efficacy of the IBC seen in isolation. But it is a marked improvement on the earlier bad loan resolution process. A World Bank estimate says the old law used to take an average 4.3 years to resolve insolvency and recovery was 25.7 cents for every dollar – implying an average haircut of 75 per cent for every creditor.

Mardia Chemicals Ltd, the first defaulter taken to a DRT in the 1990s, is a classic case that illustrates how helpless the lenders were then. ICICI Bank had slapped a claim of ₹1,400 crore on Mardia Chemicals. The company made a counter-claim of ₹5,600 crore against ICICI Bank and moved the Supreme Court against notices sent by the bank, arguing that Section 17 (2) of the SARFAESI Act was blocking its ability to take legal recourse against seizure notices. In April 2004, the Supreme Court upheld the constitutional validity of the SARFAESI Act, but struck down a provision in the Act that required borrowers to deposit 75 per cent of the amount claimed by lenders before they could file appeals with DRTs.

Before that, Mardia Chemicals had filed a reference with the BIFR in May 2003. A decade later, in February 2013, the DRT upheld the company's appeal against the recovery suit filed by ICICI Bank on the grounds that the BIFR was yet to complete its proceedings in the matter!

We have mentioned earlier in his chapter how many days the cases are taking to get resolved under IBC and what has been the recovery rate so far. Let us take a look at global practices for context and comparison.

Japan, which introduced a bankruptcy law in 2004, takes six months to settle a case and the recovery rate is close to 93 per cent. The UK introduced a new bankruptcy law in 2002. There, the recovery rate is 88.6 per cent and settlement is usually within a year. In the US, where insolvency law is more than four-decades old, it takes 18 months to settle with a recovery rate of 80.4 per cent.

IBC is just four years old. As the stakes are very high, there is a huge and unprecedented volume of judicial precedence created since the insolvency law came into force. This has been delaying the process of recovery.

But the time taken to resolve the cases is reasonable compared with global standards. There is room for improving the recovery rate. India has, however, caught up with others or even scored over other nations in reducing the cost of recovery. This is now 1.5 per cent of recovery, down from 9 per cent in pre-IBC days and comparable with developed markets.

Arguably, the biggest achievement of the new law has been the change in the body language of promoters. They are afraid of losing their empires. The bankers are using the threat of IBC as a tool to instil fear among promoters, forcing them to the discussion table, and thereby reversing the tradition where banks had to chase defaulters.

While the IBC is still fraught with challenges as defaulting promoters are always seeking ways to game the system, the banks have started using it as a stick to settle cases faster outside NCLT. The law is evolving and once pre-packs, group insolvency and cross-border insolvency laws are in place, one can hope that it will match up with global best practices.

■ ■ ■

Two Curious Cases

Even if no stakeholder takes recourse to the judicial system, there are many reasons why resolution takes a long time.

Take a look at two illustrative cases from the list of 28 defaulters the RBI wanted the commercial banks to take up at the NCLT by end-December 2017, if these were not resolved by mid-December.

The Mumbai bench of the NCLT admitted bankruptcy resolution petitions for these two companies – Uttam Value Steels Ltd and Uttam Galva Metallics Ltd – in June and July 2018, respectively. The banks were given 20 more days to complete the resolution process after the 270-day deadline ended.

This is one of the rare instances of a resolution being worked out for two companies simultaneously. They are interlinked in terms of production and the two sister companies together owed ₹6,113 crore to the lenders.

SBI was the lead lender. Other banks with significant exposure included PNB, Canara Bank and Andhra Bank. The resolution professionals of the two companies needed to get the resolution plan approved by the NCLT.

These twin cases succinctly illustrate the progress of the single-window insolvency and bankruptcy resolution process which aims at minimising cost and time for resolution/liquidation.

The most valuable of the assets was a one-million tonne hot-rolled production capacity of Uttam Value Steels at Wardha, Maharashtra. It used to purchase pig iron from Uttam Galva Metallics to be processed at this facility.

When the assets were put up for sale, there were bids and counter-bids. One of the bidders, a consortium of SSG Capital Management of Singapore, Synergy Metals & Mining Funds, ART Special Situations Fund and Investment Opportunities IV Pte Ltd, offered a ₹3,300 crore resolution plan. But this was rejected as it came late.

JSW Steel Ltd and the Liberty House Group of the UK had shown early interest but both backed out.

The winning bid came from a team consisting of distressed assets investor, CarVal Investors LLC and Nithia Capital Resources Advisors LLP. Their bid document said CarVal would set up a trust called Arcil Trust ARC, 15 per cent of which was to be held by India's oldest ARC, the Asset Reconstruction Company (India) Ltd.

Until late 2019, CarVal was the investment arm of Cargill, a food and agriculture conglomerate which is the biggest closely-held US company by revenue. In 2019, Cargill decided to exit the asset management business, selling CarVal to a group of 17 CarVal employees.

Nithia Capital is a London-based investment company. It was incorporated in 2010, with a net worth of £1,000. In 2018, it posted a loss of £2,76,829, a shade less than the loss it had recorded in 2017.

The winning bidders had committed ₹2,541 crore. Of this, ₹625 crore was upfront payment. The lenders would get the money but it would be given in the form of a loan to the two defaulting companies at 15 per cent interest. Another ₹1,200 crore would flow to the lenders over a period of five years, out of the internal accruals of the two companies. This is common enough in the IBC resolution process.

One key question: After repaying the high-cost loan of the bidders, would the companies make enough money to pay the bankers?

Other components of the package included ₹198 crore trade receivables, outstanding for at least three years. Another ₹248 crore was advances given to 'suppliers', which were group companies such as Lloyds Steel Industries Ltd and Frontline Roll Forms Pvt Ltd, almost a decade ago. Incidentally, SSG's bid of ₹3,300 crore included ₹748 crore of such trade receivables.

These chunks were included as part of the payment plan to bankers, if they could be recovered within one year. If they were not received, they would be written off. Incidentally, some of the trade receivables and advances have been pending for several years.

Finally, ₹270 crore would be realised in the form of subsidy from the Maharashtra state government. Receipt of this subsidy had several performance conditions attached.

The operational creditors to whom the companies owe ₹1,017 crore were promised ₹3 crore, in line with what the non-essential creditors – who are not secured – typically receive in such cases.

Essentially, the bankers were assured of ₹625 crore as upfront cash and the rest of the ₹2,541 crore was based on the performances of the defaulting companies as well as external parties. The haircut could be much more than the projected 60 per cent.

Some questions arise about the contours of this case:

- Why would CarVal with at least $10 billion in assets under management and three decades of experience team up with Nithia which had just £1,000 net worth and limited experience?
- Did Nithia inform the banks that its chairman, Johannes

Sittard, known to be a confidant of Lakshmi Mittal of ArcelorMittal, resigned in April? It seems that the resolution plan was submitted after his resignation.

- Nithia Capital founder CEO, Jai Krishna Saraf, lives in London. His LinkedIn profile does not say much about him. Is he competent to run a one-million-tonne steel plant? People familiar with him defend his credentials, saying he had spent decades on the job with Sittard.
- The resolution plan demanded repayment of money to the investors with hefty interest ahead of anything else. Won't that impact the company's ability to pay back to the bankers?
- Why was ₹248 crore (shown as advances) and ₹198 crore (receivables) in the books of the company payable to bankers, with caveats?
- Why was the higher bid by the SSG-led consortium rejected even though it proposed more payments?
- Finally, the liquidation value of the two companies is around ₹1,350 crore – more than double of what the banks are assured of getting as upfront cash. The rest would come in over time.

Allowing new bids after sealing the process does lead to inordinate delays and kills the sanctity of the process but it also helps the price discovery. While the debate on value maximisation versus early resolution is very much alive, these two cases illustrate what ails India's insolvency process.

The story does not end here.

On 6 April 2020, the New Delhi principal bench of the NCLT, headed by acting president BSV Prakash Kumar, approved the resolution plan (RP) for Uttam Galva Metallics and Uttam Value Steels. The resolution plan is a mix of an upfront settlement amount and deferred and contingent payments to the lenders of ₹1,567 crore and ₹1,078 crore, respectively. The CoC for the twin companies approved the plan in April 2019.

Split Judgment

This is also a rare case of a split judgment, with two NCLT judges taking different views.

While the joint resolution plan was approved by the CoC in April 2019, the SSG-led consortium contested the decision for several months, largely on the basis that the CoC did not follow the appropriate process.

The case to decide on SSG's claims was then heard by a two-judge bench in Mumbai NCLT – M.K. Sherawat, member (judicial) and Chandra Bhan Singh, member (technical). Despite pleas from the RP, bidders and the CoC to hasten the process, it took four months for the hearing to happen, and the bench took almost five months to pass its order.

The climax was the two judges taking opposing views. Sherawat found the decision to shortlist CarVal and rejecting SSG was 'in violation of (the) insolvency process'. He found the resolution plan of SSG better than CarVal and ordered the CoC to reconsider the resolution plan of SSG and give both bidders 'equal opportunity of explaining the feasibility, viability and effective implementation' of their resolution plans.

Taking 'a conscientious decision of granting equal opportunity to all stake holders', Sherawat ordered for a CoC meeting on 18 December 2019 to examine both plans, the decision by 19 December and submission of it before the bench on 20 December. Incidentally, the order was delivered on 31 December, his last day in office before superannuation.

However, Singh 'respectfully disagreed' with the order of his 'learned brother'. He found CarVal's resolution plan superior to that of the SSG Group and held that the CoC conducted the whole process 'in a fair, transparent and complaint manner'.

Finally, it was sent to the NCLT principal bench in New Delhi which dismissed the SSG Group's plea and approved the sale of twin assets to the joint consortium of CarVal Investors and Nithia Capital Resources Advisors.

The details of the resolution plan are as follows:

Uttam Value Steels

An upfront settlement of ₹275 crore, an equity infusion of ₹40 crore and a bank guarantee of ₹3.19 crore. This pegs the total upfront fund commitment at ₹318.19 crore.

Besides, there is ₹500 crore deferred payment to the creditors and a contingent payment available for the financial creditors in the form of recovery of trade receivables, etc., of ₹160 crore.

They have also been offered 5 per cent equity participation. The equity of the company is ₹2 crore.

Uttam Metallics

An upfront settlement of ₹350 crore, an equity infusion of ₹60 crore and a bank guarantee of ₹1.17 crore, making it a ₹411.17 crore upfront commitment of funds.

There is a ₹700 crore deferred payment to the creditors and ₹456 crore contingent payments.

Here too, financial creditors have been offered a 5 per cent equity participation. The equity of the company is ₹3 crore.

■ ■ ■

16

Does the RBI Need New Clothes?

On 12 December 2018, when Shaktikanta Das took over as the 25th governor of the RBI, he tweeted: 'Assumed charge as governor, Reserve Bank of India. Thank you each and every one for your good wishes.'

A few days later, after chairing his first board meeting, he tweeted again: 'Good meeting of RBI central board. Wide ranging issues discussed.'

This was the first time an RBI governor used social media to communicate. If this was unheard of in the RBI's history, the series of events that led to Das' arrival at the central bank was also unprecedented.

RBI governors have resigned on several occasions in the past. But there had never been public displays of acrimony between the government and the central bank governor before the events that led to the exit of Das' predecessor, Urjit Patel. Patel quit nine months ahead of the end of his three-year term after a bitter series of board room battles.

Since its establishment in 1935, three RBI governors have resigned before their terms ended. The first was Sir Osborne Smith

(30 June 1937), and then Sir Benegal Rama Rau (14 January 1957) and finally, Patel (11 December 2018). At least two governors – K.R. Puri (2 May 1977) and R.N. Malhotra (22 December 1990) – also had their tenures cut short because of changes in the government.

The first governor, Smith, could not stomach the government's tendency to give orders to the central bank. Rau resigned due to differences with the finance minister, T.T. Krishnamachari.

Patel cited personal reasons but few observers were convinced about that.

The Autonomy

RBI's 'fight' for autonomy and the government's periodic iteration of 'respect' for its authority are as old as the central bank itself. The last round was unique because the government threatened to use Section 7 of the RBI Act and 'direct' RBI to do certain things that the central bank did not think fit to be done.

The government has never wielded this particular weapon. Section 7 gives power to the government to 'give such directions to the Bank as it may, after consultation with the governor of the bank, consider necessary in the public interest'.

Combining two sections of the Bank of England Act, 1946, and Commonwealth Bank of Australia Act, 1945, this clause was inserted in 1949 into the RBI Act of 1934 when the central bank was nationalised.

C.D. Deshmukh, who was then the RBI governor, wanted the government to take responsibility for its actions, if it ever decided to act against the advice of the governor. But the idea did not find favour with then finance minister, John Mathai.

So, Section 4 of the Bank of England Act was grafted into the RBI Act as Section 7. In full, it says, 'The Treasury may from time to time give such directions to the Bank as, after consultation with the Governor of the Bank, they think necessary in the public interest [except in relation to monetary policy].'

The government also has the power to appoint/reappoint the governor and deputy governors and to remove them, as well as the power to appoint/remove any other director, or member of one of the local boards. The RBI has four local boards for east, west, north and south zones of India. If the RBI fails to carry out its obligations under the Act, the government can even supersede its central board.

The IMF's 'India: Financial System Stability Assessment Update' report in February 2012, dealt with these issues extensively. It said:

> The reasons for the removal of the RBI governor are not specified in the law. Although there have been no instances where the governor has been dismissed without a valid reason and the rules of natural justice apply, the explicit specification of the reasons for dismissal in the law would be better aligned with good international practice. The governor is also not appointed for a minimum term but for a maximum term with the possibility of reappointment.

The government's right to 'direct' is, of course, not confined to the RBI alone. This is true when it comes to other regulators as well. For instance, Section 16 of the Securities and Exchange Board of India Act, 1992, empowers the government to issue directions on 'questions of policy as the central government may give in writing to it from time to time'.

Under the SEBI Act, the central government can also issue directions on 'matters of policy' and the views of the government are final.

The SEBI Act, in fact, offers more sweeping powers to the government. In the case of the RBI, the direction can be issued if considered necessary in the public interest. But as per the SEBI Act, the government does not need to assign any specific reason to issue directions to the market regulator.

Also unlike in the case of the RBI (where the governor must be consulted), there is no compulsion for the government to consult the board or chairman of SEBI before issuing any direction. The relevant section of the SEBI Act envisages that consultation can be done 'as far as practicable' in contrast to the RBI Act which says consultation is mandatory.

What are the consequences if the government's direction is not followed? Section 30 of the RBI Act provides for supersession of the RBI board and Section 11 for the removal of the governor and deputy governors. Similarly, Section 17 of the SEBI Act cites 'persistent default in complying with the directions of the Central government' as one of the grounds for the supersession of the board.

Other regulators can also be 'directed'. The Insurance Regulatory & Development Authority Act, the Life Insurance Corporation Act, the State Bank of India Act and the Competition Act – all have similar provisions.

Even the non-financial regulators such as the Telecom Regulatory Authority of India (TRAI), the Petroleum & Natural Gas Regulatory Board (PNGRB), International Airports Authority (IAAI) and the Central Electricity Regulatory Commission (CERC) – can face such direction.

What is unique about the RBI Act is that the government must 'consult' the governor before directing it and the action must be in 'public interest' as opposed to the matters of 'policy', as in the case of other regulators.

Consultation ensures that the government gets the benefit of the governor's views on matters of public interest. But the Act is silent on what happens if the governor's views differ from that of the government. It also does not define what 'public interest' is.

History of Fights

The history of central banking in India is replete with many fights between the government in power and the RBI. The title of the book of former governor D. Subbarao, *Who Moved My Interest Rate?* itself is a testimony to this. His predecessor Reddy too, was involved in similar fights – which were more severe than an India–China war, a colleague of Reddy says in jest – but the details are not in the public domain. Reddy's run-ins with the finance ministry were more on specific issues while Subbarao fought on broader policy issues.

Reddy always downplayed the fights, terming them 'creative tension' but those who had seen the period from close quarters vouch that there was nothing creative about it and the tension was at times unbearable. Reddy fought hard against the government's plan to create sovereign wealth funds and use of foreign exchange reserves for infrastructure development. The finance ministry went to the extent of reaching out to the board of the central bank, seeking help to convince Reddy but he did not budge an inch from his stance.

When P. Chidambaram, former finance minister, called the then deputy governor Rakesh Mohan for an 'interview', which the ministry was conducting through a committee to identify Reddy's successor, Reddy was not kept in the loop. That was the finance ministry's way of insulting Reddy.

The ministry did the same thing to Subbarao – by not accepting his recommendation for giving another term to his deputies, first Usha Thorat and then Subir Gokarn. In Subbarao's own words, this is the price he paid for asserting autonomy.

His first brush with the ministry came in June 2010 when an ordinance was promulgated empowering the finance ministry to resolve all disputes between the regulators. This was when the Financial Stability and Development Council (FSDC) was being constituted.

Subbarao immediately wrote to Pranab Mukherjee, then finance minister, saying 'the very existence of a joint committee (the council) will sow seeds of doubt in public mind about the independence of regulators'.

'The ordinance has seeming implications for regulatory autonomy and sows seeds of doubts where none exist. My earnest request to you is to allow the ordinance to lapse. If that option is not acceptable, the portion of the ordinance relating to the RBI Act may be deleted.'

Mukherjee did not pay heed.

The Core of the Dispute

The 2018 dispute revolved around the RBI balance sheet. That was at the core of the dispute. How much in the way of capital and reserves should the RBI keep on its balance sheet and how much can it pass on to the government to help bridge the fiscal deficit? RBI's total reserves stood at ₹9.6-lakh crore as of June 2018. Until June 2020, the RBI followed a July–June financial year.

There are three contributing factors to its reserves – interest on government bonds held for conducting open market operations, fees from government's market borrowings and income from investment in foreign currency assets; earnings retained after giving dividends to the government; and revaluation of foreign assets and gold. The government felt that the RBI was more than adequately capitalised and should pass on the surplus to it.

There were other areas of disagreement as well but this was the most intractable.

In the run-up to Patel's resignation, the government sent three notes to the RBI citing Section 7 of the RBI Act, leading to long, acrimonious board meetings.

It wanted the RBI to relax the PCA or prompt corrective action norms that restrain a troubled bank's activities, including fresh lending. Around that time, a dozen banks were under PCA (11 of them were PSBs), and the government was keen that these banks be freed up from the PCA controls to be able to lend to credit-starved medium and small enterprises.

The banking regulator's decision that all banks must abolish all loan recast schemes and take the loan defaulters, including the power companies, to insolvency court, also did not go down well with the government. It wanted the RBI to soften its stance on bad loans. The power companies also moved the Allahabad High Court against the RBI move.

The government also wanted the RBI to open the liquidity tap for NBFCs, which were reeling under asset–liability mismatches.

The RBI's 'dissent' on the recommendation of a government

panel on changes to payment and settlement laws had already come into the public domain. The panel had recommended sweeping changes in the legal framework governing payments and settlements in the country. It even proposed the creation of an independent Payments Regulatory Board, to be headed by a person appointed by the government in consultation with the RBI.

The fight came into the open at the 23 October 2018 board meeting of the RBI and spilled over to the next meeting on 19 November.

In one of his speeches in 2012 ('Remembering Dr. I.G. Patel') then RBI governor D. Subbarao paraphrased former governor Patel's views on the governor's responsibility this way: 'Don't nitpick. Pick your battles. Once you have picked your battles, fight those battles valiantly.'

Urjit Patel's book *Overdraft: Saving the Indian Saver* has chronicled the fight but one thing is for sure. He did not follow I.G. Patel's advice; he opened too many fronts and, therefore, could not come up a winner. Some seasoned bureaucrats and central bankers feel that these disputes would not have escalated to such an unprecedented level of distrust had the protagonists acted with the maturity expected of the positions they held.

While the government threatened to direct the central bank under Section 7 of the RBI Act, it did not actually happen because Patel resigned, defusing the eyeball-to-eyeball confrontation. The interplay of powers of the finance minister as chairman of the FSDC with the provisions of the RBI Act is yet to be seen.

Disputes between regulators are not uncommon but disputes between the regulator and the government rarely enter the public domain in this fashion. After a spat between SEBI and IRDA over unit-linked insurance plans (ULIP), the FSDC was set up in 2010 through an ordinance. The Indian version of a super regulator subsumed the High-Level Co-Ordination Committee on financial markets. In case of a dispute between two regulators, the decision of the FSDC chairman is final.

Open Board Meetings

The US Federal Reserve periodically holds 'open' board meetings. Typically, these begin at 10 am at the Fed's headquarters, the Marriner S. Eccles Building, on 20th Street and Constitution Avenue, NW, in Washington DC.

The agenda of the open board meeting is released to the public in advance. If anyone wants to attend such a meeting, that person can register by providing date of birth, and social security number, or passport number. One can even carry a camera with the approval of the US Public Affairs Office.

The Freedom of Information Office keeps audio cassettes of such meetings up to past two years; one can buy such tapes for the princely sum of $6 per copy.

The Indian system is much more opaque, which means that we have less idea of what exactly occurred and who was aligned in which direction at the critical RBI board meetings. Minutes give only a sense of what was put on the record – there are often interchanges that are recorded in one sentence or just glossed over.

Going by the events leading to the October board meeting and the proceedings of the subsequent meetings, it was however obvious that the government would not let up on an attempt to alter the governance style of the central bank. It wanted the board to play a dominant role. Cynics said this chain of events was an effort to turn the RBI board into an extension of the finance ministry.

Technically, the board can have 21 directors, including the governor and four deputy governors, two government nominees, four from RBI's local boards and 10 appointed by the government.

The four deputy governors and two government nominees do not have voting rights; in the case of a tie, the governor has the casting vote. In RBI's history, no resolution has ever been put to vote.

The Monetary Policy Committee of the RBI, which is organised on the lines of the Federal Open Market Committee, can have members of the board of governors, apart from experts chosen from academia.

The disputes assumed significance in the context of the observations made in 2017 reports of the Financial Sector Assessment Program, run by the IMF and the World Bank.

Among other things, two reports released in December 2017, pointed out the checks and balances on the RBI, saying: 'The RBI Act contains a number of powers enabling the central government to supersede the decisions of the RBI. Although these powers have not been used... their existence undermines the RBI's legal independence.'

This observation was probably made keeping in mind Section 7 of the RBI Act which the government threatened to invoke to 'direct' RBI. The reports also said that 'the RBI governor is not appointed for a minimum term but for a maximum one and may be dismissed at will by the government without disclosing the reasons for such actions.'

Does the RBI's board have the competence and skill to guide its management? Do the directors have expertise in central banking? Historically, don't some of the directors have conflict of interests when it comes to issues such as liquidity and interest rates, as they run their own business houses?

One may argue that with the Monetary Policy Committee firmly in place, it is time for the RBI to have an operational board. If indeed the government aims to have a board-managed RBI, it should take a close look at the Federal Reserve System.

The Fed has a two-part structure. The central authority is the Board of Governors in Washington, DC. There is a decentralised network of 12 Federal Reserve Banks located all over the US.

The seven-member board of governors is an independent agency which oversees the Federal Reserve System. The president designates a chairman and vice chairman. Each serves four-year terms. These appointments are subject to Senate approval and may be renewed.

The members are appointed by the US president and confirmed by the Senate, serving staggered 14-year terms. The long terms are designed to shield them from political pressures.

Jerome Powell, the current chairman is a former partner at Carlyle Group, and served in the US Department of Treasury between 1992 and 1993. The other members are a mix of economists, attorneys and management consultants. Many have served in government administrations under both Republican and Democrat presidents.

The Power of the Board

The RBI board draws the power from two sections of the RBI Act.

Section 7 (2) says:

> Subject to any such directions, the general superintendence and direction of the affairs and business of the Bank shall be entrusted to a Central Board of Directors which may exercise all powers and do all acts and things which may be exercised or done by the Bank.

And, Section 58 (1) says:

> The Central Board may, with the previous sanction of the 1[Central Government], 2[by notification in the Official Gazette,] make regulations consistent with this Act to provide for all matters for which provision is necessary or convenient for the purpose of giving effect to the provisions of this Act.

This section also says that every regulation made by the central board should be forwarded to the central government and a copy of the regulation must be laid before both the Houses of Parliament within 30 days.

What is more, the government can also call for an audit by the Comptroller and Auditor General (CAG) of the RBI's books.

Section 51 of the RBI Act allows appointment of special auditors by the government. 'Without prejudice to anything contained in section 50, the 1[Central Government] may at any time appoint the 2[Comptroller and Auditor General] 3[***?] to examine and report upon the accounts of the Bank.'

As mentioned above, there can be up to 21 members, including governor and four deputy governors, two government nominees, four from RBI's local boards and 10 appointed by the government.

Originally, the RBI Act provided for only one government director on its board without voting power. But after the Department of Financial Services was carved out from the Department of Economic Affairs in the Ministry of Finance, a provision was made for a second non-voting government director on the RBI board. The second government director stepped in after the Factoring Regulation Act 2011 came into being.

Another amendment to the RBI Act in 2013 made it mandatory for directors to demit office after their four-year term ends, even if their successors have not yet been appointed. Prior to this, a director could continue beyond four years until a successor was appointed. As a result, the board was always full. That is not the case anymore.

Unlike companies, the concept of independent director does not exist in the RBI Act. Anyway, it is a 'legal fiction' as a truly independent director for the central bank can only come from Mars!

Who can be a Director?

There is no explicit qualification for a director. There are disqualifications though – a government employee, an insolvent person, someone attached to a bank either as an employee or as a director, and a mentally challenged person cannot be on the RBI board.

The board is expected to meet six times a year. A committee of the central board, consisting of the governor and deputy governors and at least one other director, is expected to meet every week to 'transact' 'current business'.

This committee discusses issues through a close-loop blog every week and meets once in a month.

The government has been cavalier in its dealings with the central board and the local board positions. Often, it has not bothered to fill up many positions on the central board as well as local ones.

Going by the RBI Act, the governor and not more than four deputy governors are full-time official directors on the board, which typically meets six times a year. Apart from them, there are 10 non-official directors, nominated by the government 'with expertise in various segments of the economy'; four other government-nominated directors to represent the RBI's four local boards; and two representatives of the government.

In April 2020, while the central board had 14 directors, the local boards of east, west and north had two directors each, and the south, just one.

On the lines of the central board of directors, five members on each of the four local boards are supposed to be nominated for a term of four years. After being appointed by the central government, they advise the central board on local matters and 'represent territorial and economic interests of local cooperative and indigenous banks'.

If the board of the central bank needs to play a supervisory role, as opposed to the current advisory role and the RBI governor dons the role of the CEO of the central bank, changes are needed to effectively implement this new system.

For instance, the governor's position could be made constitutional like that of CAG and judges of Supreme Court and high courts, who can be removed only by a two-thirds majority in both Houses of Parliament.

On several occasions, there has been debate about according Cabinet minister rank to the RBI governor's post. This has merit since this person is in charge of the monetary authority and the systemic lead regulator (*primus inter pares* or first among the equals in the world of regulators). Many have also argued for constitutional protection to the office of the governor.

Other important questions arise:

Should the search committee for the governor include the leader of the Opposition in Parliament?

Should half the board members be co-opted by the board itself instead of being chosen by the government?

The appointment of nuclear and space scientists, and CEOs of

IT companies to the board of the RBI lends credence to the belief that it is a ceremonial board. Most board members seem to feel that way and interpret the board position as a recognition of their contribution to society in their respective fields – especially so if those fields are far removed from the domains of central banking and financial markets. Shouldn't this change if the board is to be actively operational?

But even while such policy decisions are debated, they are less urgent than the high-priority task of reviving the almost-defunct local boards and ensuring the central board is at full strength.

Cosmetic Changes

These issues have all been swept under the carpet after Das took over the mantle. But certain changes are being made, some of them cosmetic. For instance, to make operations more transparent, the RBI, for the first time, released the minutes of its 579th central board meeting held on 11 October 2019 (although it did so in January 2020). Earlier, such minutes were available only in response to applications under the Right to Information (RTI) Act.

In the new regime, the minutes are placed on the RBI website within two weeks from the date of its confirmation in the next meeting of the central board, and upon being signed by the chairman in the same meeting.

Contrast this with the practice of the securities market regulator SEBI where the chairman generally holds a press conference after each board meeting to explain the major discussions held, and decisions taken at the meeting.

The minutes of October 2019 showed the RBI board discussed issues such as the liquidity situation and credit flow from banks and NBFCs to the economy and the regulatory supervision of commercial and cooperative banks. This was definitely a sanitised version of the actual discussions. But at least a nod towards transparency has been made.

This is not the only new development. There have been quite a few recent changes in the organisational structure of RBI.

For instance, in April 2017, it set up a formal enforcement department – a centralised department to speed up regulatory compliance. Earlier, this was a loose unit within supervision.

While this is a valuable addition to the organisational architecture, the RBI's market intelligence machinery is poor compared with that of most central banks in developed countries. A dedicated cell, and the development of more active institutional and informal networks through consultations with the market players are necessary. Earlier, the RBI board's secretary department had a market intelligence cell.

In May 2018, the RBI appointed its first CFO – the National Securities Depository Ltd Vice President Sudha Balakrishnan. A chartered accountant, Balakrishnan holds the rank of an executive director.

Raghuram Rajan had wanted to have a chief operating officer (COO), holding the rank of a deputy governor, but the government shot down the proposal.

In late 2017, RBI advertised for a CFO, who was to be responsible for accurate and timely presentation and reporting of financial information of the bank and flagging risks to the finances – operational, market, etc. – and developing strategies to mitigate them, among others.

Does the RBI's balance sheet structure call for a CFO? Or, does this show a reluctance on the part of the governor to sign off on the balance sheet?

Specialised Cadre

The initiative for the biggest organisational recast was taken in November 2019 when the RBI decided to integrate the supervision functions into a unified department of regulation to take care of supervision and regulatory functions. By being posted in this department throughout their careers, the staff will develop sufficient domain skills and expert knowledge.

The 576th meeting of the RBI board in Chennai on 21 May 2019 reviewed the structure of supervision in the context of growing diversity, complexity and interconnectedness within the

Indian financial sector. The trigger was probably the PNB fraud.

The board decided to create a specialised supervisory and regulatory cadre or SSRC within the RBI to strengthen the supervision and regulation of commercial banks, urban cooperative banks and non-banking financial companies.

The plan is to recruit 35 per cent of the SSRC from the market, and the rest from its employees. Out of the 14,000 employees on the RBI's payroll in 2020, there are 750 supervisors. The RBI wants to ramp up the figure to 1,200.

Until this recast, supervision used to be conducted through three separate departments – department of banking supervision, department of non-banking supervision, and department of co-operative bank supervision.

The newly created department of supervision is divided into four categories – very large, large, medium and small. Regulation too was carried out by three separate departments.

Offsite surveillance is also being modernised with a research wing being set up, backed by expertise on analytics and use of artificial intelligence (AI). The focus is on six risks – credit, market, liquidity, operational, governance and conduct and cyber security.

Specialisation Vs Generalisation

The debate about whether the RBI needs well-rounded central bankers or specialists in chosen areas is as old as the central bank itself.

At the initial stage, the focus was on specialisation. During the first decade after its inception in 1935, the RBI had three departments – banking, issue and agricultural credit. The last one was trifurcated into three branches from August 1945: The agricultural credit department, the department of research and statistics and the department of banking operations.

The departments were regrouped again into three groups in April 1951. The group I consisted of staff attached to the department of research and statistics, group II of the staff of the department of banking operations, banking development and the agricultural credit department and group III of the employees of all other departments.

Four years later, in April 1955, the agricultural credit department was reconstituted into a new group, making it group IV. The industrial finance department and the department of non-banking companies were added to group II in September 1957 and March 1966, respectively.

Yet another group or group V was created for the staff of the erstwhile Industrial Department Bank of India with effect from April 1965. Around the same time, the composition of the five groups was also fine-tuned for greater administrative efficiency.

In 1978, through an office order (dated 27 April) the RBI abolished the group-wise system of seniority and opted for a combined seniority for certain segments with retrospective effect. A section of employees challenged this in the Supreme Court as violative of Articles 14 and 16 of the Constitution of India. Article 14 deals with equality before law and 16, equality of opportunity in matters of public employment. However, Chief Justice Y.V. Chandrachud squashed the petition.

For the past four decades, the central bank has rejected specialisation and focused on generalisation in contrast to global practices in major central banks. Only its legal department is a specialised one while the economic and statistics department is a semi-specialised group of professionals.

The latest development indicates that the RBI is attempting to return to specialisation – and the move is reportedly facing stiff resistance from its employees. It is starting with the supervisory cadre; if it succeeds, the practice can be replicated in other areas.

The RBI needs to strike a balance between specialisation and generalisation. There is a trade-off between creating a holistic view and specialisation, which runs the risk of missing the wood for the trees. Career central bankers have been usually been the jack of all trades and master of some.

Some RBI employees feel they will miss out on exposure to different facets of running a full-service central bank while others are weighing the risks of the new department morphing into a separate entity, which is carved out of the RBI.

Some seasoned central bankers feel the new framework could have been avoided had the RBI put in place a cluster approach, based on longer tenure and capacity building.

There could be a debate on the design of the framework but one thing is for sure: There must be an entry barrier. Executives should not be placed in a department simply because they have opted for it. They must pass a qualifying test and should periodically undergo refresher programmes to be able to keep abreast with developments in an era of dynamic central banking.

The immediate trigger for setting up such a system could be the flak the RBI has got for the series of large, high-profile frauds that hit the financial sector.

RBI Caught Napping

It started with PNB. While the RBI was still grappling with this, the Punjab and Maharashtra Cooperative Bank went belly up. The ED said in its prosecution complaint that Housing Development & Infrastructure Ltd (HDIL) had laundered at least ₹2,500 crore of the ₹6,700 crore that the company had taken as loans from Punjab & Maharashtra Cooperative Bank between 2007 and 2013.

The bank allegedly replaced 44 loan accounts of HDIL and its group of companies with 21,049 fictitious loan accounts. The RBI is also being blamed for taking too long to eject Rana Kapoor from Yes Bank.

Historically, the RBI has tried to keep crooked bankers at bay by issuing a circular a day. What it actually needs is more on-site supervision. Only checking high-frequency data with the help of technology is insufficient.

Earlier, on-site supervision was the mainstay of RBI supervision; now it has been reduced and replaced by reliance on offsite inspection, which essentially consists of tracking data – daily, weekly, fortnightly, monthly.

The RBI ought to revive its comprehensive on-site supervision, particularly of the cooperative banks, where inspection and supervision is weak. It can do so nowadays since the cooperative banks are no longer subjected to the dual control of the RBI and the respective state government. The RBI became the sole regulator of the cooperative banks through an Ordinance in June 2020.

On-site supervision must be done across India and not restricted to bank headquarters alone. The assumption that everything is centralised in all banks (because they have a centralised processing system) is simply not correct. The regional offices and select branches must also be put under the scanner.

Earlier, on-site supervision was theme-based, across banks – say with a focus on treasury, priority sector lending, etc. That must be restored along with city-specific, geography-specific scrutiny of bank practices.

The RBI used to carry out transaction testing but it stopped after it set up a new supervisory framework SPARC (Supervisory Programme for Assessment of Risk and Capital). This was based on the recommendations of a high-level steering committee for the supervision of commercial banks, chaired by Deputy Governor K.C. Chakrabarty. After this committee submitted its recommendations, the RBI shifted to the so-called risk-based supervision (RBS) creating the IRISc (Integrated Risk and Impact Scoring) model.

A Complex Model for Risk

The risk-based supervision is a rather complex model. In the first phase of the roll-out, 29 banks were brought under the framework from the financial year 2013. Earlier, these banks had been grouped into five categories, according to their business models and not according to size and profile (such as State Bank of India, other PSBs, old private banks, new private banks and foreign banks). Later, the number of groups was increased to eight.

The revised framework underscores a comprehensive evaluation of both present and future risks, identification of incipient issues, determination of a supervisory stance based on the evaluation and facilitating timely intervention and corrective action.

This marked a radical shift from the earlier CAMELS supervision, which was compliance-based and oriented towards transaction testing.

Under CAMELS, the banks were grouped based on their business model. In the new supervisory regime, the banks were re-grouped, based on homogeneity. For instance, Citibank, Standard Chartered and HSBC had earlier been grouped as foreign banks; under the RBS, they migrated to the group of medium-sized banks.

Until 2016, 15 banks were covered by RBS; by April 2020, all banks have been brought under this. Historically, the RBI has been an on-site inspection heavy and off-site supervision light regulator. The RBS reversed the trend.

Along with this, the focus shifted from on-site inspection to off-site supervision and the transaction testing samples shrank. The inspections were made mostly headquarters-oriented and all designated foreign exchange and treasury branches, administrative offices and sensitive branches which were under the scanner of on-site inspection were excluded.

This is why PNB's Brady House branch, the fountainhead of the largest-ever fraud in Indian banking, was never brought under the RBI inspection scanner.

Against Global Trend

The 2008 global financial crisis taught many central banks to intensify on-site examination but the RBI did exactly the opposite. The upgrade of the off-site surveillance system is welcome but it should not have coincided with the dilution in the rigour of on-site examination.

The problem was not with RBS model per se; the problem was with its implementation. The implementation was not very smooth. The banks were not prepared for it; nor were they consulted. The rating model was not shared with them, making it difficult for them to comprehend the new supervisory regime. It was a paradigm shift but neither the regulator nor the banks had clarity on how to approach the change.

A degree of subjectivity is also involved in measuring risks under RBS. This brought down the ratings of banks by at least one notch. A bank which was earlier getting 'A' rating under CAMELS started getting 'B' under RBS but it did not know why, and the RBI did not explain the methodology clearly.

Since the focus of CAMELS inspection was on earnings, among other things, it might have encouraged banks to show high profitability, even at the cost of higher risks, to get a higher rating. That could be one of the reasons why RBI shifted to risk-based supervision. Many banks got downgraded even though there was no significant deterioration in health.

Incidentally, a 19 January 2018 IMF report captioned 'India's Financial Sector Assessment Program', commended RBI for the 'remarkable progress in strengthening banking supervision'. Stating that supervision and regulation by RBI remain strong and have improved in recent years, it lists the implementation of a risk-based supervisory approach as the key achievement.

The challenge is how to create capacity, with continuity and convergence between off-site supervision and on-site inspection. Only data analytics and transaction testing can red-flag impending dangers. Closer coordination with the capital market regulator to track the flow of funds across the financial system will also help this cause.

A Reticent Regulator?

The RBI seems to be a 'reticent' regulator, not a 'reluctant' one. It does not consult market participants as it should. At least that was the trend in the past. Raghuram Rajan tried to change this but after he left, the push to engage with market participants reduced. However, under Das, the RBI's engagement level with the market players seems to have increased.

In contrast, SEBI has close to a dozen standing advisory committees offering inputs for all major policy changes. At the second stage, the capital market regulator seeks public comments for the policies.

The RBI's excuse for avoiding active consultation is perhaps the fact that this process takes time. But since policy changes are made without much consultation, the circulars often need to be revised again and again. The circulars relating to dealing with stress assets and NPAs come in handy, as examples of this issue. Though there were consultations, they were private and with a select few banks, rather than being public and wider in scope.

For instance, in the matter of resolution of bad assets, there were consultations with the banks but not with the industry. Of course, the AQR was kept secret by design.

The RBI needs to inculcate a culture of wider consultation – a ginger group can always challenge the central bank's wisdom. Greater communication within and outside the RBI and deeper consultations with all stakeholders will help draft directives better.

Issues Galore

There are several other issues that the central bank needs to tackle.

- There is a technical committee on financial markets but does anyone know how many meetings it has held in the past few years? Its conclusions may not gel with market participants but what is the harm in listening to them?

  RBI executives, both senior and junior, have for quite sometime, also stopped attending the meetings of industry bodies such as Fixed Income Money Market & Derivatives Association of India (FIMMDA) and Foreign Exchange Dealers' Association of India (FEDA), which represent the community of bond and foreign exchange dealers.

  This restriction was based on the apprehensions that too much familiarity with market participants could be the source of regulatory capture. That may be so, but by avoiding such interactions altogether, the RBI misses out on valuable informal and formal inputs necessary for policy formulation and effective implementation.

- The RBI vision document on payments (covering the period between 2015 and 2018) spoke about setting up an external committee on payments. But there has been no further action on this front.
- It may also need to create a panel, including external members with impeccable integrity and expertise, to study the regulations and policies for banks and NBFCs. Currently, the Board for Financial Supervision (set up in 1994), a sub-committee of the central board, looks after financial regulation and supervision but its focus is primarily inspection and audit. Based on feedback from different participants, there could be a framework for regulations.
- There is a need for creating a framework for three other critical issues – inflation forecasting, liquidity management and RBI's interventions in the foreign exchange market. On several occasions in the past few years, the RBI's inflation forecast has been well off the mark. This dents its credibility and also influences the Monetary Policy Committee's approach to the policy rate.

  The overnight call money rate has been used as the prime measure of systemic liquidity. But call money is a very small portion of the entire system. Shouldn't we have a more robust and transparent framework for managing both transient and durable liquidity?

  What is the right level of local currency to be released into the system? How do we measure volatility in the foreign exchange market? The RBI doesn't need to tell the market the preferred rupee–dollar exchange rate according to its calculations. But there could be a framework to decide this, and more particularly a framework for the measurement and management of volatility.
- The RBI can also welcome investment bankers, private equity managers, treasury experts, et al. to serve stints at a senior level. Globally, central bankers do this to build in-house expertise.

- Similarly, RBI executives should be encouraged to have stints in the private sector to hone their skills. The RBI has been ultra conservative in this regard. Even retired senior executives have been barred from taking up senior board/ executive positions in regulated entities for up to three years after their superannuation to avoid potential conflict of interest.

  Also, junking a democratic transfer policy where executives are periodically rotated through different departments, making some of them stick to certain assignments will help build domain expertise. Although the RBI has high quality manpower, the lack of a pipeline of capable leaders with domain expertise with well thought-out succession plan has been an Achilles' heel. A good omen is that a policy focus on specialisation has been initiated.
- Purists will shudder, but should the RBI consider setting up an appellate body to deal with bankers' dissatisfaction? This need not be like the Securities Appellate Tribunal, a separate body to which one can appeal against SEBI orders. Instead, it can be on the lines of the Regulatory Decisions Committee of the FSA, UK. That is an FSA board committee but kept operationally separate from the rest of the UK regulator.

Such a body can be the first stop for resolution before a bank moves court against the RBI. In the recent past, Kotak Mahindra Bank took RBI to court on issues related to the dilution of promoter's shareholding in a commercial bank. This was later settled but a commercial bank taking the banking regulator to court is a rare phenomenon in India.

Globally too, this does not happen often even though instances of other financial sector regulators being dragged into legal battles are not rare. For instance, the Builders Bank in Chicago sued the Federal Deposit Insurance Corp, claiming the agency's risk profile determination for the bank was 'flawed'. Similarly, the Independent

Community Bankers of America challenged regulations issued by the National Credit Union Administration in a court of law.

In 2019, an Australian court dismissed allegations that Westpac Banking Corporation had approved mortgages without adequate credit checks. This dealt a blow to the Australian Securities and Investments Commission's efforts to raise lending standards.

A Full-Service Central Bank?

The last question is: Should the RBI remain a full-service central bank?

It was constituted on 1 April 1935 under the Reserve Bank of India Act, 1934. The main purpose, as stated in the Preamble of the Act, was:

> To regulate the issue of bank notes and the keeping of reserves with a view to securing monetary stability in India and generally to operate the currency and credit system of the country to its advantage.

Over time, newer functions kept on being added to its portfolio to meet the growing needs of an expanding economy. It is a monetary authority, a banking regulator, the lender of last resort, a foreign exchange and exchange rate manager, financial inclusion facilitator, banker to the central and state governments and a sovereign debt manager, apart from other functions such as currency issuer and payment system regulator and facilitator.

Does it have too much on it its plate in terms of managing commercial banks, cooperative banks, regional rural banks, non-banking financial companies and even housing finance companies?

Also, it has time and again taken upon itself the task of focusing on new frontiers as new technologies has created new challenges. Indeed, sometime back an RBI unit was created called 'New Frontiers' to deal with crypto currencies, banknotes printed on plastic, fin-techs, reg-techs, sup-techs, central bank money, etc. (Not too much is known about the progress of such projects.)

Globally too, central banks have struggled to find their ideal roles. However, after the 2008 financial crisis, most countries have leant towards full-service central banks. The UK had tried to find an alternative by creating the Financial Services Authority. But this was abolished after the global financial crisis, and the Bank of England's regulatory and supervisory functions, restored.

The European Central Bank, too, is no more a pure-play monetary authority; it plays the role of supervisor as well. The RBI's handling of NBFCs and cooperative banks in the recent past has raised questions about its ability to manage this broad range of responsibilities.

The Financial Sector Legislative Reforms Commission (FSLRC) report in October 2012 made a string of recommendations to clip the wings of the RBI and pitched for a new regulatory architecture. There were heated discussions and debates but we have not moved forward. Rajan found the FSLRC recommendations on the appropriate size and scope of regulators 'somewhat schizophrenic'.

In the two years between February 2018, when the $2 billion Nirav Modi scam hit state-owned PNB, and March 2020, when the private sector Yes Bank was placed under moratorium, every facet of India's financial system was exposed and revealed as vulnerable. IL&FS, a shadow bank, collapsed; DHFL, a housing finance company, went under; the multi-state Punjab and Maharashtra Cooperative Bank crumbled. All under RBI's nose.

An apple a day may keep the doctor away but a circular a day issuing frequent directives to the banks cannot keep the financial system in the pink of health.

There is no definitive answer to the question of categorising central banking as either an art or a science. However, it is apparent that the RBI is struggling to manage the complex challenges it is facing, without transforming itself. The RBI is the full-service central bank of a country aspiring to be an economic superpower. It cannot just dry clean its uniform and carry on – it needs a full makeover.

■ ■ ■

17

The Way Forward

The Reserve Bank of India and the Securities and Exchange Board of India are closely monitoring recent developments in financial markets and are ready to take appropriate actions, if necessary.

– A (rare) joint statement by the banking and markets regulators on a Sunday, 23 September 2018

There are rumours in some locations about certain banks including cooperative banks, resulting in anxiety among the depositors. RBI would like to assure the general public that Indian banking system is safe and stable and there is no need to panic on the basis of such rumours.

– A press release by the Reserve Bank of India, 1 October 2019

Concern has been raised in certain sections of media about safety of deposits of certain banks. This concern is based on analysis which is flawed. Solvency of banks is internationally based on Capital to Risk Weighted Assets (CRAR) and not on market cap. (1/2)

RBI closely monitors all the banks and hereby assures all depositors that there is no such concern of safety of their deposits in any bank. (2/2)

– Tweets by the RBI on 8 March 2020 – again, a Sunday

Your money is safe. Let me reiterate that the Indian banking system is safe and sound

– RBI Governor Shaktikanta Das,
in his address to the press, 27 March 2020

The press releases, tweets and the RBI governor's statement between September 2019 and March 2020 stressed the same point: The Indian financial system is safe and sound.

When was the last time that the RBI had to issue such reassurances? There is no precedent, at least not after the economic liberalisation of 1991.

More than a decade ago, on 30 September 2008, the RBI did issue a release, assuring depositors about the safety of their money, but that concerned a particular bank, not the banking system as a whole.

> There are reports in some sections of the media that based on rumours regarding the financial strength of ICICI Bank, depositors are withdrawing cash at its ATMs and branches in some locations.
>
> It is clarified that the ICICI Bank has sufficient liquidity, including in its current account with the Reserve Bank of India, to meet the requirements of its depositors. The Reserve Bank of India is monitoring the developments and has arranged to provide adequate cash to ICICI Bank to meet the demands of its customers at its branches/ATMs.
>
> The ICICI Bank and its subsidiary banks abroad are well capitalised.

This was just after the collapse of Lehman Brothers, when the US subprime crisis became the global financial crisis, or as it is sometimes referred to, the transatlantic crisis. The trigger for the rush to withdraw deposits was ICICI Bank's exposure to the US investment bank (which was actually very small), and its struggle to tide over short-term asset–liability mismatches in its overseas operations.

A Crisis of Confidence

That moment of doubt about ICICI Bank did not translate into broader concerns about the sector in 2008. Now there seems to be a crisis of confidence about the entire Indian banking industry.

The nervousness about the Indian financial sector started in the second half of the calendar year 2015 when the RBI forced the banks to come clean with its AQR. But even before the banks could shore up their balance sheets, PNB discovered it had been the victim of the biggest fraud in Indian banking history, in February 2018. The money involved was initially pegged at little over ₹11,000 crore but as the details emerged (and the rupee depreciated), the amount grew, to at least ₹14,000 crore.

Before the media had finished dissecting the PNB fraud, another company, this one a shadow bank, went into free-fall in early September 2018. IL&FS, a company that had been floated to catalyse infrastructure creation but dabbled in many more things, defaulted in its debt servicing.

That default set off a forest fire that spread through the NBFCs. It charred the bigger ones in that shadow-banking forest and turned the smaller bushes into ashes. The casualty list included India's fourth-largest mortgage financier DHFL, which was a triple-A rated company like IL&FS.

A year later, in September 2019, the Punjab & Maharashtra Cooperative Bank, a scheduled urban cooperative bank operating across six states, went belly up, forcing the RBI to prevent depositors from withdrawing their money. Similar curbs were imposed on the depositors of Yes Bank in March 2020, when the fourth-largest private lender by assets took the fast lane to insolvency.

Banking crises are hardly new in India. In the first three years of Independence, between 1947 and 1950, 183 banks failed, out of which 70 were in West Bengal. The next decade witnessed the collapse of 315 banks, including the Palai Central Bank, the biggest in Kerala and the 17th largest among 94 scheduled commercial banks at the time. On 8 August 1960, when Kerala High Court approved bad loans-laden Palai Central Bank's liquidation, most banks in the southern state and even elsewhere faced a run on their deposits.

There were 339 banks at that time. Many went into extinction and depositors lost money. This led to the passage of the Deposit Insurance Act by Parliament in 1961 and also the formation of the Deposit Insurance & Credit Guarantee Corporation to protect bank depositors.

Similarly, the gross NPAs of the Indian banking industry hit 19.07 per cent in 1994, two years after the RBI introduced the prudential norms on income recognition, asset classification and provisioning, following the international banking regulations issued by the Basel Committee on Banking Supervision.

For PSBs, the gross NPAs as a share of total loans were even higher – 21.11 per cent. The gross NPAs for the industry remained in double digits for six years, until 2002.

Meanwhile, the second half of the 1990s witnessed a shake-out in the NBFC sector, triggered by the collapse of CRB Capital Markets Ltd, a financial services conglomerate, which had been granted a provisional banking licence. The triple-A rated NBFC, ran a family of 133 subsidiaries. It was exposed as duping millions of small investors of their investments in its mutual fund and fixed deposits.

The number of NBFCs, which had increased from 7,063 in 1981 to 55,995 by 1995 but dropped to 7,855 in 1999 after the RBI tightened the regulations, asked for more equity and cancelled thousands of licences.

Trouble in the cooperative banking sector is also not new. Remember the Madhavpura Mercantile Cooperative Bank, the largest urban cooperative bank in Gujarat? It was set up in September 1967 as a cooperative society, and got the status of a scheduled bank in 1999. Within two years, its massive exposure to stockbroker Ketan Parekh led to a collapse when the dotcom bubble burst and the stock market crashed.

By March 2001, the bank had a negative net worth of₹1,147.13 crore. A run on the bank led to 90.9 per cent deposit erosion even as the gross NPAs as a percentage of total advances hit 88.2 per cent.

To check contagion, RBI issued this release on 4 April 2001.

> In the wake of the recent events that have affected a few urban co-operative banks in Gujarat, it had been reported that some co-operative banks may face liquidity problems in their day-to-day operations. To obviate any such difficulty, the Reserve Bank had already advised all concerned that these banks may approach public sector banks and also primary dealers for repos facilities against eligible government securities held by them.
>
> In case the co-operative banks are unable to meet their liquidity needs from the money market, including through repos with other banks and primary dealers, such banks have further been advised to approach the Reserve Bank of India, Central office through the RBI Regional Director in Ahmedabad. On the advice of Regional Director, RBI will provide special liquidity support to such banks against their eligible holdings of appropriate assets for temporary periods up to 90 days.

An Acrimonious Fight

The new dimension in the latest turmoil is its backdrop – this is an acrimonious fight between the finance ministry and the RBI. Things came to such a pass that the government threatened to use a particular section of the RBI Act to 'direct' the banking regulator.

The points of conflict were many – ranging from the government's uneasiness with the RBI not allowing weak banks to lend (because they did not possess sufficient capital) to the regulator directing banks to move the insolvency court against large defaulters. Disagreements between the central bank and the government on policy issues have occurred many times, but this time, it spilled over into the public domain.

Viral Acharya, a deputy governor, on 26 October 2018, had warned the government of the 'wrath of financial markets' if the independence of the central bank was curbed. Subhash Chandra Garg, the economic affairs secretary, retorted a week later on 2 November with this tweet: 'Rupee trading at less than 73 to a dollar, Brent crude below $73 a barrel, markets up by over 4 per cent during the week and bond yields below 7.8 per cent. Wrath of the markets?'

Similarly, the Indian financial system is no stranger to crises. But a crisis of confidence that forces the RBI to issue a press statement assuring the safety of deposits, tweet on a Sunday and get the governor to issue a statement is something new and alarming.

PNB and Punjab & Maharashtra Cooperative Bank were hit by outright frauds. In one sense, the scope for fraud cannot be eliminated though it can be reduced. Still, one cannot condone the RBI's role. Many blame the shift to risk-based supervision for such frauds. While off-site surveillance system is welcome, it cannot be done at the cost of on-site supervision and transaction testing.

While the creation of a specialised supervisory and regulatory cadre may help plug some loopholes, market intelligence is something the Indian central bank cannot afford to ignore.

A December 2016 paper of the Bank for International Settlements, the central banks' bank, says:

> Central bank remits necessitate that policy and operational decisions are made with an understanding of the financial market context in which central banks operate. Gathering intelligence on financial markets makes a vital contribution to that understanding. It enhances and extends insights that come from the analysis of market data and from published commentary and research, and thereby informs a range of policy and operational objectives.

According to the paper, market intelligence is most important for market operations and analysis, monetary policy analysis, and foreign exchange reserve management. Market intelligence is used to support a very wide range of functions, including financial stability.

Had the RBI had a sufficiently efficient system for gathering and analysing market intelligence, it could have sensed the rot in the banking system even before the CRILC was set up.

Similarly, it could have flagged potential trouble in the NBFCs that were borrowing short and lending long, riding on a liquidity sugar rush after the November 2016 demonetisation. At the same time, the bankers were watching haplessly as they did not have the capital to support lending.

The Crux of the Problem

How long will India allow this zombie credit culture to continue? Japan started the so-called zombie credit culture in the 1990s. Europe followed in the wake of Japan, where low interest rates and the banks' refusal to write-off bad debt has stymied growth for decades.

Economists claim the European Central Bank's Outright Monetary Transactions (OMT) programme induced zombie lending by banks, which remain under-capitalised. Italy, Portugal and many other Organisation for Economic Cooperation and Development (OECD) countries have witnessed this.

The basic lesson from Japan's experience is that if the banks lack sufficient capital, they end up doing zombie lending and evergreening loans. India does not seem to have learnt this lesson (for that matter Japan does not seem to have learnt it either!).

There is an incentive to not declare a loan bad even after the borrower defaults, as the banks need to set aside money to provide for such bad loans. That hits their profits and, more importantly, erodes their capital.

The banking regulator asks the banks to maintain a minimum capital. To ensure that, the banks look the other way to avoid taking a hit on their balance sheets and they hope that borrowers, with the support of fresh money, will be able to get back to profitability and repay their loans.

Credit Misallocations

Zombie banking always leads to credit misallocations. The insolvent firms keep on getting bank credit and stay alive and those who need loans are turned away.

The Japanese story happened when Japan's real estate bubble collapsed in the early 1990s. The banks were affected as they were holding real estate assets, either as collateral for loans, or they had direct exposure to real estate. The government introduced a series of measures to stabilise the banking system and spur growth. But under-capitalised banks preferred zombie lending.

The story of the Indian banking system is more complex but the lessons are much the same: An ultra-loose monetary policy and regulatory forbearance cannot substitute bank capital. Bank must be adequately capitalised. If they are not, we see zombie lending which, in turn, creates zombie lenders.

The NBFC crisis in India is an offshoot of the banking crisis. As under-capitalised banks were not allowed to lend, the NBFCs rushed to grab market share. Easy money was a big incentive for them. Until the RBI launched AQR, the banks were doing zombie lending.

Many observers have asked if the RBI was too aggressive in its mission clean up? In the mid-1990s, the Indian banking industry had an even higher basket of bad loans – as a percentage of their loan book – but they were still nursed back to health without much noise.

In the second half of the current decade, was the RBI under Urjit Patel, too obsessed with the demonstrative effect of what the central bank could do, rather than the effect of the action itself? Could the clean up have been done without exposing bank vulnerability so crudely?

The Japan Story

While there is no definite answer to these questions, the Indian banking story does, in many ways resemble the story of Japan and of Europe. The banks remained under-capitalised; the RBI kept on devising different restructuring plans for stressed assets and the banks kept on zombie lending until the regulator changed approach and tackled the problem head-on.

A large part of the banking system is owned by the government. Indeed, India is unusual among large economies because of the large government ownership of banks. Unlike some of the large private banks, PSBs lack the balance sheet health and strength to attract capital from the market. So, the government needs to infuse capital but its own fiscal weaknesses prevent it from doing so in liberal fashion.

Acharya's maiden speech as RBI deputy governor, on 'Some Ways to Decisively Resolve Bank Stressed Assets', was delivered at an IBA conference in February 2017. He spoke about resolving the bad loan problem in a time-bound, decisive manner.

Some banking sector analysts found the proposal too academic and infeasible in the Indian context while 'status quoist' bankers also did not see merit in what he proposed. His suggestion was to create special structures to deal with stressed loans, keeping in mind the possibility of revival of the companies that had borrowed money from banks.

One such structure is a private asset management company to handle the creation, selection and implementation of a feasible resolution plan for a quick turnaround of the largest troubled companies in telecoms, metals (iron and steel, in particular), engineering-procurement-construction and textiles within a fixed time frame.

One or more credit rating agencies would rate the resolution plans in which the promoters of these companies would have no say. The banks had to choose from among those resolution plans to ensure adequate credit rating of the restructured entity, and take a deep haircut which would be approved by the government and accepted by the vigilance authorities. Of course, the resolution would have to pass through the insolvency law.

In sectors such as power, which suffer from excess capacity and need long-term solutions, the plan was to create a quasi-government body such as a national asset management company with a minority government stake. This would raise debt, possibly government-guaranteed, and manage the asset reconstruction companies and private equity firms responsible for turning around stressed companies.

The proposal was a radical departure from measures that RBI had actually adopted to resolve the bad loan problem before the insolvency law was put in place. It shifted the focus from banks to the larger economic scenario, taking notes of the fact that a banking crisis could morph into a larger crisis that hits industrial growth in Asia's third-largest economy.

Acharya had a point. He did not look at the health of the banking sector in isolation. He wanted to treat the zombie lenders and zombie borrowers – sick banks and sick industries – simultaneously.

If we want to save the banks first and take care of industry later, it could be too late to boost economic growth and create jobs. We can have healthy banks but who will they lend to? So, there has to be an attempt to dissect the economic viability of underlying assets and find ways of restructuring them to become productive.

The proposal also called for a significant restructuring of PSBs, including raising private capital, sale or securitising of assets, merging banks and getting rid of non-performing workforce by offering voluntary retirement schemes and inducting a younger, digitally-savvy talent pool.

It spoke about 'tough love' and allowing market forces to decide which banks should survive.

Political Animal

Nobody looked at Acharya's proposal seriously because the PSBs are political animals. While RBI looks after regulations and supervision, the PSBs are run by the government in power. The problem does not lie in the public sector character of these banks but in how they are governed. As we know, IDBI Bank Ltd has been 'privatised' by giving its majority ownership to the state-owned LIC, while 13 PSBs have been merged to create five relatively large banks.

Will it change the way they are run? What will happen to other PSBs such as UCO Bank in West Bengal, Punjab & Sind Bank in Delhi, Indian Overseas Bank in Tamil Nadu and Bank of Maharashtra in Maharashtra? Given the state of their balance sheets, can they fend for themselves?

There are too many questions. Is there really a crisis or is this a game being played by India Inc.? The bottomline is, the bank crisis spilled over to the real sector and created a crisis of confidence.

What lies in the future? Should development financial institutions be revived as a concept? Should the new landscape of banking be one of co-existence of big banks and small banks? Should we have more banks or fewer banks? Will the bad banks and good banks continue to cohabit due to the government's indulgence?

If all state-owned banks cannot be capitalised, the government must choose who should live and who should die. Can a few of these be privatised?

The quality of assets of the Indian banking system showed marginal improvement in the financial years 2019–20 and 2020–21, leading optimists to believe that the phase of bad-loan recognition is over and it is time for resolution.

But balance sheets of banks will deteriorate again, quite severely, following the impact of the general lockdown prompted by the Covid-19 pandemic. Even prior to the lockdown, the NPAs of Indian banks as a percentage of the loan book was the worst among the G-20 nations after Russian Federation.

Through the past decade and more, corporate India continued to leverage by taking on more debt. The banks changed their preferred asset class from steel, to infrastructure, to telecom, and the RBI kept on displaying forbearance. In an easy money regime, treasury profits have helped banks clean up their balance sheets at periodic intervals. But if this story continues, at some point, there won't be anybody to lend to, barring the government. That is the last bastion – signalling fiscal dominance and debt stagnation.

If the government as the majority owner wants to run banks as an agency for social good, let it not pretend these are commercial entities. Alternatively, it should put in place enabling conditions to allow the banks to run as business enterprises.

DBS Bank Ltd, the largest bank in Southeast Asia by assets, was set up by the Singapore government as a development financial institution in 1968. It is run by its board. The government has nothing to do with operations, except for earning handsome returns on its investment.

What should the government do with the PSBs? Vitor Gaspar, Paulo Medas and John Ralyea, all officials of the IMF's fiscal affairs department, have made some interesting suggestions at the IMF Blog in May 2020. Although they have written on the role of state-owned enterprises in saving lives and livelihoods in the time of the Covid-19 pandemic, the points they make are relevant even otherwise.

> In a time when governments are facing increasing demands and struggle with high debt, a core principle for state-owned enterprises is not to waste public resources. We make four main recommendations for how countries can improve the performance of state-owned enterprises:
>
> Governments should regularly review if an enterprise is still necessary and whether it delivers value for taxpayers' money. For example, Germany conducts biennial reviews. The case for having a state-owned enterprise in competitive sectors, such as manufacturing, is weaker because private firms usually provide goods and services more efficiently.
>
> Countries need to create the right incentives for managers to perform and government agencies to properly oversee each enterprise. Full transparency in the activities of the enterprises is paramount to improve accountability and reduce corruption. Including state-owned enterprises in the budget and debt targets would also create greater incentives for fiscal discipline.

> Many aspects of these practices are in place, for example, in New Zealand.
>
> Governments also need to ensure state-owned enterprises are properly funded to achieve their economic and social mandates, such as in Sweden. This is critical in responding to crises – so that public banks and utilities have enough resources to provide subsidised loans, water, and electricity during this pandemic – and in promoting development goals.
>
> Ensuring a fair playing field for both state-owned enterprises and private firms would have positive effects by fostering greater productivity and avoiding protectionism. Some countries already limit preferential treatment of state-owned enterprises, like Australia and the European Union. Globally, a potential way forward is to agree on principles to guide state-owned enterprises' international behaviour.
>
> The stakes are high. Well-governed and financially healthy state-owned enterprises can help combat crises such as the pandemic and promote development goals. However, to deliver on these, many need further reforms. Otherwise, the costs to society and the economy can be large.

Half a decade has been lost since the RBI decided to remove the tumour of bad loans in 2015. The RBI's desire to act decisively was not to the liking of the government. If the government continues to remain in denial about the state of public sector banking, India will go the Japan way. It is high time that both government and the central bank aligned their actions to recognise the mess and clean up banking, once for all.

The government uses its clout as the majority owner to make the PSBs act in an unsustainable manner. Meanwhile, the RBI goes overboard, tinkering with regulations to make up for supervisory failures.

Many say that excessive regulations stifle India's banking industry in somewhat the same way that over-regulation has prevented the free development of the labour market. As a result, while the informal economy is the biggest source of employment, a large section of the population continues to depend on informal sources of finance – they do not have full access to the formal banking system.

At the end of this book, I am still seeking an answer to a question: Has India let down its banking system or, is it the other way round? Probably, the blame should be shared.

The banking regulator could have encouraged competition by allowing many more banks to set up shop. It has not done so and hence, financial repression continues. The banks too have not explored the phenomenal opportunities that the world's second most populous nation offers.

There are millions of borrowers and savers in the hinterland of India but very few banks seek to identify and exploit the business opportunities there. Some banks go there only under compulsion; while others stay away. Everyone ends up losing as a result.

■ ■ ■

PART VI
CHARTING THE ILLS

'A picture is worth a thousand words' is an adage which means that a picture or image often tells a story better than words. The graphics and charts in this segment should be able to convey more than what I have tried to through 400-plus pages.

Quite a few of the graphics focus on bad loans – where India stands among the G-20 nations, how the bad loan piles grew, how banks brushed them under the carpet of restructured loans and which are the most affected banks. The graphics also show how the PSBs have been losing their market share and the private banks have been moving ahead – privatisation by stealth.

Then, there are other important aspects of the Indian financial system – the government support to the PSBs by infusion of capital since the mid-1980s, the world of shadow banks, the increasing incidents of frauds, loan write-offs and how rating agencies are first caught napping and then go overboard in downgrading corporations.

And, don't miss the chart that maps how long it take the government to appoint a successor to the boss of a PSB. (In one case, it took 264 days!) Had the subject not been critical for the Indian economy, I would have probably titled the book, 'Pandemonium: The Great Indian Banking Comedy'!

PSB Recapitalisation

Going by the Economic Survey 2019–2020, in 2019 every rupee of taxpayer's money invested in PSBs, on average, lost 23 paise.

Year	Recapitalisation (in ₹ cr)
1985-86 to 1992-93	**4,000**
1993-94	**5,700**
1994-95	**4,363**
1995-96	**850**
1996-97	**1,509**
1997-98	**2,700**
1998-99	**400**
1999-00	-
2000-01	-
2001-02	**1,300**
2002-03	**770**
2003-04	-
2004-05	-
2005-06	**500**
2006-07	-
2007-08	**10,000**
2008-09	**1,900**
2009-10	**1,200**
2010-11	**20,117**
2011-12	**12,000**
2012-13	**12,517**
2013-14	**14,000**
2014-15	**6,990**
2015-16	**25,000**
2016-17	**25,000**
2017-18	**90,000**
2018-19	**1,06,000**
2019-20	**70,000**
Total	**4,16,816**

Source: Reserve Bank of India

Bad loans, India vs Rest of the World

In 2019, among G-20 nations, India was only slightly better than Russian Federation in bad loans.

G20 Countries	2010	2011	2012	2013	2014	2015	2016	2017	2018	2019	2020 Estimates
Argentina	2.12	1.40	1.73	1.73	1.99	1.74	1.84	1.83	3.11	5.75	
Australia	2.15	1.97	1.75	1.40	1.05	0.92	0.98	0.86	0.90	0.96	
Brazil	3.11	3.47	3.45	2.86	2.85	3.31	3.92	3.59	3.05	3.11	4.00
Canada	1.19	0.84	0.65	0.57	0.52	0.52	0.60	0.45			1.00
China, P.R.: Hong Kong	0.83	0.69	0.60	0.54	0.51	0.73	0.85	0.67	0.55	0.57	10.00
China, P.R.: Macao	0.39	0.34	0.19	0.09	0.12	0.12	0.20	0.23	0.22	0.24	
China, P.R.: Mainland	1.13	0.96	0.95	1.00	1.25	1.67	1.74	1.74	1.83		
France	3.76	4.29	4.29	4.50	4.16	3.98	3.64	3.08	2.75	2.47	3.00
Germany	3.20	3.03	2.86	2.70	2.34	1.97	1.71	1.50	1.24		1.00
India	2.39	2.67	3.37	4.03	4.35	5.88	9.19	9.98	9.46	9.23	13.00
Indonesia	2.53	2.14	1.77	1.69	2.07	2.43	2.90	2.56	2.29	2.43	
Italy	10.03	11.74	13.75	16.54	18.03	18.06	17.12	14.38	8.39	6.75	11.00
Japan	2.46	2.45	2.43	2.13	1.75	1.53	1.40	1.19	1.07		2.00
Korea, Rep. of	0.59	0.48	0.59	0.57	0.49	0.46	0.47	0.35			
Mexico	2.04	2.12	2.44	3.24	3.04	2.52	2.09	2.09	2.05	2.15	
Russian Federation	8.23	6.59	6.03	6.00	6.73	8.35	9.44	10.00	10.12	9.29	
Saudi Arabia	2.97	2.22	1.67	1.31	1.08	1.24	1.38	1.61	1.95	1.86	
South Africa	5.79	4.68	4.04	3.64	3.24	3.12	2.86	2.84	3.73	3.89	
Turkey	3.49	2.58	2.74	2.64	2.74	2.99	3.11	2.84	3.69	5.02	
United Kingdom	3.95	3.96	3.59	3.11	1.65	1.01	0.94	0.73	1.07		2.00
United States	4.39	3.78	3.32	2.45	1.85	1.47	1.32	1.13	0.91	0.86	4.00

Source IMF, S&P Global Ratings, Global Banking Outlook, July 2020
NOTE: Estimate for India is for March 2021; other countries for December 2020

*All figures in %

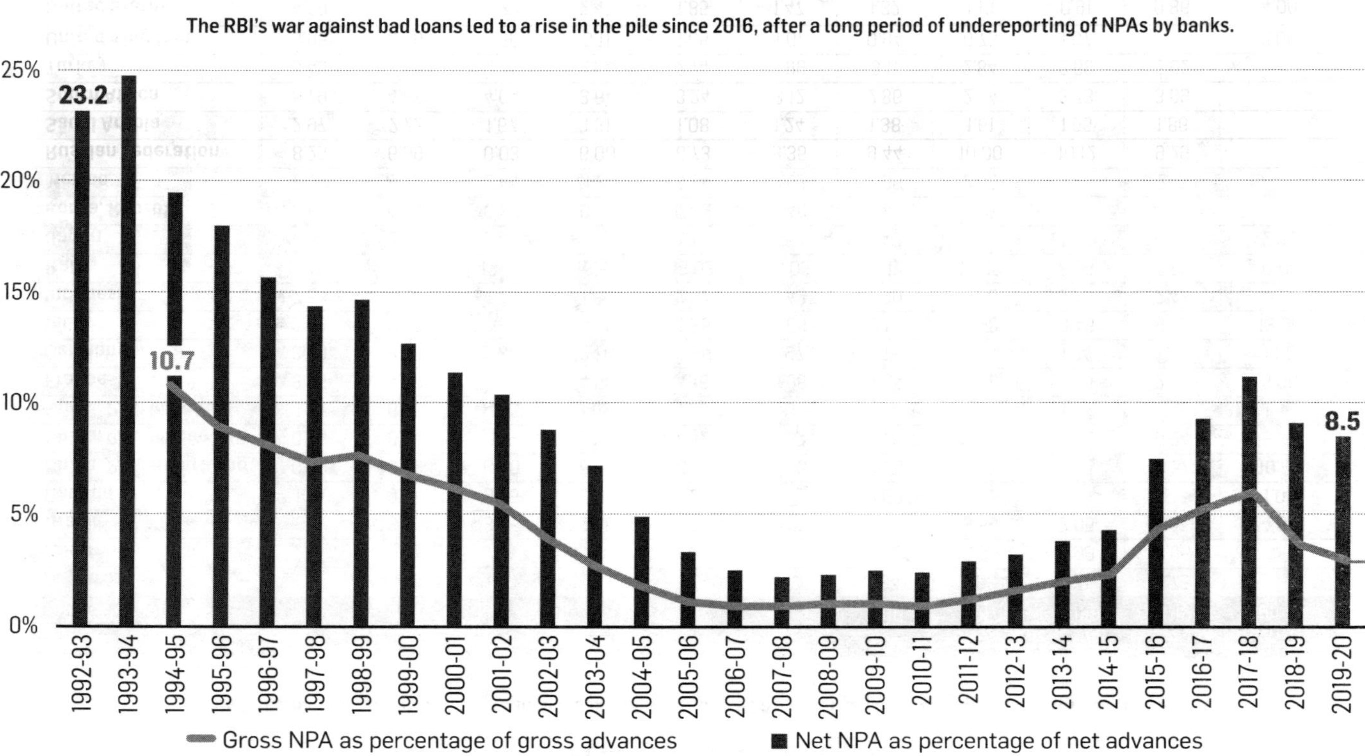

Source: Reserve Bank of India

Clever Concealment

Until 2015, banks were hiding their bad loans under restructured assets. The scene changed from 2016 onwards.

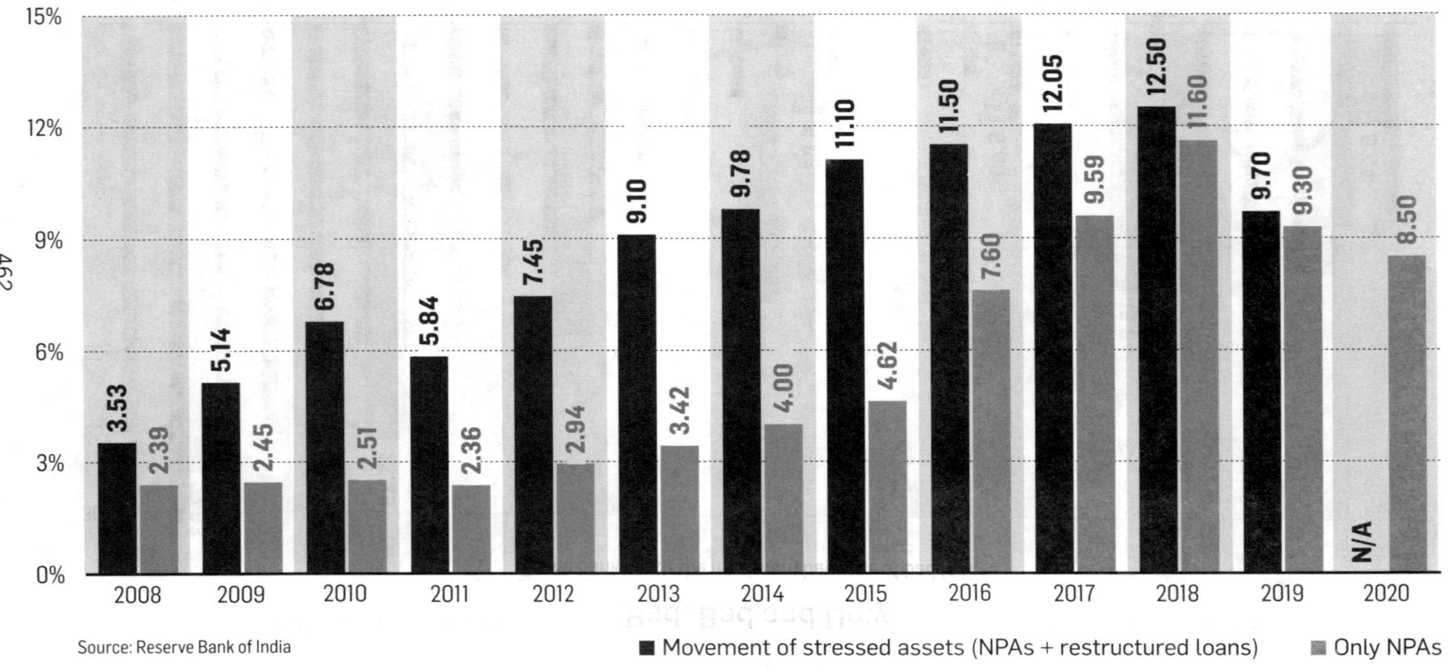

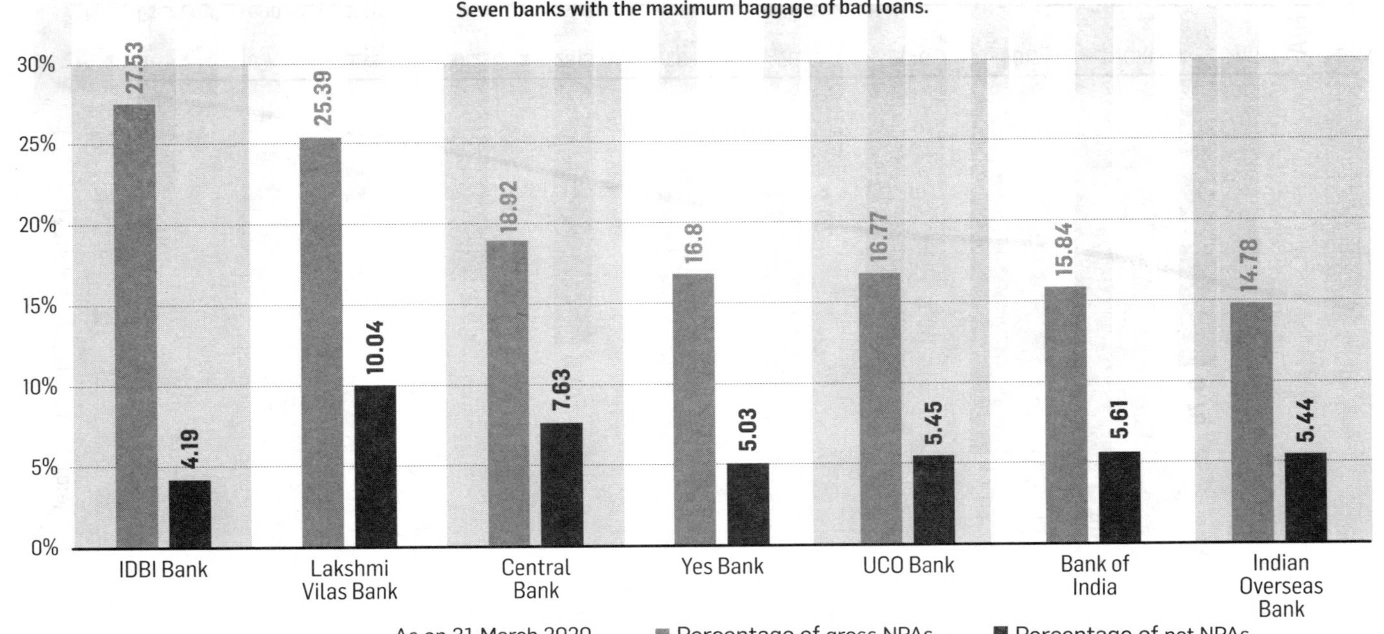

Bad, Bad and Ugly
Seven banks with the maximum baggage of bad loans.
30%
25%
20%
15%
10%
5%
0%
27.53
4.19
IDBI Bank
25.39
10.04
Lakshmi Vilas Bank
18.92
7.63
Central Bank
16.8
5.03
Yes Bank
16.77
5.45
UCO Bank
15.84
5.61
Bank of India
14.78
5.44
Indian Overseas Bank
As on 31 March 2020
Percentage of gross NPAs
Percentage of net NPAs
Source: Bank balance sheets

On the Back Foot

Banking industry's credit growth has been slowing since 2016 as mountain of bad loans is staring at them. Many bankers are reluctant to lend for fear of piling up of bad loans.

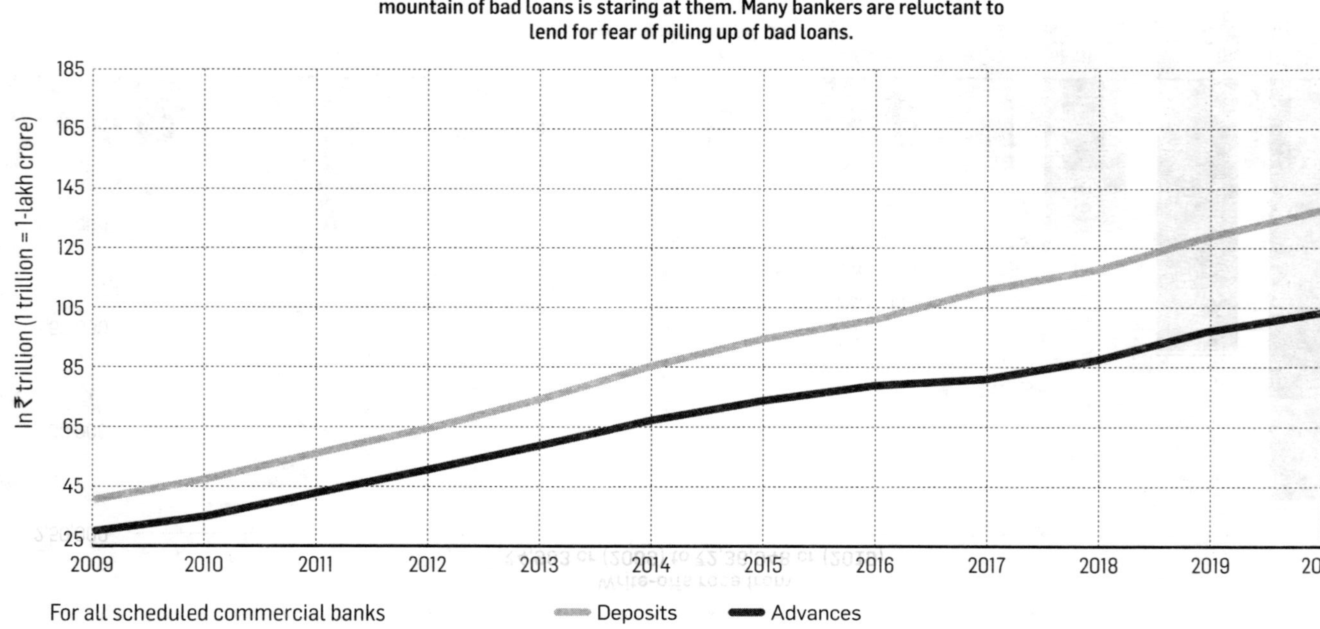

Source: Reserve Bank of India

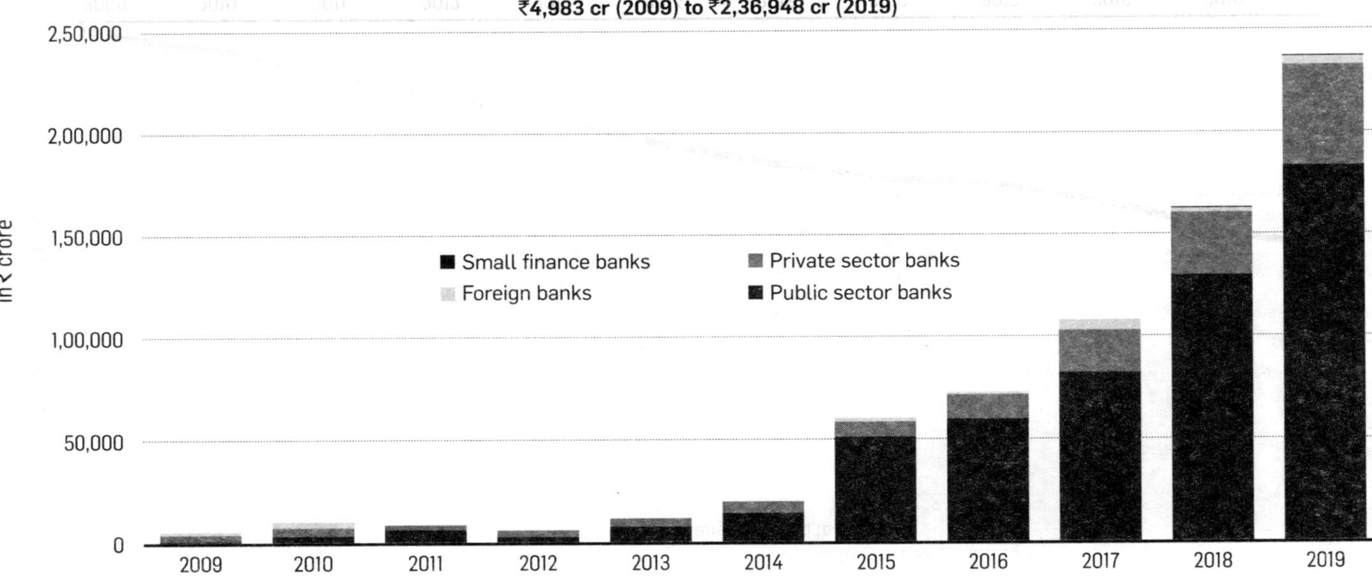
Write-offs Balloon from 2016 to 2019
This creates an optical illusion of lower NPAs.
Write-offs rose from
₹4,983 cr (2009) to ₹2,36,948 cr (2019)
In ₹ crore
2,50,000
2,00,000
1,50,000
1,00,000
50,000
0
Small finance banks
Foreign banks
Private sector banks
Public sector banks
2009
2010
2011
2012
2013
2014
2015
2016
2017
2018
2019
Source: Reserve Bank of India

The Lion's Share

In 2019, PSBs held 61% of advances but were responsible for 77.4% of all write-offs.

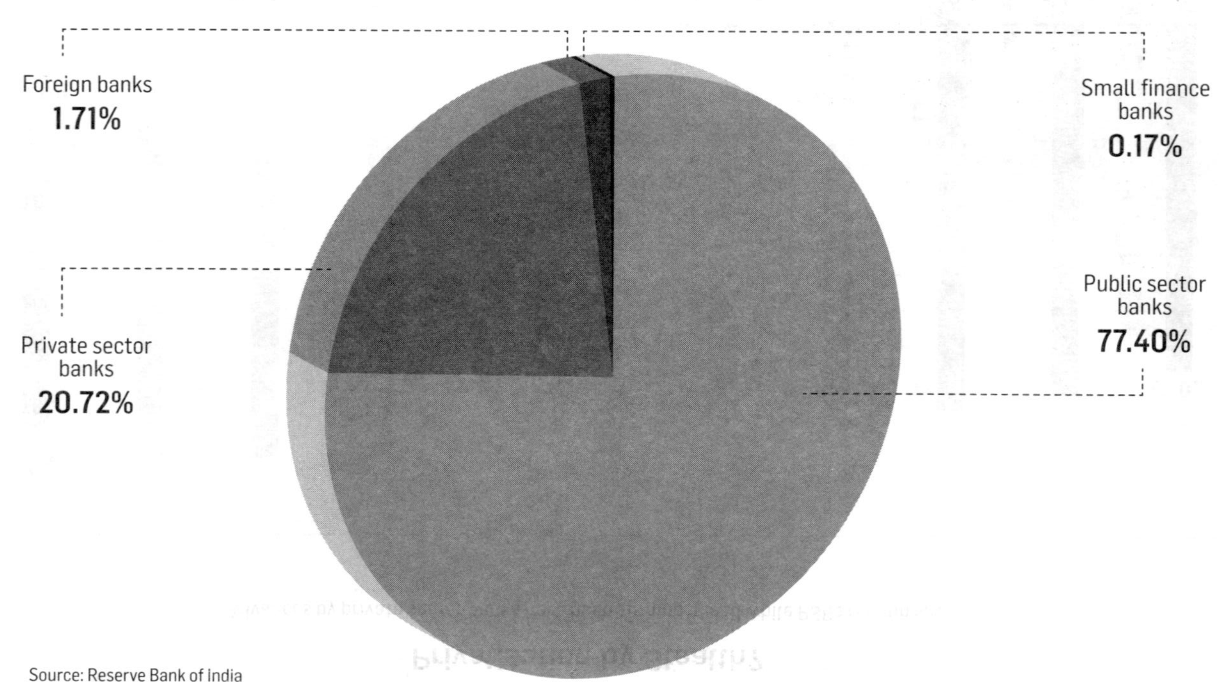

Source: Reserve Bank of India

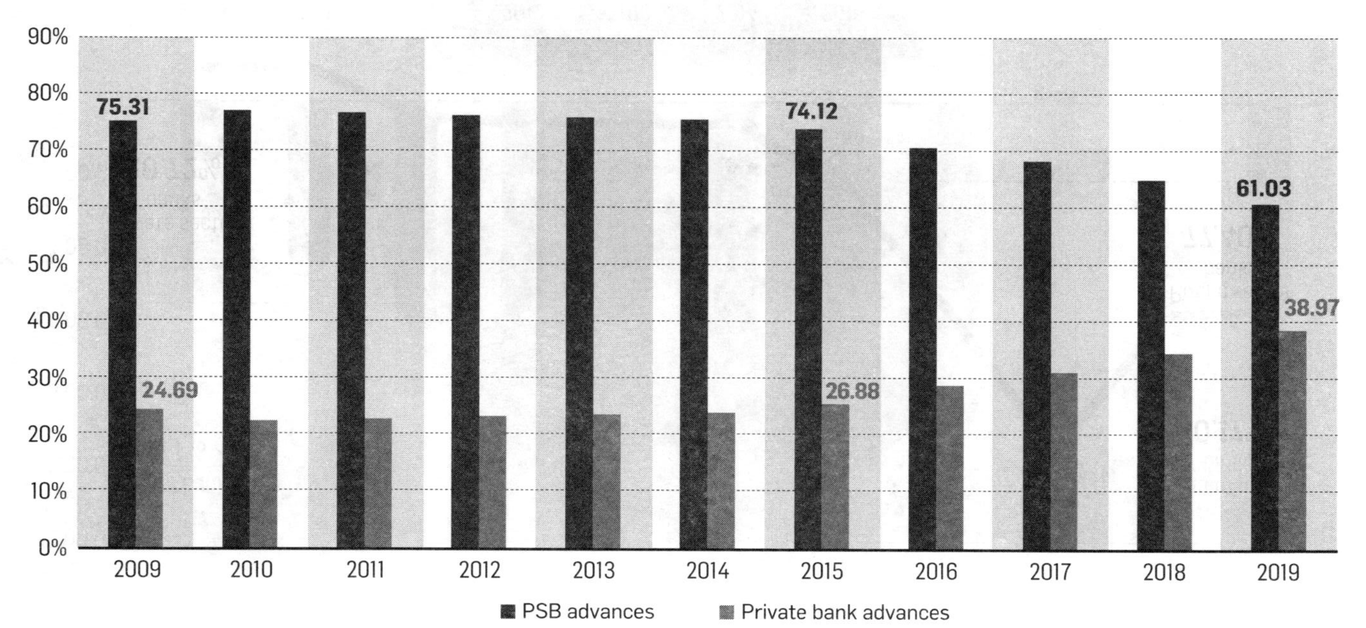
Privatisation by Stealth?
Advances by private sector banks have been surging ahead while PSBs remain shy.
90%
80%
70%
60%
50%
40%
30%
20%
10%
0%
75.31
24.69
74.12
26.88
61.03
38.97
2009
2010
2011
2012
2013
2014
2015
2016
2017
2018
2019
PSB advances
Private bank advances
Source: Reserve Bank of India

Incremental Advances: Advantage Private Banks

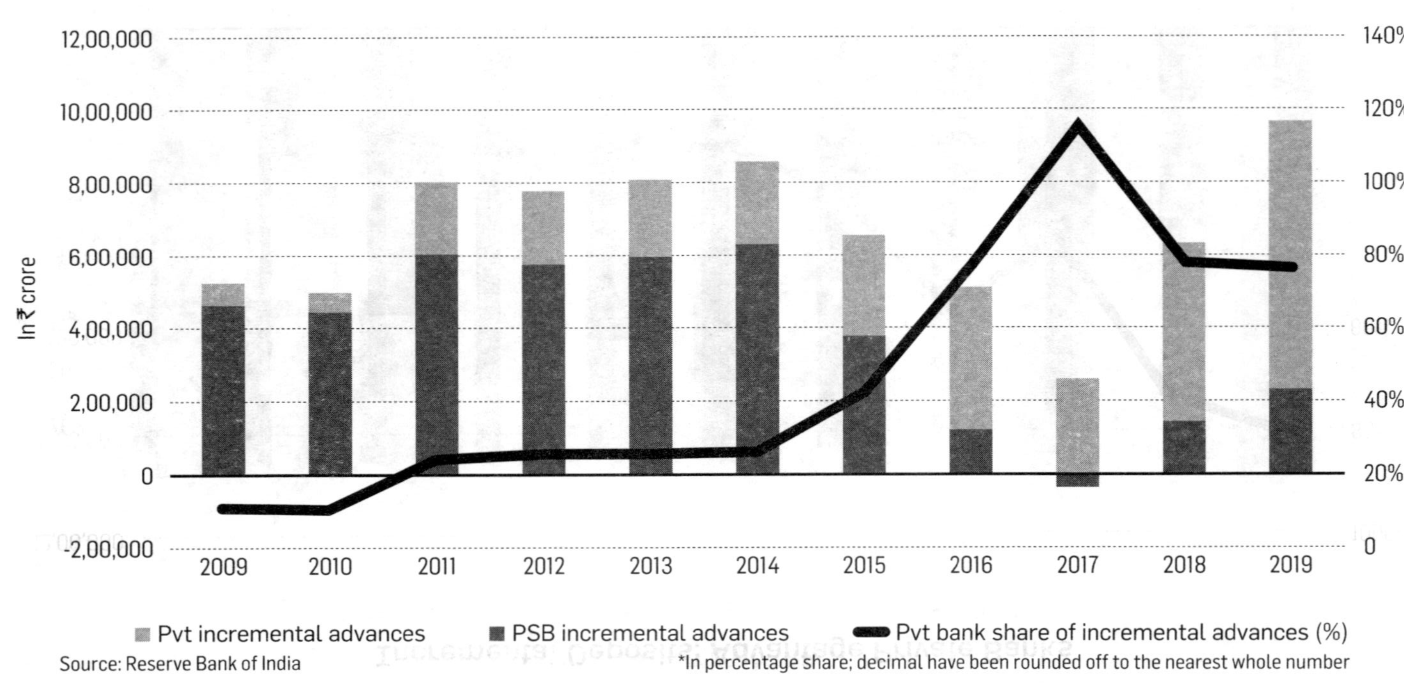

Source: Reserve Bank of India

*In percentage share; decimal have been rounded off to the nearest whole number

Incremental Deposits: Advantage Private Banks

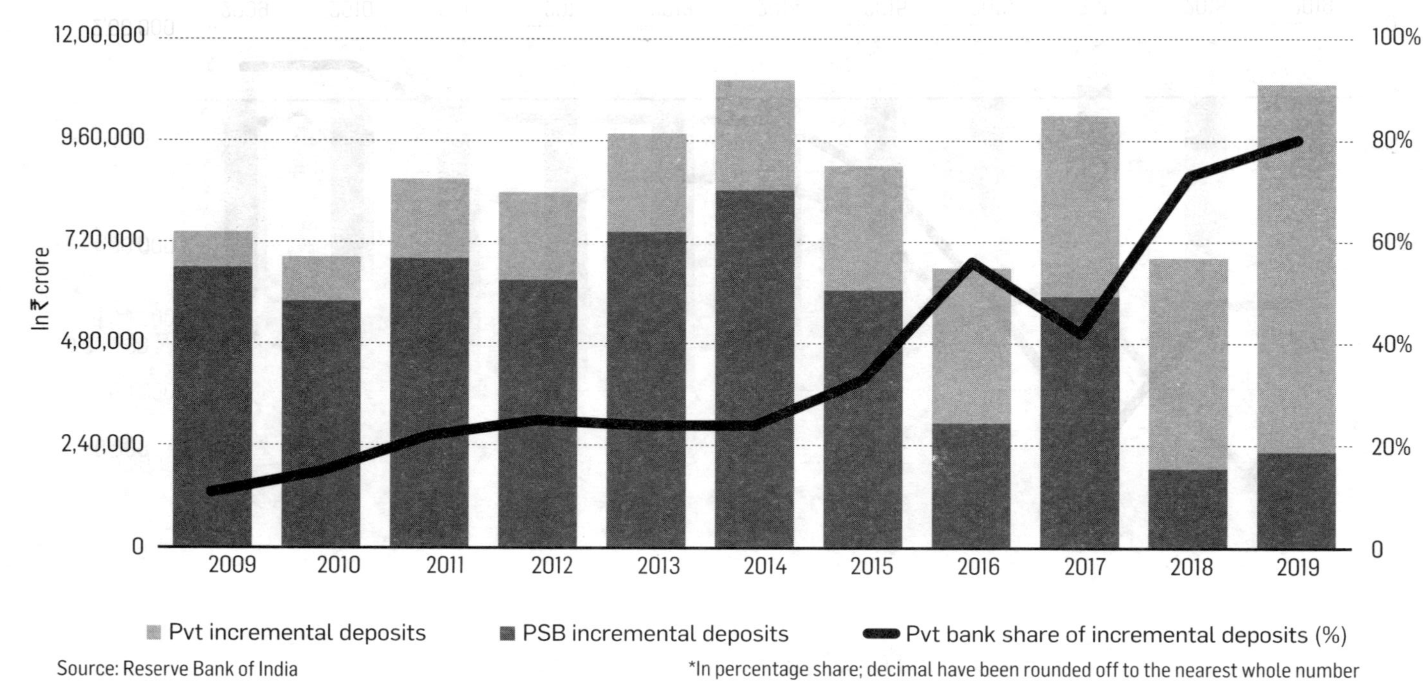

Source: Reserve Bank of India

*In percentage share; decimal have been rounded off to the nearest whole number

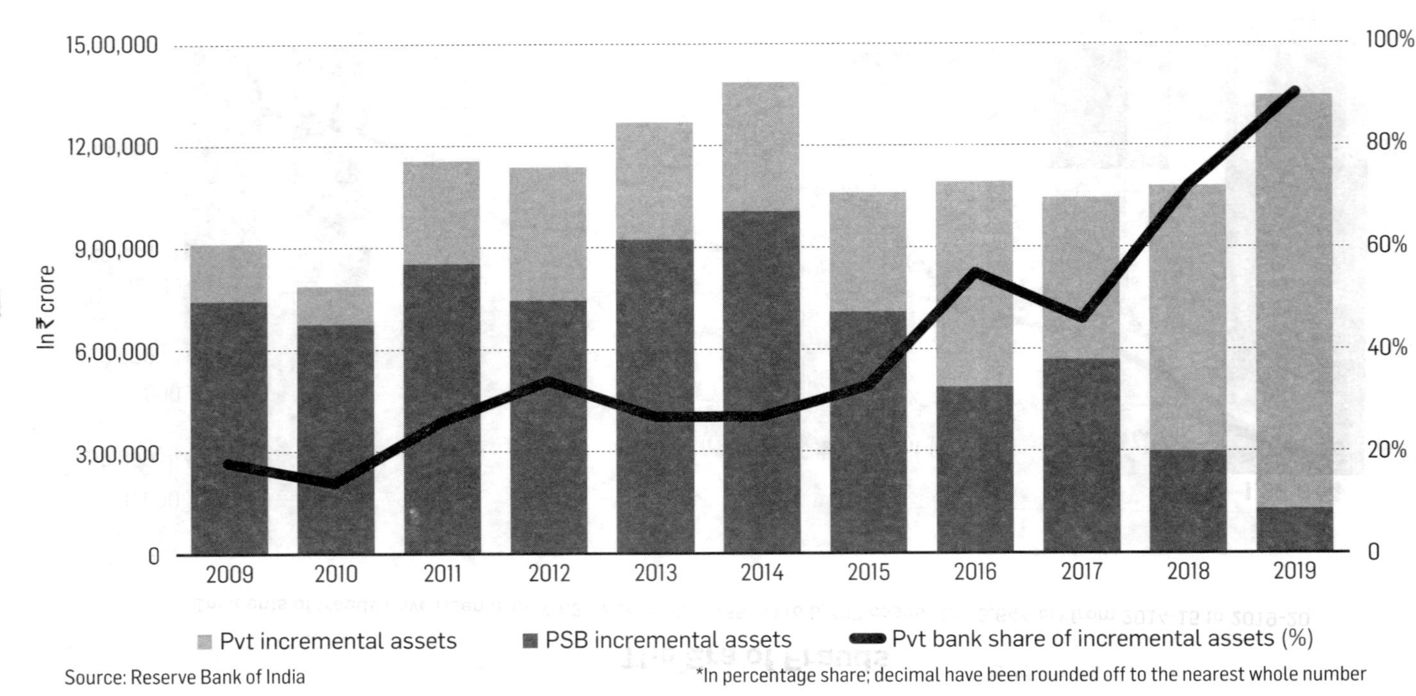

Incremental Assets: Advantage Private Banks
In ₹ crore
15,00,000
12,00,000
9,00,000
6,00,000
3,00,000
0
100%
80%
60%
40%
20%
0
2009
2010
2011
2012
2013
2014
2015
2016
2017
2018
2019
Pvt incremental assets
PSB incremental assets
Pvt bank share of incremental assets (%)
Source: Reserve Bank of India
*In percentage share; decimal have been rounded off to the nearest whole number

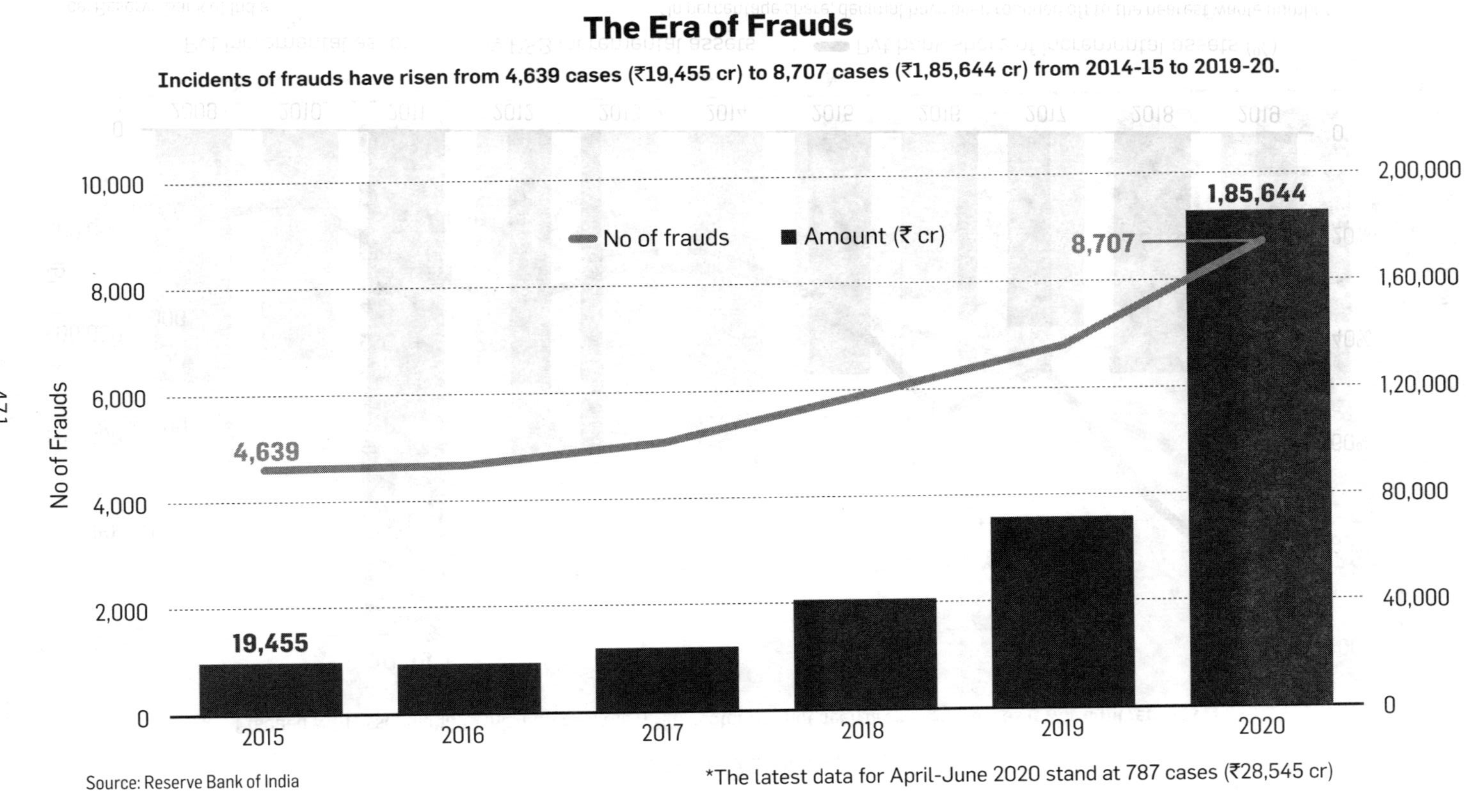
The Era of Frauds
Incidents of frauds have risen from 4,639 cases (₹19,455 cr) to 8,707 cases (₹1,85,644 cr) from 2014-15 to 2019-20.
No of frauds
Amount (₹ cr)
No of Frauds
In ₹ crore
10,000
8,000
6,000
4,000
2,000
0
2,00,000
1,60,000
1,20,000
80,000
40,000
0
4,639
19,455
8,707
1,85,644
2015
2016
2017
2018
2019
2020
Source: Reserve Bank of India
*The latest data for April-June 2020 stand at 787 cases (₹28,545 cr)

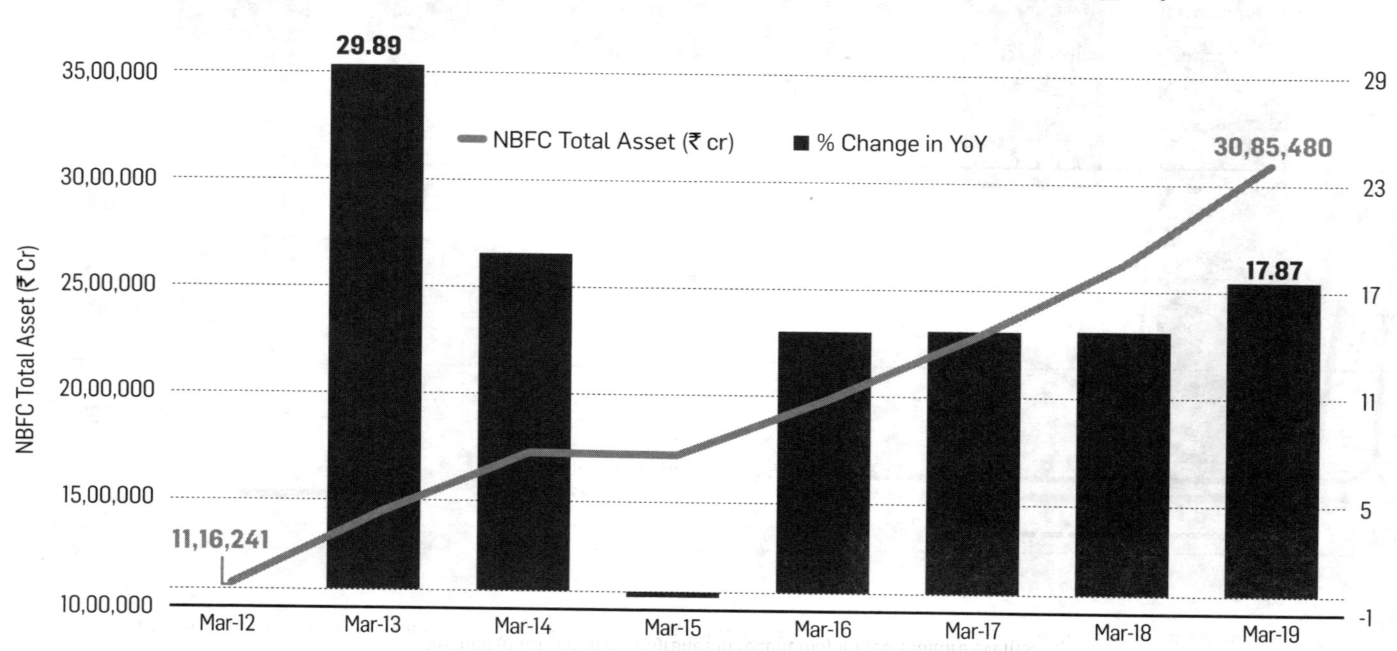
Shadow Banking
Plagued with asset–liability mismatches, the NBFC sector has not been growing as fast as it was until recently.
NBFC Total Asset (₹ cr)
% Change in YoY
29.89
17.87
11,16,241
30,85,480
35,00,000
30,00,000
25,00,000
20,00,000
15,00,000
10,00,000
NBFC Total Asset (₹ Cr)
29
23
17
11
5
-1
% Change in YoY
Mar-12
Mar-13
Mar-14
Mar-15
Mar-16
Mar-17
Mar-18
Mar-19
Source: Reserve Bank of India
*Total assets of NBFC in September 2019: ₹32,57,642 crore

Credit Falling off the Cliff

Sudden multi-notch downgrades in recent major credit failure events.

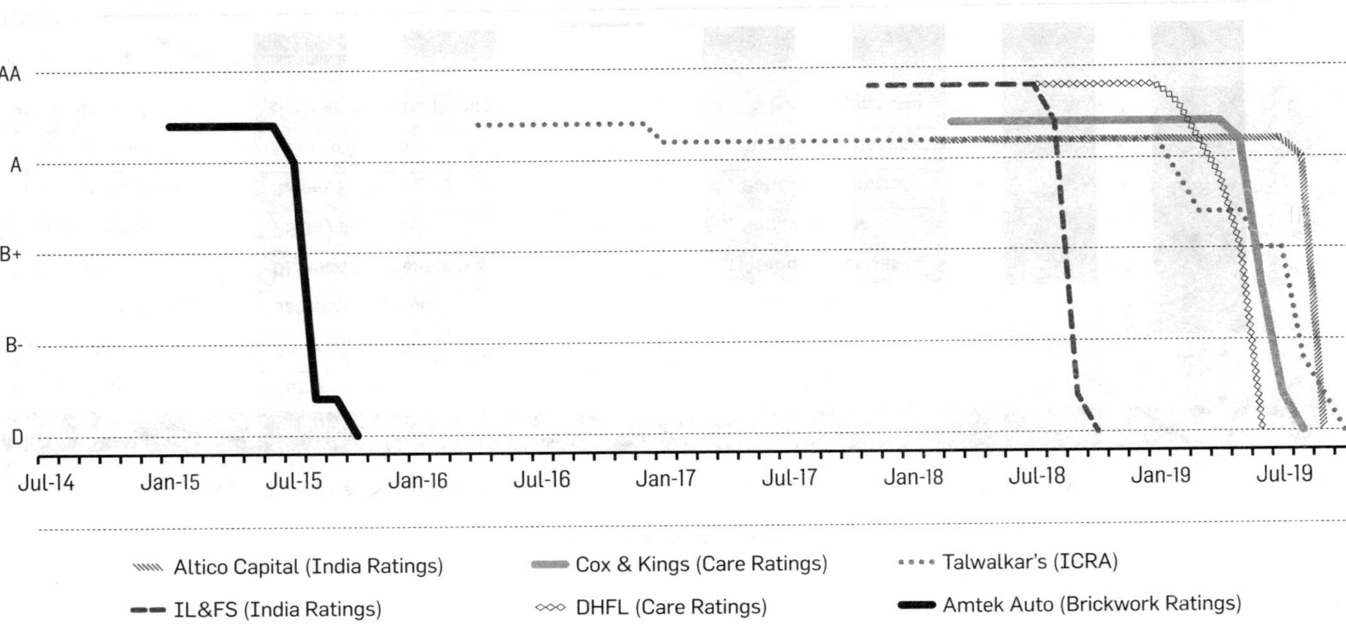

Source: Rating Releases of Rating Agencies

The Change of Baton

The gap between a PSB CEO leaving office and the successor coming in could be as much as 264 days.

Bank	Incumbent	Last Day in Office	Successor	Appointed on	Gap (in days)
Andhra Bank	**Suresh Patel**	12/31/2017	**J Packirisamy**	9/21/2018	**264**
Dena Bank	**Ashwani Kumar**	12/31/2017	**Karnam Sekar**	9/19/2018	**262**
Punjab & Sind Bank	**Jatinderbir Singh**	12/31/2017	**S Harisankar**	9/19/2018	**262**
Bank of India	**Dinabandhu Mohapatra**	6/30/2019	**Atanu Kumar Das**	1/20/2020	**204**
Bank of Baroda	**PS Jayakumar**	10/12/2019	**Sanjiv Chadha**	1/20/2020	**100**
Central Bank of India	**Rajeev Rishi**	8/1/2018	**Pallav Mohapatra**	9/21/2018	**51**
Syndcate Bank	**Melwyn O Rego**	8/13/2018	**Mrutyunjay Mahapatra**	9/21/2018	**39**
Allahabad Bank	**Usha Ananthasubramanian**	13/8/2018	**SS Mallikarjuna Rao**	9/19/2018	**37**

Source: Banks Board Bureau and bank balance sheets

Epilogue

Postponing the Inevitable?

As the book headed for printing in September 2020, I decided to focus the Epilogue on how the COVID-19 pandemic will impact Indian banking. This black swan event will have a bearing on the global banking system.

Borrowers are finding it hard to repay their loans with the economy going into a tailspin, leading to large-scale job losses. But India's banks will get a bigger shock than their peers elsewhere, as the banking system here is more fragile and vulnerable. India has the second-worst ratio of gross NPAs to total loans among the G-20 nations after the Russian Federation.

In late 1992, after Hurricane Andrew struck the Bahamas and the US states of Florida and Louisiana, and exposed the frailty of the US insurance industry, Warren Buffett famously said: 'It is only when the tide goes out that you learn who's been swimming naked.'

This was an apt description of what happened: The insurance industry was masking its adventurism but it was exposed when the good times ended. I am tempted to reference his quote and add, 'It is only after two years that we will learn which banks are healthy and which are not.'

As the pandemic hit, the RBI allowed banks to offer a six-month moratorium for all term loans. The moratorium was first given for March–May 2020 and then extended by three months to August 2020.

After the moratorium ended, a new window was opened for restructuring those loans that the borrowers were not able to service because their businesses were affected by the pandemic. The loans were to be restructured by funding interest, converting part of debt into equity and giving the borrowers more time – up to two years – to pay up.

In percentage terms, the number of borrowers opting for the moratorium began progressively decreasing but, as I write this, there is no clarity on how many would seek restructuring of their loans, and the impact this exercise would have on the banks' health.

As of 14 August, the commercial credit portfolio of the Indian banking system was a little over ₹101.5-lakh crore. Everybody and their uncle is offering guesstimates of how much of the total outstanding bank loans will be restructured. The banking community estimates that 5–8 per cent of its loan assets can end up for restructuring.

This means a little over ₹5–8-lakh crore worth of loans will be restructured. What will be its impact on the banks' balance sheets? Since the banks have to provide for 10 per cent of the loans restructured, they would need ₹50,000–80,000 crore in fresh capital. If restructuring rises to 10 per cent of loans, ₹10-lakh crore will be restructured. For that, the banks will need ₹1-lakh crore provision.

A few may need capital for credit growth after this but overall the operating profits of most banks should be able to cushion the shock of this provision. The 32 listed universal banks had a combined operating profit of close to ₹3.12-lakh crore in the financial year 2020. The share of PSBs in this was ₹1.58-lakh crore.

On the positive side, many of the banks have already taken care of the provision required for their legacy of bad loans. The so-called provision coverage ratio of SBI in the April–June quarter of the financial year 2020–21 was 86.3 per cent. For IDBI Bank, it is even higher – 94.71 per cent. Most PSBs have provided for around 80 per cent, or more, for the bad loans already recognised. Also most banks started setting aside money to provide for COVID-19-affected loans, from the March 2020 quarter.

Anatomy of the Loan Recast

Let us take a closer look at the composition of loans that are likely to be restructured. Very few corporate loans (typically ₹100 crore and above) are likely to be restructured, primarily for two reasons.

One, only those loans that were 'standard' in banking parlance as on 1 March 2020, may be restructured. Two, they need to be restructured within two years. These norms rule out deep restructuring, which some of the corporate loans require. Those loans, which had turned bad by March and need a longer timeframe for a recast, cannot be covered by this scheme.

For such loans, I assume the banks will insist on a change in ownership of the borrowing companies as outlined in the RBI's June 2019 restructuring guidelines. They will be taken to the insolvency court or there could be out-of-court settlements. Simply put, corporations that were already sick before the COVID-19 pandemic cannot gatecrash into the new restructuring scheme.

The experts' committee headed by K.V. Kamath, appointed by the RBI to work out a resolution framework for banks' corporate loans, has outlined parameters to deal with 26 sectors buffeted by COVID-19.

The panel, after 12 meetings in less than a month, recommended thresholds for different financial parameters for borrowers to get the benefit of restructuring and exceptions were made for the five most-affected sectors – automobile, aviation, roads, real estate and wholesale traders. In an interview with *Mint*, Kamath has said a deadline of March 2022 is enough to restructure the cash flows of COVID-19 affected companies.

Retail loans such as mortgage and auto loans, among others; and loans given to MSMEs may see large-scale restructuring.

Typically, retail borrowers are careful about their credit score/

ratings as any default will close the door for bank loans on them forever. Hence, there is unlikely to be any wilful default (where they have money to service the loans but are not doing so). There could be cases of customers losing their jobs or self-employed persons going through a rough patch. Some of them may quit their vocations and close the loans, while others will look for restructuring.

MSME Complexity

The most complex piece is the MSME segment. Until the government redefined such enterprises in May 2020, there were about 63.05 million micro enterprises, 0.33 million small ones and about 5,000 medium ones. The sector is the second-biggest employer in the country after agriculture with 31 per cent share of the GDP.

Even in normal times, the MSMEs have problems with cash flows as they are forced to wait to collect bills and, quite often, the government is the culprit in holding back payments. The MSMEs lack the balance sheet strength to carry such receivables.

The pandemic has played havoc in this segment. Under a ₹3-lakh crore, four-year, fully government-guaranteed loan scheme (with one-year moratorium), the banks sanctioned ₹1.58-lakh crore by August-end and disbursed at least ₹1.11-lakh crore. Even this may not be of great help to all the MSMEs. A simple extension of the moratorium will not end the woes of those who have eroded their capital.

The ₹20,000 crore sub-debt scheme with a 90 per cent government guarantee, part of the Atmanirbhar Bharat package, may come in handy for them. Under this scheme, MSME promoters can be given money equal to 15 per cent of stake in the company or ₹75 lakh, whichever is lower, for a maximum of 10 years, with a seven-year moratorium on principal payment. The borrower has to pay the interest only for the first seven years and repay the principal within three years after the moratorium ends.

Some of the MSMEs and retail customers were not paying back the banks until August as they preferred to conserve cash in uncertain times. Some of them might have started servicing bank loans after the moratorium was lifted.

One thing is for sure that the latest restructuring of loans is very different from any past schemes. Since 2001, the RBI has come out with a string of schemes at regular intervals – CDR, S4A, 5/25, SDR – till it withdrew all of them in February 2018 to stop their rampant misuse.

There are enough filters in the COVID-19 loan restructuring scheme to prevent misuse, both by the borrowers and banks. Still, will this tool delay growth in banks' bad loans? We will have to wait for two years to find out.

Meanwhile, a public interest litigation entertained by India's highest court on waiver of interest on interest, or compounding interest on loans during the moratorium period, has added a new dimension to the debate on what the judiciary can do and how helpless is the banking regulator.

A commercial bank does not run currency printing presses. It is a financial intermediary or the so-called pass-through that takes money from depositors and lends that money to borrowers, keeping a margin. How can it waive the interest on loans given to the borrowers when it is paying interest to depositors on money kept with it? Should the depositors subsidise the borrowers?

One thing is for sure though, the cost of waiving compounded interest during the moratorium period will be borne by the government and not the banks.

The case will create a precedent that encourages borrowers to seek some legal option to avoid paying interest in the future, if they are hit by drought, flood or any other calamities.

This will also shake the confidence of investors in banks. The quality of loan assets of banks has often been suspect. But the intervention of the judiciary in the banking business will make investors even more nervous and more likely to question projected flow of interest income.

Barring a few, most banks saw a drop in NPAs in the June 2020 quarter. They made hefty provisions, anticipating deterioration in the quality of assets. Will that protect their balance sheets? It all depends on how fast economic activities pick up and how borrowers who have availed themselves of the banks' offer for moratorium behave.

NPAs to Rise

The gross NPAs of the banking system, which rose to 12.5 per cent in March 2018, dropped to 9.7 per cent a year later. By September 2019, NPAs were at 9.3 per cent and 8.5 per cent in March 2020.

The corona virus changed the scene dramatically. The graph will reverse again and gross NPAs could spike to as much as to 14.7 per cent of bank loans by March 2021, the RBI's July 2020 Financial Stability Report says. However, that is the worst-case scenario. A more conservative estimate puts the gross NPA figure in March 2021 at 12.5 per cent.

If indeed Indian banks' gross NPAs rise to 14.7 per cent, it will be a 22-year high. The last time banks had a worse higher gross NPAs was in 1999 – 15.9 per cent. That dropped to 14 per cent in 2000, and to a single-digit 9.4 per cent in 2003.

The government-owned banks are worse off than their private-sector peers. Their gross bad loan ratio could increase to 15.2 per cent by March under the baseline scenario, the RBI report says.

This has always been the pattern. Almost immediately after the introduction of income recognition norms, the gross NPAs of the entire banking industry turned out to be 19.07 per cent in 1994. But for PSBs, NPAs were 24.8 per cent.

In addition, many Indian banks, particularly in the public sector, do not have enough capital. As their bad loans grow, their capital will erode (due to the need for provisions), and this will cripple their ability to lend.

The capital-to-risk-weighted-assets ratio of Indian banks will drop from 14.6 per cent in March 2020 to 13.3 per cent in March 2021 under the baseline scenario and to 11.8 per cent under the very severe stress scenario, the RBI report says. 'Stress test results indicate that five banks may fail to meet the minimum capital level by March 2021 in a very severe stress scenario.' It does not name the banks but one can easily guess which ones are referred to.

Most private banks have already raised dollops of capital. In mid-September, the government sought Parliament's approval for infusing ₹20,000 crore in PSBs in financial year 2020–21. Will this be enough? The Union Budget in February 2020 did not make any provision for it even as the number of PSBs has shrunk following the mergers, in sync with the drive for consolidation

Global rating agency Moody's Investors Service pegs the capital requirement for India's PSBs at between ₹1.9-lakh crore to ₹2.1-lakh crore over the next two years to shore up their balance sheets. This takes into account the rising bad loans due to the pandemic and lockdown. The most likely source of capital, it says, will be the government.

Banks which do not get capital will be caught swimming naked.

Risk Aversion Vs Prudence

Meanwhile, India's banking regulator is upset with the extreme risk aversion of commercial banks, which is holding back the flow of credit to the productive sectors. This undermines the role of banks as the principal financial intermediary in the economy, the RBI says. However, the bankers have a different story to tell. They are not risk-averse; they are just being prudent.

Who is right? Probably, both.

It is a Catch-22. Bankers are not giving credit to those who are perceived to be capable of playing a role in pushing growth and creating employment as they do not find these businesses credit-worthy. And, the banks are willing to lend to those businesses which are not asking for money!

At the root of the debate on risk averseness versus prudent banking is a belief that credit growth can push economic growth. Can it? Shouldn't this be the other way round as in industry asks for credit when it wants to invest, seeing growing demand?

Historically, whenever bank credit has been used as a vehicle for economic growth, banks have ended up piling bad assets. This had happened in the 1990s, after the economic liberalisation, and also in the recent past when after the global economic crisis, banks were encouraged to open the tap to all and sundry to fuel growth and insulate the Indian economy from the impact of the crisis.

Cheap money flooded the system and bankers merrily gave loans to undeserving borrowers who took on debt instead of putting up their own equity. Essentially, the banks ended up providing risk capital. Their indiscretion was exposed after the RBI conducted an AQR, the first-of-its-kind audit of banks' books, in the financial year 2015–16. By then, the bad loans had ballooned and 11 PSBs were restrained from giving fresh loans.

In mid-August 2020, the deposit portfolio of the Indian banking system was a little over ₹140-lakh crore, growing at 3.8 per cent over the past year. In contrast, credit growth has been a negative 1.5 per cent. In the financial year ending March 2020, bank credit had grown at 6.1 per cent, less than half of the previous year's growth (13.3 per cent).

The RBI data on credit flow to different sectors, based on the businesses of 33 large banks with 90 per cent share in bank credit, show that in May 2020 loans given to agriculture and allied activities grew at 3.5 per cent, down from 7.8 per cent in May 2019. The credit flow to industry had grown by only 1.7 per cent, against 6.4 per cent in the same period of the previous year. Growth in loans to the services sector, and personal loans, too, has dropped.

The MSMEs is the only segment to which bank loans have grown. The catch is that banks have been giving the MSMEs money only because the government is standing guarantee. The banking system is expected to give ₹3-lakh crore collateral-free 'revival' loans to those units that have bank loans on their books already. The four-year loans, including a one-year moratorium, is fully backed by a government guarantee.

If a customer defaults, the government will compensate the bank. The government will make good 75 per cent of such losses immediately, and pay the rest after all attempts at recovery have failed.

Any business unit – it may or may not have the MSME tag – which has a turnover of ₹100 crore and ₹25 crore outstanding bank credit as on 29 February 2020, can get up to 20 per cent of its outstanding debt as a fresh loan from the banks, no questions asked. This pegs the maximum fresh credit for one unit at ₹5 crore. Any unit that had not delayed paying an instalment for its existing loan beyond 60 days is eligible for this facility.

However, the MSMEs alone cannot push up credit growth, as the banks' exposure to this segment is less than a fifth share of the bank credit market. Barring MSMEs, a few road projects and some public sector undertakings are the only customers of bank credit at the moment. Most well-rated large industries to whom the banks would love to give credit are deleveraging instead of asking for loans.

What are the banks doing with their money? They are parking it in the RBI's reverse repo window and earning a measly 3.35 per cent interest. If there are opportunities to earn more by giving loans, only a fool will settle for 3.35 per cent, and we must assume that bankers are no fools. They are doing this because the options are limited.

Policy Rate at a Historic Low

The RBI went for a deep 1.15 percentage points rate cut at two off-cycle meetings in March and May 2020, paring its policy repo rate to a historic low of 4 per cent to spur demand for loans and drive economic growth.

The repo rate is the rate at which commercial banks borrow money from the central bank and the reverse repo rate (at 3.35 per cent, this too is at its lowest) is the rate at which commercial banks park their excess money with the central bank. When the banking system is flush with liquidity – which has been the case in the financial year 2020–21 – the reverse repo becomes the de facto policy rate.

Yes, indeed some of the banks (primarily those in the private sector) have been growing their loan books handsomely, but the story behind the growth is neither the absence of risk averseness, nor lack of prudence.

They are smart enough to snatch away corporate borrowers from public sector peers by offering cheaper credit. Simply put, the overall credit pie is not growing but a few banks are eating into others' market share by repricing loans at lower rates.

Some believe that the fear of being hounded by the investigating agencies is contributing to the government banks' lack of enthusiasm for giving fresh credit. (All accounts exceeding ₹50 crore, if classified as bad loans, must be examined by the banks through a forensic audit for possible fraud.) This may not be true. Most banks have now started following the quantitative model for risk assessment, laced with qualitative inputs. The CEOs do not take the credit calls; credit committees do.

It is unfair to expect risk capital from the banks to prop up the economy. Once there is demand and companies are willing to invest to put up factories, keeping their own equity on the table, the banks will offer credit. The demand will be created only after consumers are convinced that the pandemic is tamed. In its fight against the novel coronavirus, the government has not exactly covered itself with glory so far.

Appendix
The Stressed Sectors

Four stressed sectors contributed the most to the pile of banks' bad assets. Here is a close look at these.

Telecom

India is the world's second-largest telecommunications market. The banking sector's exposure to the telcos was ₹1.3-lakh crore as of January 2020, according to a Credit Suisse report. The industry's overall indebtedness is close to ₹4.4-lakh crore (inclusive of amount payable to government towards spectrum purchased).

Over the years, the rating agencies have taken negative actions on some telcos. Intense competition has dented revenue prospects and the so-called interest coverage ratio – calculated by dividing a company's earnings before interest and taxes (EBIT) by its interest expenses – for the sector was around 1 in financial year 2018–19 (for a sample of three private telcos as well as state-owned operators, tracked by rating agency ICRA Ltd). Any interest coverage ratio of 1.5 or lower calls into question a company's ability to meet interest expenses.

In addition, the telcos face a burden centred on the definition of their adjusted gross revenue (AGR). The telecom service providers pay a percentage of their revenues as licence fee, as well as spectrum usage charges to the government.

According to them, non-core business such as rent and income from the sale of handsets or roaming charges should be excluded from the revenue of which they pay a percentage.

The Supreme Court has come through with a judgment giving ten years to telcos to pay AGR with annual payments. In the same order, the court said decisions on spectrums were referred to the Telecom Regulatory Authority of India (TRAI).

The DoT has pegged Bharti Airtel Ltd's dues at ₹43,980 crore, Vodafone Idea Ltd's at ₹58,254 crore and the Tata Group's at ₹16,798 crore aggregating to around little over ₹1.19-lakh crore.

This adds to pressures on an industry already struggling with elevated debt levels and pressures on revenue and profitability. The aggregate revenue of the telecom sector has been coming down. Going by the Cellular Operators Association of India (COAI) data, the industry's average gross revenue dropped from ₹1.91-lakh crore in financial year 2017 to ₹1.56-lakh crore in 2018. In the first half of 2019, till September 2019, it was ₹1.08-lakh crore.

Quoting Parliamentary questions, COAI pegs the debt of the telecom industry at ₹7.7-lakh crore in 2018. An April 2020 ICRA report says the debt level of the industry, which moderated to ₹4.4-lakh crore in March 2020, from ₹5-lakh crore a year ago, would rise to ₹4.6-lakh crore by March 2021 on account of expected participation of telecom operators in upcoming spectrum auctions (towards 4G renewals in select circles) as well as AGR dues. This is despite an improvement in cash flow and moderation in capital spend.

Predatory pricing by one telecom operator resulted in the bankruptcy of several others resulting in drastic consolidation. In June 2020, the NCLT approved a resolution plan for Aircel Ltd – submitted by an ARC – at just 1.5 per cent of the total bank dues of ₹20,000 crore owed by the company which had moved the insolvency court after it failed to repay loans.

Another telco, Reliance Communications Ltd, filed its resolution plan with the bankruptcy court in March 2020 with ₹46,000 debt to 53 financial creditors including banks, NBFCs and various funds.

Power

The power segment is in equally bad shape. There are coal-based projects worth 15,200 megawatt (MW) which have been completed, but do not have the power purchase agreements (PPAs) and hence are not eligible for fuel-supply agreements. A power project without a fuel supply agreement is a dud asset. The cost of imported coal is prohibitive and makes it unprofitable.

Another set of coal-based power projects with total capacity of 13,700 MW are in various stages of construction. Captive coal blocks will reduce costs but rupee depreciation (these power plants were planned in 2010-11 when the rupee-dollar exchange rate was 44/45 vs. 75/76 now) and delays have made them unviable.

Besides coal-thermal, there are stranded gas-based thermal power plants which were slated to produce 15,000MW. Similarly hydro power projects for 2,000MW are stalled.

The UDAY (Ujwal Discom Assurance Yojna) Scheme announced in November 2015 by the central government for the stressed electricity distribution companies (discoms) envisaged taking over 75 per cent of the debt of power distribution companies or discoms by Indian states. The plan has been to bring down interest costs and push up the revenue by raising tariffs. But although they have reduced interest costs, many discoms are facing regulatory hurdles for increasing tariffs and the aggregate technical and commercial losses have risen.

After the implementation of the UDAY Scheme, the discoms' ratings have taken a beating as the tariffs have not been hiked.

According to ICRA, the median tariff hike for discoms at all-India level had reduced from 8 per cent for financial year 2015 to 4 per cent for financial year 2016 and 2017 and further to 3 per cent and 1 per cent for 2018 and 2019, respectively. ICRA also said recently, that out of the 14 states which issued tariff orders for financial year 2020, the median tariff hike was as low as 1 per cent. Regulators in five states did not approve any tariff hike for the year and two states lowered tariff rates.

The total outstanding dues owed by distribution companies to power producers rose by around 37 per cent to ₹69,558 crore in September 2019 over the same month of the previous year (September 2018), reflecting the stress in the sector.

Distribution companies owed a total of ₹50,583 crore to power generation companies in September 2018, according to web portal and app namely PRAAPTI (Payment Ratification and Analysis in Power Procurement for Bringing Transparency in Invoicing of Generators). The portal was launched in May 2018 to make power purchase transactions between generators and discoms transparent.

The Department of Financial Services of the ministry of finance prepared a list of 34 coal-based power projects, mostly private, with a 40,130 MW capacity which were considered 'stressed' by power ministry in March 2017. They had ₹1.88-lakh crore outstanding debt. Fourteen stressed power projects, with a capacity of 16,450MW, and outstanding debt of ₹66,811 crore were resolved by June 2020. Thirteen more, with a capacity of 16,227MW and ₹93,095 crore outstanding debt could be resolved at the insolvency court or outside it, while no resolution has been rolled out for seven of them, with 7,410MW capacity and ₹27,868 crore exposure to the lenders.

In January 2019, Germany, one of the world's biggest consumers of coal, announced that it would shut down all 84 of its coal-fired power plants over the next 19 years in the fight against climate change. Two years before that, China had dropped its plan to build at least 100 coal-fired plants. But India continues to run old thermal power plants with small capacity which present a threat to the environment. Many of the old power plants of NTPC Ltd have outlived their rated life-cycle and need to be decommissioned. It will take a while for new plants to start running, and tariffs will be relatively higher.

NTPC Vidyut Vyapar Nigam Ltd, NTPC's trading arm, can buy from the 15,200MW power projects that do not have PPAs. The blended cost – the cost of power purchased from these plants and from NTPC's new generation plants – will be lower and bring down the cost for the discoms.

EPC

Over ₹1-lakh crore bank loans is stuck in the engineering, procurement and construction segment. This is not showing signs of resolution. In August 2016, the Cabinet Committee on Economic Affairs, headed by Prime Minister Narendra Modi, approved a series of initiatives to revive the construction sector.

The National Institution for Transforming India, or NITI Aayog, quickly followed up to address the delayed payment or non-payment by the government departments and public sector undertakings after completion of projects. Typically, all these projects are affected by disputes which delay payments.

It was decided that 75 per cent of the payments to the contractors must be released against bank guarantees, where the arbitration awards have gone in their favour but are being challenged. The payment will flow into an escrow account and the lenders' dues will be cleared on priority.

However, no progress is seen as yet. As the EPC companies have no assets, there is hardly any option before the lenders but liquidation. When they become sick, these EPC firms face an outflow of talented engineers and employees with superior technical knowledge. In addition, the flow of potential orders dry up, bank guarantees are invoked and indebtedness rises. They also cannot bid for new projects.

Structurally, the solutions for this sector lie outside the purview of NCLT. While the credentials of the EPC companies will also be important, resolution ultimately rests on policy changes to address the known problems.

Steel

The only segment which has seen substantial improvement is steel, where the banks' exposure is to the tune of around ₹3.3-lakh crore. Steel companies' earnings doubled following anti-dumping measures in the shape of a minimum import price, coupled with availability of raw material following regular auctions by iron ore miners.

The government's decision to give preference to domestically manufactured iron and steel products is also helping the steel producers. There is demand for the alloy due to ongoing and upcoming projects of Indian Railways, the dedicated freight corridor, regional airports, smart cities, and the mushrooming of affordable housing projects, among others. This is why stressed steelmakers are seeing faster resolutions of bad assets.

However, the promoters of steel plants do not want the lenders to smell money while the NCLT process is on. They have been trying to delay the IBC processes in order to enjoy the good times for as long as possible before having to pay up, or lose their assets.

List of Abbreviations

AGR : Adjusted Gross Revenue
AM : Alternative Mechanism
AMC : Asset Management Company
AML : Anti-Money Laundering
AQR : Asset Quality Review
AUM : Assets Under Management
BBB : Banks Board Bureau
BFS : Board for Financial Supervision
BIFR : Board for Industrial and Financial Reconstruction
BIS : Banks for International Settlements
BSNL : Bharat Sanchar Nigam Limited
CAG : Comptroller and Auditor General of India
CAGR : Compounded Annual Growth Rate
CAMELS : Capital adequacy, asset quality, management, earning and liquidity and sensitivity
CAR : Capital Adequacy Ration
CASA : Current Account and Savings Account
CBI : Central Bureau of Investigation
CBS : Core Banking Solution
CCEA : Cabinet Committee on Economic Affairs
CCI : Competition Commission of India
CDR : Corporate Debt Restructuring
CEIB : Central Economic Intelligence Bureau
CET1 : Common Equity Tier 1
CP : Commercial Paper
CRA : Credit Rating Agency

CRAR : Capital to Risk-weighted Assets Ratio
CRILC : Central Repository of Information on Large Credits
CRR : Cash Reserve Ratio
CTR : Cash Transaction Report
CVC : Central Vigilance Commission
DBS : Department of Banking Supervision
DBS : Development Bank of Singapore Ltd
DCA : Debtor–Creator Agreement
DCCO : Date of Commencement of Commercial Operation
DEA : Department of Economic Affairs
DFI : Development Finance Institutions
DFS : Department of Financial Services
DICGC : Deposit Insurance and Credit Guarantee Corporation
DIPAM : Department of Investment and Public Asset Management
DoPT : Department of Personnel and Training
DPR : Detailed Project Report
DRT : Debt Recovery Tribunal
ED : Enforcement Directorate
EMTN : Euro Medium Term Note
EPBG : Export Performance Bank Guarantee
EPC : Engineering, Procurement and Construction
EPFO : Employees Provident Fund Organisation
EWT : Employees Welfare Trust
EY : Ernst & Young
FASB : Financial Accounting Standard Board (US)
FDI : Foreign Direct Investment
FEDA : Foreign Exchange Dealers' Association
FERA : Foreign Exchange Regulation Act
FICCI : Federation of Indian Chambers of Commerce and Industry
FIMMDA : Fixed Income Money Market & Derivatives Association of India
FIU-IND : Financial Intelligence Unit of the Government of India
FSDC : Financial Stability and Development Council
FSLRC : Financial Sector Legislative Reforms Commission
FSR : Financial Stability Report
GDP : Gross Domestic Product
GRAF : Governance, Reward and Accountability Framework
HDFC : Housing Development Finance Corporation Ltd
HFC : Housing Finance Company
HSBC : Hongkong and Shanghai Banking Corporation
IBA : Indian Banks' Association
IBBI : Insolvency & Bankruptcy Board of India

IBC : Insolvency and Bankruptcy Code
ICA : Inter-Creditor Agreement
ICBA : Independent Community Bankers of America
ICD : Inter-Corporate Deposits
ICICI : Industrial Credit and Investment Corporation of India Ltd
IDBI : Industrial Development Bank of India
IFCI : Industrial Finance Corporation of India
IIFCL : India Infrastructure Finance Company Limited
IMF : International Monetary Fund
InvIT : Infrastructure Investment Trust
IPPAI : Independent Power Producers Association of India
IRAC : Income Recognition and Asset Classification
IRDA : Insurance Regulatory and Development Authority
IRDP : Integrated Rural Development Programme
IREDA : Indian Renewable Energy Development Agency
IRP : Interim Resolution Professional
ISIN : International Securities Identification Number
JLF : Joint Lenders' Forum
KCC : Kisan Credit Cards
LAP : Loans Against Property
LC : Letter of Credit
LIC : Life Insurance Corporation
LoU : Letter of Undertaking
MoU : Memorandum of Understanding
MPC : Monetary Policy Committee
MPID : Maharashtra Protection of Interest of Depositors
MSME : Micro, Small and Medium Enterprises
NABARD : National Bank for Agriculture and Rural Development
NACAS : National Advisory Committee on Accounting Standards
NAV : Net Asset Value
NBFC : Non-Banking Financial Companies
NCLAT : National Company Law Appellate Tribunal
NCLT : National Company Law Tribunal
NCUA : National Credit Union Administration
NDA : National Democratic Alliance
NHAI : National Highways Authority of India
NHB : National Housing Bank
NIIF : National Investment and Infrastructure Fund
NSE : National Stock Exchange
OMT : Outright Monetary Transactions
PCA : Prompt Corrective Action

PFC	:	Power Finance Corporation
PFRDA	:	Pension Fund Regulatory and Development Authority
PIB	:	Press Information Bureau
PMJDY	:	Pradhan Mantri Jan Dhan Yojana
PNB	:	Punjab National Bank
PSB	:	Public Sector Bank
PSU	:	Public Sector Undertaking
PTI	:	Press Trust of India
QIP	:	Qualified Institutional Placement
RBI	:	Reserve Bank of India
RDDBFI	:	Recovery of Debts Due to the Banks and Financial Institutions (Act)
REIT	:	Real Estate Investment Trust
RoC	:	Registrar of Companies
RP	:	Resolution Professional
RTI	:	Right to Information
SBI	:	State Bank of India
SBLC	:	Stand-by Letter of Credit
SDR	:	Strategic Debt Restructuring
SEBI	:	Securities and Exchange Board of India
SFIO	:	Serious Fraud Investigation Office
SIDBI	:	Small Industries Development Bank of India
SMA	:	Special Mention Accounts
SoI	:	Statement of Intent
SR	:	Security Receipt
SSRC	:	Specialised Supervisory and Regulatory Cadre
STR	:	Suspicious Transaction Report
SWIFT	:	Society for Worldwide Interbank Financial Telecommunications
UTI	:	Unit Trust of India
WRP	:	Weighted Received Premium

Glossary

5/25 Scheme: A refinancing and repayment scheme introduced by RBI in 2014, it allows banks to extend long-term loans of 20 to 25 years (to infra projects) to match the cash flow of projects while refinancing them every five or seven years. The government withdrew this scheme in 2018.

Advanced Tier-1 (AT-1) bonds: Like any other bonds issued by banks and companies, these bonds pay a fixed rate of interest at regular interval. Typically, these bonds, mostly picked up by mutual funds, pay a slightly higher rate of interest compared to similar, non-perpetual bonds. However, the issuing bank has no obligation to pay back the principal to investors. These are considered to be high-risk, high-yield bonds.

Analytic firewall policy: Chinese wall between the sales executives and the analytical team in a rating agency, ensuring that analysts do not know what the credit rating agency is earning, and the sales executives do not have access to any information about the rating beyond what is in the public domain.

Anti-Money Laundering (AML): It refers to the laws, regulations and procedures intended to prevent criminals from disguising illegally obtained funds as legitimate income. AML regulations require financial institutions to monitor customers' transactions and report suspicious financial activities.

Appeal committee: The committee which looks into the second appeal filed by any company that is not satisfied with the rating assigned by the rating committee.

Asset–liability mismatch: A mismatch that occurs when a financial institution's assets (loans) and liabilities (money taken in the form of deposits or bonds) do not match. Ideally, they should match in terms of tenure as well as amount.

Asset Management Company (AMC): A company that invests its clients' pooled fund into securities that match its declared financial objectives. Such companies are called mutual funds in India and they run different schemes for investments in debt and equity.

Asset Quality Review (AQR): A process started by RBI in June 2015, AQR is a first-of-its-kind audit of bank's books by the central bank. The banks were directed to declare their bad loans and come up clean in six quarters between December 2015 and March 2017. It was part of RBI governor Raghuram Rajan's initiative.

Asset Reconstruction Company (ARC): Is a specialised financial institution that buys the NPAs or bad assets from banks and financial institutions, and helps clean up their balance sheets. It makes money recovering such assets.

Bad assets: Assets on which a bank does not earn any interest. Additionally, it needs to set aside money to provide for such assets. An illiquid asset is also called a bad asset when its secondary market disappears.

Bad bank: A bad bank is a bank set up to buy the bad loans and other illiquid holdings of another financial institution. The entity holding significant non-performing assets sell these assets to the bad bank. By transferring such assets to the bad bank, the original institution clears its balance sheet. Bad banks are typically set up in times of crisis when financial institutions get saddled with bad loans.

Balance sheet: A statement of the assets, liabilities and capital of a business or other organisation at a particular point in time, detailing the balance of income and expenditure over the preceding period.

Banks Board Bureau (BBB): An autonomous body of the Government of India, functioning since April 2016, the Bureau was created following the recommendations of P.J. Nayak Committee (2014). With the main objective to empower the boards of PSBs, it is tasked to improve their governance, recommend selection of chiefs of government-owned banks and financial institutions, and help banks develop strategies and capital raising plans.

Basel Committee on Banking Supervision (BCBS): Headquartered at the Bank for International Settlements in Basel, Switzerland, it aims to strengthen the regulation, supervision and practices of banks and enhance financial stability. Primarily, the BCBS serves to help national banking and financial market supervisory bodies move towards a more unified, globalised approach to solving regulatory issues. It has three sets of banking regulations (Basel Accords) that help to ensure financial institutions have enough capital at hand to handle obligations. The Accords set the capital adequacy ratio (CAR) to define these holdings for banks.

Black swan phenomenon: A concept derived from the 'black swan' event or theory – a metaphor that describes an event that is a surprise (to the observer) and has a major impact. The theory was developed by Nassim Nicholas Taleb to explain the disproportionate role of high-impact, hard-to-predict and rare events that are beyond the realm of normal expectations in history, science, finance and technology.

Board for Financial Supervision (BFS): Set up in November 1994 to supervise the money market institutions in the country, the BFS is an autonomous body under the RBI. The primary objective of BFS is to undertake consolidated supervision of the financial sector comprising commercial banks, financial institutions and non-banking finance companies.

Buyer's credit: A short-term loan facility extended to an importer by an overseas lender, such as a bank or a financial institution, to finance the purchase of capital goods, services, and other big-ticket items. The importer to whom the loan is issued is the buyer of goods, while the exporter is the seller. Buyer's credit allows the buyer, or the importer, to borrow at rates lower than what would be available domestically.

Cabinet Committee on Economic Affairs (CCEA): Chaired by the prime minister, the committee reviews economic trends, problems and prospects 'for evolving a consistent and integrated economic policy', coordinate all activities requiring policy decisions at the highest level, deal with fixation of prices of agricultural produce and prices of essential commodities as well as foreign investment.

CAMELS (capital adequacy, asset quality, management, earnings, liquidity and system and control): A recognised international rating system used by regulatory banking authorities to rate financial institutions according to the six factors represented by its acronym. Supervisory authorities assign each bank a score on a scale. A rating of one is considered the best, and a rating of five is considered the worst for each factor. Internationally, 'S' stands for sensitivity for market risks.

Capital Adequacy Ratio (CAR): A measurement of a bank's available capital expressed as a percentage of a bank's risk-weighted credit exposures. Also known as Capital to Risk Assets Ratio or CRAR, it is the ratio of a bank's capital to its risk. National regulators track a bank's CAR to ensure that it can absorb a reasonable amount of loss and complies with statutory capital requirements.

CASA: Low cost current and savings accounts. Banks do not pay any interest on current account and pay relatively low interest on savings accounts. Until 2011, interest on savings accounts was mandated. The higher the CASA, the lower the cost of money for a bank.

Cash credit: A kind of perpetual loan, in contrast to a term loan, which gets repaid over a finite period. This is mainly secured by the working capital assets of a company in the form of raw materials, finished goods and receivables.

Cash Reserve Ratio (CRR): A portion of deposits a bank does not earn any interest on, and needs to keep with the RBI. The aim is to ensure that banks do not run out of cash to meet the payment demands of their depositors. CRR is also a tool used by a central bank to control liquidity in the banking system.

Cash Transaction Report (CTR): This is used by the banking system to help prevent instances of money laundering. In India, banks are required to submit this form for any transaction of ₹10 lakh and above in an account.

Central Repository of Information on Large Credits (CRILC): Set up in 2014, it is a credit information system where banks have to submit reports on all borrowers with an aggregate fund-based and non-fund-based exposure of ₹5 crore or more. They also need to classify borrowers as Special Mention Accounts (SMA) of various levels to gauge the probability of such accounts turning bad.

Collateral: A borrower's pledge (in a lending agreement) of specific property to a lender, to secure repayment of the loan.

Common Equity Tier 1 Ratio (CET1): A measurement of a bank's core equity capital, compared with its total risk-weighted assets that signifies a bank's financial strength. CET1 capital includes the core capital that a bank holds in its capital structure.

Compounded Annual Growth Rate (CAGR): The year-on-year growth rate of an investment over a specified period of time. It is calculated by taking the nth root of the total percentage growth rate, where 'n' is the number of years in the period being considered.

Core Banking Solution (CBS): A software for recording transactions, storing customer information, calculating interest and completing the process of passing entries in a single database.

Corporate Debt Restructuring (CDR): Introduced by RBI in August 2011, CDR offered flexibility to the banking system for restructuring bad debt. The idea was to pool all the banking creditors in large accounts for restructuring. It is often achieved by way of negotiation between distressed companies and their creditors, such as banks and other financial institutions, by reducing the total amount of debt the company has, and also by decreasing the interest rate it pays while increasing the period of time it has to pay the obligation back.

Cost-to-income ratio: An efficiency measure, similar to the operating margin, defined by operating expenses divided by operating income. Unlike the operating margin, lower cost-to-income ratio is better. The cost-to-income ratio is most commonly used in the financial sector, and can be used for benchmarking by a bank when reviewing its operational efficiency.

Credit Guarantee Enhancement Corporation: Formed by RBI to help companies boost credit rating and raise cheaper funding.

Credit rating: An assessment of the creditworthiness of a borrower in general terms or with respect to a particular debt or financial obligation. A credit rating can be assigned to any entity that seeks to borrow money – an individual, corporation, state or provincial authority, or sovereign government.

Credit Rating Agency (CRA): An entity that assesses the ability and willingness of the issuer company for timely payment of interest and principal on a debt instrument. It evaluates and assesses an individual's or a company's creditworthiness.

Cumulative redeemable preference shares: A preference share is called cumulative when the outstanding payment of a dividend is cumulative. If a company does not have the financial capability to pay a dividend to the owners of its preference shares at any point of time, then it will not pay a dividend to its common shareholders, as long as the preference shareholders are not paid.

Debtor–Creditor Agreements (DCA): An agreement between creditor and debtor, entered into during the period of corporate debt restructuring scheme. Under the agreement, the debtor agrees not do certain things without the prior consent of CDR Empowered Group, like not to create or assume additional indebtedness, make any investment or divert funds except in ordinary course of business, transfer or alienate assets, take steps to reorganize the company, etc.

Deferred payment guarantee: A guarantee issued by a bank at the request of a customer for buying goods or machinery, with a commitment to pay after a specified time in either lump sum or instalments. The bank undertakes to pay the instalments due under the deferred payment schedule.

Department of Financial Services (DFS): It is a department under the Ministry of Finance, Government of India. DFS deals with issues relating to PSBs, financial institutions, public sector insurance companies, pension reforms, etc.

Development Finance Institution (DFI): A special class of lenders created in Independent India, these were promoted, owned and assisted by the government to offer long-term project financing, particularly for infrastructure. Banks were meant to focus on short-term loans such as the working capital needs of commercial borrowers.

Dividend distribution tax: Tax levied on dividends paid by a company to its shareholders out of its profits.

Due diligence: An investigation or audit of a potential investment. Due diligence serves to confirm all material facts with regard to a sale.

Escrow account: A third-party account where funds are kept before they are transferred to the ultimate party. It provides security against scams and frauds, especially with high asset value and dispute-prone sectors like real estate. Escrow accounts can hold money, securities, funds, and other assets.

Evergreening: This refers to the practice of 'managing' the balance sheet through disbursing fresh loans to book artificial profits by recovering interest on previous loans. This is basically a process of showing loans as standard or performing by crediting the loan accounts with monies from seemingly unknown sources.

Face value: The nominal value of a security as stated by the issuer. For stocks, it is the original cost of the stock; for bonds, it is the amount paid to the holder at maturity.

Financial inclusion: A process of ensuring access to financial products and services for all sections of the society, regardless of their income and savings, at an affordable cost and in a transparent manner.

Financial Stability Report (FSR): A biannual report published by RBI that reviews the health of banks for macroeconomic management.

Fiscal deficit: The shortfall created when a government's total expenditure exceeds the revenue it generates in a fiscal year. This deficit or gap is taken care of by borrowing money from the market.

Floating charge: A charge created over a company's receivables and stocks in general.

Follow-on Public Offer (FPO): An issuance of additional shares made by a company after an initial public offering (IPO). Companies usually announce FPOs to raise equity or reduce debt.

Foreign Exchange Management Act (FEMA): The Act was passed in the 1999 winter session of the Indian Parliament to replace the Foreign Exchange Regulation Act. It seeks to make offences related to foreign exchange civil offences.

Foreign Exchange Regulation Act (FERA): The 1973 legislation passed by the Indian Parliament under the Indira Gandhi government, that came into force with effect from 1 January 1974. The Act imposed stringent regulations on certain kinds of payments, such as dealings in foreign exchange and securities and transactions, that had an indirect impact on foreign exchange and import or export of currency.

Great Recession: It refers to the economic downturn from 2007 to 2009 after the bursting of the US housing bubble and the global financial crisis. The Great Recession was the most severe economic recession in the United States since the Great Depression of the 1930s.

Gross NPAs: The bad assets of a bank which have not been provided for. See non-performing assets (NPAs).

Haircut: In financial markets, a haircut refers to a reduction applied to the value of an asset. It is expressed as a percentage of the loan exposure that has turned bad. For instance, when a bank settles for ₹60 for a ₹100 exposure that has turned bad, it is said the bank has taken 40 per cent haircut.

High net-worth customer: A classification used by the financial services industry to denote an individual or a family with high net worth (wealth).

Holding company: A type of financial organization that owns a controlling interest in other companies, called subsidiaries. Holding companies are protected from losses accrued by subsidiaries – so if a subsidiary goes bankrupt, its creditors can't go after the holding company.

Housing Finance Companies (HFCs): Housing finance companies are those entities which have been set up to finance 'purchase/construction/reconstruction/renovation/repairs of residential dwelling unit…' for a whole host of functions, including giving loans to corporations and government agencies for employee housing finance projects. As per RBI's definition, not lower than 50 per cent of net assets of such entities should be 'housing finance' or 'providing finance for housing', of which at least 75 per cent should be towards housing loans in individual category.

Indradhanush Plan: The Government of India, to resolve the issues faced by the PSBs, launched a seven-pronged plan called 'Mission Indradhanush' in 2015. The Indradhanush mission for PSBs aims at revamping the functioning of the PSBs to enable them to compete with the private sector banks. It seeks to revive economic growth through the reduction of political interference in the functioning of PSBs and improving credit. The seven parts of this plan include appointments, formation of Banks Board Bureau, capitalisation, de-stressing, empowerment, framework of accountability and governance reforms.

Inflation: A quantitative measure of the rate at which the average price level of goods and services in an economy increase over some period of time. It is the rise in the general level of prices where a unit of currency buys less than it did in prior periods. Often expressed as a percentage, inflation thus indicates a decrease in the purchasing power of a nation's currency.

Infrastructure Investment Trust (InvITs): Investment instruments that work like mutual funds and are regulated by the SEBI.

Initial Public Offering (IPO): A stock market launch where shares of a private corporation are offered to the general public on a securities exchange for the first time. Through this process, a private company transforms into a public company.

Insolvency and Bankruptcy Code (IBC): The 2016 bankruptcy law of India, which has consolidated the existing framework by creating a single law for insolvency and bankruptcy. IBC applies to companies, partnerships and individuals and provides for a time-bound process to resolve insolvency. Under IBC, debtor and creditor both can start 'recovery' proceedings against each other. This law was necessitated due to a huge pile-up of non-performing loans of banks and delay in debt resolution.

Inter-corporate deposits: An unsecured loan extended by one company to another.

Inter–Creditor Agreement (ICA): Framed under the aegis of IBA, following the recommendation of Sunil Mehta Committee on stressed asset resolution, this is an agreement signed by banks and financial institutions to speed up the resolution of stressed assets.

ISIN: International securities identification numbers, a 12-digit code, which is the unique identification of a security.

Kiting or kite flying: Fraudulent use of a financial instrument to obtain additional credit that is not authorised. Kiting encompasses two main types of fraud: Issuing or altering a cheque or bank draft for which there are insufficient funds. It also refers to paying off a loan by taking another loan and then taking yet another loan. On a much smaller scale, it is same as when people use one or more credit cards to withdraw cash at an ATM and pay dues on another credit card.

Letter of Undertaking (LoU): An explicit undertaking offered by a bank to another bank on behalf of a customer who is importing goods from a company in another country. Backed by the LoU, the overseas bank gives buyer's credit to the importer.

Libor (London Interbank Offered Rate): A globally accepted key benchmark interest rate that indicates borrowing costs between banks. The rate is calculated and published each day by the Intercontinental Exchange (ICE).

Liquid funds: A type of mutual fund without a lock-in period and with a residual maturity of up to 91 days.

Liquidity sugar rush: Surplus liquidity in banks, affecting the money market instruments such as borrowing and lending.

Loans Against Property (LAP): One form of mortgage loan available for both salaried and self-employed borrowers to help them fulfil their business and personal needs by mortgaging property. It is a loan against fully constructed, freehold residential and commercial properties, for personal and business expansion and needs.

Loan restructuring: Banks restructuring or modifying the terms of loans for borrowers facing financial stress.

London approach: A set of general principles developed in the 1970s by the Bank of England that govern how a company's bankers and, when appropriate, its other creditors should respond to news that the company is facing serious liquidity problems. It is the voluntary, collective approach, adopted by banks in the United Kingdom, when faced with a company in financial difficulty.

Masala bonds: Rupee-denominated bonds issued by Indian entities in overseas markets. Masala, meaning spices, was used by International Finance Corporation (IFC) to popularise the culture and cuisine of India on foreign platforms. These bonds are used to fund infrastructure projects in India, fuel internal growth via borrowings and internationalise the Indian currency.

MUDRA (Micro Units Development and Refinance Agency): Launched by Prime Minister Narendra Modi in April 2015, it is a public sector financial institution that provides loans at low rates to micro-finance institutions and non-banking financial institutions, which then provide credit to MSMEs.

MUDRA loans: Refinance support to banks/financial institutions/NBFCs for lending to microunits having loan requirement of upto ₹10 lakh. It provides refinance support to microbusiness under the Scheme of Pradhan Mantri MUDRA Yojana.

Narrow bank: Banks that do not lend. These banks accept deposits and invest in government bonds.

National Investment and Infrastructure Fund (NIIF): India's first infrastructure-specific investment fund anchored by the Government of India, it is a collaborative investment platform for international and Indian investors who are looking for investment opportunities in infrastructure and other high-growth sectors of the country. It manages over $4 billion of capital commitments.

Nationalised bank: A government-controlled bank that is governed by the Nationalisation Act. The first set of banks was nationalised in 1969.

Net NPAs: When a loan turns bad, a bank has to set aside or provide for it. Net NPAs are bad assets net of such provision. A profitable bank can provide handsomely to bring down its net NPAs. (Also see gross NPA and NPA.)

Non-Banking Financial Company (NBFC): A financial institution that provides banking service without meeting the legal definition of a bank; one that does not hold a banking licence. In India, NBFCs are typically not allowed to mobilise deposits from the public.

Non-convertible debentures: Fixed-income instruments, usually issued by high-rated companies in the form of a public issue to accumulate long-term capital appreciation. These are debt instruments with a fixed tenure and people who invest in these receive regular interest at a certain rate.

Non-food credit: Commercial loans from banks to various sectors of the economy – agriculture, industry and services.

Non-Performing Assets (NPA): Credit facilities or loans for which the interest and/or instalment of principal has remained 'past due' for at least a quarter or 90 days.

Nostro account: An account that a bank holds in a foreign currency in another bank. Nostros, a term derived from the Latin word for 'ours', are frequently used to facilitate foreign exchange and trade transactions. The opposite term 'vostro accounts', derived from the Latin word for 'yours', is how a bank refers to the accounts that other banks have on its books in its home currency.

Payments bank: Banks that operate on a smaller scale without involving any credit risk. It can't advance loans or issue credit cards. Currently such banks in India can take up to ₹1 lakh deposit per customer.

Perpetual bonds: Bonds with no maturity date, that are not redeemable and pay a steady stream of interest forever.

Policy rates: Key lending rate of the central bank. It is a monetary policy instrument under the control of the RBI to regulate the availability, cost, and use of money and credit.

Ponzi scheme: The term 'Ponzi Scheme' was coined after a swindler named Charles Ponzi in 1919. It refers to a fraudulent investing scam promising high rates of return with little risk to investors. The Ponzi scheme generates returns for early investors by acquiring new investors.

Power purchase agreement: A contract between a government agency and a private utility company wherein the latter provides power source (for example, electricity) for the government over a long period of time.

Pradhan Mantri Jan Dhan Yojana (PMJDY): Launched in 2014 under the National Mission for Financial Inclusion, a financial inclusion programme of the Government of India, it is open to Indian citizens and aims to expand affordable access to financial services, such as basic savings and deposit accounts, remittance, credit, insurance, pension, in an affordable manner. As on 7 October 2020, 40.98 crore deposit accounts have been opened, and money kept in such accounts are over ₹1.30-lakh crore. The beneficiaries have been issued 30.06 crore RuPay credit cards. PMJDY accounts are eligible for Direct Benefit Transfer (DBT), Pradhan Mantri Jeevan Jyoti Bima Yojana (PMJJBY), Pradhan Mantri Suraksha Bima Yojana (PMSBY), Atal Pension Yojana (APY), Micro Units Development & Refinance Agency Bank (MUDRA) scheme.

Priority sector lending: Banks in India (including foreign banks) are required to lend to few specific sectors like agriculture and allied activities, micro and small enterprises, poor people for housing, students for education and other low-income groups and weaker sections, to the extent of 40 per cent of their loan assets. The definition is dynamic and the RBI has changed the sectors eligible for such loans in the past, depending on the state of the economy.

Private equity: Equity capital (or shares) of a company not quoted in the market or publicly traded on an exchange.

Private equity firms: Investors or funds that make investments directly into private companies and even listed entities. Typically, they cash out by selling their stakes in the market when the private company goes for a public issue. Private equity firms characteristically make longer-hold investment in target industry sectors or specific investment areas where they have expertise.

Quick mortality accounts: Bank accounts which become NPA within one year of original sanction or first disbursement, and in case of housing loan, within one year from the date of commencement of instalment, whichever is later.

Rating shopping: Rating shopping refers to how a company or a debt paper manages to get same or better rating from another agency within three months of it getting a poor rating. In the 25th edition of the FSR, RBI has warned of 'rating shopping' by companies for long-term bank loans based on indicative ratings given by CRAs, which are not available to the banks or investors.

Recapitalisation bond: Dedicated bonds issued by the government for recapitalising the PSBs so that they are able to meet the capital adequacy norms.

Repo rate: The rate at which commercial banks borrow money from the central bank.

Return on Asset (RoA): It is an indicator of how profitable a company is relative to its total assets. RoA gives a manager, investor, or analyst an idea as to how efficient a company's management is at using its assets to generate earnings. This is calculated by dividing the net income by the average total assets, and expressing the result as a percentage.

Return on Equity (RoE): The amount of net income returned as a percentage of shareholders' equity. Return on equity measures a corporation's profitability by revealing how much profit a company generates with the money shareholders have invested.

Revenue deficit: Excess of total revenue expenditure compared to total revenue receipts.

Reverse repo rate: The rate at which commercial banks park their excess money with the central bank. When the banking system is flush with liquidity, the reverse repo rate becomes the de facto policy rate.

Rights issue: A set of rights granted by a company to its shareholders to purchase additional new shares in the company.

Ring-fencing: The term has its origins in the ring-fences that are built to keep farm animals in and predators out. In banking, it is used to describe a number of strategies that are employed to protect a portion of assets from being mixed with the rest. Offshore banking is sometimes referred as ring-fencing assets.

Risk-Based Supervision (RBS): Introduced by RBI in 2014, RBS focuses on evaluating both present and future risks, identifying incipient problems and facilitates prompt intervention/early corrective action. It replaced the compliance-based and transaction-testing approach (CAMELS) which was more in the nature of a point-in-time assessment. RBS is a structured process that identifies the most critical risks faced by an individual bank and systemic risks in the financial system.

Round-tripping: It denotes a trip where money returns to the place from where the journey began. In the context of black money, it leaves the country through various channels such as inflated invoices, payments to shell companies overseas, the hawala route and so on, and returns in a freshly laundered form, thus completing a round-trip.

S4A (The sustainable structuring of stressed assets): Introduced by RBI in 2016, this scheme offering flexibility to the banking system, was aimed at reducing the bad loans in the economy. S4A allowed banks to convert up to half the loans of stressed companies into equity, or equity-like securities. The scheme was intended to restore the flow of credit to critical sectors including infrastructure. The RBI withdrew this scheme in 2018.

Securitisation: The financial practice of pooling various types of contractual debts, such as residential mortgages, commercial mortgages, auto loans or credit card debt obligation, and selling these consolidated debts as bonds, pass-through securities or mortgage obligation to various investors.

Securitisation & Reconstruction of Financial Assets and Enforcement of Securities Interest Act (SARFAESI): A 2002 Act, it empowers banks and financial institutions to directly auction residential or commercial properties that have been pledged with them to recover loans from borrowers. This act was made to identify and rectify the problem of NPAs through multiple mechanisms. It employs three significant tools for asset management of financial institutions: asset securitisation, asset reconstruction and powers for security interest enforcement.

Shadow banking/shadow bank: A group of financial intermediaries facilitating the creation of credit across the global financial system but whose members are not subject to regulatory oversight. The shadow banking system also refers to unregulated activities by regulated institutions.

Sick Industrial Companies (Special Provisions) Act (SICA): First enacted in India in 1985 to detect unviable ('sick') or potentially sick companies and to help with their revival, if possible, or their closure, if not. It was repealed and replaced in 2003 by the Sick Industrial Companies (Special Provisions) Repeal Act, which watered down some aspects of the original Act and fixed some problematic factors. SICA was fully repealed in 2016.

Small finance bank: A new set of banks that appeared in the banking landscape in India recently to foster financial inclusion. They need lesser capital than the so-called universal banks, and 75 per cent of their loans must be in the category of priority sector loans as opposed to 40 per cent priority loans for universal banks. Besides, 50 per cent of their loan assets must consist of smaller loans – not more than ₹25 lakh each. Currently, there are ten such banks in India. Eight out of these ten entities were microfinance NBFCs.

Special Mention Accounts (SMA): Assets or accounts that shows symptoms of bad asset quality in the first 90 days itself or before it being identified as NPA. In case a borrower is not able to pay one instalment (30 days), it signals incipient stress and the account is called SMA-0. For non-payment between 31 and 60 days, it is SMA-1; and between 61 and 90 days, SMA-2.

Standard assets: Assets of a bank are classified in terms of its repayment status. They are standard assets, substandard assets, doubtful assets and loss assets. Standard asset for a bank is an asset that is not classified as an NPA. The standard asset exhibits no problem in the normal course other than the usual business risk. Banks need to make provision even for standard assets – a very small percentage of loans.

Stand-By Letters of Credit (SBLC): It is a guarantee that is made by a bank on behalf of a client, which ensures payment will be made even if their client cannot fulfil the payment.

Statements of Intent (SoI): It is a schedule in a vested agreement that defines how the parties will work together in pursuit of their shared vision and desired outcomes. This schedule is unique to vested agreements for organisations on a vested journey; it sets the tone for how the parties intend to work together over the life of the partnership

Step-down pricing: System of banks charging higher interest rates at initial stages, when the risks are higher, and reducing the interest rate as the risks reduce.

Strategic Debt Restructuring (SDR): Introduced by RBI in 2015, SDR is one of the many restructuring schemes. It enabled banks to recover their bad loans by converting the advances into equity and taking control of distressed companies.

Sub-standard asset: Assets which have remained an NPA for less than or equal to 12 months.

Super-priority loans: High-margin loans where the lender takes the first charge on cash flow and assets, which takes precedence if the borrower defaults.

Suspicious Transaction Report (STR): A report made by a financial institution about suspicious or potentially suspicious activity. The Prevention of Money Laundering Act, 2002, and the rules thereunder require every banking company to furnish details of suspicious transactions, whether or not made in cash.

SWIFT: A messaging network run by the Society for Worldwide Interbank Financial Telecommunications. It provides a network that enables financial institutions worldwide to send and receive information about financial transactions in a secure, standardised and reliable environment.

Swiss challenge method: A selection process for a project where the highest bid in the first round of bidding becomes the base price to place counter-bids in the second round of bidding. If no other bidder can better the highest bid, the top bidder in the first round is declared the successful bidder.

Take-out financing: Model for providing long-duration finance through medium-term loans. The take-out financing model has been in existence since 2006, when IIFCL, a special purpose vehicle for infrastructure financing, was set up.

Targeted audit: Audits of certain accounts by external auditors to identify red flag misdoings.

Term deposits: A fixed-term investment that includes the deposit of money into an account in a bank or financial institution. The maturity can range from one month to a few years. Typically, such deposits earn higher interest rates than savings accounts.

Tier I Capital: Primary funding source of a bank. It consists of shareholders' equity and retained earnings. It is basically a bank's core capital and includes disclosed reserves – that appears on the bank's financial statements – and equity capital. This money is the funds a bank uses to function on a regular basis and forms the basis of a financial institution's strength.

Tri-party repo: A contract where a third entity, called a tri-party agent, between a borrower and a lender, acts as an intermediary and facilitates the transaction.

Weak bank: A bank that has accumulated losses and net NPAs that exceed its capital.

Wilful defaulter: A borrower who has the ability to pay but who refuses to service the bank debt and/or divert money for other purposes.

Index